Y0-BEA-484

THE HISTORY OF
PIANOFORTE MUSIC

Da Capo Press Music Reprint Series

GENERAL EDITOR

FREDERICK FREEDMAN

VASSAR COLLEGE

THE HISTORY OF
PIANOFORTE MUSIC

BY

HERBERT WESTERBY

𝄞 DA CAPO PRESS · NEW YORK · 1971

A Da Capo Press Reprint Edition

This Da Capo Press edition of *The History of Pianoforte Music*
is an unabridged republication of the first edition published in
London and New York in 1924.

Library of Congress Catalog Card Number 78-87624
SBN 306-71809-X

Published by Da Capo Press
A Division of Plenum Publishing Corporation
227 West 17th Street, New York, N.Y. 10011

Manufactured in the United States of America

For Distribution and Sale Only in the
United States of America

THE HISTORY OF PIANOFORTE MUSIC

THE HISTORY OF
PIANOFORTE MUSIC

BY

HERBERT WESTERBY,

Mus.Bac.Lond., F.R.C.O., L.Mus.T.C.L.

AUTHOR OF *The Piano Works of the Great Composers*

With Numerous Musical Illustrations in the Text

LONDON:
KEGAN PAUL, TRENCH, TRUBNER & CO., LTD.
J. CURWEN & SONS, LTD.
NEW YORK: E. P. DUTTON & CO.
1924

Printed in Great Britain by MACKAYS LTD., Chatham

PRELUDIUM

THE subject of pianoforte music probably includes more literature than that of all the other branches of the tonal art put together.

In treating this subject the author has endeavoured to go upon original lines and to base his classification and critical estimate of the various Schools and composers upon personal examination of the music in question. He was moved to do this by the fact that existing works on the subject are largely " steeped in the past," and by the necessity that the enormous literature of the piano should be viewed from a twentieth-century standpoint.

Moreover, the sphere of pianoforte music centres neither in the organ-like polyphonic works of Bach as written for the Clavichord, nor in the orchestrally-minded sonatas of Beethoven, but in the compositions of the modern Romantic School, and in the modern National Schools which are also permeated with Romanticism. Hence the work has been so proportioned as to treat these sections as of primary importance

Authorities.—The principal modern work on the subject has been Weitzmann's *History of Clavier Playing and Clavier Literature*, 1863. A second edition of this appeared in 1880 (the year of Weitzmann's death) and a third, enlarged by Otto Lessman, appeared in 1887. Much notable pianoforte music has been published, however, since the above dates, and passing by Weitzmann's neglect of much foreign music which was in print by the time of the second edition, whole Schools of National thought have sprung up and crystallized into shape since that time. Prosniz's *Handbuch der Clavier Literatur* (1884 Edition—Doblinger, Vienna), going only as far as 1830, has since been brought down to 1908. The Seiffert (so-called, Weitzmann) *Geschichte der Klavier Music* (1898),

Volume I (461 pages), treats only of harpsichord and clavichord music (on which it is the authority) up to the time of Handel, while Villanis' *L'Arte del Clavicembalo* (Turin—Fratella Bocca) similarly discusses the history of harpsichord music of the 17th century. Oscar Bie's *History of the Pianoforte and Pianoforte Players* (1889) (English Edition—Dent) is based on Weitzmann, and, like Fillmore's *History of Pianoforte Music* (4th Edition, 1888—Presser) and Pauer's *Dictionary of Pianists* (1895), is conservative and largely devoted to the past.

Modern National Schools.—With regard to the modern National Schools of Pianoforte Music, various articles in musical journals have appeared on the subject, and music in general has been nationally classified by Niemann in his *Music and Musicians of the Nineteenth Century* (Senff—in German), but the author believes that the present is the first up-to-date *collective* and *comparative* treatment of national pianoforte music.

Weitzmann, it should be noted in passing, treats his work from the standpoint of " clavier playing," with the resulting anomaly that the music of Field is classified with that of the other pupils of Clementi as perpetuating the style of his master, who represents, however, quite another epoch in composition.

Principal Factors.—Generally speaking, the author has searched for evidence concerning, and endeavoured to direct attention to : (1) the influence of the Italian School upon eighteenth-century composers ; (2) the development and influence of various kinds of " technique " or technical figuration in composition ; (3) the use of musical form, the harmonic aspect, and the influence of the orchestra ; and (4) the definition of the romantic element.

National Schools and Form.—The author, in his treatment of the present subject, apart from dealing with the various " Schools'" and " Nationalities," felt it was also necessary to treat historically of the various *forms* of pianoforte music in order to make the survey complete. Hence the Suite, Fugue, Sonata, Concerto, Variation, Prelude, Programme Music, Modern Dance Forms, Studies, Duets, have been dealt with separately.

Special emphasis has been laid on the original material upon which the National Schools of thought are being built, *viz.* :—The National Folk Song and Dance, and an effort has been made to treat the British School as fully as space allowed.

Educational Aspect.—The educational needs of the average pianoforte student have not been lost sight of and it is hoped that the whole of the chronological tables in particular will be found useful in this direction. Attention to any particular phase can be followed by consulting the cross references, or the Index, or through the works mentioned in the classified Bibliography. Piano Trios, Quartets, etc., as coming under the head of Chamber Music are not dealt with in this volume.

Above all, however, it is necessary that the Student should play or listen to the various works mentioned in order to form a critical and comparative estimate of the literature of pianoforte music in general.

The teacher who wishes to obtain a comprehensive survey of pianoforte music as graded and classified for *educational* purposes is recommended to study Ruthardt's Catalogue-Guide, or Wegweiser (6th Edition, 1905. Gebrüder Hug or Bosworth). No comprehensive guide, including British publications, is in existence. Webbe's *Pianist's Primer* (1900) (Forsyth) is the nearest in this respect.

Historical Aspect.—As regards the historical aspect of the subject generally, it is difficult to portray a movement which runs, so to speak, in half a dozen different channels at the same time, but it is trusted that the reader will make allowance for the necessary overlapping of the various chapters. Further, as the present work has been written without regard to the interest of any music publisher, the author has been enabled to maintain a perfectly impartial and independent attitude in the opinions herein expressed, for which he alone is responsible.

The enormous scope of the subject and the exigencies of space are responsible for a somewhat condensed treatment generally and for any faults which may have crept in. For the notification of these latter, as well as of any new work of importance, the author would be grateful, so that the work may be kept accurate and up-to-date.

Acknowledgments.—The author is obliged to Mr. J. B. MacEwen, formerly Hon. Secretary to the now defunct Society of British Composers, to Dr. Moravcsik, the Principal of the Royal Academy of Music of Budapest, for an historical digest of Hungarian Pianoforte Music furnished by him—one which, unfortunately, it was necessary to condense considerably—and to Mrs. A. A. Ginever, who made the translation for the Royal Academy ; also to Professor Philip Pedrell of Barcelona, the late Sir Hubert Parry, Sir Alexander Mackenzie, Sir Charles V. Stanford and the late Mr. J. E. Matthew, for kind help.

CONTENTS

ix

PART II

THE MUSIC OF THE PIANOFORTE—THE CLASSIC PERIOD

PART III

THE ROMANTIC PERIOD

PART IV

ERA OF NATIONAL MUSIC

PART I

THE MUSIC OF THE HARPSICHORD AND CLAVICHORD

" An organ is a despotism—your piano is the Constitutional bourgeois."— *George Meredith.*

" The study of the history of music, seconded by hearing the actual performance of the master-pieces of different epochs, will prove the most rapid and effectual cure for conceit and vanity."—*Schumann.*

THE HISTORY OF PIANOFORTE MUSIC

CHAPTER I

THE STORY BEGINS

PIANOFORTE music is the most universal, as well as the most democratic, form of the tonal art. The *study* of the *piano* is usually the first branch of musical art taken in hand by the multitude, and its literature is correspondingly voluminous. The adaptability of the instrument for the rendering of other forms of musical art makes it doubly useful. It may not, in its interpretative effect, render the rich, drawn-out sigh of the violin, nor approach the thrill of the human voice ; it cannot give the variety of tone and power of the modern orchestra, nor can it yield the thunder and roll of the organ. It is, however, superior to voice and violin in its provision both of melody and of concurrent harmonies ; while, compared with the orchestra and organ, it can produce characteristic and distinctive effects of its own of the utmost delicacy, as well as interpret the most heroic moods. Finally, in its satisfactory reproduction of all other forms of musical art, from the Handelian chorus to the string quartet, it has not inaptly earned the title of " The instrumental maid-of-all-work " ; and its democratic functions are represented in its music, since, owing to its lack of variety of *timbre* or tone-colour effects, it must rely mostly on *ideas* and their development.

The absolute ineffectiveness which much modern orchestral music betrays when reproduced on the piano is ample proof of this.

Moreover, composers who may be really great in orchestral, choral, operatic, and even in song forms, may be, and often are, pitifully lacking in pianoforte music ; while others, unknown in these larger spheres, may occupy, with justice, places in the front rank as composers for the pianoforte. It is this levelling tendency which makes it difficult to impress on the general

3

public—which goes largely by general reputations—that world-renowned composers whose *genre*, for instance, is orchestral music, may be utterly *banal* in the realm of the piano ; while others who have written works of great artistic merit, infinitely more fitted to the instrument, are comparatively unknown.

In the constant sifting process which accompanies the evolution of the fittest, much that was esteemed fifty years ago has been overshadowed by later work and is now, artistically speaking, of no avail. Hence the Author's difficulty is that of taking everything *de novo*, not from the standpoint of a contemporary of Mendelssohn and Schumann (as in the case of Weitzmann) but from that of the Twentieth Century.

Casting our thoughts back to the conditions which preceded the use of the harpsichord and clavichord, we ask ourselves— What was the general medium of musical expression similar to that now supplied by the pianoforte ?

This we find in the guitar-like lute with its usual twenty-one to twenty-four strings (including pairs in unison) which was in use from the fourteenth to the eighteenth centuries. In its day the lute, like the pianoforte, was not only much used in the orchestra and as a solo instrument, but also to represent transcriptions of vocal and orchestral works. The compositions written specially for the lute were of two classes : (1) Those in the polyphonic style of the madrigal and motet, abounding, as such, in responsive and fugal passages ; (2) Collections of dance forms and popular airs.

It is only natural that on the introduction of the early clavier instruments (the spinet, virginal and clavichord) these two styles should be transferred to them. Meanwhile the lute, as being somewhat unsuited for polyphonic composition, did much for the institution of a purely instrumental style. Composers of that time were in the habit of writing over their polyphonic compositions, " *Da cantare o suonare* " (to be sung or played). Not only were they suitable for voices (" apt for voyces or viols ") but they were supposed to be playable on the family of viol instruments (a " chest of viols ") and on the lute. The lute's lack of sustaining power, however, brought about a style which consisted of chords interspersed with single notes instead of the usual flowing vocal parts ; and to this were added various devices for eking out the transient tone of those instruments, such as turns, ornamental passages, tremolos, repeated notes, and occasionally more ambitious runs and arpeggios.

The use of the lute also as an accompanying instrument (its true *métier*, as shown in its descendant, the guitar), with its detached chords struck in support of the voices, further aided the formation of that instrumental style which was transferred to the keyboard instruments when they came into fashion.

It must not, however, be imagined that the vocal style lost its influence upon that of the instrument for some time. Indeed, up to the time of Sebastian Bach, the polyphonic style was very strongly in evidence. But the primitive instrumental style, though influenced by the madrigal and vocal forms, was also there, and was especially used in the presentation of dance forms and in transcriptions of the popular airs of the time.

The origin of the piano in its earliest form, the clavichord, is derived from the " monochord "—a *one*-stringed instrument in use in the eleventh century. A keyboard was added and *single* melodic sounds were produced by upright *wooden* tangents which struck or pushed the one string, and set the portion marked off into vibration. The primitive monochord then became a clavichord (*clavis*, a key) though it still retained the same name. In order to produce *harmonic* effects, several strings, similarly acted upon and all tuned in unison, were added and *metal* tangents were used instead of wooden.

It thus became, as it were, a set of monochords. The clavichord had already reached four-octaves compass by 1511, and, constructed as it was in the form of a chest, it was placed on a table when in use.

The instrument had usually more keys than strings. By 1720, however, it was made with a pair of strings (tuned in unison) to each key, and thus became " amenable to the equal temperament tuning preferred by J. S. Bach " (Hipkins). It was for this instrument, with its delicate tone, its infinite power of light and shade, and its variety of touch, that *Bach* wrote his immortal *Forty-eight Preludes and Fugues* (first part in 1722), described as being for the " well-tempered clavichord," and also his expressive *Chromatic Fantasia*.

The usually three-cornered *clavicembalo* or Italian harpsichord (in French, *clavecin* ; in English, *clavicymbal*) was known in England in its smaller forms as the *virginal* or *spinet*. The latter, having one string only to each key, came into use shortly after the clavichord, and was in use side by side with it. Unlike the clavichord, its strings were plucked by *quills* fastened to a wooden bar or " Jack." Its tone was clear and staccato. A legato was not possible, but in florid passages the effect was brilliant. From the larger harpsichords somewhat grandiose but expressionless effects could be obtained. It was for the smaller *virginal* (possibly so named as intended for the use of girls) and for the *spinet* that the unique School of English Elizabethan composers wrote their famous compositions.

The larger *harpsichord*, which usually had two, three or (more rarely) four strings to each note, was the grand piano of the sixteenth and seventeenth centuries, and was used as such in the orchestras of that time. Builders of that era, including the celebrated Rückers of Antwerp and (in the eighteenth century) Tschudi, the predecessor of Broadwood's, London, exercised their ingenuity by adding " Venetian swell," to swell the tone when required ; also octave couplers, as well as lute, harp, oboe and other imitative stops. On the harpsichord, unlike the clavichord, no expression could be made through the touch. Contrast was obtained by addition of other effects (as in the case of the organ) or by change of keyboard.

The swell effect was an advantage, but the tone, like the piano's and unlike the organ's, was transient. Like the clavichord and spinet, the harpsichord was made with double keyboards, and occasionally we meet with compositions designed to take advantage of the crossing of parts on the two claviers, as, for instance, in the *Goldberg Variations* of Bach, or with echo effects obtained from alternate use of the two keyboards, as in the *Italian Concerto*.[1]

We must now speak of the music written for the spinet or virginal.[2]

---

[1] *Cf. The Oxford History of Music*, Vol. IV, p. 110 *ff.*, and Villani's *L'Arte del Clavicembalo*.

[2] For a description of the old stringed instruments, *see* also Jeffrey Pulver's *Dictionary of Old English Music* (Kegan Paul); also his article on " The Destiny of the Plectrum," in *Musical News*, Sept. 15th, 1923.

CHAPTER II

THE ENGLISH COMPOSERS FOR THE VIRGINAL

Principal Composers	*Original Collections of Compositions*
Byrd, 1546–1625.	*Fitzwilliam Virginal Book*, 1550–1621.
Munday, 1550–1610.	*My Ladye Neville's Book*, 1591.
Giles Farnaby, (b. 1560).	*Benjamin Cosyn's Book*, (*c.* 1600).
Bull, 1563–1628.	*Parthenia*, printed 1611.
Peeter Philips, *c.* 1550–1624 ?*	*Will Forster's Book*, 1624.

THE introduction to the first real school of composers for the forerunner of the pianoforte takes place in our own country in the reign of Queen Elizabeth (1558–1603). In England we had, at the end of the fifteenth century, a race of organists, who, unlike those on the Continent, had got rid, to a certain extent, of the inappropriate vocal style and initiated a real instrumental technique. At this time the virginal as a domestic instrument had become immensely popular. The Tudor monarchs were excellent performers, and Henry VIII., Edward VI., Mary and Elizabeth retained the services of eminent virginal players. Mr. Van Borren in his *Sources of Keyboard Music in England* (Novello, 1915) avows that " The English virginalists . . . were admirably equipped for creating a repertory absolutely appropriate to the resources of the instrument." In truth, the source of the whole technique of the pianoforte must be sought among them ; and, moreover, it seems that this technique was not exceeded until the time of Domenico Scarlatti. England, in John of Fornsete's remarkable canon *Sumer is icumen in*, of the thirteenth century, and the outstanding choral compositions of John of Dunstable (d. 1453), had proved to be well ahead of the Continent, and now it led also as regards instrumental works. It is interesting to hear of Queen Elizabeth's pride in her power as a performer on the virginal, and how the Scottish Ambassador was introduced by " my Lord of Hunsdean " into a

*Note. Peeter Phillip's compositions in Queen Elizabeth's Virginal Book range from 1580-1605.

quiet gallery where they " might hear the Queen play upon the virginal," and how he " entered within the chamber and stood a pretty space hearing her play excellently well." Elizabeth, on discovering the Ambassador, " enquired whether my Queen or she played best. In that I found myself obliged to give her the praise."

The earliest old English virginal Piece which has survived is a " hornpipe " of about 1500 A.D. by one, Hughe Aston, of whom nothing seems to be known. Half a century later, Pieces appear in the *Mulliner Boke.*

The principal collection or storehouse of these treasures of a bygone age is the *Fitzwilliam Virginal Book* (1558–1621),[1] once known as the *Queen Elizabeth Virginal Book,* though evidently compiled after her death. It contains compositions by John Bull, Wm. Byrd, Giles and Richard Farnaby, Orlando Gibbons, Hooper, Thomas Morley, John Munday, Peeter Philips, Thomas Tallis and others.

Its contents have been summarized as follows :—" 130 Dances, 17 Organ Pieces, 46 Arrangements of Popular Songs, 9 of Madrigals, 22 Fantasias in the Ricercari Form by nine composers, 7 Fancy Pieces by four composers (early examples of the " characteristic " style), 19 Preludes and 6 Expositions of the Hexachord." *Variations* on all kinds of tunes are also there, as in the delightful composition *O Mistris Myne,* which is built on one of the popular airs of the day. To the student of folk-song the collection is of great interest. It belongs to a time when English musicians were employed at various European courts and made known there the treasures of English folk-song, such as *Fortune my Foe, Greensleeves, Packington's Pound* and *Walsingham*—all composed by William Byrd with 22 Variations, to which Dr. John Bull afterwards added 30 others. It also contains *The Carman's Whistle,* of which Oscar Bie says : " *The Carman's Whistle* is a perfected popular melody which will linger for days in our ears ; "[2] and the more stirring *Sellinger's Round* of which he says : " In the later Variations the graver movement is again taken up, but more florid and more varied, with runs which pursue each other in canon. This Piece, perhaps the first perfect clavier-piece on record, which

[1] *An Elizabethan Virginal Book,* by Ed. W. Naylor, 1899, and *The Fitzwilliam Virginal Book,* ed. by W. B. Squire and Fuller Maitland, 1890.
[2] *History of the Pianoforte and Pianoforte Players.* Dent, 1899.

had left its time far behind, was written in 1580." It must be remembered that these old-world compositions have to be approached in the appropriate spirit to get the effect of the lightly-sounding virginal or spinet and the " atmosphere " of the period. In the collection there are also "Fantasias" or Pieces in the fugal style, in which ingenuity is shown in the imitative presentation of themes at various intervals and in various keys. The Pieces are noteworthy for an early exposition of musical form and as presenting the origin of the Suite with its dance movements all in one key. The style of *technique* shown is remarkably advanced ; imitative scale passages, florid broken chords and repeated notes occurring frequently. As regards *tonality* or sense of key, both flattened and major sevenths and the " Tierce de Picardie " abound, and some of the Pieces are wonderfully modern in feeling. As regards the *dances*, these comprised the stately *Pavan* of Italian origin ; the bright *Alman* or Allemande of German origin, with its single melody well ornamented ; the *Galliard* (sung as well as played and danced) in triple time and usually following the Pavan in the early Suites ; the *Coranto* or Courante, of French origin, in triple time ; the sprightly *Gigge* or Jig, of British origin, with its spirited leaping rhythm (mostly 3/8) often used as a closing movement. It was introduced into Germany and used by Bach and Handel in their Suites, and into Italy, where its dotted rhythm became a rolling triplet measure. Finally there are the swaying *round* dances—the *Basse Danse* and *Branle*, of French origin.

There are other smaller and unique collections of this period, *viz.*, the *Benjamin Cosyns Virginal Book*, which contains 98 Pieces by various composers ; *Ladye Neville's Book*, containing 42 Pieces by Byrd written before 1591 ; and the book entitled *Parthenia* (1611), the first English engraved clavier music, containing 21 works by Byrd, Bull and Gibbons, all set out upon the six-line stave.[1]

These various collections also afford instances of early programme music, as in the well-known Battle Piece by Byrd from *Ladye Neville's Book*, in which there is a kind of melancholy duet for " Flutes and the Droome."

Another example is in the bell music by Byrd, in which the two notes of the two large bells are kept sounding throughout

---

[1] *Cf.* Rimbault's reprint, 1847.

as a kind of "ground bass." The composer begins quite
simply as in Ex. 1.

working in the imitative counterpoint in a more and more
complicated manner, till he is able to add passages suggesting
a full peal of bells in full swing against the two larger bells,
which have kept on throughout as in ex. 2.

In the Fitzwilliam collection there is also a *Fantasia* by John
Munday, depicting various kinds of weather, "Faire Wether,
Lightning, Thunder, Calme Wether," etc.

The three composers, Byrd (1546–1623), Bull (1563–1628),
and Gibbons (1583–1625), stand out as the most prominent of
this golden age of English compositions for the clavier, which
was quite unequalled in its time. Peeter Philips and Giles
Farnaby were also large contributors.

Byrd was a pupil of Tallis, and, like his master and his
contemporaries Bull and Gibbons, a contrapuntist of the first
rank. His learned and effective Variations on the interesting
theme, *The Carman's Whistle*, which were played by Rubinstein
at his Historical Recitals, sound wonderfully fresh.

Bull was a Master of the Chapel Royal and later Organist at Antwerp Cathedral. His *King's Hunting Jigg* is a charming little characteristic piece. His Variations are quite modern, and distinguished by wide, sweeping scale passages. The *Jewel Variations* are specially artistic. Oscar Bie says that these two composers, Byrd and Bull, " represent the two types which run through the whole history of the clavier: Byrd the more intimate, delicate, spiritual intellect ; Bull the untamed genius, the flashing executant, the restless madcap, the rougher artist."

The works of Gibbons, who was also a Master of the Chapel Royal, are also remarkable for contrapuntal skill and technical freedom of style.

If we put on one side the effects of incomplete emancipation from the old church modes, the *special features* of this old virginal music, composed a century before the time of Handel and Bach, are: (i) its advanced technical character, (ii) its natural and pleasant melody, and (iii) the contrapuntal skill manifested in its composition.[1]

---

[1] *Cf.* the Albums edited by Bantock devoted to Byrd, Farnaby, and Bull. (Novello.) "Fourteen Pieces for Keyed Instruments " by Wm. Byrd.—Ed. by Fuller Maitland and W. Barclay Squire (Stainer & Bell). Also Wm. Byrd, *Dances, Grave and Gay,* ed. by Margt. H. Glynn (Rogers) ; an easy selection, with notes.

CHAPTER III

THE OLD HARPSICHORD SUITES

" Ay, such a Suite roused heart to rapture."—Browning.

TOWARDS the end of the sixteenth century instrumental dance music was particularly in request. At first the old dance forms were taken *singly*, but later on the advantage was noted of performing them in *sets* or *suites*, by which interesting contrast of character could be obtained. *Sets* or *suites* of dance tunes of all possible kinds, as set for the spinet, harpsichord, clavichord, lute and viol da Gamba came into use ; and where these tunes were not particularly intended for dancing, greater finish was combined with greater working out in contrapuntal style. This grouping together of old dance tunes is important, since it led to the evolution of (1) the highest of all developed forms—the sonata, (2) the harmonic aspect of music in general.

The *History* of the Suite extends over a period of some 250 years and, as has been pointed out, takes under its wing almost the whole era of instrumental music.

Frequently these old Suites consist not only of old dance tunes, but also of the old *fugal forms* known as the *Ricerari, Canzoni*, etc.; instances of the polyphonic style referred to in Chapter I. Then again the selection of the various dances was influenced (1) by the fashion of the day, (2) by the nationality of the composer. The Suite itself seems to have originated in Italy (*c.* 1508) in music written for the lute. (See *Zur Geschichte der Suite*, Norlind.)

In Italy the collections were called *Sonate di Camera* ; in England, *Lessons* ; in Germany, *Partita* ; and in France, *Ordres*. We spoke of the old dance forms found in the collections of virginal music. We should like to quote a description of some of these given in a remarkable book entitled *Musicks Monument*, by Thomas Mace, written in 1676, some fifty years after the Virginal Collections referred to. The description occurs in connection with music written for " the noble lute."

" (1) The *Prælude* is commonly a Piece of confused, wild, shapeless, kind of intricate Play (as most use it) in which no perfect Form, Shape or Uniformity can be perceived ; but a Random, Bussines, Pottering, and Groping, up and down, from one Stop, or Key to another ; And generally so performed, to make Tryal, whether the Instrument be well in Tune, or not ; by which doing, after they have compleated their Tuning, They will (if They be Masters) fall into some kind of

" (2) *Allmaines*, or Fansical Play, more Intelligible ; which (if He be a Master able) is a way, whereby He may more Fully, and Plainly show His excellency, and Ability, than by any other kind of undertaking ; and has an unlimited and unbound Liberty ; In which, he may make use of the Forms, and shapes of all the rest.

" (3) *Pavanes* are Lessons of 2, 3 or 4 Strains, very grave, and sober ; Full of Art and Profundity, but seldom us'd in These our Light Days.

" (4) *Allmaines*, are Lessons, very Agrey, and Lively ; and generally of Two Strains, of the Common, or Plain, Tune.

" (5) *Ayres* are, or should be of the same Time (yet many make Tripla's and call them so) ; only they differ from Allmaines by being commonly Shorter, and of a more quick and nimble Performance.

" (6) *Galliards*, are Lessons of 2 or 3 Strains, but are performed in a slow, and Large Triple-Time ; and (commonly) Grave, and Sober.

" (7) *Corantoes*, are Lessons of a Shorter Cut, and of a quicker Triple-Time ; commonly of 2 Strains, and full of Sprightfulness, and Vigour, Sprightly, Brisk, and Cheerful.

" (8) *Sarabands*, are of the Shortest Triple-Time ; but more Toyish, and Light than Corantoes ; and commonly of Two Strains.

" (9) *Chichonas*, are only a few Conceited Humourous Notes, at the end of a Suite of Lessons, very Short, (*viz.*) not many in Number ; yet sometimes consist of 2 Strains, although but of 2 Semibreves in a Strain, and Commonly of a Grave kind of Humour.

" (10) Toys, or *Jiggs*, are Light Squibbish Things, only fit for Fantastical, and Easie-Light-Headed People ; and are of any sort of Time.

"(11) *The Ground*, is a set number of Slow Notes, very
Grave, and Stately; which (after it is expressed Once, or
Twice, very plainly) then He that hath Good Brains and a
Good Hand, undertakes to play several Divisions upon it
Time after Time, till he has shew'd his Bravery, both of
Intention, and Hand.

"Thus, I have given you to understand, the several sorts,
and Shapes, of most Lessons in use."

In addition to the dance forms mentioned by Mace, there were
frequently in use the *Bourrée*, "of a jovial and pleasant expression," the *Gavotte*, the *Forlane* (Venetian Gondoliers'
Dance), the *Hornpipe*, the "small stepped" *Minuet*, as well as
the Variation forms of the stately *Chaconne* and *Passacaglia*.
(*See Suites* in Grove's *Dictionary* and Prout's *Applied Forms*.)

As regards the further evolution of the Suite, we find one of the
first steps in the contrasted alternation of *Pavan* and *Galliard*,
the former described by the composer Morley as "a kind of
staid music ordained for grave dance," and the latter as "a
lighter and more stirring kind of dancing." These two forms
soon dropped out and the quiet, smooth-flowing *Allemande* in
4/4 time and the lighter Italian or French *Courante* (respectively
in 3/4 time or 3/2 mixed with 6/4) took their places and formed
a nucleus for the orthodox Suite which came to consist of
Allemande and Courante, the rhythmical and massive *Saraband*
(in 3/2 time and accented second beat) and the lively (often in
fugal style) *Gigue* (in 6/8, 9/8 or 12/8 time).

In addition to these four, which were always in the same key,
it was optional to insert other dances between the last two and
to add a *Prelude* or *Overture* at the beginning.

Variation Suites.—It should be noted, meanwhile, that the
movements of the *Partitas* of Frescobaldi, Froberger, Pasquini,
Buxtehude and other early composers were often in the form of
Variations on a stated theme, in which the characteristics of the
various dances were imitated, as in Froberger's *Auf die Mayerin*
Suite, which was built on the tune of a popular Volkslied.
(*See* Chapter VI.)

As regards *style*, the *Partitas* of Frescobaldi (1616) are very
much in organ style, but those of his pupil Froberger (who died
in 1667) show much freer technique and, on the whole, are in
what was subsequently recognized as orthodox form.

If Froberger thus " brought the Suite on its first step towards perfection " (Adler), it was reserved for his French contemporaries *Chambonnière* (in 1670) and *Couperin* (in 1713) (*see* Chapter IV) to add artistic and refined style to their *Suites*, which consisted of highly poetical and characteristic movements, and, as such, became the model for other composers of that period, including Bach.   As an example may be mentioned the quaint Characteristic Suites of *The Seven Planets*.   After the Suites of Couperin perfection was soon reached in the English Suites of *Bach* which were composed about 1726 for an English gentleman but not published till long after.

The Suites of *Handel*, which were published principally from 1720 to 1733, show more of the influence of Italian models. They are more straight-forwardly melodious than those of Bach, who is more reflective, loving to go round his periods and prolong the " linked sweetness long drawn out "—in a word, more contrapuntal in style.   Bach is most successful in the Gavottes and Bourrées, Handel in the typical Italian Giga.   Bach, again, is conservative, while the Suites of Handel are examples of the freer style adopted by the Italian composers of Chamber Music. (*See* also Chapter X.)   In Handel's Fifth Suite, for instance, occur the variations known as the *Harmonious Blacksmith*,

Air, with Doubles. (Harmonious Blacksmith, Handel).

while in his Second Suite the names of the dance forms disappear and we have movements entitled *Adagio, Allegro, Adagio Fugue*, presenting a link in the evolution of the cyclical form of the Sonata, and also resembling in this the preceding so-called *Sonatas da Camera* (1683–94) of Corelli, which are really Suites.

To summarize, the Suite, initiated in Italy, developed in Germany by Froberger, artistically wrought in France by Chambonnière and Couperin, came to its perfection again in Germany.   As the highest form of harpsichord and clavichord music composed during the polyphonic period, it finds its climax in the master mind of its leading composer, John Sebastian Bach.

The evolution of the Suite can be seen at a glance by reference to the following Table. Besides those already mentioned, the following are of special artistic and historical significance :—
Locke's *English Collection*, 1673, Pasquini's *Partite*, 1697 ; the *Suites* of Rameau, 1706 ; the *Lessons* of Babell, 1713 ; the *Suites* of Mattheson, 1714 ; and, finally, the *Lessons* of Arne, 1750. The reader is referred to other Chapters (*see* Index) for further details.

EVOLUTION OF THE SUITE

1615–37. Partite by *Frescobaldi* for cembalo, in organ style.

1649–67. Suites by *Froberger* in orthodox form.

1670. " Characteristic " Suites by *Chambonnière.*

1673. *Melothesia, Locke's* Collection of " Lessons."

1689. *Playford's* Collection of " Lessons."

1689. *Kuhlau's* Partitas.

1690–5. *Purcell's* " Lessons."

1690–5. *Buxtehude's* Suites, depicting " The Nature and Properties of the Planets."

1697. *Pasquini's* Partite.

1697. *Krieger's* Partitas.

1700. *Lessons* by *Blow.*

1700. *Lessons* by *Hy. Simmonds.*

1706–35. Suites by *Rameau.*

1710. Suites by *Loeillet.*

1713. " Lessons " by *Babell.*

1713. " Characteristic Suites " by *Couperin.*

1714. *Mattheson's* 12 Suites.

1716. *Zippoli* Suites.

1717. *Bach's* French Suites.

1726. *Bach's* English Suites.

1720–23. *Handel's* Suites.

1727. *Gottlieb Moffat's* Suites.

1750. *Arne's* Lessons.

1762. *Nichelman.* Suites, in French style.

CHAPTER IV

FRENCH CLAVECIN MUSIC

THE next step in the evolution of a perfected harpsichord style was made by the French composers, who flourished about 1750 (thirty years after the climax of the English Virginal School), as well as by the Suites of Froberger, of whom more will be said later.

The efforts of the French School resulted in a more elegant and more ornamental style, or " *style galant* " as it was called. As early as 1530, *French Dances*, Galliards, Basse Dances, Branles and Pavans, together with Transcriptions of songs, had appeared for the spinet in the *Collections* of *Attaignant*.

Programme music also came to the front as in the Pavan *La Bataille* in Susato's *Collection* of 1551, while in the Denis Gaultier Collection for the Lute we see the origin of those fancy decorative titles with which Couperin and others adorned their compositions.

Chambonnière (1620–1670), the most prominent harpsichord composer in the time of Louis XIV. (whose court clavecinist he was), is regarded as the founder of the French Harpsichord or Clavecin School. His four Pièces in *Les Maîtres du Clavecin*, *viz.*, *La Rare* Courante, Sarabande *La Loureuse* (published in 1670) have a quaint meditative and refined air. Anglebert, among whose works (1689) are twenty-two Variations on the well-known theme *Folies d'Espagne* (used by Corelli and many others), Le Bèque and Dumart contributed works of a similar kind, but it was reserved for François Couperin (1668–1733), the contemporary predecessor of Scarlatti, Handel and Bach (whom he influenced in many ways), to perfect the characteristic style in the Suite. His collections of Pièces appearing in 1713, 1716, 1722 and 1730 were termed *Ordres*. These, although containing movements all in one key, were not Suites in the usual sense of that time, but collections of usually over a dozen Pieces in which Allemandes, Courantes, Sarabandes, Gavottes, etc., are interspersed with poetical pieces such as *La Galante, Princesse d' Esprit, Enchanteresse, Idées Heureuses, Langueurs Tendres*, etc. These characteristic movements are quaint, defined, and artistic as compared with the more energetic compositions of previous composers. (*See* Table, last Chapter.) The delicate portrait pictures and characteristic sketches of Couperin[1] are unique.

His portraits of the *Lonely One, The Spectre, Wavering Shadows, Love in the Cradle, The Shepherd's Feast, Les Folies Françaises ou les Dominos*, and *Les Papillons*, suggest at once the immortal sketches of Schumann.

Couperin, in 1717, wrote one of the first modern methods in his *Art de Toucher le Clavecin*, which was compiled with a view

---

[1] *Ordres* of Couperin (Brahms and Chrysander.) (Aug.)

to improving style and technique. The exemplary Preludes attached to it foreshadow something of modern Sonata form and its development.

Marchand, who competed against Bach (Weitzmann), Loeilly and Dandrieu Daquin (1694–1772), who wrote *Le Coucou*, composed smaller clavecin works. Rameau (1713–1764) comes next to Couperin in Pavans and surpasses him in bolder technique and straightforwardness of style, though not in refinement and characterization. His *Rappel des Oiseaux* and *La Poule* are realistic, as well as tasteful examples of *Programme* Music. Rameau's *Concertos* for the clavecin, violin, and basse de viole (1741), written in the ensemble style of the old Concerto, still survive.[1]

Both Couperin and Rameau show, here and there, in their characteristic impressions, the influence of the prevailing Italian School, but on the whole they display individuality of style.

---

[1] For comparative examples, see Macdowell's *From the Eighteenth Century*, 2 Books. (Elkin.) Also *Six Eighteenth-Century Pieces*, ed. by Alfred Moffatt (B. & F.).

CHAPTER V

HARPSICHORD AND CLAVICHORD TECHNIQUE

BEFORE proceeding to the consideration of early Italian and German, and later English music written for the harpsichord, we must pause awhile to describe the *technique* of the instrument, as well as the polyphonic style in which much of the art of the period was written.

The construction and tone effects of these early instruments had necessarily a very important influence on the music composed for them. The peculiar *pizzicato* or " plucked " quality, and the usually unvarying strength of tone of the harpsichord, rendered it more effective in quick passages written in two or three parts, while the clavichord, with its clear, expressive and minutely graduated tone, was more suitable for the quiet weaving of the parts in polyphonic music.

Mattheson, in 1713, says that the light or *Galanterie* style could also " be best brought out and in the clearest manner on a good clavichord, as the latter produced the singing tone far more sustained and softened than the harpsichord and spinet."

It was this singing tone which appealed, doubtless, to Bach, for his compositions, and some of the earlier ones of his son Em. Bach, were written for the clavichord. The latter recommends practice on the harpsichord, with its heavier touch, as well as on the light action of the clavichord ; and he himself told Dr. Burney (*Burney's History*) that he had always endeavoured to write in a *cantabile* style for the clavier.

In the sixteenth century the clavichord, as successor to the monochord, was the favourite instrument in Italy, just as the " virginal " or spinet was in England. It was in connection with the latter, as represented by the School of " Virginal " Composers in Queen Elizabeth's time (1550–1621) that we have the first remarkable contribution to technique in rapid passage work in scales and broken chords, and in thirds and sixths. The Suites of Couperin added refinement and taste, but it is to

20

Italy we must look for the basis of modern virtuosity in the works of Domenico Scarlatti.

The latter's wonderfully neat style, with its crossing of hands and octave work, together with the other devices of the earlier English School intensified, made a decided advance on the past. The polyphonic style of his contemporaries, Bach and Handel (somewhat influenced by the organ), was even more boldly dealt with in that of Scarlatti. We may compare, for instance, the vigorous declamatory recitative scale passages followed by broken chord work and the periods of fugal imitation which typify the *Toccatas* and *Chromatic Fantasia* of Bach with the electric staccato, piquant phrases, rushes in double notes, arpeggios and rolling octaves of Scarlatti. These point to Scarlatti having the truer clavier style. It was reserved for Paradies and Clementi to develop his technique still further and form the foundation of that used by Beethoven.

Scarlatti was known as the greatest virtuoso of his time. Handel, his rival in Rome, whose performance is said to have been equal to that of Scarlatti, was later taken up with opera and oratorio work, and neither he, nor Bach, appeared very much in this rôle. Bach's own style of playing, as befitted his use of the clavichord and the polyphonic style, was such that he played with " a scarcely perceptible movement of the hands ; his fingers hardly seemed to touch the keys and yet everything came out with perfect clearness and a pearly roundness and purity " (Spitta).

Bach's method of touch has been thus described : " He held the five fingers so bent that the tips were brought into straight line, each finger being held in this position over its key, ready for striking " (Ad. Kullak), the tone thus being produced, not by giving a direct blow to the key as in the case of the piano, but by " causing it (the finger) to slip away from the front end of the key by gradually drawing the finger tip towards the palm of the hand." This scooping action of the fingers was combined *before* Bach's time with a horizontal position of the finger, as can be seen in various old prints.

Bach was one of the first to curve the fingers. He also reformed the method of fingering which, before his time, was somewhat primitive. Previous to Bach's adoption of the curved position of the fingers the thumb was little used.

J. Seb. Bach, and his son Emmanuel, in his *True Art of*

Playing the Clavier, practically brought fingering to what it is now.

As regards the *marking* of fingering, the earliest German fingering was practically the same as the present English method.

The *Agréments* or various ornaments used in clavier music were brought about by the thin, unsustained tone of the harpsichord and clavichord, and were particularly cultivated by the French clavier writers.

Em. Bach, in his *True Art*, makes an effort to regulate their use, remarking that " They serve to connect the notes, they enliven them and give a special weight and emphasis, bringing out the sense of the music, whether it be sad, cheerful or otherwise."

CHAPTER VI

THE POLYPHONIC STYLE AND EVOLUTION OF FUGUE

> " . . . his volant touch
> Instinct through all proportions, low and high,
> Fled and pursued transverse the resonant Fugue."
> (Milton's *Paradise Lost*.)

WE have already pointed out (in Chapter I) that early clavier music falls into two styles :—

(1) Dance forms and popular airs.

(2) Compositions in the polyphonic style of the madrigal and motet.

We have noticed that English virginal composers were contrapuntists of the first rank.

The mastery of the contrapuntal style is also manifested somewhat later in the earliest composer of the Italian Clavier School—Frescobaldi, who, through his pupil Froberger, transferred it to Germany, where it reached a climax in the Fugues and polyphonic compositions of Bach and Handel.

Beginning with the early English School, we find in the Fitzwilliam Collection that the so-called *Fantasi* s are in the strictest contrapuntal style, one Fantasia in four Parts by Gibbons (d. 1625) being a remarkable specimen of a free Fugue.

Hawkins, in his *History of Music* (1776), speaks of these old Fantasias as abounding in " figures and little responsive passages and all those other elegances observable in the structure and contrivances of the Madrigal."

The Preludes, Toccatas, and many of the Galliards and Pavans in the Fitzwilliam Collection are also in polyphonic or imitative style.

We next find compositions similar to the English Fantasias appearing as Ricercari, Canzoni (German, Canzonen) and Fantasias in the works of the Italians Frescobaldi, Pasquini and others, and in those of the German Froberger and others.

In these compositions a theme was irregularly developed in fugal style, the middle sections being in a different measure.

23

In later times, it should be noted, the term " *Ricercari* " was applied to complete and scientifically developed Fugues. Many of the early so-called Fugues are really in simple imitative or Canon form. The *Canzone alla Francese* was modelled on popular folk-tunes. An example is the melodious two-movement *Canzone Francese* of Pasquini (*Pieces by Pasquini*, Ed. by Shedlock, Novello). (*See* next Chapter), of which the following is the theme :—

In a similar manner folk-tunes were also varied in the Partitas or Suites, as in the *Auf die Mayerin* Suite of Froberger (Chapter IX), founded on the following German Volkslied :—

The *Canzone Francese*, through its usually clear formation in periods or sections, led direct to the Fugue.

Frescobaldi's (1593–1644) compositions, written, as they were, in a masterly contrapuntal style, exercised considerable influence on Bach, but Buxtehude, who was Organist for over thirty years at Lübeck (to which place Bach used to make excursions to hear him play) was apparently Bach's principal model.

The Fugue, when fully developed, still continued by the side of the less formal Canzoni, Ricercari and Fantasias. Its perfect form may be generalized as falling into three continuous sections :—(1) Exposition, (2) Middle Section, (3) Recapitulation, with intervening episodes and varying order of entry of theme ; thus, A and B representing the Subject and Answer :—

	Exposition		Middle Entries		Recapitulation
Soprano		B		A	A
Alto	A		B		
Tenor	B			A	B
Bass	A			B	A

The Poet Browning, in his *Master Hugues of Saxe-Gotha*, gives an amusing description of a Fugue which commences thus —

" First you deliver your phrase,
    Nothing profound, that I see,
Fit in itself for much blame or much praise,
    Answered no less where no answer needs be.
Off start the two on their ways.

Straight must a Third interpose,
    Volunteer needlessly help ;
In strikes a Fourth, a Fifth thrusts in his nose,
    So the cry opens, the kennel's a-yelp,
Arguments hot to the close."

Examples of Fugues of this period are the *Cat's Fugue* by Dom. Scarlatti (d. 1757) on a subject suggested by a cat walking over the keys ; *Fugue in F* by J. Bernard Bach (d. 1749) ; *Fugues in D* and *D Minor* by Kirnberger (d. 1783) ; *in F* by J. Ernest Bach (d. 1781) ; and *in F Minor* by W. F. Bach d. 1784). For modern Fugues, *see* Chapter XVIII on the " Modern Contrapuntal Element."

CHAPTER VII

EARLY ITALIAN "CEMBALO" MUSIC

Early Italian Composers	Contemporary Works
1616. Frescobaldi. *Suites*, etc.	1550–1624. English Virginal Collec-
1620–1660. M. A. Rossi.	tions.
1697. Pasquini. *Variations*, etc.	1670. Chambonnière. *Ordres*.
1716. Zippoli. *Pieces*.	1696. Purcell. *Lessons*.
1733. Scarlatti. 1st *Sonatas*.	1713. Couperin. *Ordres*.
d. 1736. Pergolesi.	1720. Handel. 1st *Suites*.
d. 1740. Alberti.	Bach (1685–1750) and Handel
1746. Paradies. *Sonatas*.	(1685–1759).
d. 1756. Durante.	Haydn. Mozart (1774. Haydn's
d. 1767. Porpora.	1st *Sonatas*.)
1770. Clementi. 1st *Sonatas*.	Beethoven.
d. 1784. Martini.	
d. 1785. Galuppi.	
d. 1812. Turini.	
d. 1816. Paisiello.	
d. 1832. Clementi.	

As will have been gathered from the last Chapter, the influence of the early Italian Cembalo or Harpsichord School was an important one. Its strength lay (1) in the melodiousness of its polyphonic compositions, which were supreme until the appearance of those of Bach and Handel ; (2) in the superiority of its harpsichord technique, one which by its leaven of quasi-Corelli violin technique was the model for Beethoven, through the Italian Clementi. Frescobaldi (1587–1640), Organist of St. Peter's, Rome (1627), was the first to initiate a freer instrumental style, though those of his works intended for cembalo the Canzoni, Ricercari, Corrente, etc.) are certainly *organlike* and fugal in *style*. Even his Partite, or Variations Suite on an Aria (as in *Alte Meisterstücke*, Un. Ed.) and the Variations (1616) on *La Follia* (a Spanish dance theme) are mainly contrapuntal.

It is not until the second half of the seventeenth century that a free harpsichord style appears in the works of Pasquini (1637–1710), an organist in Rome strongly influenced by Frescobaldi and Froberger.

Pasquini evidently had a fondness for the Variation form and his smoothly written D minor *La Follia* Variations (1697–1702)

Pasquini Cuckoo Toccata

(Pasquini vol. Novello) show a notable advance on Frescobaldi's style. Those on the Italian *Bergamesca* dance show yet more variety. The *Toccata in C* shows organ influence, with its somewhat fussy " imitation " effects, and is interesting for comparison with the Toccatas of Bach, Pasquini's immediate successor.

One interesting piece, the *Toccata con lo Scherzo del Cucco* (1702), in which the cuckoo's notes are heard, is neatly and freely written in florid style. The call of the cuckoo seems to have been a favourite device in early programme music—as in the gay *Cuckoo Capriccio* of Kerl (1679) and the older contrapuntal example of his teacher Frescobaldi (1629).

Pasquini left also some very Handelian Basso Continuos for *Sonatas* for two cembalos, one of which has been ably filled in by Mr. Shedlock in his Pasquini volume (Novello) and from which Mr. Shedlock judges that he is " really the predecessor of the German master Kuhnau as a writer of Clavier Sonatas."

The four pieces by Zippoli (*Maîtres de Clavecin*, Litolff), dated 1716, are somewhat organlike and contrapuntal in style, but Porpora (d. 1767) in his Fugues (*see* last Chapter) and Marcello in the Presto of his *C minor Sonata* (Bonawitz Coll.,

Bos.) show Scarlatti-like harpsichord technique. The style of
the former appears directly in the works of Haydn, his pupil.

Strange to relate, to secure the next link in the evolution of a
clavier style one must go back to Michael Angelo Rossi, who
lived in Rome about 1620 and died in 1660, some thirty years
before any of the Pasquini compositions mentioned were written.
Rossi was a pupil of Frescobaldi—his style is remarkably
prophetic of that of Haydn, and is to be attributed to his being
an excellent violinist. In this case the correctness of the
period assigned has been doubted, but it is certain that the real
harpsichord style received its most powerful stimulus through the
Italian School of Violin and Chamber Music, which, through
Corelli, Vivaldi, Geminiani and others was pre-eminent between
1670 and 1750. Rossi as a violinist was a contemporary of the
predecessors of Corelli : Vitali and Biber.

In Rossi's works the gigue-like broken-chord figures (*see* last
Chapter) and roving scale passages of Corelli are punctuated, as
it were, into neatly barred or phrased motives.

Another feature in the evolution of technique, which was later
much exploited, was the so-called *Alberti Bass* (Ex. D), brought
forward by Dom. Alberti (b. 1717), though used before his time
by Rossi and others, and originating in such passages as the
Bass of Ex. C. by Rossi.

The compositions of Alberti, who settled in Rome in 1737,
were very popular in their day. The Gigue from his 4th
Sonata (*Old Masters*, May. Ash.) is remarkably bold in style.

Other smaller composers of harpsichord music are :—
Alessandro Scarlatti (1659–1725), the father of Domenico Scar-
latti, who wrote Toccatas, etc., his pupil G. Grieco, and Padre
Martini (1706–1784), the historian and theorist whose tuneful

and spirited Gavotte, Ballet, Prelude and Fugue and Allegro
(*Maîtres de Clavecin, II*) are worthy of preservation.

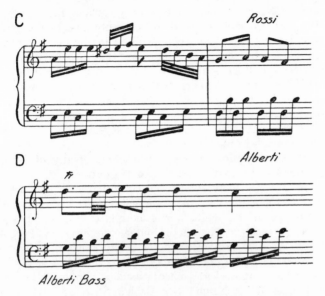

The most distinguished of the Italian School, however, is
Domenico Scarlatti (1685–1757), the contemporary of Bach and
Handel and pupil of his father Alessandro, and of Pasquini,
Domenico was reputed as the Italian virtuoso *par excellence* of
his time, and, on the visit of Handel to Rome in 1709, a contest
at the harpsicord was arranged in which the honours were
divided, though at the organ Handel was acknowledged as the
superior.   For two years Scarlatti was *Maestro al Cembalo* to the
Italian Opera in London, and afterwards he was Court Cembalist
at Lisbon, Naples and Madrid, where he is said to have died.
It was while he was in Madrid (1729–1754) that his first *Sonatas*
appeared (first ed. in Paris, 1733).   These so-called " Sonatas "
(originally *Studies*) consist mostly of single movements.
    The term "Sonata" here is opposed to " Cantata " the
former meaning to be " sounded," the latter to be " sung."   In
earlier times polyphonic compositions, both vocal and instrumental, were in the same style ; hence the vague direction *per
suonare o cantare*—" to be sounded or sung."

The position of Scarlatti's Sonatas in the *Story of Pianoforte Music* is an important one : (1) For their melodiousness, freedom of style and phrasing imbibed from the violin and Chamber Music of Corelli (1653–1713), whose first Suite-like Sonatas for two violins and bass were published in the year of Scarlatti's birth ; ` (2) for their position in the development of modern Sonata form, standing, as they do, between the Sonatas of Corelli and those of Em. Bach ; (3) for their development of keyboard *technique*. Scarlatti was the Liszt of his day. The frequent crossing of hands (*Sonata in A*), piquant staccatissimo effects, sudden leaps, bravura passages of sixths and octaves, present in most of his 300 harpsichord compositions, mark an epoch in modern technique.

Scarlatti's technique is superior to that of any of his contemporaries ; to that of the dainty Couperin (fifteen years younger), of the more robust but conservative Rameau (same age) or of the earlier and more energetic Purcell (d. 1695) who, twenty-six years his senior, wrote more in the style of Pasquini (Scarlatti's master), though his later contemporary, Pergolese (1710–1736), runs him close in his freely-written *Prelude* and *Variations* (*Old Masters*, Fl. May. Ash). Of Scarlatti's chief German contemporaries Bach approaches him most nearly in experiments in technique (*see* Bach's *Studies : Old German Composers*, Pauer.), for interlocking and quick alternate use of the hands, while Handel and his early associate, Joh. Mattheson, generally show some of the best features of Italian harpsichord technique.

Another aspect of Scarlatti's music is that of the purely *harmonic style* which, with him, takes up a definite position as compared with the half-contrapuntal style of his predecessors.

Speaking generally, Scarlatti formed the basis on which Paradies and Clementi built—the latter as founder of the modern pianoforte style.

The breezy tunefulness of Scarlatti, as in the *Sonata in A*, *Capriccio in E*, and refined *Pastoral*, his skilful contrapuntal work, as in the *Cat's Fugue*, his strong, rhythmical characteristics (*Tempo di Ballo*), combined with a wealth of interesting technical devices, all tend to make his works immortal. Scarlatti's works can be studied in the Germer Selection (12 *Sonatas*, Bos.), the 37 *Sonatas*, ed. by Barth (Univ. Ed.), 50 *Lessons* (Aug.) or in the 60 *Sonatas* (B. and H.).

Of less importance are the technically interesting *Studios* of Scarlatti's contemporary Durante, who was mostly a writer of church music.

Two later composers, Galuppi* (1706–85) and Paradies (1712–95), deserve notice. The former, who was in London from 1741 to 1744, wrote spirited and tuneful Gigues (*Old Italian Composers*) and *Sonatas* (1746. *Les Maîtres de Clavecin*, II), as well as the once popular *Toccatas* which form the subject of Browning's poem :—

" You sat and played Toccatas, stately at the clavichord.
What ? Those lesser thirds so plaintive, sixths diminished, sigh on sigh,
Told them something ? Those suspensions, those solutions, ' Must we die ? '
Those commiserating sevenths—' Life might last ! we can but try.' "

Paradies is specially noted for his bright and taking two-movement *Sonatas* (1746) which, as regards form, " would seem to form an intermediate stage between Scarlatti and Em. Bach " (Shedlock). One may note that the works of both of these composers show the influence of Scarlatti as well as the use of the *Alberti Bass Formula* and a leaning to a more modern style.

Paradies lived most of his life in London, where his twelve *Sonatas* were published in 1746. His works were studied assiduously by young Clementi and later by Cramer ; and along with the works of Scarlatti they formed the principal models for the next thirty years, after which Clementi, Haydn and Mozart became supreme. Paradies' *Sonata in F* is in what one would call " Handelian " style, with a very attractive Gigue ; and the Gigue from his second Sonata is also very bold. Light and fluent imitation is the chief feature of the interesting *Sonata in E minor*, while in the virtuoso *Sonata in D* there is a delightfully piquant first movement with much Scarlatti-like crossing of hands and a brilliant *Toccata Presto* Finale. His best-known Toccata is from the *Sonata in A*. (All these Sonatas have been published by Ash.)

Two still later composers deserve mention : Paisiello (1741–1816) and Ferd. Turini (1749–1812), both of whom trench on the Haydn period. Paisiello's works (*Old Italian Composers*) are distinctly Haydnish, probably as a result of his residence in St. Petersburg. Towards the end of the eighteenth century

* See *Musical Times* for May, 1923, article on " Round about a Toccata of Galuppi," by C. van den Borren (trans. R. Capell).

German music, though partly based on Italian models, began to be supreme, through Haydn and Mozart. The compositions of Matiello (c. 1783), Sarti (1729-1802) (six Sonatas published in London in 1762) and Sacchini (1734-1786), especially the latter (e.g., Op. 3 and 4), are modelled on Haydn.

Turini's music, however, though vigorous, is still in the pure Italian style.

The works of the old Italian School, terminating only a century ago, are interesting historically (1) as showing the material upon which Clementi and Haydn, the first two modern pianoforte composers, founded their style—the former influenced also by his entire devotion to the new pianoforte, the latter by his first love for the string quartet and its orchestra : (2) as containing much which, from its melodiousness, contrapuntal and (especially) technical importance, is permanently interesting and of lasting renown.

CHAPTER VIII

PURCELL AND ARNE

" Then Arne, sweet and tricksome ; and masterly Purcell." *Lay—Clerical Soul.—Leigh Hunt.*

" Musick is yet but in its nonage, a forward child, which gives hope of what it may be hereafter in England, when the masters of it shall find more encouragement. *'Tis now learning Italian, which is its best master, and studying a little of the French air to give it somewhat of gayety and fashion."* (*Purcell,* in his prologue to the Opera, *The Prophetess,* 1691).

1673. Locke's *Melothesia.*	*Contemporary Works*
1699. Playford's *Collection.*	1670. Chambonnière's *Ordres.*
1696. Purcell's *Lessons* (Purcell d.	1689. Anglebert's *Ordres.*
1695).	1697. Pasquini. *Variations,* etc.
1699. Blow's *Lessons.*	1713. Couperin's 1st *Suite.*
1713. Babell's *Lessons.*	1720. Handel's 1st *Suites.*
c. 1690–17. Hy. Simmonds' *Lessons.*	1733. Scarlatti's 1st *Sonatas.*
c. 1748–58. Nares' *Lessons.*	
c. 1750. Arne's *Lessons.*	

PURCELL (Introduction)

WITH the time of Purcell we come once more to an era in the history of English clavier music, which stands out conspicuously and deserves more appreciation than it secured until recently.

The old English Virginal School was, in its own era, supreme, and led the way in instrumental composition ; but by the time of the Purcell School continental composers are in full swing, and it must therefore stand on its own merits. It is curious that Oscar Bie should have dismissed the second or Purcell School with the sentence, " With John Blow, Henry Purcell, Thomas Augustine Arne, *in the following generation,* English clavier music blends with the general continental stream, till it is absorbed and must seek its nourishment from without." No wonder the English editors remark that " The author here makes a startling leap of a century or so in his chronicle of English composers."

C. F. Weitzmann, in his *History of Pianoforte Playing and Pianoforte Literature*, 1887 (Schirmer, New York, 1897), takes an equally short-sighted view when he classifies the 17th century school with the English virginalists and expresses the opinion that " The characteristic expression of this earlier English clavier school is a wearisome monotony of melody, rhythm and modulation ; it has therefore had no influence whatever on the further development of the art of clavier playing." It is only right to say that the periods are separated and a more enlightened and more detailed view is taken in Max Seiffert's later edition of the same work (Leipzig, 1899).

It is necessary to understand something of this Purcell period and what preceded it. The last of the virginal composers, Dr. John Bull, died in 1628. Henry Purcell (1658–1695) did not come forward as an instrumental composer till 1683, and then it was in Sonatas for two violins and bass and harpsichord —compositions greatly in advance of their time. His *Lessons for the Harpsichord or Spinet* were not published till 1696, the year after his decease. Meanwhile, he had been occupied principally with his powerful and masterly dramatic and church works. Looking backwards again, we note that Queen Elizabeth died and the period of the high-handed Stuarts began in 1603. The Commonwealth lasted from 1649 to 1660, when the Restoration took place and the organs in the churches began to play once more. Church music of all but the simplest type had languished, but secular and instrumental music flourished. As a matter of comparison, two elements were to be noted in the old virginal collections, *viz.*, the *polyphonic* or vocal style, and the bold and appropriate clavier technique displayed by the English masters. From the introduction of the School (about 1550) till the date of Purcell's first instrumental works (about 1683) the contest lay between these two elements. The polyphonic element was perpetuated in Madrigals for voices and Fancies or Fantasias for viols by Jenkins, Lawes and others ; but the instrumental technique stood still, so that, as Davey remarks in his *History of English Music*, " If the keyboard music had been of equal importance, then the reign of Charles I. and the Commonwealth would have been the greatest English period as regards instrumental music, but no advance seems to have been made by the English virginalists and organists." Then again, the dramatic or operatic element was ever in opposition to the contrapuntal, and the popularity of the declamatory Airs and Dialogues of Lawes and others, and of Masques and Operas leading up to Purcell's own masterly, dramatic musical works, all tended to the elimination of counterpoint.

As Dr. Walker, in his *History of Music in England*, aptly puts it, " After the Restoration counterpoint was at a discount ; and it was not until the time of Purcell that men began to see that instrumental work could be written which should combine learning with taste." Not but that " there was plenty of counterpoint in almost everything Purcell wrote, but it is counterpoint on a *consciously harmonic basis.*" (Scholes' *Introduction to British Music*.)

Purcell's style was formed through that of his master, Pelham Humphreys, who received his training in France and returned thence in 1667, and this, together with Purcell's leaning to Italian style, accounted for the new style of the School of English Harpsichord Composers from about 1683 onwards. The French influence on English music came at first through King Charles, after the Restoration, who, as Davey says, " killed the older English School, vocal and instrumental alike." Charles wanted music he could beat time to. As the composer and writer, Mattheson, friend of Handel, said, " The Italians exalt music, the French enliven it " ; and so the second English Clavier School, through foreign influence, became more exalted and more enlivened, or rather more *direct* in expression.

Italian musical influence in England was no new thing in Purcell's day. Even in Queen Elizabeth's time we find that Italy, which had learned the art from the Flemings, sent over Italian musicians. Alfonso Ferrabosco, a composer of virginal music and of Madrigals, was domiciled in Queen Elizabeth's Court in 1562, while the Italian dances, the Galliards and Pavans, were in fashion, and appear frequently in the *Fitzwilliam Virginal Book*. John Cooper (or Coperario) (d. 165 c.) studied in Italy and on his return wrote *Fancies* for viols and the organ. Italian influence had, however, so far proved a stimulus only, and the Early English Virginal School (1550–1621), as we have pointed out, stands by itself, unique. Between this " Golden Age " of English music, ending about 1625, and the publication of Purcell's *Lessons* (a period of some seventy years), compositions of no great merit, by G. Jeffreys,

Jno. Tillett, and I. Strengthfield, appeared. These, together
with Matthew Locke's method, named *Melothesia*, containing a
" choice collection of lessons " (1673) which already show
Italian influence, and the tuneful and neat *Lessons* of Locke and
Lawes in *Playford's Collection* (1689) fill the intervening
period.

Purcell, in his *Suites* (1683) for two violins and bass and in his
Lessons, acknowledges Italian influence.

Mr. Shedlock thinks that Purcell must have modelled his
Suites on the similar works of Vitali (1670).

One cannot play through the *Popular Pieces* by Purcell
(revised by Pauer in Augener's ed.) without feeling the forcible

instinct for rhythm—the rhythm which is the essence of the dance and is lost sight of in the Suites of Bach and Handel owing to the linked imitation with which they abound. Imitation is also present in Purcell, but the rhythmic and melodic interest is always greater. The florid *Preludes* of the 3*rd* and 5*th Suites*, and the *Toccata*, which was printed by the Germans as an early work of Bach, the ornamented Almands of the 3*rd*, 4*th*, 5*th* and 7*th Suites*, which surpass those of Bach and Handel in the pulsating rhythm of the dance, the unique grounds with their ever-varying melody over a repeated ground bass, and the rhythmical life of the Courante of the 7*th* and of the *Allmand and Courante in A minor* are arresting features.

Purcell's command of rhythm—the *life* of all music—in so great variety reminds one of Brahms, whom he surpasses in clarity and boldness.

Mr. Fuller Maitland, in his reference to the Chester Edition of the harpsichord music of Henry Purcell (in four volumes) mentions the fact that his successor in England, Handel, " appropriated many of Purcell's characteristic idioms " and that the movements are " full of character and originality." This Edition contains some newly-discovered Pieces. Concerning the ornamentation of the period—the student can refer to Dannreuther's work (Novello) and Dolmetsch's *Interpretation of the Music of the Seventeenth and Eighteenth Centuries* (Novello).

In conclusion we might quote Pauer's eulogy (*Popular Pieces*) : " As an inventor of harmonies he was far in advance of his time, and his melodies will find favour so long as men retain the sense of appreciating all that is beautiful and lovely in music."

Purcell's contemporaries and possible models in harpsichord music were of the contrapuntal age—and these men were Frescobaldi, Alessandro Scarlatti, Chambonnière and Froberger, to all of whom he is superior in freshness and vigour, and especially as regards melody and technique, in which he also surpassed his later contemporary Pasquini (1637–1710) (whose first representative pieces are dated 1697) and closely approaches the later Dom. Scarlatti (b. 1684).

During the period succeeding the death of Purcell (1695) and the arrival of Handel in 1710, English musical art was under the influence of Italian models as represented by Corelli,

D. Scarlatti and Handel. The poet Browning represents this
period thus :—

> " Buononcini's work is theme
> For fit laudation of the impartial few.
> (We stand in England, mind you!)   Fashion, too,
> Favours Geminiani."

To this time belong the *Lessons* of Blow (1698), the master of
Purcell, who preceded and followed his pupil as organist of
Westminster Abbey.   These are somewhat contrapuntal in style.
Also the *Lessons* of Henry Simmonds (born at the end of the
17th century), a fashionable teacher and performer in the
reign of George the Third, whose first set, though only in two
parts (May's *Old Masters*, Ash), are fresh and tuneful.   Also the
Suites of Lessons (1713) by Wm. Babell (*c.* 1690–1723), a skilful
harpsichord executant, the Preludes from which (Schloesser's
Old English Masters, Ash) show remarkable virtuosity for that
time.

The *Eight Sonatas or Lessons* (c. 1750) of Thos. Arne (1710–78),
the composer of *Rule, Britannia* (*Popular Pieces*, Arne, Aug.),
are worthy of remembrance for their fluent, neat, well-written
and melodious style, and, though showing the influence of
Handel, have something of English individuality about them.
In the *Eight Sonatas or Lessons* there is scarcely a single movement which, allowing for the thin writing of the period, is not
highly interesting.

In natural, vigorous, transparent melody they may be esteemed
superior to those of his predecessors, Scarlatti and Paradies, and
equal to those of Handel, his early contemporary ; while in
technique he is generally the equal of Paradies (but not generally
of Scarlatti) though his virtuoso Prelude to the spirited Fugue
from the *Concerto with Strings* (Ash) is quite equal to Scarlatti
or Handel.

Almost equal to those of Arne, the *Lessons* of James Nares
(1715–83) also sound remarkably fresh and modern.   Nares
was organist at York Minster and at the Chapel Royal.   He
published *Eight Sets of Harpsichord Lessons* in 1748, *Five
Harpsichord Lessons* in 1758, *Three Harpsichord Lessons* and
other works in 1778.   In the fourth volume of the *Oxford
History of Music* Mr. Fuller Maitland publishes *in extenso* a
Lesson for the Harpsichord in B♭, of which he says, " the poignant
expression of the first movement and the delicious freshness
and gaiety of the second are almost worthy of Bach."

Jeremiah Clark's (d. 1707) volume of harpsichord pieces, published in 1700 and his *Choice Lessons* published in 1711 after his death deserve attention, as also do the *Lessons* of Maurice Green (1696–1755), John Stanley (1714-86), the blind organist of St. Andrew's, Holborn, who wrote in the Handelian manner, William Bryce (1710–79), Master of the King's Music in 1755, Thomas Rosingrave (1690-1750), and Jonathan Battishill (1738–1801), harpsichordist at Covent Garden Theatre, whose compositions are, as Dr. Walker puts it, " nearly all very worthy work " compared with the similar class of music on the continent.

Sonatas by I. Burton (1766) and J. Worgan (1769) also appeared, while S. Wesley's three *Sonatas* and Cipriani Potter's *Studies* may be mentioned, though not possessing special interest. It is hardly necessary to say that Handel's arrival in England (1710) overshadowed our native composers, and it is only now that we are discovering the treasures we have in this country. Fortunately these are now appearing in our concert programmes and in the lists of teaching pieces—for instance, in the recent *Early English Harpsichord Music* revised by Alec Rowley (Rogers)—so that they may yet come into their own.

For further study *see Old English Masters*, ed. by A. M. Henderson (B. & F.) ; also J. A. Fuller Maitland's edition of *Contemporaries of Purcell*, 7 vols. [John Blow, vols. 1 and 2 ; Croft, vols. 3 and 4 ; J. Clark, vol. 5 ; Various, vols. 6 and 7 ; vol. 8, " At the Court of Queen Anne," various composers.] *See also Five Pieces* by Purcell (A.F. Co.).

CHAPTER IX

EARLY GERMAN SCHOOL

Early German Composers	Contemporary Works
1587-1648. Samuel Scheidt.	1616. Frescobaldi : *Works.*
1667. Froberger died.	1670. Chambonnière . *Ordres.*
1579. Kerl's *Cuckoo Capriccio.*	1673. Locke's *Melothesia.*
1697. *Suites*, etc., published.	1696. Purcell's *Lessons* published
1695. Kuhnau's 1st *Sonata.*	(died 1695).
1714. Mattheson, 1st *Suites.*	1713. Couperin's *Ordres.*
	1720. Handel's 1st *Suites.*

IN Germany a good foundation had already been laid in music, which, intended for either organ *or* clavichord, was, however, to all intents and purposes, organ music. The organists Paumann, Schlick, Hopheimer and especially Hans Leo Hassler (1612) and Samuel Scheidt (d. 1648) [*see Selected Pieces, Variations* and *Dance Forms* (B. and H.)] had prepared the way in everything but appropriate technique for the return of Froberger to Vienna in 1649 from Rome, where he had imbibed the freer Italian style. Froberger (1600-1667) was taken from Halle to Vienna and thence to Rome, where he was a pupil of Frescobaldi —eventually reappearing as a brilliant clavierist and organist. A legend is told of his being shipwrecked on the way to England, of his arrival in London destitute, and of his rescue by the organist of Westminster Abbey and presentation to Charles II. In the slow movements of Froberger's *Toccatas* (*Maîtres de Clavecin*, II) the influence of the organ is still apparent, as also in the original organ forms, the Canzoni and Ricercari, while the lighter characteristic triple time of the Italian Allegros is found in the quick movements.

His *Auf die Mayerin Suite*, having seven movements in Variation form (Gigue, Sarabande, Courante, etc.) on a popular song theme, shows a freer and more harpsichord (or clavichord) style of technique than that of his master Frescobaldi, and is less contrapuntal generally ; while other extracts from Suites seen in Niemann's *Frobergiana* (Senff) manifest something also of that refinement which we associate with the French clavecin school. (*See* also Adler Ed., 2 vols., B. and H.)

The organist J. K. Kerl (1627–1693), also a pupil of Fresco-baldi in Rome, shows the Italian leaven in his *Toccata, Canzoni,* etc., for organ or cembalo. His *Cuckoo Capriccio* (1679) [Three pieces by Frescobaldi, Froberger and Kerl (Shedlock, Nov.)] deserves special notice for its gay spirit and freer harpsichord style.

The clavier music of Johann Kuhnau (1660–1722) is somewhat organistic and has something of an old-world ring about it. More solid than the Italian compositions of that period, it lacks the warm glow of Italian melody and spirit ; neither has it the natural melody and energy of Purcell, nor the graceful technique of Pasquini. Kuhnau's chief merit is that his *Sonata in B♭* (1695) is the first real clavier *Sonata*, though so-called Sonatas of the nature of Suites had previously been written for two violins and bass. Thus we see that the clavier got not only its Sonata form, but much of its technique from that of the Italian violin and chamber music of the period, while its primitive instrumental style came from the lute.

Kuhnau adds the remark to his first Sonatas, " for why should not such things be attempted on the clavier as well as on other instruments ? " Other Sonatas named *Fresh Fruits* appeared in 1696. These also evince somewhat limited technique combined with contrapuntal and reflective style, and the constructive ability identified with German composers in general.

In these and the *Seven Partitas* (1695) one meets with certain expressions or idioms which we find later in the music of Handel and Bach. The *latter* master Kuhnau had preceded in Leipzig (1700) as Cantor of the Thomas Kirche. In 1700 appeared the interesting Programme *Bible Sonatas* (Shedlock Ed. Novello) in which, like the English virginal and other early composers, he adopts a definite programme. In this work he depicts graphically, in minute detail, incidents from the Bible, the first two being " The Combat between David and Goliath " and " David curing Saul by means of music."

In the former we have the whistle of the sling, as well as the thunder of the fall of Goliath.

Thoroughly German in style also are the *Suites* (Ed. published by R. Forberg) from the *Componimenti* (1727) of Gottlieb Muffatt (of probable Scottish origin), who was taught in Vienna, where he settled. They are contrapuntal and solid but not lacking in melody.

In the Suites (1714) of Johann Mattheson (1681-1764), the
early associate of Handel at the Opera House in Hamburg
(1703-9), we find something of Italian melody and vivacity.

Many of the movements in *Old German Composers* (Aug.) and
Old Masters (Ash), to which the reader is referred, are directly in
Handel's style, and are well worthy of study.   They suggest that
Handel, with his well-known faculty for assimilating what was
best in others, may have taken advantage of the many hints
which Mattheson boasted of having given him.   Mattheson was
first a singer and then conductor (at the cembalo) of the Opera
at Hamburg, then the leading Opera in Germany.   He is
also known as the writer of valuable historical books on various
aspects of music.

We must now proceed to the consideration of the principal
German composers of this period, Handel and Bach, after which
the music of their smaller contemporaries will be touched upon.

CHAPTER X

HANDEL AND BACH

> . . . "and Bach,
> Old father of Fugues, with his endless fine talk,
> . . . and the learned sweet feeling
> Of Handel."—*Leigh Hunt.*

> "Give me some great, glad subject, glorious Bach,
> Where cannon roar, not organ peal, we lack."—*Browning.*

	Contemporaries.
1685–1750. Bach.	1668–1733. Couperin.
1685–1759. Handel.	1683–1757. Scarlatti.
	1683–1764. Rameau.
	1681–1764. Mattheson.
	1685–1795. Paradies.

"Twin Giants of Polyphony" they have been termed. Both born in the same year, within a few miles of each other, their spheres of interest differed widely almost from the first, and the two countrymen were fated never to meet.

Bach, who first saw the light in Eisenach—now a pleasant tourist centre—came of a race of musicians who, for two hundred years, had been prominent in the musical history of Thuringia.

Handel, hailing from the neighbouring town of Halle in Saxony, came, strange to say, of an unmusical family.

Handel from the first was thrown into contact with Italian music. A visit to Berlin at the age of twelve made him acquainted with Ariosto Buononcini (afterwards his rival in London) ; they were members of the Court Orchestra there.

Bach, who went to a school at Lüneburg, near Hamburg, was early brought into contact with *French* instrumental music at the ducal Hof-Kapelle at Celle, though in his position as Concert-meister at Weimar (1714) he gave special attention to Italian Chamber Music.

His clavier Suites, with the exception of the *Italian Concerto*, show the influence of French rather than of Italian models (the first four of the *French Suites* being apparently modelled on Couperin, as is shown by their refined dainty melancholy) ;

43

while for the rest he was much influenced by the preceding organ
school of Germany (Buxtehude, Pachelbel, etc.).   Mr. Shedlock,
however, thinks that his *Chromatic Fantasia* was suggested by
an Adagio from a *Toccata* by Alessandro Scarlatti.

Bach's sympathies and experiences were strongly circum-
scribed, for, with the exception of a few visits to other parts of
Germany, he was domiciled and led a quiet life in one part of
the country, while Handel, who started at Hamburg as violinist
and deputy conductor of the Opera House, was almost from the
first by reason of his stay in Italy, England, and Hanover,
associated with the splendour of Courts and the publicity of the
Opera House and Concert Hall.

In 1717 Bach was appointed Kapellmeister at Anhalt-
Cöthen, where he gave special attention to the clavier, composing
the *French Suites*, the two-part *Inventions* and the similar
three-part *Symphonies*, as well as Part I of the immortal
Wohltemperirte Clavier.

In 1723 Bach was appointed Cantor (Precentor) of the St.
Thomas's School at Leipzig—a position he held till his death
twenty-seven years later.   In Leipzig he wrote the *English
Suites*, the *Concertos* for two, three and four Claviers with
Strings, and the *Musical Offering*.   With regard to the latter,
Bach had, in 1747, received an invitation from Frederick the
Great in whose Court his son was cembalist.   " On the day of
his arrival, when the usual list of visitors to the Palace was
presented to the King, Frederick was seated with his musicians
and about to play a *Flute Concerto*.   He took the list, scanned
it hastily, but, on alighting on the name of the Cantor, turned
hastily to his orchestra and joyfully exclaimed, ' Gentlemen, old
Bach has arrived! ' " (Naumann).   On arrival at the Palace,
Bach tried the new Silbermann pianofortes (then a novelty), and
then, by request, extemporized a Fugue on a theme suggested
by the King, accomplishing his task in a most masterly style.
Bach's *Musical Offering* consists of several Canons, Fugues in
three and six Parts, a Sonata and two-part Canon for clavier,
flute and violin, all worked after his return to Leipzig on the
theme given to him by Frederick and dedicated to the latter.

An interesting piece of programme music, and one doubtless
inspired by the *Bible Sonatas* of his predecessor in Leipzig, is
Bach's *Capriccio on the Departure of a Brother* (Bos), which
quaintly depicts the pleading of the friends to " remain with

us " and the " dangers in foreign lands," winding up with a lively fugue on a subject " imitating the Postilion's Horn."

The *Forty-eight Preludes and Fugues* have been termed the *Musician's Bible*, and have formed the subject of earnest study by Beethoven, Mendelssohn, Chopin, Schumann, and representatives of all musical creeds. Schumann described the *Forty-eight* as the " musician's daily bread." Beethoven said, " Play a great deal of Bach and everything will become clear to you." Bach's music, as a rule, is purely subjective and reflective in tone, while Handel's style, in consequence of his Italian models and devotion to Opera, is distinctly dramatic, straightforward and open in delineation of musical thought. Bach's is mostly the language of a poet and recluse, written, so to speak, in the eighteenth-century North German dialect. His style is, therefore, not so easily grasped as Handel's, but it is nevertheless full of poetry—depicting every mood found in the range of human emotion.

THE POETRY OF THE FORTY-EIGHT

In order to give the student an insight into the emotional nature of Bach we cannot do better than quote the *titles* suggested by " Carmen Sylva," Queen of Roumania, for the *Immortal Forty-Eight.*

1. C Prelude, *Sakuntala;* Fugue, *Her Wanderings in the Forest.* 2. C minor Prelude, *The Pathfinder cheerfully going to his Goal;* Fugue, *We should* (as Nietzsche says) *dance through Life.* 3. C♯ Prelude, *Harvest Festival, with desolate Stubble Fields;* Fugue, *The Village Dance, with Thoughts of Toil.* 4. C♯ minor Prelude, *Homesickness;* Fugue, *Comfort to world-weary Souls.* 5. D Prelude, *Mountain Stream;* Fugue, *Rustling of the Leaves.* 6. D minor Prelude, *The Conflict of Thought;* Fugue, *Answer to Doubts.* 7. E♭ Prelude, *Procession of Country Holiday-*

Makers; Fugue not named.   8. E♭ minor Prelude, *Atonement;* Fugue, *Salvation to the Sinner.*   9. E Prelude, *Lover's Declaration;* Fugue, perhaps the response.   10. E minor Prelude, *Murmur of the Sea;* Fugue, *Dialogue between Wind and Wave.* 11. F Prelude, not named ; Fugue, *A Breath of Spring.* 12. F minor Prelude, *Did I then ask to live?;* Fugue, *I have borne the Burden of Fate.*   13. F♯ Prelude, *The Lily-of-the-Valley's Summons to a Fairy Banquet;* Fugue, *Love's Young Dream.*   14. F♯ minor Prelude and Fugue, no names. 15. G Prelude, *Youth;* Fugue, *The Rover.*   16. G minor Prelude, *Eternal Questionings;* Fugue, perhaps the answers. 17. A♭ Prelude, *The Knights of the Round Table;* Fugue, *Sir Galahad.*   18. A♭ minor Prelude, *De Profundis.* Fugue, *Soft Sighs.*   19. A Prelude and Fugue, *Sunshine in the Basilica.* 20. A minor Prelude and Fugue, *The Secret.*   21. B♭ Prelude and Fugue, *Mayday Song.*   22. B♭ minor Prelude and Fugue, *Jephthah's Daughter.*   23. B Prelude and Fugue, *Sunday on the Rhine.*   24. B minor, *Vain Supplication.*   25. C Prelude, *Departure of the Exiles;* Fugue, *Their Songs on the Way.* 26. C minor Prelude, *The Fiery Cross;* Fugue, *The Coronach.* 27. C♯ Prelude, *Requiem Aeternam dona nobis, Domine;* Fugue, *Et Lux perpetua luceat nobis.*   28. C♯ minor Prelude and Fugue, *Who shall roll us away the Stone from the Door of the Sepulchre?*   29. D Prelude and Fugue, *O Death, where is thy Sting? O Grave, where is thy Victory?*   30. D minor Prelude, *The Spirit of the Storm;* Fugue, *Anarchy.*   31. E♭ Prelude and Fugue, *Portrait of a Girl-Friend.*   32. D♯ minor Prelude and Fugue, *Rustling of Autumn Leaves.*   33. E Prelude and Fugue, *Thankfulness for Beauties of Creation.*   34. E minor Prelude and Fugue, *Consolation.*   35. F Prelude, *Bridal Song;* Fugue, *Up out into the World.*   36. F minor, not named.   37. F♯ Prelude and Fugue, *Quiet Joys of Happy Home.*   38. F♯ minor Prelude, *Lovers' First Quarrel;* Fugue, *Reconciliation.*   39. G Prelude and Fugue, *Glad Tidings.*   40. G minor Prelude and Fugue, *Via Crucis.*   41. A♭ Prelude and Fugue, *A Glorious Career.* 42. G♯ minor Prelude, *Scheherazade;* Fugue, *Clouds from the Narghileh.*   43. A Prelude and Fugue, *Crusader's Return.* 44. A minor Prelude and Fugue, *Anxious Mother and Wilful Son.*   45. B♭ Prelude and Fugue, *Idyll of Love.*   46. B♭ minor Prelude and Fugue, *Parting and Tears.*   47. B Prelude and Fugue, *Parting and Tears* [sic].   48. B Prelude and Fugue,

Domestic Peace and Joy. 48. B minor Prelude, *Retrospect of Life;* Fugue, *Last Words.*

It is a remarkable fact that very few of Bach's compositions appeared in his lifetime, and that forty years after his death he was almost forgotten. It was not until 1779 that some of the *Forty-eight* were first published in London, where they were made known by Samuel Wesley—the next edition appearing at Zurich. Mendelssohn was the means of a general *resurrection of Bach's works* and the beginning of a cult which has now deservedly assumed enormous proportions.

Speaking generally, Bach's *clavier technique* is that of the *organ.* Practically speaking, his whole life was devoted to the organ, which embodied the spirit of the polyphonic tendencies of the age, and both his vocal and instrumental works are reminiscent of it. Nevertheless Bach brought the technical figuration embodied in his style to a high pitch of perfection. He was among the first to introduce the modern method of execution by systematizing the use of the thumb and the position of the hand. Previously the hand had been held horizontally and the thumbs hung down in front of the keyboard.

Both from a technical and contrapuntal point of view his *Goldberg Variations* form one of the most remarkable instances of this type of execution. Both these and the *Italian Concerto* bear evidence of being intended for the double-keyboard harpsichord in the necessity for transfer of one hand to a second manual and in the echo *p* and *f* effects. Every third variation is a Canon and Bach's sense of humour appears in the " 30 " which is a *quodlibet*—one made up of snatches of popular airs of the day.

That Bach took an interest in musical education is proved by the *Klavierübung,* an *Exercise Book* containing " Inventions, Preludes, Suites, etc." He commends the Inventions and Symphonies to the amateur who is anxious to learn—" that he may not only learn to play properly in two parts, but also, with further progress, to perform well in three, and, above all, to attain to a good *cantabile* style in execution."

The elegant canonic style of the Inventions and Symphonies is exchanged for a more robust and bravura one in the *Toccatas* (the *D major*), also the *Chromatic* and *C minor* Fantasias—a style in which the organ technique is particularly prominent in

the declamatory recitative and improvisatory bravura passages
which lead off to the usual Fugue.

A still more generally attractive style appears in his gay
Bourrées and Gavottes, Gigues, etc., in the *Partitas*, the 5*th* and
6*th French Suites*, and the larger *English* ones, reputed to have
been written for an English gentleman.   In these we note the
fine Preludes of the 2*nd* and 4*th English Suites* and the Saraband
and Allemande of the latter.   Mr. Fuller Maitland, in the
Oxford History of Music, Vol. IV says, " It has been shown that
the *English Suites* of Bach are, in several cases, adaptations of
movements from a book of Suites by Charles Dieupart (d. about
1740), which are proved to have been in Bach's possession, and
from the accident of Dieupart's living in England may well
have been known in Bach's family as the *English Suites*."

The *Italian Concerto* was written on the old Italian model,
which consisted of two quick movements with an intervening
slow movement.   The great *Concertos* for two, three and four
claviers with stringed orchestra (*see* Part III, Chapter XXII),
especially the one in D minor for three claviers, performed by
Mendelssohn, Thalberg and Moscheles in London and since
revived several times, are a monument to Bach's unequalled
powers as a contrapuntist.   Bach, indeed, must almost always
have looked at composition from a horizontal point of view.
Here again he differs from Handel.   The latter, though he does
not have the *variety* of harmony which we find in Bach, is really
more modern in style ; his more varied experience keeps him,
to some extent, more clear of the contrapuntal yoke, and Handel
thus " unites in himself the perfect blending of both epochs,
of the old one of strict polyphony and of the new one of
accompanied melody " (Riemann).   Owing to Handel having
modelled his style on the melodious contrapuntal works of the
Italians, Carissimi, Scarlatti and others, Handel excels Bach in
his vocal polyphonic works (the oratorios, etc.), while he created
instrumental works in his various sets of Concertos for Strings,
for Organ, and for Oboe soloists, " which hold an equal rank
with those of Bach " (Riemann).

Where Bach excels is in harmonic invention.   Purcell, who
admittedly copied Italian models, and died when Bach was ten
years old, specially excelled as chromatic harmonist in his day,
and it was left for Bach to build, though independently, on
Purcell's foundations.   There is this difference, however, that

Purcell's harmonies were produced more perpendicularly and those of Bach more horizontally or contrapuntally. In *manner* Purcell, like Handel, was the more modern ; in *result* Bach comes nearest to the present time.

Handel wrote little clavier solo music. There are two sets (16) of Suites, six Fugues and twelve smaller pieces [*see* the *Handel Gesellschaft's Collection*, Vol. II ; also Selection from second set of nine *Suites* and the smaller pieces ed. by Bülow in *Twelve Easy Pieces* (Augener).] These represent all that his busy life of concerto and opera, and oratorio work apparently left time for. His Suites are in the *style* of the *Italian* Chamber Music Suites, and are consequently free in style, showing the influence of the Ricercare of the Fugue Suite in which various contrapuntal movements appear. Hence we find Fugues, Variations, Adagios, and Allegros in his Suites. The *Harmonious Blacksmith* Variations in the *5th Suite* were so named by Lintern, a publisher in Bath, who wished to associate with the title the memory of his father—a musical blacksmith and lover of Handel. (*See* Part I, Chapter III.) Deserving special mention are a fine sweeping Prelude (*3rd Suite*), a free and Toccata-like Allemande (*8th Suite*), an energetic and interesting Presto (*2nd Suite*), the brilliant E minor Fugue (*4th Suite*), a Fantasia in C, and several very spirited Gigues.

Handel's clavier music possesses the virtues of the *Italian style*, its clearly defined and periodic melody, as compared with the usually more indefinite " linked sweetness long drawn out " of Bach, while his association with the " virtuoso " of the harpsichord, Scarlatti, possibly made him bid for the necessary " effect " on the clavier. Apart from this, Handel's whole mood was of the " heroic " order and his music (vocal and accompanimental at least) of the strongly " characteristic " style—his subjects always interpreting *in themselves*, *i.e.*, in their contour, the emotions implied.

In this feature of " characterization " Bach was certainly less prominent than Handel. On the other hand, his method of interpretation is not usually by *contour* of melody, but the more modern one of *harmonic colour*.

While Bach makes less use generally of this more modern method of characterization, he surpasses Handel in the depths of his emotions. Neither Handel nor Bach, however, are what would be called " characteristic " writers for the clavier, but the comparison may help in an estimate of the " twin giants of polyphony."

[The student may refer to *The Pianoforte Works of the Great Composers, Bach and Handel to Beethoven* (W. Reeves), in which the works of the above are treated in detail.]

In the Story of Pianoforte Music the period succeeding the death of Handel in 1759 begins at once to take on a crowded aspect. In the year mentioned, 1759, Haydn had already written his 1*st Symphony*. Em. Bach, whose work " at the parting of the ways " is discussed in Part III, Chapter III, had already been at work for twenty years, and his second set of Sonatas appeared the year after, in 1760. Clementi (Part II, Chapter V) appears on the scene ten years later, while the first Piano Sonatas of Haydn and Mozart follow close afterwards.

Musical evolution now assumes a new course. The era of polyphony, summed up in Bach and Handel, gives way to an harmonic age in which Sonata form becomes the all-in-all.

New centres of interest and comparison are formed and the works of many previous composers, popular in their day, are completely overshadowed. Meanwhile, it remains only to mention briefly the German contemporaries of Bach and Handel, whose names still survive. The chief of these, Em. Bach and Haydn, are referred to elsewhere. J. Adolph Hasse (1699–1783), whose pleasant *Sonatas*, Op. 6 and 7 (1754) (*Maîtres de Clavecin*, I), like those of Haydn, combine Italian melody with German solidity, was, like Mattheson, a tenor at the Hamburg Opera. In 1724 he became a pupil of Porpora and of Alessandro Scarlatti. His popularity as a clavecinist was the means of his earning the endearing title of " Il caro Sassone " (" the beloved Saxon ").

The Sonatas (1757) of Benda (1721-1795) have something of a Mozartian sweetness about them and also show Italian influence through his service in the King of Prussia's Court in Berlin (1742), where Italian tastes prevailed.

Benda resembles in some measure Em. Bach, whom he quite equals in style. His work, moreover, is more sympathetic and leans rather towards Mozart than Haydn. The *Suites of* Nichelmann (1717–62), who wrote in Couperin's style ; and the contrapuntal compositions of Marpurg (1712–95), Kirnberger (1721–83) (except the two and three-part Fugues), Eberlin (1716–62), Krebs (1713-80), and Rolle (1718–85) are of no special interest, while the tuneful but empty *Sonatas* of Wagenseil are now quite forgotten. The sons of Bach, other than Emmanuel—J. Chr. Fr. Bach (1732–95), Joh. Christian Bach (1735–82), known as the " London Bach," and Friedmann Bach (1710–84), the eldest and most talented son, are all composers for the clavier. Of these the latter is the most important. Friedmann had much of the masculine grip of his father, enriched also by a more modern feeling.

His remarkable *Grand Fantasia in E* and *A minor* and *major* (Ash), the bold *D minor Caprice and Fugue*, the *Fugue in F minor* (Bos), and the *Polonaises* (Bos), deserve to be kept in remembrance.

The works of Joh. Chr. Bach, who was an organist and settled in London in 1759, are mostly light and trivial in style. The three-movement *Sonata in C minor* (*Maîtres de Clavecin*, I), with the Fugue and Gavotte, in which he leans towards Mozart, are noteworthy for their solidity and melodiousness. J. C. F. Bach, in his Rondo and Variations [*Alte Meister* (Steingräber)] approaches Haydn in tuneful and neat, but also light style.

Finally, the art of writing an excellent *Fugue* seems to have been instinctive in the numerous branches of the Bach family, judging by the *F major Fugue* of John Bernhard Bach (1676–1749) (cousin of Sebastian) and the *Fantasia and Fugue in F* of his son *Joh. Ernst. Bach* (1722–81).

" Ye look your last on Handel ?——
Why wistful search, O waning ones, the chart of stars for you,
While Haydn, while Mozart occupies Heaven ? "—*Browning.*

CHAPTER XI

ONE important aspect of the preceding period is that of technique.

With Bach we have essentially an organ style and almost always a smooth-flowing one accordingly.

Handel, again, from his travels in Italy and his associations with Scarlatti, had acquired more of the true harpsichord style (though this was to some extent based on that of the Italian Chamber Music of the period) and consequently we find in his Fugal compositions more of that boldness and piquancy which we associate with the non-sustaining harpsichord and piano.

If one only compares, for instance, Bach's comparatively brilliant *Fugue in A minor* (Steingräber, Ed. No. 8, Vol. I) with Handel's *E minor Fugue* of the *4th Suite*, we shall see the nearer approach to the true harpsichord style in the latter, though Bach gets glimpses of it occasionally, as in Nos. 3, 10, 15 and 39 of the " 48."

What applies to Handel in this way is also applicable to his Italian models, to his predecessor Pasquini, his contemporaries Porpora and Durante, his later contemporaries Martini, Galuppi, and Paradies, and his successors (in this style) Turini (b. 1749) and Clementi (b. 1752).

The technique of the polyphonic style, as applied to the harpsichord, clavichord and pianoforte may be divided into three periods : (1) that of Frescobaldi (organ style), perfected in Bach ; (2) the quasi-violin style, probably initiated by Pasquini in the *D minor Follia Partita* Variations (*c.* 1697), which were founded on or suggested by the violin technique of Corelli (*Sonatas*, 1683), extended by Haydn and adopted by Clementi ; (3) the modern style initiated by Clementi, combining polyphonic with modern pianoforte style.

The essence of the Corelli influence is in the typical Italian fiddle-like Gigue (*Geige*, a fiddle) with its winding and piquant broken chord figuration as in *Allegro* 1683, one branch of which appeared in the subsequent *Alberti* bass.[1]

This freer, leaping style of technique is continued in the *Fugues* of Porpora (1685–1767), a contemporary of Handel and teacher of Haydn, especially in his *Fugue in B♭* (*see* Example) and similar compositions of Martini (1706–84).

Haydn based the *technique* of his chamber music on Porpora and the Italian models, and transferred it to his piano Sonatas, just as Handel used his violin harpsichord style in his organ Concertos. Meanwhile, Clementi brought over the same style to England and adapted it to the new pianoforte, and the result can be seen in the greater sweep of style in some of his Fugues, and in the contrapuntal studies in his *Gradus*. Mozart and Beethoven both founded their technique on Haydn, and Mozart's *Fugue in C* (*Fantasia in C*) might much more appropriately have been intended for string quartet or orchestra. Beethoven however, also assimilated the new pianoforte *technique* of Clementi's Sonatas, and the *Fugue in E♭*, Op. 35 (Variations,

[1] The broken chord style is, however, foreshadowed in Bull's *Les Buffons* Variations (1621) and Gibbons' *A minor Gallliards* (1621), and slightly in Froberger's (d. 1667) Gigue in the *Auf die Mayerin* Suite.

1803) is probably the first fugal classic written for the piano in something like real pianoforte style—a style which is also seen, though somewhat uninspired, in the Fugue to the *Sonata*, Op. 106.

Noteworthy Fugues by German composers in the *intermediate* (No. 2) technique mentioned above are two Fugues by Kirnberger (*Maîtres de Clavecin*, I), one in E♭ by Krebs (*Old German Composers*), and a *Capriccio in C* by Marpurg. Strange to say, the next great composer of Fugues, Mendelssohn, except in in the *F minor*, copied the organ style in consequence of his devotion to Bach.

Technique, or the bravura element, is pre-eminent in that old polyphonic form, the Toccata (from *toccare* = to touch or to play), of which the earlier examples begin with organ-like full chords and then, as in the later examples, run off through passage work into fugal periods. This form was most exploited by A. Gabrieli (1557–1613) and Merulo (1533–1604), and it remained popular until Bach's time. There are examples by G. Pietri in the Italian style, *tutta di salti* (*Fitzwilliam Virginal Book*), a spirited one by Kerl (1628–93), pupil of Frescobaldi (*Old German Composers*), the massive one in A minor by Froberger (1600–67), the light and fluent *Cuckoo Toccata* by Pasquini, and similar compositions by Paradies: but the most important, though composed in organ style, are the brilliant and florid Toccatas of Bach (Vol. I, Steingräber Ed.). After falling somewhat into disuse, the Fugal Toccata has been resuscitated by the excellent example of Rheinberger's Op. 12 in C. The florid *Prelude*, which is found in the old Suites of contrapuntal pieces and was later attached to the Fugue, somewhat resembled the Toccata, as did also the vague, imitative *Allegro* of Handel's and other *Suites*.

PART II

THE MUSIC OF THE PIANOFORTE

THE CLASSIC PERIOD

" The pianoforte is the modern foundation of all musical training."—
Hauptmann.

> " . . . A musician with flying finger
> Startles the voices of some new instrument.
> . . . . In one string are blent
> All its extremes of sound." . . .
> *W. C. Roscoe.*

CHAPTER I

THE pianoforte, harpsichord and clavichord existed together for several decades side by side. The earlier *primitive pianos* suffered somewhat in comparison with the comparative perfection to which the other keyboard instruments had been brought. Türk in his *Methode* of 1789 gives the preference to the *clavichord* because of its " delicate execution " and " pleasing singing tone," while Em. Bach in 1753 had said, " During the last few years my chief endeavour has been to play the *Pianoforte* as much as possible in a *singing* manner, in spite of its deficiency in sustaining the sound, and to compose for it accordingly."

In 1787, thirty-four years later, Em. Bach says that he still thinks " a good clavichord, saving its weaker tone, has all the beauties of the other (the piano) and has the further advantage of the " *Bebung*," and the sustained tone ; because after striking I can press down on any note."

It is evident from this that the earlier pianos were deficient in sustaining power.

The *Bebung* was a tremulous tone produced by the balancing or pressing down of the finger, as already mentioned.

The first we hear of the *invention* of the *Pianoforte* is from Count Maffei, who, in 1711, describes a new cembalo brought forward by Cristofali [*sic*], the cembalist to the Prince of Tuscany, in which, instead of the usual arrangement for plucking the strings with quills, there is " a row of small hammers " for striking the strings, also the new instrument has the power of playing *piano* or *forte*—which facility was absent from the usual cembalo (harpsichord), though not from the clavichord. The early piano did not make much headway because of its lack of power and its new style of touch, and it was not until 1767—fifty-six years afterwards—that the Silbermann pianos, as improved upon originally at the suggestion of Bach, became at all popular.

It will be remembered (Part I, Chapter 10) that twenty years previously Bach had tried the Silbermann pianos at the Palace of Frederick the Great at Potsdam. In the year 1767 already mentioned, one of Zumpe's pianos—" A new Instrument call'd Pianoforte "—was used at a concert in London. On May 19th, 1768 Mr. Henry Walsh of Dublin gave a public pianoforte recital in Dublin, and later in the same year, I. Christian Bach made his first appearance as a pianist in London. Schroeter, also known as a pianist, appeared there in 1772.

In 1753, as we have quoted, Em. Bach was already endeavouring to write for the piano, but it was not until 1770, in the first Sonatas of Clementi, that the genius of the instrument was divined.

Erard made his first piano in Paris in 1777, but the important " double escapement " action did not appear till 1823. Previous to this, Americus Backers (c. 1776) invented in London the " English " or single-escapement action which was perpetuated by Broadwood and " demands higher finger movement from the player " (Hipkins) than the Erard or later actions. It was this *English action* which favoured Clementi in his more sonorous style of technique.

The piano containing the light *Viennese* or Silbermann-Stein action, as praised and adopted by Mozart in 1771 (and as continued by Streicher), favoured the easy and brilliant execution of the Viennese School of playing founded by Czerny.

A further step in the evolution of the piano was the invention, in 1820, of the cast-iron frame, designed to meet the titanic demands of virtuosos of the Liszt School.

The latest development seems to be the typewriter-like Janko keyboard, which, with its closely-packed rising tiers of keys, promises to make the extended technique of Henselt and Liszt quite a matter of ease.

CHAPTER II

" Ye know why the forms are fair, ye hear that the tale is told ;
It is all triumphant art, but art in obedience to laws."
                                    Browning, " Abt Bogler."

THE second period in the story of pianoforte music is bound up with the Sonata form.

In the first era we found ourselves confronted by two apparently irreconcilable elements—the old dance form and the polyphonic forms culminating in the Fugue.

By the time of Handel and Bach, however, these two forms have become more or less blended in the freer style of Suite from which came the notion of the cyclical nature of the Sonata. The Sonata, as now known, is by no means a haphazard conglomeration. Centuries of deeply thought-out experiment have gradually evolved the fittest presentation of the highest of all musical forms. The title " Sonata " with its meaning " *to sound* " rather than " *to sing*," as in " Cantata," early became applied to the old *Suites* of dance forms, especially when they were intended for stringed instruments ; and they retained the name when the titles of the dance forms were changed. As Marpurg puts it, in 1762, " Sonatas are Pieces in three or four movements, marked merely Adagio, Allegro, Presto, etc., although in character they may be really an Allemande, Courante and Gigue."

The feature of the old Suite was that the dance forms were all in one key.

The placing of the middle Adagio (referred to by Marpurg) in another key was the first step towards the modern cyclical form of the Sonata.

A collection of movements, however, does not necessarily form a modern Sonata. For this latter it is generally expected that the first movement should be in what is called " Sonata

Form," that is, built on two themes, which, roughly speaking, are treated in this manner in three sections :—

Exposition	Development	Recapitulation
A. 1st Theme	Development of both themes	(1) Repetition of A as before
B. 2nd Theme in contrasted key		(2) Repetition of B now in key of Tonic

The evolution of this form is seen in its embryo stage in some of the double-themed movements of Corelli's so-called *Sonatas* for two violins and bass (1683), while in 1696, Handel's Sonatas for two oboes, and movements of his third harpsichord Suite, show attempts at development and recapitulation after the modern manner.

It should be mentioned here that what is called the " *Old Sonata Form* " of this period differs mainly from the modern form thus :—

Exposition	Recapitulation
A, 1st Theme	A in key of B
B, 2nd Theme (often fragmentary in contrasted key)	B in key of A

The one-movement so-called *Sonatas* of Scarlatti are written mostly in this form, though the 2nd Theme is usually ill-defined.

It is in 1695 that Kuhnau's *Sonatas* (*see* Part I, Chapter V)— the *first real clavier Sonatas*—appeared.   In these Sonatas some approach is made to the modern form, only the nebulous second subject is neither developed nor repeated.   Sonatas were written by Pasquini, Galuppi and Paradies, the latter showing an advance on Scarlatti in matters of form (*see* Chapter VII) ; but the next link, an important one, comes with Em. Bach, whose work is described in the following Chapter.

In Em. Bach's *Sonatas for Students and Amateurs* (*see* next Chapter), the second subjects are usually clear, while the development and recapitulatory sections cause the form to approximate to that used by Beethoven, whom he anticipates also in his unexpected modulations and sudden contrasts. Em. Bach is also much less contrapuntal than Kuhnau in style. Haydn (*see* Part II, Chapter IV) built on and imitated Em.

Bach, but in his later works (1776 and 1780) he comes nearer to his pupil Beethoven both in development and in spirit of expression.

Mozart, with the exception of the C minor (1784), wrote his Sonatas (see Part II, Chapter IV) apparently for the " long ears "—in a light and popular style. His best work, however, surpasses that of Haydn.

Mozart and Haydn together enlarged the scope and development of the three sections of the typical 1st movement, while they greatly improved the slow movements and finales. Both composers were strongly influenced by Italian models and by their own devotion to violin and chamber music ; the result being (1) a more *melodious* style ; (2) the cultivation of a more fluent and more highly *phrased* and punctuated style. Clementi was the first to furnish the appropriate *technique* of the *Sonata* as written for the new pianoforte and utilized by Beethoven, and in Rust we find some anticipation of the depth of feeling presented in Beethoven's works.

It was Beethoven himself, however, who perfected the Sonata (*see* Part II, Chapter VII), by experimenting both as regards the number and kind of movements, by enlarging the bounds of key and modulation, by weaving into it an intensely animated weft of thematic development, and by filling the form with a greater range of feeling—from the tragic despair of the Adagios to the light-winged play of the Scherzos, while he also considerably developed the technique, introducing the virtuoso element with artistic effect.

The work of Em. Bach, Clementi, Haydn, Mozart and Beethoven in connection with the Sonata is further dealt with in the respective Chapters devoted to them. It will help the student to grasp in his mind the rapidity of the evolution of the Sonata, occupying little more than fifty years (from Em. Bach to Beethoven), if he will consult the following Table :—

THE SONATA

Homophonic	Polyphonic
For Harpsichord or Clavichord	
	1695. Kuhnau. *Sonatas.*
	1703. Pasquini. *Sonatas.*
	1713. Mattheson. *Sonatas.*
1733. D. Scarlatti. *Lessons* or *Sonatas.*	1730. Couperin. 3rd Collection *Suites.*

Homophonic   *Polyphonic*
For Harpsichord or Clavichord

1742. Em. Bach. *Sonatas* (1st-set).   1741. Rameau. *Concertos.*
1746. Paradies. *Sonatas.*   1744. Bach's " 48," Pt. II.
1754. Paradies. *Sonatas.*   1752. Bach's *Art of Fugue.*
1760. Em. Bach's 6 *Sonatas.*
1770. Clementi's *First Sonatas.*
1774. Haydn's 6 *Sonatas.*
1776. Mozart's 6 *Sonatas.*
1775. Rust's 1st *Sonata.*
1778. Rust's *D minor Sonata.*
1780. Haydn. 6 *Sonatas.*
1781. Em. Bach's *Sonatas for "Forte
     Piano."*
1780–90. Hässler. 3 sets *Sonatas.*
1784. Mozart. *C minor Sonata.*
1796. Beethoven to *Op.* 2.
1802. Clementi to *Op.* 40.
1802. Beethoven to *Op.* 31.
1808. Dussek. *Le Retour à Paris.*
1821. Clementi. Last *Sonatas.*
1822. Beethoven, *Op.* 111.

CHAPTER III

DEVELOPMENT OF THE MODERN SONATA

Emmanuel Bach (1714–88)

" The form is the mould in which genius is cast."—*Schumann*.

THE position earned by Emmanuel Bach (1714–88) in the story of pianoforte music is that of having enlarged and settled the *form* of the *Sonata*.

In this way he stands intermediate between his father, J. Sebastian Bach, who, in his Preludes, experimented in what we now call modern Sonata form, and Clementi and Haydn.

Em. Bach came early under Italian influence. In 1740 he was cembalist to Frederick the Great, accompanying, as part of his duties, that monarch's performance on the flute.

Italian music at that time was much in favour at the Prussian Court. It was in 1740 also that his first set of Sonatas (dedicated to Frederick) were composed, Haydn at that time being eight years old; but his best-known collection, *For Connoisseurs and Amateurs*, were composed between 1773 and 1787, when representative works by Clementi and Haydn were already in existence.

As a link between the old and the new *styles, fortes, pianos, crescendos and diminuendos*, together with unexpected modulations and enharmonic transitions, are of special interest. The restless modern spirit is also present, though only in outline ; but his work is marred by the formal nature of the theme and by its fragmentary working out.

As regards his share in the evolution of the modern Sonata, we have not space to go into great detail, but it is interesting to note how, with Em. Bach, the second subject becomes more clear and definite. We note how the old form, as in Scarlatti, with its direct double transposition of both first and fragmentary second subjects in the second half (*see* Chapter II) takes the intermediate method of interposing some development of the chief theme in its transposed key, and how this then leads direct to a full recapitulation of both subjects in the tonic, as in the modern form.

With Haydn and Clementi the transposed fragmentary first theme gives way at once to the more modern development of the second, or portions of both subjects.

In Em. Bach's Sonatas the somewhat vague and comparatively undeveloped slow movements also eventually emerge into the more developed form as used by Haydn and Beethoven, though on the whole they are thinner and not so richly harmonized in style as those of his successors. In one particular, however, viz., emotion, his slow movements, being more reflective and Teutonic than those of the Croatian Haydn or of the Italian Clementi, come nearer to those of Beethoven, as is pointed out in detail in the excellent Schenker Edition (U. Ed.).

In Emmanuel Bach's quick movements the prevailing Italian fashion is noticeable, as it is also in his technique, which is old-fashioned and partly resembles that of his father.

In Style of Composition Em. Bach broke away from the fugal style of his father. In his introduction to the Science of Accompaniment and Free Improvisation (1762) he says, " The taste of to-day has brought into vogue a style of harmony quite different from that formerly in use."

This " homophonic " or galant style, inculcating a more, purely harmonic method, was particularly developed by him, and in this he became the model for his immediate successors : Haydn, who remarked, " I owe much to him," and Mozart, who said, " He is the father and we are the children."

Besides the Sonatas he wrote some very modern Rondos, the form of which he solidified, introducing, after the manner of Couperin, much variety of key and treatment in the repetitions of the chief theme. His gay, almost Haydnish Fantasias, though modern in spirit, are mostly built on the plan of the old Fugued Toccata.

As an executant on the clavichord Em. Bach is known to have shown extraordinary skill and neatness. His critical study of the Italian and French composers of that period and the confusion arising from the various methods of interpreting the " Manieren " or " graces " then in use led to the appearance of his important work, The Correct Method of Playing the Clavier

(1753), in which explanations are given of the various embellishments. Preferring always the clavichord, both as a performer and composer, he stands at the parting of the ways as compared with Clementi, who wrote always for the new " Fortepiano," and thus inaugurated the modern Pianoforte School. Mozart did not adopt the piano till after 1777 and his leaning towards the harpsichord was particularly noticeable in his Sonatas and lighter works.

Em. Bach's chronological position is seen as follows :—

EM. BACH, 1714–88.

1732. Haydn born.
1733. D. Scarlatti's 1st *Sonatas.*

1740. 1st set *Sonatas.*

1741. Rameau's *Concertos.*
1746. Paradies' *Sonatas.*
175e. Mozart born.
1770. Haydn's 1st *Sonatas.*

1773–87. *Sonatas* for " Connoisseurs, etc."

1774. Mozart's 6 *Sonatas.*
1781. Beethoven's early *Sonatas,*
etc.

CHAPTER IV

HAYDN AND MOZART

" Every composition reveals the model from which it is derived."—
C. M. Von Weber.

	1685. Bach and Handel born.
	1750. Bach died.
1732–1809. Haydn.	1759. Handel died.
1756–91. Mozart.	1770. Clementi. 1st *Sonatas.*
	1788. Em. Bach died.
	1795. Paradies died.
	1796. Beethoven. *Op.* 2, dedicated to Haydn.
	1804. Field settles in St. Petersburg.
	1808. Weber. *Polonaise in E♭* and *Variations.*

IN the last Chapter we discussed the part taken by Em. Bach in the evolution of the Sonata.

The clavier history of Haydn and Mozart is likewise summed up in the development of that tonal structure, and, in a smaller way, in the Variation form.

Formal development, however, is not everything. Harmonic style also counts for much.

At an earlier stage we classed together Bach and Handel as leaders of polyphony. In a similar way we can associate together their successors Haydn and Mozart, as *initiating modern harmonic style.*

New forms and new harmonic style do not yet, however, suffice to distinguish the leaders of a new era. We must look, in addition, (1) to the *influence* of the *orchestra*, introducing a more minutely-phrased structure, which, in its turn, paved the way for the thematic development of Beethoven ; (2) in the case of Haydn, to a new humanizing element—that of *folk-song* or *folk-tune*, representing the virgin store of melody hidden in the hearts of the people. The gay-spirited music of Haydn, the Croatian—of Slavonic origin and peasant stock—appealed to the world at large because of the ingenious Croatian folk-song melodies hidden therein. Mr. Hadow, in his *A Croatian Composer*, says, " Some of his tunes are folk-songs altered and improved, the vast majority are original, but display the same general characteristics of Croatian folk-song," and he adds that the folk-tunes " find their way into everything—hymns, quartets, divertimenti—not because Haydn had any need to take them, but because he loved them too well to leave them out." When we consider how much of the phraseology of Mozart and Beethoven comes from Haydn, especially in their earlier works, we cannot overestimate the influence of this *national* element.

Apart from this, the music of Mozart (who was of Bavarian stock), shows also his attractive personality. This doubtless was much influenced by his career as a prodigy in nearly every European Court, where, as *virtuoso* and composer, he was the spoilt child of fortune.

We have spoken of *Italian influence* on these composers. Haydn was a pupil of Porpora in Vienna (whose Italian music at that time was much in request), and studied Clementi and Paradies as well as the works of Em. Bach who, as we have already said, influenced him strongly in the architecture of the Sonata form. Porpora's influence is perhaps the strongest, and it is interesting to note how the phrases of Porpora permeate Haydn's work. For instance, whole sections of Porpora's *Fugue in B♭* appear in Haydn's *Creation* (" The Heavens are telling " and " Achieved is the glorious work "). Mozart, again, through his sojourn in Italy and his composition of Operas in the Italian style, was thoroughly imbued with Italian melody. It will be noted that Haydn was the senior of Mozart by some twenty-four years, and that he also outlived his junior by eighteen years. Owing to this, the music of the two, who were great friends, reacted one on the other. Mozart learnt much from " Papa " Haydn, and subsequently Haydn showed that he had profited by the work of Mozart before the latter's untimely death.

Haydn's interest as a composer was chiefly centred in the symphony and string quartet, and it was not till 1774, four years after the *Op.* 2 of Clementi, who was twenty years his junior, had appeared, that he wrote his first Sonatas for piano.

Haydn's thirty-five Sonatas for piano do not equal those of Beethoven, though his last two in *E♭*, the *Genziger Sonata* and the *Op.* 78, approach him closely in some ways, while they again are surpassed by the best of Mozart.

Some of Haydn's, like some of Mozart's, are rather old-fashioned, and in both cases the pianoforte technique is not equal to that of Clementi, owing to their use of the harpsichord and the light-actioned Vienna piano.

Mozart's first six Sonatas appeared six years after those of Haydn. It may be said that the weaker ones by both were written for educational purposes and therefore to some extent in the fashion of the period.

Regarding the influence of Em. Bach, we recall that Mozart had said, " He is the father and we are the children," while Haydn acknowledged how much he owed to him ; and it is therefore interesting to find that Haydn was accused of caricaturing his model in his earliest Sonatas.

Apart from limits in form, the resemblance could probably be traced in little tricks of manner, surprise modulations, un-expected pauses, *sudden pianos* and *fortes*, in which Em. Bach was trying to make the most of the resources of the new piano-forte. In general style, however, Haydn is really nearer to Clementi than to the half-contrapuntal Em. Bach.

One special feature with Haydn is that the left hand is almost invariably employed with accompanimental work. It occasion-ally initiates, alternates with, or imitates a phrase, but it lacks the interchange and inversion of theme so characteristic of Beethoven's thematic work. Haydn looks on his work, as it were, from the point of view of a first violinist ; Mozart, to continue the simile, gives more attention to the 'cello or double bass ; while Beethoven divides the work and interest among all the parts. Mozart's left-hand part is more independent, and dialogue or imitation of that part is more frequent.

Haydn's Sonatas graduate in merit according to their date of appearance. Those of 1776 are better developed than the first set, and his finest works, as we have mentioned, are the last two in E♭ which, for Haydn, show unusually deep feeling.

As regards Mozart's Sonatas, Mr. Shedlock singles out three as of surpassing interest, the *A minor* (1778), the *C minor* (1784) and the one in *F* (1788). " In the first, as regards the writing, virtuosity asserts itself, and in the third contrapuntal skill ; but in the second the greatness of the music makes us forget the means by which that greatness is achieved " (*The Pianoforte Sonata*). The *C minor* comes nearest to those of Beethoven in nobility and unity of ideas. Mozart and Haydn both improved much on the thin style and disconnected subject-matter of Em. Bach. Their completeness of idea and greater fullness of style, together with some thematic development, make a step forward in the evolution of the Sonata (*see* Part II, Chapter III) ; while, to discriminate in our summary a greater depth of feeling and a realization of some of the possibilities of pianoforte technique mark out those of Mozart as superior to those of Haydn.

The model for Mozart's technique is contained in his own words : " Above all things a player should possess a quiet, steady hand, the natural lightness, smoothness and gliding rapidity of which is so developed that the passages flow like oil."

Haydn was so much of the violinist that in writing to his publisher in 1788 he says, " I was obliged to buy a new forte-piano, that I might compose your clavier Sonatas particularly well " ; while Mozart, as we know, was a virtuoso on the clavier from his childhood.

Mozart's superiority as a pianist is maintained also in his classic Concertos (*see* Part III, Chapter XXII) of which he founded the present form. In these he shows to advantage the art of displaying the brittle " tone " of the piano against that of the orchestra. Those of Haydn belong rather to the older style in which the piano part is more in the nature of an obbligato than of a solo part.

The favourite *Concerto in D minor*, the *Coronation*, and the last *in B♭* by Mozart are still heard in the modern concert room.

The *Variations* of Mozart and Haydn, following, as they do, Italian models, are mostly of the embroidery order and in the melodic style (*see* Part III, Chapter XXIV). With Mozart especially, by means of various technical figures, the melody is broken up into many various forms. Haydn, however, leans more to the harmonic style of treatment. His *F minor Variations*, those for " scholar and master " in Duet, as well as the Duet Variations of Mozart, stand out prominently.

Of the other works of Mozart, the energetic *Sonata in D* for two pianos is one of the classics in that form, while his Duet Sonatas, the first Duets written (No. 1, 1765), still rank as important in Duet literature (*see* Part III, Chapter XXIII).

There are also the quaintly sweet *Rondo in A minor* and the noble (2nd) *Fantasia in C minor* and the similar one attached to the *C minor Sonata*.

Haydn wrote less than Mozart for the piano, and his other miscellaneous pieces are of no particular merit.

Generally speaking, Haydn's works are especially characterized by an ever-flowing sprightly wit and humour, by perfect finish and development ('' according to his lights ''), and by a fund of refreshing melody in which, as we have pointed out, Croatian influence was strong.   Mozart was the soul of sincerity. If Haydn was the first apostle of wit, Mozart was the first in the modern style to bring out depth of feeling combined with grace and delicacy of expression ; in the former he anticipated Beethoven, as, for example, in his fiery and passionate *C minor Sonata*.

Mozart's *melody*, though Italian in cast, was always spontaneous and sincere, and in chromatic *harmony effects* he was, for his times, a daring experimenter, but in this he was always effective.   Finally, as a whole, Mozart's style was essentially diatonic.   His saying, '' Melody is the essence of music,'' is in keeping with his own general inclination to favour the beautiful at the expense of the characteristic, to revel, as it were, in sheer beauty of sound rather than in its power of interpreting or depicting in itself the various human emotions.

For this latter power, however, we must look ahead to Beethoven, .and especially to the romantic composers who succeeded him.

We shall require now to anticipate a little with regard to the position of Clementi, who was really the senior of Mozart by some four years.

It is characteristic of the subject of pianoforte music that not only do its historical periods overlap each other, but its schools also.   For instance, we note that, while Scarlatti and Paradies in Italy, with Clementi in England, are developing one style of art, Em. Bach, Haydn and Mozart in Germany are working out another.   Or, to quote an earlier parallel, while Frescobaldi in Italy is writing Suites with primitive, organlike technique, the English Virginal School is already reaching a climax in technique and developing a real harpsichord style.

Clementi, therefore, stands for us (1) as the successor of Scarlatti and Mozart, (2) as the originator of a genuine pianoforte style both as composer and executant.

Unlike most composers, Clementi lived a long as well as a most useful life, and on a stage which is already becoming crowded he occupies a unique position in the story of pianoforte music as bridging over the interval between the old and the new.

CHAPTER V

CLEMENTI, THE "FATHER OF THE PIANOFORTE," DUSSEK, RUST, ONSLOW AND HÄSSLER

1739–96.	F. W. Rust.	1770.	Clementi. 1st *Sonata*.
1747–1822.	I. W. Hässler.	1775–8.	Rust. 1st *Sonatas*.
1752–1832.	Clementi.	1780–90.	Hässler. Three sets *Sonatas*.
1761–1812.	Dussek.	1792–8.	Dussek. *Sonatas, Op.* 35.
1784–1852.	Onslow.	1796.	Beethoven. *Op.* 2.
		1806.	Dussek. *Elégie Harmonique*.
		c. 1800.	Onslow. *Op.* 2 and *Duet Sonatas*.
		1821.	Clementi. Last *Sonatas* (*Didone Abbandonata*).
		1822.	Beethoven. Last *Sonatas*.

It is significant of the rapid rise and perfection of the youngest of the arts that the life-time of one man should witness the transition from the skeleton Sonatas of Scarlatti to the perfection of that art form by Beethoven, and that this man—Clementi—should (1) have been born while Handel and Scarlatti were alive, should (2) have survived the decease of Beethoven as well as Schubert and Weber, and (3) should have been living while Liszt was at work on his *Paganini Caprices*.

The " Father of the Pianoforte," as he is styled in his epitaph in Westminster Abbey, left Italy at the age of fourteen, in 1766. Already a youthful virtuoso, he had also written several contrapuntal works as a pupil of Cordicelli.

The rest of his life, with the exception of visits to the Continent, was spent in this country, where he was trained at the expense of a " Sir Beckford " (as Marmontel terms him), the cousin of the author of *Vathek*.

For four years young Clementi studied most assiduously at the house of his benefactor in Dorsetshire. Here he had a rich literary and musical library at command, and it is said that Bach, Handel, Scarlatti and Paradies—the leading lights of his day—were his favourite composers. Added to these, no doubt, were other Italian composers for clavecin that he had known in Italy, including Martini and Marcello. The works of these

71

composers he is said to have played with ideal perfection, " the clearness of his touch and the variety of his nuances being without parallel."

Clementi's chief pupils, John Field and Cramer, also possessed the same degree of clarity of touch. In playing the Fugues of Bach they brought out each part distinctly with the necessary tone, accent, etc., to ensure its individuality. As a result of Clementi's study in private, there appeared, in 1770, (the year he left Dorset for London), his remarkable *First Sonatas*, Op. 2.

Technically in advance of all notable works of the time, the first *Sonata in C* contains features of interest which reappear in Beethoven twenty-six years later.

It is evident, from a comparison of the works of Em. Bach, Haydn and the Italian clavier composers, that the remarkably advanced style here shown by Clementi was the result of the study of the free, fluent style of Durante, Galuppi and other Italian composers. Clementi, the Italian, did for the pianoforte technique of his day what Liszt, the Hungarian, did later on. At that time the Italian School was in the ascendant. The style of Handel, who was also resident in this country, was Italian, and Bach himself, although a stay-at-home, looked with favour on the pleasant and learned Italian style and endeavoured to write his Italian Concerto in that manner. The *technique* which Beethoven adopted from the Sonatas of Clementi was therefore Italian in its origin, and it may be that he also acquired some of his vigour of style and his special use of the *sforzando* from Clementi, whose compositions he much admired.

Young Clementi was ambitious and he showed the virtuoso tendency of Scarlatti and his confrères in rapid passages of thirds, broken octaves in the bass, quick alternate flights of octaves and sixths, telling broken-chord and scale passages. He was throughout, in his piano Sonatas, ahead of the more *orchestrally*-minded Haydn and Mozart, both as regards technique, form and style ; and this probably arose from the fact that he gave all his energies to the piano and did not share the manifold activities of the two South German composers. The difference is also due to the fact that Clementi composed for the English piano, which allowed of more sonorous effects than the lighter action of the Vienna piano in use on the continent.

The first piano recital in London was given in 1768 by

J. Christian Bach, son of the great Sebastian, but Clementi's Sonatas (Op. 2, 1770) were the first published in this country as written exclusively for the piano.

The piano was yet in its infancy, and previous works had been inscribed as " For Pianoforte or Harpsichord," so that Clementi was the " Father of the Piano " in a double sense : (1) as the founder of its *technique*, and (2) as the first to write for it in a real piano *style*. Clementi played upon Broadwood's earlier and smaller instruments. Later, he became associated with the firm of piano manufacturers since known as Collard's, and it was through his advice that Broadwood was enabled by 1820 to perfect his grand piano, which had such an influence on the development of technique in the time of Liszt.

It is interesting to note the mutual influence which Clementi and Beethoven exercised on each other as composers. While Clementi was Beethoven's immediate model in technique and form, there is no doubt that the lofty style of the latter influenced Clementi at the close of his career, when his naturally sunny and vigorous style took on something of the pathos of Beethoven in his last *Didone Abbandonata Sonata*.

Mr. Shedlock (*The Piano Sonata*, J. S. Shedlock) is also of opinion that, " with the exception of Mozart's *Sonata in C minor*, Haydn's *Genziger* London Sonatas, both in E♭, and one or two of Rust's—there are none which in spirit come nearer to Beethoven than some of Clementi's."

On the other hand, there are whole passages in Beethoven's earlier works which can be traced to similar passages in Clementi.

Like the Sonatas of Haydn and Mozart, those of Clementi may be classed as (1) technical, (2) educational, and (3) artistic. As regards features of general interest, the Op. 2 are principally technical, Op. 9 and 10 contain " foreshadowings " of Beethoven, Op. 12 (No. 2) and Op. 14 (No. 2) developments of form, and so on.

It goes without saying that some of Clementi's works have been overshadowed by the richly harmonized and more reflective works of Beethoven and the Romantics, but there are still some works of his which deserve attention. The famous *B minor Sonata*, the E♭, Op. 12 (No. 4), the *F minor*, and the *Didone Abbandonata*—" one of the finest Sonatas ever written "—should be in every student's library. Clementi's early Op. 12, No. 1, is notable for the Variations which are in advance of anything

written in that style for some time afterwards. The Op. 47
(No. 2) in B♭, with Toccata, is the one played by Clementi
(then nineteen years of age) at the Court of the Emperor
Joseph V. in 1781. Mozart, then fifteen, who was also present,
played alternately with Clementi at sight, and both extemporized on a given theme—the palm of victory being undecided.
It seems that Mozart, after this (being always prejudiced against
Italians), derided Clementi's superior technique, while Clementi
generously praised Mozart's singing touch. The theme of the
Sonata played by Clementi was afterwards taken by Mozart
as the subject of his *Zauberflöte* overture, in which his superiority
in thematic development is shown ; and it is through the want
of this, and also of modern harmony and of deeper and more
reflective emotion, that Clementi's work suffers in comparison
with the best work of Mozart ánd Beethoven. It will be noted
that his Andantes are especially weak points.

Clementi's pupils—John Field, whom he took to St. Petersburg
(where his widely different style of composition anticipated that
of Chopin), J. B. Cramer, who was brought up and lived in
London, Bertini, who was also born in London, Berger (the
teacher of Mendelssohn), Klengel and Kalkbrenner—became the
first pianists in Europe and spread abroad his modern method of
technique, which had been developed in his unique and invaluable *Gradus ad Parnassum* (1817) and in his *Preludes and
Exercises*. These publications were based on the contrapuntal
style already out of date, and were soon left behind by Czerny,
but they were useful, from a technical point of view, as studies
in independence of the fingers, and generally for the Concertos
and Sonatas of Mozart and Beethoven.

After his arrival in London Clementi was busy as a virtuoso
and teacher ; and from 1777 to 1780, as cembalist of the Italian
Opera, he conducted the Operas of Porpora, Sacchini and
Pergolese, as well as the Oratorios of Handel. In 1781 he began
his concert tours on the Continent, including the one to Russia
in 1802. These occupations, together with composition, filled
an active life till he died at the age of eighty. Moscheles relates
how, at a dinner given in his honour in 1827, " Smart, Cramer
and I conducted him to the Piano. Everyone's expectation is
raised to the utmost pitch, for Clementi had not been heard for
many years. He improvises on a theme of Handel and carries
us all away to the highest enthusism. His eyes shine with the

fire of youth, those of his hearers grow humid. Clementi's playing in his youth was marked by a most beautiful legato, a supple touch in lively passages and a most unfailing technique. The remains of these qualities could still be discerned and admired, but the most charming things were the turns of his improvisation, full of youthful genius."[1]

DUSSEK (1761–1812)

In comparison with Clementi Dussek appeals to us generally as putting mere brilliant technical figuration less in the foreground, and substituting for it a more *lyrical style* (in which Clementi was deficient), greater repose, more sentimental feeling, and richer harmonies. In Dussek's works thematic development often has to retire in favour of a succession of passages of great melodic charm, mostly constructed on basses, with frequent use of the sustaining pedal. In short, though Dussek wrote in classic style, he had a distinct leaning towards the romanticism to which Weber later gave so powerful an impetus.

His lyrical style in composition was reflected also in his playing. The Bohemian Fanaschek writes, " In the year 1804 my countryman, Dussek, came to Prague " ; and, remarking on his " charming grace of manner " and " wonderful touch," he adds that " his fingers were like a company of ten singers," and that " his fine declamatory style, especially in cantabile phrases, stands as the ideal for every artistic performance."

Not that the *bravura* element in composition was wanting, as may be seen in his *Sonata in D minor*, Op. 9 (No. 3), where there are rapid passages of octaves, thirds and sixths. His use, too, of tenths and extensions, like those of Woelfl, foreshadow, in some degree, Weber's and Henselt's technique.

At the present day Dussek is somewhat neglected. He is now known by the Rondos *Consolation, The Adieu* and *Matinée*, and the *B♭ Sonata*, Op. 24. Other Sonatas there are, however, which, in spite of diffuse workmanship, deserve resuscitation, if only for their melodic charm. Some of them are equal to the best of those by Mozart and Haydn. Most are in two movements, though his very expressive Adagios in the three-movement *Invocation* and *Le Retour à Paris* are very attractive. Besides those already mentioned, the *F♯ minor Sonata*, Op. 61, con-

[1] From Moscheles' Diary.

taining the *Elégie Harmonique*, written on the death of Prince
Louis Ferdinand of Prussia (who was himself no mean composer),
the *Op*. 35 in *B♭* and *G*, the latter with attractive contrapuntal
first movement and Rondo, the bravura one *in A, Op*. 43, the
Moto Perpetuo of the *Op*. 9 (*No*. 3), the *Presto* of the *Op*. 10
(*No*. 3), *Op*. 45 (*No*. 1), and *Op*. 47, *No*. 1 are still worthy of a
hearing.   The *Op*. 70 *Sonata in A♭*, known on the Continent as
the *Retour à Paris*, was given the name *Plus Ultra* by an
English publisher, in answer to the *Ne Plus Ultra* Sonata of
Woelfl then recently published.

Dussek was originally an organist at a Jesuit Church at
Kuttenberg, and obtained an appointment in Holland.   He
eventually appeared in Amsterdam as a virtuoso.   Subsequently
he studied with Em. Bach and then appeared in Berlin.   In
the course of a roving life Dussek played before Marie Antoinette
in Paris and settled in London as teacher and publisher for a
period of twelve years.   Concert tours in Europe followed, and
in 1803 he became the companion and adviser of Prince
Ferdinand of Prussia, himself a composer.   In 1806 he returned
to Paris and remained in the service of Talleyrand till his death
in 1812.

Dussek's historical importance lies (1) in his introduction of
the lyric, quasi-romantic element into the Sonata form, and
(2) especially in the advancement of technique, in which he is
ahead of Mozart and Haydn, and which, through him, reached
its climax in Liszt—not by way of Clementi and Beethoven,
but through Weber, Hummel, Chopin and Henselt.

F. W. RUST (1739-96)

A forgotten composer, but one who helped in the evolution of
the Sonata, is F. W. Rust, a pupil of Friedeman and Emmanuel
Bach. Rust wrote eight Sonatas for piano, of which, as Mr.
Shedlock points out, it is sometimes " difficult to believe that
the music belongs to a pre-Beethoven period."   In freedom of
form and modern feeling the *D minor* (1788), the *Lamentation
in D* (1794) and the *C minor* (1796), so closely anticipate the
style of Beethoven, and even of Schumann, that the question
has been asked whether Beethoven was acquainted with and
influenced by them, or whether it was the result of later editing
by Rust's grandson.   The earlier Sonatas written in 1775,

1777 and 1784 are not so advanced, and the problem remains unsolved.

Another composer of the Clementi School, as far as works for piano are concerned, is George Onslow, a grandson of Lord Onslow, born in France in 1784. His dignified *Sonata, Op. 2* (Joubert) and *Variations on an Ecossaise* (Schles.), which show leanings to the chromatic style later exploited by Spohr, were probably written during a stay of some years in London, where he was a pupil of Dussek and Cramer. His *Duet Sonatas, Op. 7* and 22, are still played. Onslow lived mostly in France, and his reputation as a composer of Chamber Music secured to him the directorship of the *Institut* in Paris in succession to Cherubini. The three sets of Sonatas by J. W. Hässler (1747–1822) deserve mention as constituting another link between those of Em. Bach and Beethoven. Though they appeared (*c.* 1780) shortly after the first set of Haydn, they partake of his neat orchestral style in all its piquancy, rhythmical vigour and humour. [See *Three Sonatas* (Hompesch, R. F.)]. His spirited *D minor Gigue* is well known.

CHAPTER VI

MODERN PIANOFORTE TECHNIQUE

" In endeavouring to conceal its defects and bring out its merits, an artist will play compositions which are most suitable to (that) instrument."
—*Spohr.*

THE natural continuation of Clementi is to be found in Beethoven. An interlude, however, is necessary here to consider the practical side of the art which Clementi did so much to further.

Modern piano technique may be regarded as being initiated by Em. Bach and placed on a firm foundation by Clementi, both of whom built on Scarlatti and Paradies.

The younger by 38 years, Em. Bach had recognized the advantages (and the deficiencies) of the early piano and composed for it, though it is not until 1781 that he named his Sonatas only " for the Forte Piano." It is interesting to note how Em. Bach avails himself of the characteristic figuration of Scarlatti's technique, though in the earlier works the organ-like recitative scale-passages of his father present themselves. Like Scarlatti's works written for the harpsichord, they are also decidedly thin in their effect, being mostly written in two parts. His later slow movements, however, are fuller and are more reflective and also more reminiscent of his father's style.

Clementi presents many similarities, but is bolder, fuller and more sonorous in style than Em. Bach. The first page of his *Sonata in C* (1770) is in octaves, and there is more variety of technique. In his *Gradus* he has rapid continuous successions of thirds and sixths, and makes great demands on muscular force in general.

The filling modern effect of the Alberti bass is often present in Clementi, though quite absent from Em. Bach. We note also the rolling effect of the broken octave passages and other effects copied by Beethoven, who founded so much of his earlier style on Clementi.

78

In Mozart and Haydn we have a similar technique to that of Clementi, but a more elegant and ornamental style, influenced by the light action of the Vienna piano, and by the composers' devotion to the Violin and Chamber Music. Mozart's technique is also influenced by his more lyrical, or song-like, and expressive style. Clementi, again, wrote almost entirely for the piano, while Haydn and Mozart's compositions were manifoldly distributed.

With Beethoven the technique is that of Clementi at first, strongly influenced by his piecemeal or analytic style of thematic figuration, in which chordal or scale-passages are broken up and, passing through various keys, appear again in a new guise. Beethoven's technique was, therefore, his own and, though it has been imitated, it has never been equalled in its own way, because of its psychological character. The language of the orchestra (*see* Chapter IV) also plays a strong part in his technique (as did the organ in that of Bach), especially in the slow movements. As pianoforte executants, no doubt Clementi and Beethoven were superior to Haydn and Mozart.

Clementi's cantabile and muscular style of playing became refined through his pupils Cramer, Berger and Field—especially the last. Cramer's quiet and smooth, yet firm, style of touch was specially commended by Beethoven, while Field, who used an almost perpendicular position of the fingers, was noted for his sweet, sustained and delicate style, which is said to have resembled that of Chopin. Kalkbrenner and Mayer combined virtuosity with a perfectly quiet position at the piano, the former notably cultivating octave playing in a new manner from the wrist ; while Dussek possessed the art of making the piano sing and was given to the use of extensions and leaps, thereby anticipating Weber and Woelfl.

Weber also considerably extended the bravura style, which he combined with greater animation and dramatic fire. The bravura element was continued by Moscheles and Mendelssohn and was combined in both with a refined classic element. The light Vienna style of execution and composition was continued by the Mozartean Hummel and by Czerny (in his studies) as well as by the arabesque adornments of the cantabile compositions of Thalberg.

Thalberg's extremely polished but cold style of execution caused quite a sensation for a time, but this was eventually far surpassed by the unequalled technical power and style of the virtuoso Lizst.

Liszt's elevated sloping hand gave great power, his equalization of fingering over black and white keys gave better methods of phrasing, while his great energy and variety of technical treatment (see Part III, Chapter XV) brought the instrument to be regarded as almost orchestral in power and resources.

Schumann, in his rich romantic style, betwixt the massive and grand, invested with contrapuntal interest a gambolling and graceful broken chord figuration peculiar to himself. (See Part III, Chapter VI.)   He initiated a new style and bore out in practice his own saying, " Executive passages alter with the times."

The original alternating, sparkling and iridescent languorous technique of Chopin, as interpreted through his poetical compositions, has been partly perpetuated through Henselt with his special development of extensions, and through the Russian School, which is founded on the works of both.

Many great virtuosos exist, as in the past, but no specially new technical style seems to have appeared since that of Chopin, the somewhat unpianistic technique of Brahms being based on a mixture of Schumann, Bach and Liszt.

Pianoforte styles having thus attained a climax in technique, are now being diverted into other channels.   Impressionism and imitation of the orchestra seem to be pre-eminent at present, and as these depend mostly on harmonic colouring, they are somewhat antagonistic to the development of technique.

In our last Chapter we were discussing Clementi, while our next is on Beethoven ; so that at first glance our intervening mention of Liszt, Schumann and Chopin would seem to be out of place.

Perhaps, therefore, the reader requires to be reminded of this *stretto* in our story—how that, while yet Clementi was alive, the virtuoso Liszt had received Beethoven's blessing, and how that, before the death of the latter, many of the best works of the Romantics, Mendelssohn, Schumann and Chopin, had already appeared.

CHAPTER VII

THE CLIMAX OF FORMAL MUSIC

" Emotion suits women only (forgive me!) ; music ought to strike fire from the soul of a man."—*Beethoven Letters.*

	1788. Death of Em. Bach.
	1791. Death of Mozart.
	1802. Field with Clementi at St. Petersburg.
1770–1827. Beethoven.	1809. Death of Haydn.
	1826. Death of Weber.
	1828. Death of Schubert.
	1832. Death of Clementi.

IT was in 1790 that the venerable Haydn, then nearly sixty years of age, in response to repeated invitations, made his first journey to England, and his first outside his Austrian fatherland. On the day of departure from Vienna (December 15th)—and at that time Vienna was the capital of the musical world—his friend and pupil Mozart took an affectionate farewell, exclaiming prophetically, " This is probably our last farewell in this life." A year later the news of the lamented premature death of Mozart reached Haydn, who was still in England. Haydn turned his steps homeward in 1792 and was entertained to a breakfast given in his honour at Bonn on the Rhine. It was in this quiet, old-fashioned town that he first became acquainted with young Beethoven, then twenty-two years of age, who submitted a Cantata for his approval ; and at this time an arrangement was made that the young aspirant should go to Vienna and study under Haydn. Six years previously Mozart had heard young Beethoven extemporize on a given theme and had prophetically announced to his friends, " Take note of him! he will make a stir in the world later! "

Previous to this Beethoven had already (at eleven years of age) written the three " Haydnish " Sonatas which he dedicated to the Elector of Cologne, as well as the *Dressler Variations*. His youthful show piece, his rhythmic *Variations*, in which he shows greater resource and command of pianoforte technique

than either of his seniors, Mozart and Haydn, was written in
1789, three years before this visit of Haydn.

On the occasion of his leaving Bonn, Count Waldstein, who
had proved himself a friend, wrote as follows :—

DEAR BEETHOVEN,

You are going now to Vienna in fulfilment of your long-
combated wish. The kind, protecting genius of Mozart still
laments the death of his pupil.

Through unremitting zeal you may receive Mozart's genius
from Haydn's hands.

Four years later Beethoven dedicated the first three *Sonatas*
(*Op.* 2) to Haydn, who, however, had proved a somewhat
intermittent teacher. It is not matter for wonder, therefore,
that these, as well as later works by the younger master, should
show strongly the influence of the symphonist as well as of
Mozart—the two most prominent composers in the style of
the period.

Coming to the consideration of Beethoven's Sonatas as a
whole (not inaptly termed the " New Testament " of music,
in distinction from the " Old Testament " of Bach's " 48 "), we
must point out that Beethoven's unapproached pre-eminence
in the modern musical world lay in his ability to develop lofty
thought and powerful emotion within the restricting bounds of
Sonata form ; just as, in a similar way, the genius of Bach was
able to express itself within the rigorous chain-bound limits of
the fugal style.

From an architectural point of view Beethoven's Sonatas
surpass all other similar structures ; while in range of emotion,
sincerity, manliness, joy, pity, pathos and humour they fully
equal and in some respects (notably in humour) surpass all
other composers' efforts. That the Sonatas are not all of equal
merit goes without saying. If we omit those in Sonatina form,
the *Op.* 49 and 79, there are thirty left. Of these the early
works distinctly show the influence of Haydn and Mozart in
their general style, while in technical figuration they are
modelled principally on Clementi, and in form on Em. Bach
and Haydn.

What have been described as the three styles of Beethoven
are exemplified in (1) the Haydn and Mozart period, *Op.* 1 to

Op. 20 ; (2) *Op.* 21 to *Op.* 100, in which the real Beethoven comes to the front ; (3) *Op.* 101 to *Op.* 135, the reflective or mystical period, in which Beethoven, withdrawing within himself, becomes subjective and mysterious.

The opus numbers, however, are not to be trusted altogether as showing progressive development, and the periods overlap each other to some extent. In the first period we have the light-heartedness of Haydn in the quick movements, and the lyrical pathos in the slow ones, with occasionally a forecast of his own deeper individuality, as in the solemn *Largo Appassionata* of the *Op.* 2 (No. 2) (1795), the touching and dramatic *Largo* in the *Op.* 7 *in E♭* (1797), the sorrow-laden *Largo* of the *Op.* 10 (No. 3) in which the struggle with fate is powerfully depicted, and in the pathetic Sonata (1799) as a whole.

Something also of the individual combination of boisterous humour with the deeper emotions is exemplified in the Scherzo-like *Prestissimo* of the *C minor, Op.* 10 (No. 1) (1798). The second period opens with the Clementi-like *B♭ Sonata*, in which is prominent the mysterious double-bass-like *motif* accompanied by rolling chord figures in the treble—an exploitation of the lower regions of the instrument fully developed by Schumann and Brahms.

There are also the lovely *Air with Variations* and *Hero's Funeral March* of the *A♭ Sonata*, and the so-called *Moonlight Sonata* dedicated to the Countess Guicciardi, in which, as Marx says, " Beethoven shows that love—a secret flame burning itself out in the consuming fire of insatiable desire—lived on in his heart." The *Allegretto*, described by Marx as a song of farewell, and by Liszt as " a floweret 'twixt two abysses," is succeeded by the *Prestissimo* in which

" . . . tempestuous passion,
The raging flood, longs to lay hold of heaven."

The *Pastoral Sonata*, a favourite with Beethoven, is a good example of the orchestral style of treatment so often found in him. Traces of this, partly derived from the symphonist Haydn, are found in his frequent use of the rolling broken octaves as a substitute for the *tremolando* of the strings ; in the sustained bass notes with superadded wavy 2nd violin accompaniment figuration ; in the short melodic figures in octaves in the bass ('cello and double-bass),and in the inversion of themes in what is called " double counterpoint "—a device constantly used by Beethoven and probably derived from the interchange of melody and accompaniment among the various instruments of the orchestra.

In the Andante of the present Sonata one may notice specially the *pizzicato*-like bass and the gambolling flute-like triplets.

The *D minor Sonata*, Op. 31 (No. 2) was prized by Beethoven as his best work and was often played by him in the salons of the Viennese nobility.

A restless dramatic spirit, " tumultuous mutterings and rollings," characterize the first movement, while the peaceful poetical Adagio is followed by a restless, perpetual motion (" galloping," Czerny called it), and over the whole there " breathes a spirit of phantasy " (Elterlein).

Mendelssohn's fairy Scherzos are anticipated in the Scherzo of Beethoven's *Op*. 31 (No. 3) ; while the virtuoso element is seen in the concert *Waldstein Sonata* with its somewhat orchestral first movement, inspired by the whirlwind and distant storm, its becalming *Adagio*, and the village fête depicted in the final Rondo, in which we have the village bell, the merry trills and the mad " wind-up " of the *Prestissimo*.

The scanty two-movement *Op*. 54, after the introductory *Minuetto*, is nothing more than a merry Dance in octaves, while the second movement is a *Study* or *Toccata* after the Italian style.

The *Appassionata* is a picture of stirring emotions ; the *F♯, Op*. 78, an experiment in modern technique on the black keys, and in interlocking of hands—a device used by Bach and developed by Liszt.

The *Adieu Sonata* is one of those in which Beethoven indicated a definite programme—the pathetic *Lebewohl* (or Farewell) *Adagio*, the earnest and exciting emotions of the leave-taking *Allegro*, the pining melancholy of the *Andante*, portraying " absence," and the joy of the return movement. One wonders if this Sonata was suggested by the *Capriccio* of Bach entitled *The Departure of a Brother*.

Scarce seventy years separate the two and yet there is a vast gulf between them in point of style.

The Sonatas beginning with *Op*. 101 open the third period, in which the reflective element holds powerful sway, as, for example, in the tender and romantic *A major Sonata*.

The titanic work in B♭, Op. 106, conceived in symphonic style, in which Beethoven begins to indulge in the somewhat ineffective fugal movements, is probably the result of his study of Bach. The E *major Sonata*, Op. 109, contains in the Adagio one of the finest Variations ever written.

We have spoken of Bach inspiring the fugal and imitative work in Beethoven's later Sonatas. It would also seem as if Mozart (who, next to Bach, made the most successful use of Fugue form in combination with the symphonic style) had been the *raison d'être* of the first movement of Beethoven's last Sonata, written in 1822. In any case, it would certainly seem that Beethoven was endeavouring in his latest years to combine the mastery of the polyphonic élement with that of the thematic. It was a consummation hardly to be expected, and perhaps the most natural effect is the first portion of the Fugue in the *Op.* 110.

Beethoven's influence on the Sonata, of which he was perfection personified, was that of *development* in all respects. He was by no means confined by the mere form, and all the various aspects were enlarged. Movements and sections of movements are boldly introduced in unheard-of related keys ; his modulations are most unexpected and take unusually wide scope ; the cadences are full of surprises and deferments ; the Codas are similarly treated and much elaborated ; while, finally, the masterly thematic development of the whole renders the work the embodiment of perfect balance of design. Beethoven's influence is further seen in the change from the Minuet to the Scherzo, the elaboration of slow introductory movements, the tendency to the encroachment of the programme element, and the development of the contrapuntal and symphonic style.

He also specially developed rhythm, giving it extraordinary variety of effect ; and, on the whole, his Sonatas are cast in the grand style—reaching occasionally to the sublime.

The student may study the various aspects of the Sonatas in the works of the writer and Elterlein (Reeves), Lenz (*Three Styles*), Nageli, Marx (*Biography*), and in the article in *Grove*.

For academic study perhaps the Germer Edition (Lit.) is the most suggestive, and St. Macpherson's Edition (Jos. Williams) and D'Albert's Edition probably come next in general usefulness.

Besides raising the pianoforte Sonata to a pitch of perfection, Beethoven did no less for the form of the Concerto.

The " modified Sonata form " of the Concerto (*see* Part III, Chapter XXII, on *The Concerto*) he improved in various ways, and, while keeping in view the *virtuoso* character of the solo parts, he did not neglect to build up in masterly fashion the orchestral portion as a whole, besides bringing forward in interesting dialogue-fashion the constituent orchestral instruments.

The " heroic nobility " manifested in the *improvisatore G major*, and the rich and complex *Emperor Concerto in E♭* form, as it were, a continuation of the virtuoso *Waldstein Sonata*.

The variation form also reached perfection in his hands. His early devotion to and mastery of this form have already been mentioned. Following Haydn's lead, Beethoven gave more attention to the harmonic aspect (*see* Part III, Chapter XXIV) and these works, which are interesting both as regards ingenuity, technique and musical effect, are among the most noteworthy of his compositions for piano.

His fifteen Variations, with a *Fugue in E♭*, Op. 35, are founded on the bass part of a Quintet by Steibelt and were the result of an improvisation made in Steibelt's presence. A set of Variations written by Steibelt on a theme occurring in Beethoven's *Trio in B♭* had aroused enthusiasm in the uncritical audience, and Beethoven's *Op.* 35 was the reply. The origin of the *Diabelli Variations* was that in 1822 Diabelli, the composer and publisher (now known by his Duets), applied to the most eminent Austrian composers for a set of fifty Variations on a theme of his own. The publication finally appeared in two volumes, thirty-three in one volume by Beethoven and fifty in the other by various composers, including one by the young virtuoso Liszt. According to Liszt (who tells the story), Beethoven appeared with the MS. of the thirty-three Variations at Diabelli's door, exclaiming, " There! You asked for one Variation ; here are thirty-three, and now, for God's sake, leave me in peace." Bülow speaks of this work as evincing " all the evolutions of musical expression from the highest sentiment to the broadest humour."

Beethoven's Duet Marches and Variations, though attractive, are comparatively unimportant (Part III, Chapter XXIII). Of his miscellaneous pieces, the short, sketch-like *Bagatelles*, the Mozartean *Rondo in C*, the lyrical but very characteristic *Polonaise in C*, and the noble *Andante in F*, intended for a Sonata, are specially noteworthy.

There is a story connected with the latter of Ries, his pupil, having heard Beethoven play it in private shortly after its composition. Ries went to Prince Lichnowsky's house and played what he remembered of it to him. The next day Lichnowsky, as a joke, asked Beethoven to listen to a piece he had just composed—with results that may be imagined rather than described. Beethoven's contributions to *characteristic* clavier music consist of a playful *Caprice, Op.* 129, entitled *Rage Over a Lost Penny*, concerning which Schumann said, " It would be difficult to find anything merrier than this whim ; I laughed heartily over it the other day " ; and the *Pathetic*, *Pastoral* and *Adieu* Sonatas which also come within this category.

It is interesting to observe, in these days of nationality in music, that Beethoven was of Flemish descent, his family having come from Louvain and Antwerp, where his grandfather, who was alive in young Beethoven's time, had been made Capellmeister in 1737.

His father had been a singer in the Elector of Cologne's Chapel.

This is another instance of the musical Flemings carrying the art into various countries—a century and a half earlier they had been the means of founding the Italian polyphonic school.

Bach and Handel the Saxons, Haydn the Croatian, Mozart the Bavarian, and Beethoven the Fleming, though adhering more or less to the pattern of the period, have all left some characteristics of their nationality in their works.

To return to Beethoven's characteristics, we note that though his brusque and untempered personality is reflected in his music, it is not shown in his workmanship. His work, as we know, was polished and repolished (often for a considerable period) with the utmost care. His discrimination of essentials was brought out in his teaching. Ries relates that not wrong notes, but only neglect of expression, exasperated him. Concerning his improvisations, Czerny recounts that " there was something wonderful in his expression. . . . Frequently (he says) not an eye remained dry, while many people would break out into loud sobs."

His method of composition was aided by his phenomenal memory, which enabled him to carry the various themes in his head till he had worked them out to the right form. " The original idea," he said to Schloesser, " never leaves me, but rises and grows until I can see it in my mind as a complete picture."

It was this concentration of purpose, this devotion to and elaboration of some central thought, which distinguishes Beethoven from Haydn and Mozart. While the latter appear to be aiming at *contrast* only of the various themes, movements and sections, Beethoven aimed at the *unity* and symmetry of the whole, while at the same time securing variety of interest.

Beethoven's style, too, is on a grander scale ; not only are his ideas loftier, his themes broader and his feeling deeper— plumbing the depths of despair—but the outlines are altogether on a larger scale than those of his contemporaries and successors.

To conclude—we have, in Beethoven, the climax of the various aspects of the Sonata form ; and just as, in Bach and Handel, the polyphonic age came to its height and then decayed, so, notwithstanding later meritorious efforts, the mastery of the Sonata style has declined, never again apparently, to reach the height it attained with Beethoven.

" All art constantly aspires towards the condition of music—which most completely realizes this artistic ideal, this perfect identification of form and matter."—*Walter Pater.*

NOTE.—Descriptions in detail of Beethoven's Sonatas, etc., appear in the Author's *Pianoforte Classics, from Handel to Beethoven* (Reeves).

PART III

THE ROMANTIC PERIOD

Music " speaks not to our thoughts as words do : it speaks straight to our hearts and spirits, to the very core and root of our souls."—*Kingsley*.

CHAPTER I

Romanticism " exacts only that the Form should be adequate to the expression of the sentiment."—*Liszt*.

BEFORE describing the romance-writers of modern pianoforte music, it is necessary to define the meaning of the word *Romanticism* as used in this connection.

Romanticism implies a comparison. In literature the word *romantic* was originally applied to that of the Middle Ages as distinguished from the *classics* of Antiquity.

The orderly, clear, and matter-of-fact style of the latter was compared with the love of the mysterious and marvellous in the so-called Romantic School.

In Modern Art romanticism is represented by the ideally and mystically beautiful, as compared with the formal and realistic.

It should, however, be remembered that " classical form does not exclude romantic matter ; and disregard of classical form does not constitute romance " (Niecks).

It is the idealistic appeal to the *imagination*, as manifested in the love of the poetic and beautiful which is the touchstone of separation. In music, the most romantic and the most fully developed and organized of all the arts, our definition of the romantic must be : That which is poetically beautiful, which ever shows the cultivation of the *ideal* or the aspiration to perfection in the portrayal of the human emotions or of various aspects of nature.

The definition must of necessity include the " characteristic " element in music, and the extension of the latter known as " programme music," but this only in the highest plane (*see* Chapter VIII), since directly this programme element becomes " realism " we transgress the bounds of romanticism as the expression of the ideal.

Realism and classicism are diametrically opposed to one another.

The true romantic element may be said to occupy the golden

mean between classical formalism on the one hand and " rank realism " on the other.   It will be seen from the above that the true element of romance is not confined to modern works. (The subordination of the formal or realistic and the presentation of the ideally beautiful can be found, for instance, in the works of Bach and Handel, who knew how to evolve the ideally beautiful out of the bonds of polyphony, not to speak of Beethoven, who could wield the sceptre of the emotions over the highly artificial structure of his Sonatas and Symphonies.)

On the whole, however, the Older Masters incline to the side of Classicism rather than of Romanticism.

In the pure Romantic composers the romantic element stands forth prominent, unfettered and unsubdued.

One noteworthy feature of the Romantic movement is that its most advanced exponents, Schumann and Chopin, were profoundly influenced, not by Beethoven—the greatest representative of " thematic " composition—but, on the contrary, by Bach, the giant of Polyphony.   One result, however, of the recent cult of Brahms was to make Beethoven again the model for the modern composer.   Possibly in future both heads of the two great divisions of Classicism will rightly share this formative influence on the Romanticism of the twentieth century.

At present composers are more influenced by the " emotional content " than by organic unity, formal coherence or mastery of counterpoint ; and, with the modern tendency to the programme and realistic element, it remains to be seen whether the artistic pendulum will swing back once more to Classicism or proceed to the other extreme of Realism.

The *Romantic Movement* in pianoforte music may be said to have been initiated as a whole by the Nocturnes of Field (*c.* 1802–6), and to have been fully matured by the time of the death of Schumann in 1856.

In looking through the works of the essentially Romantic composers we find that they present great contrasts in harmony, modulation (changes of key), melody and rhythm—as in the startlingly new and rich harmonies of Chopin and Schumann, and the unexpected modulations of Schubert.

Contrast of rhythm and a lighter chromatic style of melody is seen in Weber, while the smaller forms, in which sentiment and emotion readily find first place, are initiated by the Nocturnes of Field.

Schumann by his writings and compositions did much to develop the campaign against " Philistinism," as Classicism was then called.

The general tendency of the age, as shown in the French Revolution, the struggle for Polish nationality, the movements in Literature, originating with Goethe and Schiller, and the dawn of democracy and of a wider outlook generally, favoured the upheaval in the most reflective and sensitive of all the arts, and this upheaval we shall refer to as the Romantic Movement.

CHAPTER II

DECAY OF THE CLASSICAL SCHOOL—HUMMEL AND OTHERS

" Unless music exalt and purify, it is not under St. Cecilia's ordinance, and it is not, virtually, music at all."—*Ruskin* (" Pleasures of England.")

BEFORE proceeding to the music of the first Romanticists we must again remind the reader of the necessary overlapping of the various periods and schools. The evolution of musical Romance was more or less slow, while the lingering of Classicism and its blending with Romanticism was prolonged over a considerable period of time.

Following Beethoven, but also, to a certain extent, contemporary with him, we notice the crowd of shallow dabblers in the prevailing Classic or formal composition, whose hollow and trifling pieces already indicate the decay of the movement which found its climax in Beethoven.

A passing reference will suffice to the similarly trifling and trashy Herz School, which found its home in Paris. With regard to J. B. Cramer, the writer of noble studies commended by Beethoven, we find that his Sonatas are written in the shallow taste of the salon music of the period, though probably they were meant for educational purposes only. A significant *Petit Rien* still survives. Daniel Steibelt's name (1765–1823) lingers yet as that of one who made a speciality of battle and storm pieces with tambourine and triangle accompaniments. His compositions, including a *Concerto Militaire*, were very popular but are now forgotten. L. Kozeluch (1753–1814) wrote pretty, trivial Mozartean Sonatas in the educational taste of the period. Similar pieces by the Abbé Sterkel (whose *Rondo in A* is still known), J. B. Wanhal and Pixis (b. 1788) had a passing interest only.

Jos. Woelfl (1772–1812) stands on more solid ground. His compositions (Sonatas, Concertos, Variations, Fugues, etc.), noted for their technical daring (skips and extensions), were completely overshadowed by Hummel, and his works are now forgotten, with the exception of a striking Introductory, Fugue and Allegro from the *Sonata Op.* 25 (Ash).

In J. Nepomuk Hummel (1778–1837) we have the true succession as well as the termination of the style of Mozart. Hummel was only eight years younger than Beethoven and twenty-two years younger than Mozart, whose pupil he was ; but his highly finished and ornamental style shows the first step in the decay of the Classical age. He succeeded Haydn as Kapellmeister to Prince Esterhazy, and travelled much on concert tours as a virtuoso, gaining great fame as a pianist, especially in extemporization, in which branch he was reckoned the equal of Beethoven. During 1791–2 he resided in London and was much influenced by Clementi, who was also living there.

In his compositions Hummel has the virtues of his models— mastery of form and part-writing, the brightness of Haydn, the lyrical qualities and, to some extent, the harmonic effects of Mozart and Beethoven ; but lack of warmth of feeling, soul and inspiration, has caused his works to be neglected for the more strongly-coloured productions of the Romantic School.

The outstanding feature of his compositions is his charming use of modulation, often unexpected but always effective, as in his *La Bella Capriccioso.*

Other works still surviving are his *A minor* and *B minor Concertos* (now of educational interest only), the interesting and useful *Rondo Op.* 56 with Orchestra (St.), bravura *Oberon Fantasia*, the *E♭, F♯ minor* and *D Sonatas*, the *Duet Sonata in A♭, La Galante*, the *Capriccio Op.* 49, *La Contemplazione* (Lit.) and *La Centerola Variations.*

Hummel's style is best described in the words of Riemann :—

" His compositions are a faithful reflection of his playing ; garlands of passages hide a lack of passion and atone for an absence of warmth of feeling. The influence of his teacher (Mozart) upon his style of writing is undeniable ; nevertheless he does not approach Mozart by a long way in nobleness of melody, while the mechanical element most likely brought about by the easy action of the Vienna piano predominates."

Hummel was the last of the purely Classical School. It is interesting to remember that his contemporary, Field, the first of the Romantics, was only four years younger, while Weber, the other apostle of Romanticism, was again four years younger than Field.

CHAPTER III

THE FIRST ROMANTICISTS

" Be Fields, write what you will; be poets, be men, I beseech you."—
Schumann.

John Field (1782–1837), Weber (1786–1826), and Charles Mayer (1799–1862).

LISZT, in his preface to his edition of *Field's Nocturnes* (Schubert), has said: " Formerly it was necessary that all pianoforte compositions should be Sonatas, Rondos, etc. Field was the first to introduce a species which belonged to none of the established classes, in which feeling and melody reigned alone, liberated from the fetters and encumbrances of a coercive form. He opened the way for all those productions, which have appeared since, under the titles of *Songs without Words, Impromptus, Ballads*, etc., and to him we may trace the origin of those pieces designed to paint individual and deep-seated emotions." In other words, the Irishman, John Field (1782–1837), initiated the Romantic Movement in pianoforte music—his compositions were the direct predecessors of the smaller lyrical pieces of Mendelssohn, Chopin and Schumann.

Field was born in Golden Lane, Dublin, a dark tumble-down street near St. Patrick's Cathedral and not far from the dwelling of Tom Moore, and the house where Oliver Goldsmith had lived thirty years before. Field's father was a violinist at a Dublin theatre, his grandfather an organist. Intended to be an infant phenomenon, young Field, at the hands of his parents, experienced a severe training from an early age. He became a pupil of Giordano at the age of nine and in the following year appeared in a Concerto composed by his teacher. His parents removed to London in 1794, and at the age of twelve Field was apprenticed for ten years as pupil and salesman to

96

Clementi, who had commenced business as a piano manufacturer. He appeared in public in London in April, 1794, and five years later he appeared again in his own " Concerto for the grand forte piano, composed for the occasion."

At his earlier appearance he was introduced as the " ten-year-old " pupil of Clementi, in company with the young mulatto violinist, Bridgetower (who later was the first to perform Beethoven's *Kreutzer Sonata* in public with the composer) and the celebrated singer, Madame Mara. He appeared once more in 1801, and the astute Clementi, who had started a branch business in St. Petersburg, proceeded there in 1802, taking Field with him. On the way, Field's appearance in Paris and Vienna was hailed with enthusiasm, his exquisite performance of Bach's and Handel's Fugues being greatly admired. His first three years in St. Petersburg, where he arrived in 1804, were spent in drudgery. Spohr has recorded his visits to Field when in St. Petersburg. " Often in the evenings," he says, " I accompanied Clementi to his pianoforte warehouse, where Field had to play for hours to show off the pianos to purchasers. I have in my remembrance a vivid picture of the tall, pale youth who appeared to have grown out of his clothes—a very English and awkward figure. As soon, however, as his soul-stirring playing began, everything else was forgotten and we became all ear."

At this time Field had blonde hair, blue eyes, fair complexion and pleasing features. Later he became easy-going, indifferent to personal appearance and somewhat of a spendthrift ; while, as a man of fifty, he is described as indolent, heavy-featured, worn out and vulgar in appearance, owing to intemperate habits. He was reputed to be somewhat cynical, good-natured and droll in manner, but uneducated.

Field remained in St. Petersburg, where he became in great request as a teacher and pianist, for nineteen years, and thence he went to Moscow, where his concerts were a great success. During this time he composed (in 1814) his first three Nocturnes, a Sonata and some Concertos. In 1817 appeared the Concerto known as *L'incendie par l'orage*. Other works followed, and he led a busy life as concert-giver till 1822, when he settled in Moscow. The charm of Field's playing was aptly characterized in the qualities of his Nocturnes—perfect finish and cantabile style. Fétis speaks of his " elegant playing and beautiful manner of singing on the piano . . . although his execution had not the power of the pianists of the Modern School."* It is significant also of the similarity of his style to that of Chopin that the latter was asked by Kalkbrenner if he were a pupil of Field. In 1831 Field returned to London and appeared in public. The *Musical World* of March 31st, 1831, says in a critique : " His wonderful, and in some degree most lovely and dreamlike, trifles require throughout a perfect and beautiful touch, a singing tone, and that delicate, decided and often piquant expression so peculiar to the composer. His style of pianoforte playing has been compared to Catalani's singing." There is a reference also in 1832 to the *Concerto in E♭* (" The middle of it is exceedingly delicious ") ; and as regards his seven Concertos, Bülow writes enthusiastically about the second *in A♭* which served, he says, as the model for Chopin's *F minor*. The Rondo of this Concerto (Peters) is justly celebrated. Schumann also rhapsodizes on the *7th Concerto*. (*See* Chapter XXII.)

Leaving London in 1832, Field entered on a successful concert tour on the Continent ; but he was taken ill and lay stranded at Naples, whence he was rescued by Russian friends and taken to Moscow, where, without fully recovering, he died in 1837.

Although the Concertos and Sonatas of Field were popular in their day, he is known now almost entirely by his Nocturnes. He did not possess the logical nature and the grand style more or less necessary to the formally-developed Sonata and Concerto. Isolated movements, however, survive ; for instance, the Rondo of the *2nd Concerto* (*in A♭*) praised by Bülow, the sprightly Rondo from the *Sonata in E♭*, which contains some charming modulations, the *Scherzo* (No. 7 *Popular Pieces*, Augener) which suggests the *4th Scherzo* of Chopin, and a characteristic, pleasing *Polonaise* (G.R.).

The *Nocturnes* have been universally praised. Liszt says that " they still exhale a balsamic freshness, a sweet fragrance." " Where else," he says, " do we find such perfection of inimitable *naïveté* ? No one else has succeeded in seizing these intangible harmonies of the Æolian harp, these half-sighs floating away in air, gentle plaints dissolving away in sweet pain."

Apart from their own virtues, the idyllic Nocturnes of Field proved to be the direct models and predecessors of Chopin.

* *See* Article by Miss D'esterre Keeling in *Girl's Own Paper*.

In Chopin's hands, however, the " charming ingenuousness of his melodious reveries " underwent an emotional change. " The Irishman plucked a bunch of field flowers, daisies and buttercups twined with sweet honeysuckle and wild roses ; their beauty was their fragrance and childlike simplicity. The Pole took the flowers and fostered them in the hot-house of his morbid imagination. When they came forth once more they were exotics of rare and wonderful beauty, but they had lost their innocence " (Keeling).

Apart from emotional significance, the type of melody and accompaniment (the latter spread out in extended wavy form and supported by the sustaining pedal), together with the simple lyrical form which he used, proved, as was pointed out by Liszt, to be the foundation of the special forms representative of the lyrical Romantic School ; just as certainly as the bravura style of his contemporary Weber led to that of Liszt through Moscheles, Mendelssohn and Chopin.

Of the twenty compositions of Field which have appeared under the title of *Nocturnes* only twelve were so called by the composer, but of the seventeen in Peters' Collection we would willingly lose none ; so charming are they in their way, though they are not all equally good. The first five (in $E\flat$, C minor, $A\flat$, A, and $B\flat$) seem to be the most characteristic. " They are indeed poesies in tunes," or, as they have been termed, " the very essence of all idylls and eclogues." Nos. 13 to 17 seem to have been inspired by Mozart, but it is Mozart at his best. They are more cloying, and, if anything, more alluring than the earlier ones, besides being more richly harmonized ; but they are not so individual in style. To come to detail—No. 13 uses " imitation " effects, No. 14 has the later Chopin device of the melody in sixths, and the elaborate and beautiful No. 17 also reminds one of Chopin in line 4, and page 64 (line 7), in the latter case suggesting the style of his *Impromptu in F*♯. Of the intermediate numbers the opening melody of No. 6 and the accompaniment of No. 9 remind one of Chopin's early *Nocturnes* in $E\flat$, and portions of No. 11 (*in* $E\flat$) of Chopin's first Impromptu. The sweeping left-hand Arpeggios in No. 12 recall the *Spianato* of Chopin's first Polonaise, while the independent recurring *motif* in Nos. 3 and 7 appears in some of the Polish composer's *Preludes* and in the *F major Nocturne*. Many other instances might be given, and one is forced to the conclusion that Chopin based the style, not only of his Nocturnes, but of many of his other compositions, on those of Field. (*Vide* also Bülow's remark on the *2nd Concerto*.)

As the teacher of Glinka, the founder of the Russian School, and of Mayer, one of the founders of modern technique, Field

C minor Nocturne—Field.

exercised an important influence on the development of pianoforte style ; though Field's style, as Fétis, who heard him, said, was essentially his own.   Fétis said his school was " neither the school of Dussek, nor of Clementi, nor of Steibelt ; Field is Field—a school of his own."   A style " exquisitely *spirituelle*— coupled with surprising aplomb and coquetry."*

Field was buried in Moscow on January 11th, 1837.   The

* I am indebted for details to a recent little work, the first memoir in English on *John Field of Dublin*, by Dr. W. H. Grattan Flood.   (Dublin : Lester, Ltd.)

following inscription is engraved on a monument to the inventor
of the *Nocturne* :—

JOHN FIELD

BORN IN IRELAND IN 1782

DIED IN MOSCOW IN 1837

ERECTED

TO HIS MEMORY

BY HIS

GRATEFUL FRIENDS AND SCHOLARS

WEBER (1786–1826)

The contribution of Weber to the Romantic movement was
made (1) through his characteristically animated and dramatic
style as compared with the lyric meditations of Field, and
(2) through his enlargement of pianoforte technique by means
of the *bravura* element. A contemporary of Field, and only
four years his junior, Weber had a much wider scope. By his
efforts Germany became supreme in Opera, and he made the
evolution of a Wagner possible. Moreover, his devotion to
Opera, in which Sonata form and thematic development are at
a discount, led to his *free treatment* of *form* and the substitution
of contrasted themes for the development of one or two. His
efforts at dramatic expression led also to stronger *harmonic
colouring*, and all these were prominent features in the Romantic
movement. In this way Weber anticipated Schubert—his
junior by eleven years, while his seniors, Clementi, Hummel
and Moscheles kept up the traditional classic style. The
feature of Weber's *technique* as a virtuoso was his capacity for
extensions, wide leaps and passages of thirds, all designed for
showy effect, and foreshadowing Henselt and Liszt. The
characteristic element appears in his piano music in the *Invitation
to the Dance* and in the *Concertstück*, which he associated with
the anxious expectancy of a lady awaiting her knight's return
from the Crusades.

Generally speaking, his works glow with animation and
brilliancy and are always full of rhythmical and dramatic effect.
His piano *Sonatas* which, as Mr. Shedlock says,* present rather
the " letter than the true spirit of a Sonata," " enchant the ear "

* *The Pianoforte Sonata.*

by means of their "romantic themes" and "picturesque colouring" "intensified by grand technique."

The *1st Sonata* may be termed a drama without words, interpreted by the dramatic attitudinizing of the 1st Movement, the love duet and pervading happiness of the slow Movement, the obstructive and apparently out-of-place minuet leading to the gay frolic of the *Moto Perpetuo*.

The *2nd Sonata* has its legendary *Andante* and airy *Presto* telling of sprites and hobgoblins and thereby anticipating Mendelssohn ; while the national *Volkslied* and dance element is present in what might be called the *Patriotic Sonata*, composed at a time (1816) when his songs of war and liberty had rendered him popular. The *4th Sonata*, written while he was recruiting his health at Hosterwitz, shows some falling off.

Weber's early works consist of *Variations, Valses* and *Ecossaises*. Those written before he came of age are in the Hummel-Mozart style, but afterwards his characteristic chromatic appogiaturas and vamping bass became prominent. It is remarkable that in these early Variations there is far more *variety* of technique than in his later works generally.

Weber's first characteristic works of importance are the *Op. 12 Momento Capriccioso* and *Op. 21 Polonaise in E♭*, both written in 1808 when he was twenty-two years of age. Though warm in harmonic and brilliant in technical and rhythmical effect, they seem simple in thematic treatment and technical variety as compared with Hummel's *Capriccioso Polonaise* and Beethoven's *Polonaise* (1815), but doubtless the spirit of Romanticism is present in them. His best works after these are the *Sonatas* (1812), the *Variations, Op.* 28, 37 and 55, the *E major Polonaise*, the *Rondo Brilliant*, the *Invitation to the Dance*, and lastly, the *Concertstück Op.* 79. The main features may be said to be (1) wonderful gift of melody ; (2) limited range of *harmonic* effects—though these are always warm and appropriate ; (3) influence of the *orchestra*, shown in the frequent quasi-bowed violin passages, use of the tremolo and muttering double-bass passages ; (4) limited (though advanced) *variety* of technique ; (5) limited formal development ; (6) effective use of the *crescendo* ; (7) frequent repetition of certain chromatic appogiatura figures with repeated chord-basses, by which his music can always be recognized.

Weber came of a good family (apparently South German in

origin). His early years were embittered by a wandering
existence with his father in an Opera company.

Later, he held several conductor's positions which he filled
with distinction, especially in Prague, Dresden and Vienna.
Worn out by overwork, he died in · London when he was
conducting a performance of *Oberon* in 1826.

Weber was a contemporary of his seniors, Beethoven and
Hummel, though he died a year before the former. Haydn's
work was done when Weber's first work appeared.

His *Duets* (Chapter XXIII) have much of the charm of the
solos and are educationally valuable.

Of the Concertos the *F minor* is best known as a standard work,
although the other Concertos contain beautiful movements.

CHARLES MAYER (1799–1862)

The significance of Charles Mayer lies in his direct succession
from Field as a modern *lyric* Romanticist, and in his development of modern technique. Born at Königsberg he was, at an
early age, a pupil of Field in St. Petersburg, and at the age of
fifteen he made a series of concert tours.

If we remember that Mayer was only seventeen years younger
than Field and compare the lyric simplicity of the latter with
Mayer's modern harmonies and modern technique, we shall
realize how quickly this branch of the art came to maturity.
Mayer's playing is said to have been distinguished by the great
purity of style of his master Field; his *technique*, however,
must have considerably developed, as his Studies rank among
the most modern and prepare directly for the bravura School
of Henselt and Chopin. Mayer, like many others, wrote a
number of trifling works to meet the popular taste of the time,
but the best of his works, in the *Langley Edition* (Aug.), deserve
to rank for their warmth and purity of style with the best works
of the smaller lyrical Romanticists of to-day.

His *Valses, Etudes* and *Concertos* deserve attention. After
several concert tours Mayer settled in Dresden, where he died
in 1862.

Our story of Romance in pianoforte music now assumes a
crowded aspect and the attention of the reader must be devoted
to the many developments of the Romantic movement, from
the lyric Schubert to the virtuoso Liszt and the nationalist
Chopin.

CHAPTER IV

THE ROMANTIC MOVEMENT IN PIANOFORTE MUSIC

I	1782–1837 Field (Lyric-Nocturnes)	III	1811–1886 Liszt (Virtuoso-Transcriptions)
	1786–1826 Weber (Dramatic)		1814–1889 Henselt (Virtuoso-Lyric)
	1797–1828 Schubert (Lyric-Impromptu)	V	1814–1888 Heller (Nature-Poet)
	1799–1862 Charles Mayer (Virtuoso-Technique)		1816–1875 Bennett (Idyllic)
II	1809–1847 Mendelssohn (Classic)	V	1822–1882 Raff (Virtuoso-Lyric)
	1810–1856 Schumann (Characteristic)		1830–1894 Rubinstein (Virtuoso-Lyric)
	1810–1849 Chopin (National)		

The composers in Group I (all contemporaries of Beethoven) laid the foundations. Those in Group II perfected the movement. Groups III and V are concerned with the perfecting of the virtuoso element and concert interpretation ; Group IV with the later Idyllic and Poetic aspect.

Lyric-Romance

SCHUBERT (1797–1828)

" My musical works are the offspring of my genius—and my misery."— *Schubert.*

THE various features of the pianoforte music of Schubert, with its weaknesses and excellences, can be best studied in his *Sonatas*. Schubert was pre-eminently a song-writer, and it is the song or *lyric element* in inexhaustible beauty that first appeals to us in his pianoforte works. Next to that comes his wealth of charming unexpected modulations and harmonies. At the keyboard, however, one is made aware of a sense of very limited command of technique. Short-fingered as Schubert was, and blessed with but " little technique," as Hiller avows, we find the result in the constantly repeated chords, the limited use of extended arpeggio and scale figures, which are either spasmodically introduced, as in the first movement of *Sonata Op*. 120, or used throughout without much variation. His technique, as a rule, would seem to consist of firm chord work, cantabile melodies and variation figures combined with both ; in short, his technique was mostly of an accompanimental style.

This want of effective technique is doubtless the reason why Schubert's Sonatas are very rarely performed in public. As regards the development of theme, Schubert is indeed the antithesis of Beethoven, for instead of the piecemeal dissertation and the almost too minute analysis of the orchestrally-minded Beethoven, Schubert usually takes the theme as a whole and treats it according to Variation form, either varying the form of the melody or the harmonies, presenting the harmony alone in various aspects, or keeping the bass and altering the melody or the harmony or both. A favourite method of his is to put the theme in the bass. The same tendency is seen in the ornamentation of the chief theme in the recapitulation section of the Sonatas. Perhaps it is too much to expect that the intensely lyrical mind should express itself in the analytical thematic manner, and therefore his method may be considered as an evolution of that style of development which was later brought into further prominence by Liszt.

If strict " thematic " presentation be regarded as the distinguishing characteristic of the Sonata type, Schubert's *Sonatas* must be reckoned as Fantasias (his *Op. 78 in G* is so described) rather than as Sonatas.

As *developed* compositions not one of these we should say is equal to the average of Clementi, but they are undoubtedly graceful and attractive as music, especially the first two movements of *Op.* 42 (No. 1 Univ. Ed.), the *Con Moto* of the *Op. 53 in D* (No. 2), the first movement of No. 5 (*Op.* 143 *in A minor*), the *Andantes* of Nos. 6 and 7, and the last *Sonata* No. 10 *in B♭*.

Despite many entrancing melodies and modulations, one cannot overlook the fact that most of the movements have a patchy effect, owing to systematic lack of development and unequal technical figuration.

The *Sonata* No. 4 *in E♭* and the last three posthumous Sonatas, written in 1828 and inspired by the visit of Hummel, are more homogeneous, but, with the exception of the one in *B♭*, they are, unfortunately, not so characteristic.

The last movement of the latter, by-the-by, shows Hungarian influence.

Beethoven had written twenty-seven of his Sonatas before

Schubert commenced works of this type, but, except for the
C minor Sonata and the slow movement of the great *Duo in C,*
Schubert would seem to have built rather on a foundation of
Mozart and Haydn than on Beethoven.

Schubert felt, indeed, the overshadowing genius of Beethoven.
As a youth he exclaimed with a sigh, " Who can do anything
after Beethoven ? "—and a visit to Beethoven's house later on
with his *Duet Variations* ended in his impetuously leaving the
room overcome with emotion.

The *Fantasia* or *Sonata in E Op.* 78 is one of the most
poetical of his works, although it has the usual patchy technical
style, even in the Andante.

The *Fantasia Op.* 15 is best known for the fine dramatic
Variations in the Andante, on the theme of his own Lied,
The Wanderer.

We now come to those smaller lyrical works, the *Impromptus*
and the *Moments Musicaux,* in which, as not particularly requiring
thematic and formal development, Schubert excels. It will be
seen that they are mostly in his favourite Variation form.
The title *Impromptus,* by the way, like the *Fantasia Op.* 78,
was given by the publisher. We note that the first of the
Op. 90 (built on a very Schubertian theme) has the characteristic
repeated notes and chords, accompaniment figures, theme in
the bass and frequent charming modulations. The Etude-like
No. 2, with the spice of Hungarian rhythm in the Episode, the
Song without Words No. 4 (originally in $G\flat$), the pretty salon-
like one in $A\flat$, with the characteristic $C\sharp$ *minor* Episode,
complete the *Op.* 90.

As regards the *Op.* 142, Schumann thought that the 1st,
2nd and 4th were intended as Movements of a *Sonata in F minor,*
as the 1st Movement has some resemblance to Sonata-form.
He says it " seems to have been written during a pensive hour,
as if, while meditating on the past." The favourite short
" Contemplative " No. 2 *in* $A\flat$, the $B\flat$ theme with Variations,
and the elusive *Scherzando* No. 4, in Hungarian style, are well
known.

No. 3 of those slight improvisatory sketches termed *Moments
Musicaux* is also decidedly Hungarian in style. These popular
short pieces contain much of what is best in Schubert. The
miscellaneous pieces in Vol. 3 of the Litolff Collection, the five
Pieces in Sonata style, *Adagio* and *Rondo, Op.* 145, etc., together

with the Variations, are not at all Schubertian in style, but are apparently modelled on Mozart and Haydn. The artistic *Waltzes*, like the immortal *Lieder*, have been transcribed by Liszt, the former appearing as the *Soirées de Vienne*. Schubert contributed very largely to the realm of *four-hand* music (*see* Chapter XXIII) through the fine duet Marches, Divertissements, Sonatas, etc.

Schubert's place in pianoforte music is that of a supporter of the *Romantic* movement, which had already been stimulated by his contemporary Weber (1786–1826), who, though eleven years older, died only two years before him. While Weber advanced the bravura and dramatic elements, Schubert developed the lyric or song-like structures, which were later so largely utilized by Mendelssohn, Chopin, Schumann and many others. He also, by means of his charming modern *modulations*, did much for modern music—and modern *harmony* especially. In the latter he surpasses Mendelssohn, who was only nineteen years of age when Schubert died.

Mendelssohn, however, was the " backwash of Classicism " in his time, and it is to Chopin and Schumann that we must look for the further progress of the Romantic movement.

An Austrian by race, and born in Vienna, Schubert never left his native country except for two short visits to the neighbouring state of Hungary. These visits left their influence in the *Hungarian* style already noted in his works, and in the *Divertissement à la Hongroise*, Op. 54, which was built on Hungarian melodies and was a favourite with Liszt.

Schubert's music reflects the genial atmosphere of the South as clearly as that of Brahms reflects the sterner North, though the latter settled in Vienna and was strongly influenced by Schubert's work. Schubert was a chorister at the Imperial Training School for Court Singers till 1813, a teacher at his father's school till 1816, and from then till his death twelve years later he was engaged in a perpetual struggle with adversity, existing chiefly on the proceeds of his wretchedly-paid compositions.

It was true enough, as he himself said, that " his music was the offspring of his misery." He was of a reserved though genial disposition and it is sad to relate that not until nine months before his death was the first public concert of his compositions given.

Comparatively untrained as a composer, Schubert made up for weakness in powers of development by a gift of unlimited melody and by charming *modulations* ; and in so doing he became, not a " Classic " composer, but one of the most charming contributors to the Romantic School.

" Schubert," declares Schumann, " will always remain the favourite of youth. He gives what youth desires—an overflowing heart, daring thoughts and speedy deeds. He tells of what youth loves best—of knights and maidens, romantic stories and adventures. He gives wings to the performer's own fancy as no other composer since Beethoven."

No wonder, then, that he should be known as " the most lovable of composers."

CHAPTER V

MENDELSSOHN (1809-1847)

THE music of Mendelssohn has been aptly described as a
" backwash of Classicism." This description appears, at first,
to be somewhat contradictory. In the hitherto distinguishing
form of Classicism—the Sonata—Mendelssohn was not a success,
though his *G minor Concerto*, which is practically in Sonata
form, is one of the standard works of its kind. On the other
hand, where one would not look for Sonata form, as in the
B minor Capriccio for Piano and Orchestra, the three *Capriccios
Op. 33*, the *Capriccio in F♯ minor, Op. 5*, the *Fantasia in
E minor, Op. 16*, and the third movement of the *F♯ Fantasia*
(Op. 28), we have more or less regular Sonata form used with
that mastery which distinguishes his hand. Allied to this
representative mark of Classicism is the general style of his
writing which shows more than any other modern, the influence
of Bach, as in his clever and effective Preludes and Fugues ;
while another distinction—though a negative one—is his
limited range of harmonic modulatory effects as compared with
his contemporaries of note, all of whom, except Hummel,
were Romantics.

On the other hand, we must claim Mendelssohn partly also as
a Romanticist, because (1) of his thoroughly *lyrical* style ;
(2) of his sentimental, airy and brilliant manner in works of a
non-formal nature.

We may gain some insight into Mendelssohn's music through
his personality. At the age of fifteen, young Mendelssohn
came into contact with Moscheles, then described as the
" Prince of Pianists," who acted as his teacher for some time.

Moscheles describes the family as " such a one as I have never
known before ; Felix a mature artist and yet but fifteen ;
Fanny extraordinarily gifted, playing Bach's Fugues by heart
with astonishing correctness. The parents gave me the
impression of the highest cultivation."

A comfortable home, wealth and ease of circumstance,
personal charm and love for the sunny side of nature are
specially reflected in Mendelssohn's music.

At the age of twenty he came on a visit to England, one of

many to our country, where he made many friends, and where many of his greatest successes as a composer were achieved.

Some of his well-known pieces were written while staying with friends in Wales, and a letter (p. 264, Vol. II, Grove) describes his entering " into the beauty of the hills and woods." *The Rivulet*, which he wrote at that time, was " a recollection of a real rivulet." The *Andante and Allegro* " was suggested by a bunch of carnations and roses," the *arpeggio* passages conveying a " reminder of the sweet scent of the flowers rising up."

The *Capriccio in E minor*,* again, was suggested by " a pretty creeping plant covered with little trumpet-like flowers," Mendelssohn drawing " a little branch of that flower all up the margin of the paper," and saying that this was " the music that the fairies might play on those trumpets."

A happy, lovable nature, " not a bit sentimental though he had so much sentiment," full of fun (" nobody enjoyed fun more than he, and his laughing was the most joyous that could be ") explains much of what we feel when we hear his unique fairy music in the *Midsummer Night's Dream* and his inimitable Scherzos and Caprices.

Mendelssohn possessed a rare individuality, a fascinating and affectionate manner, and an extraordinary passion for taste and neatness in everything he did. Clever as a pianist, he was too modest to play before virtuosi ; but his performance was distinguished by " lightness of touch and a delicious, liquid pearliness of tone," developed with the lightest of wrists and never from the arm. His technical figuration in composition was, however, somewhat limited, and in his busy fidgety broken chord figures and rapid arpeggios of the diminished 7th we miss the sweep of Chopin and Beethoven, though it is suitable enough for a good Scherzo style. This technique, however, is improved upon in the *G minor Concerto*, which was modelled on Moscheles, and in the *B minor Capriccio, with Orchestra*, which was inspired by Weber's *Concertstück*.

Like his technique, Mendelssohn's *harmonic* and *modulatory* effects are limited. Out of twenty-eight bars of the Allegro of the *B♭ Sonata*, ten and a half bars consist of diminished 7ths, while his great fondness for the minor key, probably due to his Jewish descent, is shown also in his almost stereotyped modulation to the supertonic and other minor keys.

---

* The three pieces mentioned form the Op. 16 written during his visit to Wales.

On account of these deficiencies Mendelssohn's best works, apart from those in playful Scherzo style and the brilliant ones with orchestra, are the smaller Pieces known as the *Songs without Words*. These delightful and highly-finished Pieces more than any others have made his name a household word. Oscar Bie, in his *History of the Pianoforte and Pianoforte Players*, in a somewhat severe criticism, describes Mendelssohn as a "composer for young girls, the elegant Romanticist of the drawing-room" and as exhibiting a "gilt-edged lyricism." Speaking of the *Songs without Words* he says, "The *Funeral March*, compared with that of Beethoven, is as if it were written for a set of marionettes." "The *Spring Song*," he says, "is, so-to-speak, set on wires." This seems unduly exaggerated, while something also must be allowed for interpretation or manner of performance. There should be room, in pianoforte music, for all aspects of nature. We have the tragedy of Beethoven and the romantic gloom of Schumann, and we trust there will always be a place for the sunshine and light-hearted fascination of Mendelssohn. (*See also* Chapter VIII.)

Mendelssohn's best and most characteristic pianoforte music seems to come in the early part of his life ; later on he appears to have been much absorbed in orchestral and choral works.

One might mark the dividing point after the *Concerto in G minor*, Op. 25, written at the age of eighteen. Before this, and including the Concerto, the best are the *Op.* 14 (*Andante and Rondo Capriccioso*) and the three *Capriccios, Op.* 16 and the *B minor Capriccio, with Orchestra*. With these come also the *Songs without Words* (Bk. I, 1830, written at the age of twenty-one) ; the melodious *Preludes and Fugues*, Op. 35, which show remarkable facility in this difficult branch of the art and were written between 1832 and 1836, when he was less than twenty-seven, and finally, the *Variations Sérieuses, Op.* 54, one of the best works of its kind in the Classic style.

With the exception of the *Lieder ohne Worte*, Fugues and Variations already mentioned, the works after *Op.* 25 seem to have lost their freshness through lapse of time.

On the whole, though Mendelssohn's music is never deep, it can boast of warm sympathetic melody and of a sunny nature ; and, in spite of its limitations in technique and harmony, it is always truly pianistic and suited to the instrument.

CHAPTER VI

REFLECTIVE AND CHARACTERISTIC ROMANCE

Schumann

" If heaven has gifted you with lively imagination, you will often, in lonely hours, sit as though spellbound at the pianoforte, seeking to express the *harmony* that dwells in your mind."—*Schumann*.

ROBERT SCHUMANN, *the greatest of the Romanticists*, was born in the same year as Chopin, 1810. His father was a bookseller at Zwickau. Already, at the age of six, the boy was a pianist, while at seven he was a composer and extemporized at the instrument.

A few years later, when at school, he showed that literary faculty for which he also became famous in after-life.

At the age of eighteen he was sent to Leipzig to study law, and there he became acquainted with Clara Wieck, then a girl of nine only, and already known as a pianist and composer.

Schumann, neglecting the law, devoted himself to harmony and counterpoint, the pianoforte, and the study of Bach. Removing to Leipzig, he attended the lectures of Thibaut, who had written a treatise on " *Purity in Musical Art.*"

Schumann had already been hard at work at the pianoforte when in Heidelberg, and had there written the *Abegg* Variations, the *Papillons* and a sketch of the *Toccata*. It was not long before he revolted against the law and determined finally to take up music in earnest in Leipzig.

The career of a virtuoso now attracted him and, in order to hasten his progress, he originated a device for holding up one finger while the others were energetically employed.

The resultant laming of this finger and consequent abandonment of the rôle of virtuoso made a change in his career, which was fortunate for the musical world, since he was obliged to take to composition instead of becoming merely an executant.

In 1832 appeared his first set of *Caprices after Paganini*, the result of hearing Paganini's performance at Frankfort in 1830. Next year followed the *Intermezzi* and *Impromptus on a Theme of Clara Wieck;* the *Toccata* was finished, the *Concert-Allegro in B minor*, and a second and more virtuoso-like set of *Paganini Caprices* were written, while the *G minor* and *F♯ minor Sonatas* were begun.   Schumann was thus, at the age of twenty-two or twenty-three, already in full career.

A year later began his connection with the musical journal, *Neue Zeitschrift für Musik*, which lasted for eleven years without a break and did so much, in many instances, for the cause of unknown aspirants to fame, such as Bennett, Brahms, Chopin and others.   The Journal represented progressive musical art. Schumann invented certain imaginary musical personalities : the enthusiastic, heaven-storming and humorous " Florestan," the gentle, reflective " Eusebius," the philosophic " Raro " and " Jonathan," who were supposed to meet together in critical conclave.   Essays and criticisms appeared over these signatures considering   musical   art   from   different   standpoints ;   and compositions, as, for instance, in his *Carnival*, were marked " Florestan," " Eusebius," etc., according to their inner meaning. The traits of these " Davidsbündler " or " League of David," as they   were   jointly   termed,   were   also   perpetuated   in   the *Davidsbündler Tänze*, Op. 6.

The *Carnival* and five *Etudes Symphoniques* appeared in 1834, and in 1836 his romantic engagement to Clara Wieck began, only to encounter for four long years the decided opposition of her father.   The struggle, however, was not without value for art.   As Schumann himself wrote : " Much music is the result of the contest I am passing through for Clara's sake."

The *Fantasia in C, Concerto without Orchestra, Fantasiestücke, Noveletten, Kreisleriana, Kinderscenen, Arabeske, Blumenstück* and *Humoreske*, comprising all the best of his works, were written   at   this   time.   Immediately   after   his   marriage Schumann's vein of composition seemed to have changed.   His facile pen produced in quick succession 130 Songs, 3 Symphonies, a Pianoforte Concerto, and some Chamber Music.   In 1843 he became Professor of Composition at the Conservatorium with Mendelssohn as Head, and his *Variations for Two Pianofortes* now appeared.

In 1844 came the successful tour to Russia, under Imperial patronage.

Yourie Arnold, a theorist, relates that during a concert given in St. Petersburg, " Clara Schumann took part in her husband's *Pianoforte Quartet*, and played his *Kreisleriana* and several other pieces. She made a deep impression on us, although we were growing accustomed to lady pianists. . . . Schumann was silent and morose the whole evening. He scarcely spoke at all. . . . He sat in a corner by the piano, his head bent forward, his hair falling over his face, his lips pursed up as if about to whistle. He seemed lost in stern reflection. As I saw him that night, Schumann was exactly like the life-size medallion taken by the Sculptor Dondorf. Clara Schumann was more talkative, and made up for her husband's taciturnity. At the piano she proved a truly great artist, possessed of virile energy and feminine instinct both in reading and execution, though she was at that time not more than five or six-and-twenty. But one could hardly describe her as a gracious or sympathetic woman."

The world-famous *Kinder-Album, Op.* 68, appeared shortly after this tour.

An appointment at Düsseldorf in 1850, as successor to Ferd. Hiller, was only held by Schumann for three years, when he was obliged to resign owing to symptoms of incipient insanity. A year later the unfortunate man tried to drown himself ; and he died in an asylum near Bonn some two years afterwards, in July, 1856, at the early age of forty-six.

It is worthy of note that practically all Schumann's piano music was written before his marriage, and that his sympathies afterwards seemed to have turned in a new direction, when his energies were bestowed mostly on works which required, so to speak, a bigger canvas.

In Litzmann's *Life of Clara Schumann* appears a letter showing how she wished her husband's genius to obtain full recognition. This is what she wrote : " Listen, Robert ; will you not, just for once, compose something brilliant, something easy to understand, and something without a superscription—a piece which hangs together well, neither too long nor too short ? I should so like to have something to play at concerts for the public. For a genius this is certainly humiliating, but policy sometimes requires it." Fortunately for art Schumann was apparently unable to carry out this behest. He owes his niche in the temple of fame to the reflective and characteristic forms of musical art—forms made for the solitary chamber rather than for the concert hall, which naturally is a more suitable environment for the " brilliant " and " easy to understand."

Whether a further devotion to pianoforte composition would have been a gain, had he lived longer, is problematical. His later piano works, with the exception of the *Kinder-Album*, show signs of that obscurity of style which we believe must have been occasioned by the approaches of his terrible malady.

The key to Schumann's *style* is to be found in his cultivation of the mystic element in life under the influence of the Romanticist Jean Paul Richter.

It has been said that " the tunes of Schumann, like the colours of Rossetti, are always trembling on the verge of symbolism " (Hadow), and Schumann was, indeed, the leading representative of the " Characteristic " School. (*See* next Chapter, dealing with the " Characteristic " Composers.)

Two obstacles stood in the way of the perfect recognition of his music : (1) the employment of polyphony (an extension of the traditions of Bach), with its ever-tangling web of the various parts, and (2) obscured rhythmical effects. Schumann himself said, " only study Bach thoroughly and the most complicated of my works will seem clear." He must needs, then, be an educated musician who would understand Schumann in all his moods. The persistent *cross-rhythm* effects do not, however, come direct from Bach, though they are the outgrowth of his style ; and these were later used to exhaustion by Brahms, who modelled much of his style upon Schumann. The principal musical virtue of Schumann was his modern feeling for *harmony* in all its rich and varied colouring. The moods which he wished to instil into his hearers were obtained, as he himself said, " by penetrating more deeply into the mysteries of harmony." Chopin resembles him to a certain extent in harmonic feeling, but does not go so far, the attraction in his case being made complete by his more effective technique.

With Schumann it is otherwise. Harmonic feeling comes first, polyphonic effects next and pianistic technique last.

Both composers, however, were as decidedly lyrical as Bach and Beethoven were instrumental (loving the organ and the orchestra respectively.

As regards *classical structure*—in which, no doubt, Schumann was much influenced by the master-hand of his confrère Mendelssohn—we may say that Chopin and Schumann stood further apart, the latter showing a much wider grasp of instrumental and orchestral forms on a large scale.

Another comparison may be made between the influences which prompted these two Romantic composers. For Schumann it was the poets Jean Paul Richter, Byron and others who reflected the trend and attitude of the age. For Chopin it was his intense devotion to his native land, the spirit of whose songs is reflected in his art.

Schumann's works may be divided into two classes : (1) those which are avowedly " characteristic," the great majority, and (2) formal works such as Sonatas, Fugues, etc.

Taking Vol. I of the Litolff collection of his works, we have, first, the *Jugend-Album*, *Op*. 68, containing those little characteristic sketches, so true to life, from the desolate *Poor Orphan* to the run-away *Wild Horseman*, and the mysterious *Old Goblin*. Then there are the similar *Kinder-Scenen* with their charming Miniatures—*The Entreating Child*, *Perfect Happiness*, and a dozen others equally inspired. The *Forest Scenes* belong to a different sphere, the realm of nature. The simple little tone-poem *Solitary Flowers* recalls Burns's *Ode to a Daisy*, while the sweet but melancholy song of the dainty *Prophet Bird* takes all hearts captive.

The delightful *Album-Blätter* portray all manner of little scenes ; the beautiful *Schlummerlied*, the fantastic *Elves* and *Burla*, the fluttering *Vision* and the sympathetic *Presage of Sorrow*. It is not too much to say that here is Schumann at his best. Modulations, harmonies and expressive features are here refined and polished to the last degree. In technique Schumann is also at his best in the light, pleasant and original, a manner or style which, springing from the nature of his compositions, was practically unforestalled by any composer. Here there is none of the massive, somewhat clumsy, technique which marks many of his other works and is unfortunately the feature most often copied by his numerous imitators.

In the next volume (No. 2), comprising the *Fantasiestücke*, *Noveletten* and *Nachtstücke* we are conscious of a greater energy, a greater striving, a more massive style and a richer colouring ; as well as of something quite different from all which had appeared before in Pianoforte Literature. What a picture-gallery of the emotions the *Fantasiestücke* present : the twilight *Eve*, the strenuous Excelsior-like *Soaring*, the pleading *Why* ? the many-hued *Whims*, the ghostly *Night*, the mystifying *Fable*, the happy entrancing *Dream Visions* and the jovial *Finale !*

The title *Novelettes* was suggested by the dramatic short story which had become popular in Germany under that title. The 1st and 2nd themes of the first *Novelette* have been compared to a " rugged German baron " and a " mild, elegant, domestically-inclined Fräulein " ; No. 7 tells of dashing cavaliers and courtly dances ; No. 8 is a mediæval mystery with tragic ending ; and No. 9 " a sprightly dance and frolic of forest elves round a secluded chapel."

The ghostly and mysterious *Nachtstücke* (Nocturnes or Night Pieces) are, like all Schumann's characteristic pieces, quite unique ; the tiptoe entry of No. 1, with its stealthy dialogue, the frolicsome yet tender No. 2, the dramatic No. 3 with the legendary and merry episodes, and finally the heaven-inspired *Finale*—an evening prayer.

In the favourite *Carnival* (Vol. III) we find a series of cameos or miniature pictures of various personalities—the " David's-League " family, Chopin and Paganini, with reminiscences of the merry Harlequin and Columbine, and of others who masquerade in the *Papillons* and the *Faschingsschwank aus Wien.*

The only connecting link appears to be the insertion in the pieces of the musical notes (in the usual German nomenclature) —A, E♭ (*es*), C, B (*h*), or A♭ (*as*), C, B(*h*), representing in each case the word " Asch." Schumann himself describes it as follows : " The name of a city, in which a musical friend of mine lived, consisted of letters belonging to the scale, which are also contained in my name ; and this suggested one of those tricks which are no longer new, since Bach gave the example. One piece after another " (he says) " was completed during the Carnival season of 1835, in a serious mood of mind and under peculiar circumstances. I afterwards gave titles to the numbers, and named the entire collection *The Carnival.*"

Referring to Liszt's performance of it in Leipzig, he expresses the opinion that " its musical moods change too rapidly to be easily followed by a general musical public."

Happily, however, owing to Madame Schumann's later

interpretation of her husband's works, the *Carnival* became a favourite.

Browning, who makes an interesting study of Schumann's *Carnival* in his *Fifine at the Fair*, speaks of the

> Columbine—Pantaloon,
> She toe-tips and, *staccato-legato*, shakes his poll,
> And shambles in pursuit, the senior. *Fi! la folle.*

In the *Faschingsschwank aus Wien* (" A Carnival Jest from Vienna ") we have more glimpses of the " fun of the fair " and of similar experiences in the gay student life of Heidelberg. The description ends in the Finale with " The noise of the Carnival dies away., the church clock strikes six." Humour and sentiment appear also in the *Davidsbündler Tänze*, in which the sketches are signed " F." (Florestan) or " E." (Eusebius), according to their character. The *Kreisleriana* are of a different type—truly poetical and reflective sketches suggesting in their languor and refined melancholy the influence of Chopin to whom they are dedicated. They seem to have been named after the eccentric Kapellmeister Kreisler, who was also of a literary turn of mind.

To complete the principal characteristic works, we have the rich, songful *Romances*, the fine original *Marches*, more forceful and dignified than those of Schubert, the ornamental tracery of the *Arabeske*, the genial and really humorous *Humoreske*, and the descriptive *Bunte Blätter, Op.* 99.

Of the non-formal romantic works the beautiful rhapsodic *Fantasia, Op.* 17, stands supreme—that " mingled earthly dream " which was originally written in connection with a proposed memorial for Beethoven. The nature of the work comes out in the titles intended for the three movements, viz., *Ruins, Triumphal Arch, The Starry Crown.*

Besides this we have the discursive *Op.* 8 *Allegro*, and the *Etude Toccata*, which is written, by the way, in Sonata form. In the first book of the *Paganini Studies* Schumann, as he himself says, " copied the original, perhaps to its injury, almost note for note, and merely enlarged a little harmonically." In the poetical, yet bravura, 2nd Set, which are intended more for the concert room, he " broke loose from a too-closely imitative translation of the themes selected from the original 24 *Caprices*," which also inspired Liszt and Brahms to unheard-of technical feats in composition. Schumann, in his own notes on these

Etude-Transcriptions of his, says (*Music and Musicians*, p. 360, Reeves), " it is impossible that those who have once heard them executed perfectly should not often think of them with pleasure."

In these, and especially in the *Études Symphoniques* (dedicated to Sterndale Bennett), which are Variations on a theme in C♯ minor, we have displayed before us the originality of Schumann's technique with its almost orchestral fulness of tone, extensions, skips and massed chords, its inner melodies and imitation dialogue and pervading *sostentante* style.

The " Abegg " *Variations Op.* 1 are earlier in style ; but the *Impromptu Variations* (*Op.* 5) on a theme of Clara Wieck and the charming *Variations for Two Pianos* are characteristic and are written in the free style of small Fantasias (*see* Chapter XXIV on " Variations "). Of the formally developed cyclical works, the *Sonatas*, especially the *G minor*, are full of glowing colour and rich in imagination, though they suffer somewhat from want of unity of style. (*See* Chapter XXI, " Modern Sonatas "). The *Concerto in A minor, Op.* 54, is one of the most charming of Schumann's works (*see* Chapter XXII, " Concertos "), technically attractive—showing the influence of Chopin—warm and romantic in feeling, and structurally artistic.

The *Concertstück* and *Concert Allegro*, both in Concerto style, are more classic in feeling and manner.

Schumann's *Fugues* are characteristic in feeling, but lack somewhat of the contrapuntal fluency of Mendelssohn (*see* Chapter XVII, Part III). In his *four-hand* music (Chapter XXIII) he provides increased pleasure for " young and old " in the attractive *Children's Ball* and *Ball Scenes*.

Generally speaking, one cannot but be struck by the composer's warm romantic glow, sincere expression and fund of humour, as exemplified in the noble and original harmonies and the truly lyrical style.

It is true that he falls somewhat short of unity of *form* in his larger works, that he inclines rather much to the creation of small phrases, to occasionally over-complex weaving of the parts and to rhythms coloured by a certain sombre melancholy, while his *technique* is also sometimes difficult without being correspondingly effective ; but, on the whole, we have, in his best works, very much of what the musical world would not willingly let die. Schumann will always be known as an original genius and as the greatest of the Romanticists.

CHAPTER VII

CHARACTERISTIC, IMPRESSIONIST AND PROGRAMME MUSIC

" The Poet's word-mesh, Painter's sure and swift colour and line-throw
Outdo both of them music!—*Browning*, (" Charles Avison.")

FROM the earliest periods in the history of the tonal art both
instrumental and vocal composers have striven to represent in
music the objective side of nature, or, in other words, not
content with appealing direct to the emotions, they have also
endeavoured to recall what goes on in the world around us.
This portraiture of the external is secured (1) through direct
imitation, or (2) through some effect which will call up, by
association, the mental picture desired. The direct imitation
of thunder is an instance of the first, that of a flash of lightning
an example of the second class.

In the latter case the natural phenomenon of light is usually
interpreted in sound by an extremely swift scale passage, or a
glissando.

The limitations of such imitation are very obvious.

In the words of Ambros : " Music is the best painter of the
soul's state and feeling—*and the worst of realistic objects.*"

Within the same category as the imitation of lightning we
must place also the imitation or suggestion of the emotions such
as joy, sorrow, humour and happiness, which can only be
recalled by association of ideas—slow music for sorrow and quick
for joy, etc. As early as the fourth century B.C. this was
recognized by the Greek philosopher Aristotle, who says :
" It is in rhythms and melodies that we have the most realistic
imitations of anger and mildness, as well as of their opposites
generally."

Simple modern examples of these musical representations of
emotions occur in Schumann's *Poor Orphan* and *Merry Peasant*.

Some distinction requires to be made between Characteristic
and Programme music, and between these and Impressionist
music. The line of demarcation between the two former is by-
no means easy to draw, but, speaking generally, *characteristic*
music would seem to imply that which is characteristic of, or

associated with, definite states of the mind, its moods and emotions.

Programme music, on the other hand, treats rather of definite events, occurrences or phenomena in Nature, while *Impressionism* hovers between the two in its vague presentation of a picture, a picture which may partake of both classes.

" Music is a very imperfect language; it is all adjectives and no substantives; it cannot delineate the objects themselves."—*Dr. Crotch.*

Bearing in mind this dictum of a once-famous English church composer and former instrumental prodigy, we would say that in Programme music we naturally, first of all, look for representations of sounds in Nature, such as the rolling of thunder, the noise of the sea, the crash of the storm, the music of bells, the song of birds, etc

Early examples are to be found in the *Fitzwilliam Virginal Book* (1550–1621) as, for instance, Munday's *Fantasia* containing *Faire Wether, Lightning, Thunder,* etc.

In the *Susatos Collection* of 1551 there is the Pavan *La Bataille,* and we have also the *glissando Jacob's Ladder* of Froberger, the descriptive incidents in the *Bible Sonatas* by Kuhnau—Bach's predecessor at Leipzig—as well as Bach's own Capriccio *The Departure of a Brother* (*see* Part I, Chapter X). The call of the cuckoo has ever been a favourite device, as in the *Cuckoo Capriccio* of Frescobaldi (1626), the *Cuckoo Capriccio* of Kerl (1679), the *Cuckoo Toccata* of Pasquini, 1702, and *Le Coucou* by Daquin, the contemporary of Rameau (*c.* 1705).

Rameau, also, in his artistic suites, has imitated the call of the birds and the cackle of the hen; and Couperin likewise wrote a *Hunting Scene* and the *Bells of Cythera.*

With later composers artistic Programme music is more scarce. Weber's *Concertstücke* and *Invitation to the Dance,* Beethoven's playful *Rage Over a Lost Penny,* Henselt's descriptive *Thanksgiving after a Storm,* and Liszt's *Les Cloches de Genève* and *Mazeppa Étude* stand out as examples. During this same period and, indeed, up to the present day, we are confronted with *Realism,* which one may describe as Programme music carried to an inartistic extreme. This development of a legitimate device brings out emphatically the weak points and limitations of the art. Music's sway lies in its power over the

emotions and not in material trickery. The announcement of
a Programme naturally takes away from the interest of the
music itself and concentrates attention on the Programme
device ; while rank Realism dethrones the divine art and
substitutes for it another deity and a false one. Examples
of this are not difficult to find. Kotzwara's *Battle of Prague*,
Steibelt's *Bacchanals* with tambourine accompaniment,
Dussek's guillotine scene in *The Sufferings of the Queen of
France* suffice without quoting later instances.

Music " characteristic " of the moods and emotions and of
their associations may be said to be first prominently illustrated
in the dainty Suites of Chambonnière, Couperin, Rameau and
Em. Bach.

In the Suites of Couperin we have, indeed, a complete
portrait gallery.

The failings and graces of Nannette, the gossiping wife, the
Soeur Monique, the *Enchanteresse*, *Le Turbulent*, *Les Dominos*,
and many others are depicted. Impressions aroused by
association with nature are given by the *Butterflies*, the *Bees*,
and the *Grasshopper*, while the varied emotions of *Les Sentiments*,
Les Regrets, *L'Ame en Peine*, etc., are faithfully related.

Rameau again, in his *Les Tendres Plaintes*, *La Timide*, etc.,
and Em. Bach in his *Les Langueurs Tendres* and *La Complaisante*,
have displayed similar powers of characterisation.

In the same class we may also mention the *Consolation* and
Adieu Rondos of Dussek, the *Lamentation* Sonata of Rust, the
Adieu, *Pathétique* and *Pastoral* Sonatas of Beethoven.

Schumann was pre-eminently a depictor of the *characteristic*.
His important *Kinder-Album*, *Kinder-Scenen*, *Carnival*, *Davidsbündler*, etc., are full of charming music and artistically " true
to nature."

Schumann himself, in his literary articles, pleaded the cause
of both Programme and Characteristic forms. In " Florestan's
Shrovetide Speech " occurs the following :—

" ' Did not Beethoven write a Battle Symphony, also, sir ? '
' Yes, sir, the *Pastoral Symphony*, ' answered Eusebius
indifferently."

Schumann also laughed heartily over Beethoven's *Rage over
a Lost Penny*. " Now I have you, Beethovenians," he says ;
" I could be angry with you in quite another way when you
turn up the whites of your eyes and rave about Beethoven's

freedom from earthliness, his transcendental flight from star to star."

Schumann recognizes the living tone-landscapes of Bennett— the " lake " the " mill-wheel " and the " hundred voices prattling and splashing " of the *Fountain ;* and his far-seeing literary criticisms display as much characterization in his description of works by " the manifold pictures which arise in my mind " as in his own compositions. Heller, in his *Forest and Hunting Scenes,* Jensen, Volkmann, Nicodé and Hiller, in their happy characterization of scenes in childhood and youth, not to mention characteristic works by Reinecke, Tschaïkowsky, Saint-Saëns, Huber and many others, are examples of this delightful class.

Impressionism in pianoforte music aims at no definite picture of an occurrence or of an emotional state, but rather at creating " a vague general impression " on the listener, as, for instance, in Debussy's description of one of his pianoforte pieces as " movement, rhythm, dancing in the atmosphere, with sudden flashes of light."

It is this nebulous atmosphere, with its various possible tendencies and interpretations, that Impressionism succeeds in creating. Its evanescent tone-images are produced by music of a somewhat (but not totally) formless character, which is void, in extreme instances, of any sense of key and rhythm, and often of grammatical succession, while its shifting harmonic progressions are usually characterized by extreme chromaticism. The French School, with Debussy at their head and accompanied, to some extent, by the Belgian César Franck, who settled in Paris, have led the way here and have been closely followed by the British School, as described in Part IV, Chapter XIV.

(The reader is further referred to the works of French composers mentioned in Part IV, Chapter VIII.)

In the present age, tending to the purely *harmonic* in music, there is, doubtless, much scope for development of this interesting phase of art—one which has its parallel in the important impressionist school of painting.

The only danger lies in the neglect of design ; and, as Franz says, " Colouring without a design would be as absurd in music as it is in painting."

In any event, this special development of Harmonic colouring in pianoforte music will be awaited with considerable interest.

CHAPTER VIII

LYRICAL AND POETICAL FORMS

"No music is conceivable without melody."—*Wagner*.

MANY of the non-formal pieces, and the smaller poetical forms of pianoforte music are obviously derived from the corresponding forms written for the voice ; *i.e.*, from the realm of Song in all its varied forms.

Perhaps the most prominent is the " Song without Words " as popularized in the charming and artistic examples of Mendelssohn and other more recent composers.

As regards the *lyrical* manner, these small pieces were anticipated to some extent by the *Bagatelles* of Beethoven, the *Nocturnes* of Field, and some of the smaller works of Schubert ; but in the important distinguishing marks of style, character, or mood, they were almost unanticipated up to that time. Of varying styles, these works of Mendelssohn present, on the whole, the spirit of the simple, unaffected German *Lied*. One may recall the *Spring Song*, No. 30, *Spinning Song* (No. 34), *Hunting Song* (Book I, No. 3) and *Duetto* (No. 18) as examples. Stephen Heller has suggested some interesting and appropriate titles as far as No. 42, *viz.* :—

(1) *Sweet Remembrance*, (2) *Regrets*, (4) *Confidence*, (5) *Disquiet*, (7) *Contemplation*, (8) *Restlessness*, (9) *Consolation*, (10) *The Wanderer*, (11) *The Rivulet*, (13) *The Evening Star*, (14) *Lost Happiness*, (15) *The Poet's Harp*, (16) *Hope*, (17) *Appassionata*, (19) *On the Shore*, (20) *The Vision*, (21) *Presto Agitato*, (22) *The Sorrowful Soul*, (23) *Triumphal Chant*, (24) *The Flight*, (25) *May Breezes*, (26) *The Departure*, (27) *Funeral March*, (28) *Morning Song*, (31) *Meditation*, (32) *Lost Illusions*, (33) *The Pilgrim's Song*, (35) *The Wail of the Shepherd*, (36) *Serenade*, (37) *A Reverie*, (38) *The Farewell*, (39) *Passion*, (40) *Elegy*, (41) *The Return*, (42) *Songs of the Traveller*.

The origin of these instrumentalized vocal forms may be assigned to the popular tunes and arias represented in the old

Suites which, on repetition, were treated in various ways by means of ornamentation, variation and imitative work.

The legendary Lay and Roundelay, the Minstrel's Canzone, and especially the narrative Ballad (*Ballata*) have also received illustration on the keyboard.

The latter, as usually conceived, in heroic·or dramatic vein, is exemplified in the Ballads of Chopin and in the Nocturne-like compositions of Brahms. The slighter form of the French *Chanson*, resembling the German *Lied*, but not so subjective nor reflective in style, and the meditative, concisely-built *Cavatina* are also used.

The *Romance* and *Novelette*, specially typified in those of Schumann, resemble the Ballad, but are more chivalrous in style and more glowing in spirit. The antithesis of this is found in the *Nocturne* which, while equally lyrical, is mostly dreamy in style.

Chopin founded his Nocturnes on the ideally quiet-breathing poetical Nocturnes of Field. An air of slumber and restful night hangs also over the more massive but characteristic *Nachtstücke* (Night Pieces) of Schumann.

The Serenade, in which French composers seem to excel, together with the dawn-of-day *Aubade*, breathe forth a similar atmosphere, but they are delicate and ethereal compared with the *Nachtstücke*, and usually have a kind of guitar accompaniment to the melody. Still another piece connected with slumber is the frequent *Berceuse*, exemplified by Chopin and others, a soothing song-form of simple character. Finally, there are the gently-rocking boat songs, which, under the name of *Barcarolles* and *Gondolier Songs* or *Gondellieder*, were favourites with Mendelssohn and Rubinstein.

We now come to those forms, not essentially lyrical, in which suggestive, almost " programme effects " have a part.

Of these the *Pastorale* and allied Pieces, the elevated and refined *Idyll*, the shepherd's musing *Eclogue*, the simple country tune in the *Villanetta*, all express the placid delights of the country, the piping drone of the shepherd, the humming of the bee and the rippling of the brook, etc. The Pastorales of Kullak, the Idylls and Eclogues of the Nature-poet Heller, with pieces under distinctive names, such as the *Fountain* and the *Lake* of Bennett, illustrate what has been done in this branch of art.

Another class of programme tendency which has arisen consists of the interpretative and light-winged sketches called *Papillons* (" Butterflies "), the fantastic *Fantasiestücke*, the *Scenes from Childhood* and *Kinder-Albums*, all having suggestive titles originating in the glowing imagination of Schumann and since imitated by many composers.

Another descriptive piece is the *Humoreske*, which was also illustrated by Schumann, but which in the compositions of many imitators scarcely justified its title.

The much imitated *Novelettes* of Schumann have been classified with the descriptive *Fantasiestücke*, but they seem to resemble more closely the chivalrous Romances and Ballads.

Of the many indefinite small pieces which do not express any special emotions, there are the *Album Leaves* (Kirchner and Schumann), the *Bagatelles*, the *Aquarellen* (" Water-Colour Sketches " exemplified by Gade), the *Sketch* or *Esquisse* (Heller), the delicate and ornamentally worked *Arabeske* (Schumann), and the *Apparitions* (" Visions " of Liszt), to which the more serious but disconnected and rambling *Rhapsody* (*see* Part IV, Chapter III), and the convivial *Dithyramb* are also allied.

The varying form and style of all these outgrowths of Romanticism can only be studied from the actual examples of the masters ; to which reference should be made.

CHAPTER IX

NATURE POETS

" His Fatherland is that of Shakespeare."—*Schumann.*
" He seems to have overheard and reproduced Nature in her most
musical scenes."—*Schumann.*

I.—*W. Sterndale Bennett* (1816–75)

STERNDALE BENNETT is not only the chief exponent of the
English element in pianoforte music, but is also one of the most
conspicuous ornaments of the realm of Pianoforte Literature.
As a pianoforte composer alone he fills a unique position, by
reason of his thoroughly individual character and as being the
chief representative (with Field) of the Idyllic element. English
pianoforte music in the past has suffered somewhat from the
decided leaning of its composers to church and vocal music, as
well as from its bondage to the art of other nations from the
days of Purcell onwards.

It says much for Bennett, as a contemporary of Mendelssohn,
Chopin, Schumann and Henselt, that his technical and individual
style should have remained distinct and that in balance of
form he should have been surpassed only by Mendelssohn.

Much has been said as to Bennett having been indebted to
Mendelssohn without apparently taking into account the general
musical influences of the time. Doubtless, like Mendelssohn's,
his style was formed mostly on those of his predecessors—in his
case Mozart—of whom he was especially fond—Scarlatti and
Bach (as he avowed), Beethoven and Dussek. Mendelssohn
himself was only six years older and had paid a visit to London
when twenty-two years of age, some three years previous to the
composition of Bennett's *Concerto* in 1832. It would seem that
only an indiscriminating examination would confuse the style
of Bennett with that of his contemporary. Rather is it true
that both had imbibed the Romantic spirit of the age, both
were lyrical in style and artistic by nature, and both were exceptionally smooth-fingered, light-wristed pianists.

But the melody of Bennett did not, like that of Mendelssohn, tend " towards sentimentality," but always remained lofty, almost cold, in its idyllicism. Again, Bennett, in his use of *harmony* is distinctively more characteristic ; compare, for example, his oscillating use of Super-tonic (on 2nd Dominant) and Dominant harmony, and his fresh and poetic use of the Diminished 7th, with Mendelssohn's mere technical use of the latter and general weakness in harmonic variety.

On the other hand, Mendelssohn surpasses him in formal structure, and in breadth of style in larger works. A similar comparison apparently held good with regard to his playing. Schumann said, " The Englishman excels in delicacy and finished details, Mendelssohn in energy and grasp of the entire scope of the piece."

Bennett is, above all, the Musician's Tone Poet ; the delicate finish and idyllic art of his mind appealing rather to the critical than the popular mind.

For general comparison's sake the student would do well to compare the *Fountain*, by Bennett, with the *Rivulet*, by Mendelssohn, the *Maid of Orleans Sonata* with the similarly meditative *Sonata in G minor*.

Born in Sheffield, where his father was organist of the Parish Church, young Bennett was sent to the Royal Academy of Music in London at the age of ten. Two years afterwards he appeared as pianist in one of Dussek's *Concertos* ; at the age of sixteen he had written his first *Concerto in D minor*, and three years later he had already completed a goodly list of works, including a *3rd Concerto*, two *Overtures*, the *Sextet in F♯ minor* and a *Symphony in G minor*. On September 21st, 1836, after ten and a half years' study at the Royal Academy, Bennett left London for Leipzig, where he again met Mendelssohn as well as Schumann, who gave him a hearty welcome. Many of his compositions were performed on the occasion of this stay, as also on succeeding visits in 1838 and 1842. The relations of Bennett and Mendelssohn were of " surpassing friendliness." The latter wrote at that time that Bennett " seems to have made his friends and admirers at one stroke, for you hear only *Bennett* everywhere." In the words of Mr. O'Leary (Mus. Assoc. 1874), " The famous Gewandhaus concerts, brought, under Mendelssohn, to the highest pitch of perfection, the knot of famous musicians to be met with, the hospitality of the wealthy and educated families who welcomed him to their homes, all combined to make this one of the happiest periods in his life." Schumann championed Bennett's cause in his famous *Allgemeine Musikalische Zeitung* under the pseudonym of Eusebius. He speaks of him as " a very delightful individuality," " a gentle quiet spirit, that labours on high, no matter how storms gather below him."

One of Bennett's earliest works, the three Sketches, *Op.* 10 (*The Lake, The Millstream* and *The Fountain*), proved to be a universal favourite. The first number, with its placid, undulating figures in 6ths, the last with its sparkling broken-chord passages, the *Millstream* with its turgid imagery expressed in a tumble of wild *arpeggios*—all three show forth Bennett's characteristic harmonies.

Schumann speaks of these as " the three most lovely pictures which have appeared in Germany, true to nature-colour, poetic in conception, musical Claude Lorraines, living tone-landscapes." The *Impromptus, Op.* 12, he also speaks of as " true poems " and " not inferior to them."

The three *Romances, Op.* 14 (Ash) are grateful to play, requiring a supple wrist for *agitato* elements, and are by no means easy. Schumann speaks of them as marking " a great step in advance as regards deep, even *strange, harmonic combinations*, and a bold broad construction, " possessing richly flowing melody " and " highly impassioned character." The light wrist-work in most of Bennett's compositions resembles that of Mendelssohn, and it is valuable in both cases from an educational point of view.

As to the four-hand *Diversions*, Schumann declaims on their " imaginativeness," their " refinement in detail " and " art in the whole ; " and concerning the *Fantasia, Op.* 16, he says : " As for lovely melodies, it rings with them as richly as a nest of nightingales."

The *Suite de Pièces, Op.* 24, and *Capriccio in A minor, Op.* 28, are also interesting as regards technique, besides containing many of his characteristic touches. While speaking of educational value, the useful and loose-fingered *Toccata*, the charming yet precise *Rondeau à la Polonaise* and the interesting *Rondo Piacevole* should also be kept in mind.

Schumann speaks of " genuine creative power " manifested in the *Suite*. " Here is," he says, " not the profound, the sublime, that awakens thought and imposes on us, but the delicate, playful, often fairy-like grace, that leaves small yet deep traces behind it in our hearts." If Bennett may be compared with Mendelssohn for the excellence of his technique, it is interesting to note also his fine feeling for balance of form, together with his avoidance generally of the actual form of the Sonata.

His one successful effort in this direction, which, like the *Lake* and the *Fountain*, is pure characteristic music, is the *Maid of Orleans Sonata*, *Op*. 46 (Cramer), wherein the different movements are described as follows by extracts from Schiller's poem

I. *In the Field*.   Andante Pastorale in A♭.

" In innocence I led my sheep
Adown the mountain's silent steep."

The Andante opens in a quiet, idyllic frame of mind.   (Note the characteristic harmony in bar 2 of the Example.)

II. *In the Field*.   Allegro Marziale in A♭ minor.

" The clanging trumpets sound, the chargers rear
And the loud war-cry thunders in mine ear."

Here two strongly contrasted themes are heard—one portraying sharp strife, contention and the " clanging trumpets sound," the other an agitated and anxious prayerful melody.

III. *In Prison.* Adagio Patetico in E.

" Hear me, O God, in mine extremity,
In fervent application up to Thee,
Up to Thy heaven above, I send my soul."

A simple, prayerful melody leads to an episode illustrating the passage

" When on my native hills I drove my herd,
Then was I happy as in Paradise."

In the final movement—

The End. Moto di Passione in A♭.

" Brief is the sorrow, endless is the joy "

the composer hardly rises to the level of his theme as the climax of the poem, although the movement is characteristic as far as it goes.

The most popular of Bennett's *Concertos*, that in *F minor*, possesses a charmingly brilliant and sparkling 1st Movement, while the beautiful Barcarolle—an afterthought—deserves to live in perpetuity. (*See* Chapter XXII.)

The *Studies, Op.* 11, are artistic and brilliant in style, but seem to be founded mostly on the older Clementi technique.

On the other hand, the *Preludes and Lessons* (Ash) are among the most artistic and delicately wrought of their kind, ranking next to those of Chopin.

Bennett, in 1851, reluctantly refused the conductorship of the Gewandhaus Concerts ; five years later, however, he became conductor of the London Philharmonic Society and Professor in the Chair of Music at Cambridge. In 1866 the erstwhile student and professor became Principal of his old School, the Royal Academy. It is thus delightful to relate that honours for the greatest English pianoforte composer were not allowed to wait until his death.

Time has flown since Bennett's name had become " a household word in the musical circles of Germany," but there will assuredly come a time when the blare of Tschaïkowsky and Richard Strauss will give way to reflection, and the genuine artistic claims of the " musician's poet " will again come to the front. Bennett was a born pianist and his pianoforte music, for genuine originality, individuality of style, subtlety and finish within the limits of his genre, are difficult to equal.

It is something of a reflection on us as a nation that Bennett's works should still lack presentation in a collective edition. Let us hope that this may soon be remedied.

CHAPTER X

NATURE POETS (*continued*)

" True poetry—without which all art is lifeless—can express itself as
well in the Sonnet as in the Epic."—*Fétis.*
" Heller has indeed penetrated the mysteries of Nature . . . the
beneficent influence of the forests, of the fields, and of the streams has
transformed his meditations into melodic transports."—*De Maiter.*

II. *Stephen Heller*

STEPHEN HELLER stands next to Schumann as a master of the
" characteristic."

His music shows the power to depict certain situations and
moods, to create an atmosphere, so to speak, by means of
certain melodic, harmonic and rhythmic traits.

Certain rhythms awake echoes of the dance, the chase and
martial tread ; gloomy and thick turgid *harmony* suggests
tragic or mournful events ; while bright, spirited, sparkling
figures in the upper registers stimulate joyful associations,
terrestrial and celestial.

Heller's power lay, not in the mastery of the thematic, fugal
or formal development, nor in the management of huge choral
or orchestral effects, but in his command of the pictorial art
of " characterization."

Take, for instance, the " Chase "—a favourite theme with
many composers—with its wayward echoes of " the tumult of
the chase."

" The deep-mouthed bloodhounds' heavy bay," the clattering
steeds, the horn's merry peal, the echo " from rock, glen and
cavern," the wild halloo, the doe cowering in her covert, the
falcon on high, the labouring stag down darksome glen—all go
to make up an exciting picture, such as Sir Walter Scott knew
so well how to depict. All these wild, moving incidents of the
chase seem to be ideally interpreted in Heller's *Jagdstück, Op.* 102
(Ash-Senff), as compared, for instance, with the straightforward

ding-dong *Jagdlied* of Schumann, the *Die Jagd* of Rheinberger
or the third *Song Without Words* of Mendelssohn.

Each of the latter is artistic in its way, but gives only a
general impression of the galloping rhythm and the forms.
Heller's *Jagdstück*, while equally artistic, is much more minute
and true to nature—though his *La Chasse* is rather courtly
than wild.

Heller was essentially a *poet of nature*. In his *Op.* 86, *In the
Woods* (Aug.), which is full of imagination, a series of reveries
is given thus : (1) *The Mystery of the Forest*, (2) *An Unfortunate
Encounter*, (3) *The Hunter's Rest*, (4) *Lost in the Wood*, (5) *In
Forest Glades*, (6) *The Supernatural Huntsman*. Of these,
Nos. 1, 5 and 6 are delightfully naïve and characteristic, while
No. 5 has been described as " an amorous lament, exhaled in a
morning landscape of springtide." These nature studies are
interestingly continued in the *Op.* 128 and 136, in the latter of
which Heller shows his devotion to scenes of the forest and the
chase by taking the characteristics of Weber's similar Opera,
Der Freischütz, and reproducing them in miniature. These
should be distinguished from the studies from *Der Freischütz,
Op.* 127, which are transcriptions of the features and style of
the original.

Heller's ability to idealize nature is exemplified in his
Promenades d'un Solitaire, Op. 78, and the continuation, *Op.* 80,
Wanderstunden, as well as in the *Op.* 89, *In Wald und Flur*.
These " solitary walks," or " Nature reveries " were apparently
inspired by that student of Nature, Rousseau.

In *Op.* 78, Nos. 1 and 2, we find the key to the series, namely,
the knelling of the horns, a hunting refrain and a forest reverie,
in which the recluse penetrates Nature's mysteries. In
Germer's Edition of the *Wanderstunden* (André) titles are given
which assist the interpretation of the atmosphere surrounding
these walks in the depths of the forest. A collective edition
of these Nature studies would be a boon.

The *Scènes Pastorales, Op.* 50, the *Rêverie d'un Promeneur
Solitaire* (Rousseau), *Op.* 101, the delicately written *Eclogues,
Op.* 92, and the original *Bergeries, Op.* 106, all likewise deserve
study in this connection. While Heller was always lyrical in
style—and his fund of melody is always fresh—his works are
not all descriptive.

We come now to those which are simply expressive and

generally lyrical in style. To these belong the delightfully contemplative *Nuits Blanches, Op.* 82—a type which, like his nature music, stands unique, being quite different in style from the Songs without Words, the Nocturnes, Impromptus, etc., of other composers—though, in general, bearing some resemblance to the Etude, the Impromptu and the Rêverie. This style also includes the *Op.* 83, 110, 123 and 114.

Then there are the collections of short *characteristic* pieces in which Heller rivals his contemporary Schumann ; the charming *Album à la Jeunesse, Op.* 138, the *Petit Album, Op.* 134, and the *Scènes d'Enfants*, in which dramatic characterization in miniature is skilfully depicted.

A comparison with Schumann's similar works is most interesting. The work of the latter, both in his slight children's character-sketches and in his forest scenes, is more boldly outlined—more " square-cut "—and the colours are laid on with no uncertain hand. Heller, on the contrary, may be ranked almost as an impressionist in water-colours : he creates an atmosphere, and the suggestive details are most delicately wrought out. Heller does not, perhaps, present the variety of material, but it is equally well, if not more artistically used.

Schumann was probably the first to initiate successfully the two branches of this art of delineation, but Heller helped to perfect them. Many of Heller's pieces are in the Song-without-Words style, as, for example, his *Op.* 73, 105, 120 and several of the *Studies*, *Preludes*, etc.

Stephen Heller was born at Pesth, in Hungary, in 1815, of mixed Bohemian and Austrian parentage, and at the age of nine we find him appearing in public as a prodigy. Three years later he had already made extensive tours, playing the then fashionable Concertos of Moscheles, Hummel and Ries, and the usual firework pieces by Herz, etc. At seventeen years of age he began the study of composition and was befriended by a Count Fugger in Augsburg, who made him acquainted with Beethoven's and Chopin's works. There he wrote the *Scherzo* and three *Impromptus, Op.* 7 and 8 (Ash.) which he sent to Schumann for criticism. This was in 1836. Schumann, as Eusebius, in pointing out Heller's individuality, declaims in his usual style : " Thank Heaven! our young composer knows nothing of that vague, nihilistic no-style behind which many scribblers ape Romance. . . . We feel that there is in the background of his compositions a peculiar, attractive twilight or rather dawn—a kind of ' mental halo.' He finishes off finely and carefully ; his forms are new, fantastic and free." He has not the " harmonious euphony " of Henselt, but " has more wit and knows how to mingle contrasts in unity." Schumann aided the young composer by finding him a publisher.

Two years later Heller arrived in Paris, but his reserved manner prevented his becoming popular in the Salons as Chopin had done. Charles Hallé helped to spread Heller's fame and to alleviate the last hours of the retiring artist who had done so much for pianoforte music. With the exception of two visits to London in 1849 and 1862 the rest of Heller's life was spent in Paris, where he died in 1888.

Heller, like Chopin, wrote only, or almost only, for the pianoforte. Both these composers were dreamers, both noble and refined in style, and both breathing the element of the Salon. Chopin was popular in the Parisian Salons, while Heller kept mostly in retirement. Chopin's works are more fitted for the concert room, Heller's for the quiet of the study and boudoir. Chopin, with a Slavonic temperament, was the more enthusiastic ; Heller, likewise of Slavonic descent, but reared in a Hungarian revolutionary atmosphere, is more fitful. Nothing is more characteristic of Heller than those strange, fitful and forceful rhythmical passages which are continually appearing in his music in the shape of reiterated chords, as, for example, in No. 17, of *Op*. 47, and the alternating quiet and forceful passages, as in No. 2 of the *Preludes*, *Op*. 81.

Heller's music throughout is permeated by strong contrasts. The alternating impetuous and languorous changes of mood are seen in the *Wanderstunden*, for instance (André Ed.), pp. 10, 13, 14, 16 and 17, while strongly marked recurring short phrases occur in Nos. 3 and 4 of the same series and in the *Études*, *Op*. 137. Instances of Hungarian colouring are noticeable in most of the numbers.

Despite some alleged Mendelssohnian leanings Heller is more allied to Weber on account of the warmth of his harmonies and rhythms ; but his technique is restrained and artistic and never merely showy. Heller's light fashionable pieces consist of Variations, Caprices, Rondos, and Improvisations on the popular airs of the day—mostly operatic.

His transcriptions of Schubert's *Lieder*, including the well-known concert work, *Op*. 33, *The Trout*, the Mendelssohn *Wings of Song*, the Beethoven *Variations*, *Op*. 130–133, and the Schumann *Improvisation*, *Op*. 98, are of more than passing interest. Heller's best-known Sonata, *Op*. 88, is the least developed, but all four movements (except the *Allegretto*) are individual in style.

The third and fourth *Scherzos* are especially interesting, though idyllic in manner as compared with those of Chopin. The individual *Caprices*, the somewhat Chopinesque *Valses*, and especially the *Tarantellas* (including the *Vénitienne*) show much of the inspired vigour and dash of Heller's best style. The *Polonaises*, the *Impromptus*, the second *Intermède*, the poetical *Nocturnes* and *Nocturne Serenade*, the refined and original *Serenade*, *Op*. 56, the *Ballades* and the *Canzonettes*, *Op*. 66, might be mentioned as containing much individual writing.

The charming *Studies*, *Op*. 16 (The Art of Phrasing), about which the others, *Op*. 45, 46 and 47, are introductorily grouped, are of world-wide fame. After the *Op*. 16 appeared, Heller was besieged by the publishers for more and it seems they were not averse from cutting out passages which were too difficult. Is this the reason, one asks, why they are so practical? (!)

The *Op*. 90 *Studies* are singularly expressive and pathetic; the *Op*. 125 resemble his Preludes in delicacy, while the *Op*. 116 is more technical.

Heller's Preludes are unique, surpassing those of Chopin in poetical character and in finished perfection of detail, both harmonic and melodic. Each of the twenty-four *Preludes*, *Op*. 81, is a gem—a perfect miniature in itself. They have been described as " delicious genre pictures, painted with the most exquisite care—fifty bars at the most, a passing shadow, an azure vapour curling upwards, a will-o'-the-wisp, which dances, is extinguished and then laughs mockingly further on " (De Maiter). Chopin's *Preludes*, though given in all the keys, are unequal in style and length, and they are really more in *Étude* form, while Heller's present all styles in poetical form. Bennett's *Preludes* and *Lessons*, together with Chopin's *Preludes* come nearest to them, and Bennett's, from their perfectly finished style, run them very close.

The pieces in *Op*. 119 of Heller are on a similar scale.

Last, but not least, there are the similar dainty *Arabesques* and *Traumbilder* (Aug.), intended, like the *Studies*, for the formation of expression and taste in style.

The works of Heller, as may be gathered from the foregoing account, stand by themselves. Original, noble, refined, clear, and, withal, genuinely poetical in style, they stand supreme as examples of the art of painting in miniature and as representing nature in all its moods.

CHAPTER XI

ADOLF JENSEN (1837–1879) may be classed as one of the principal smaller writers in the Romantic vein. In his early works, such as the attractive *Op*. 5, *Innere Stimmen*, the *Op*. 7, *Fantasiestück*, and the charming *Op*. 18 (F.S.), he shows traces of the influence of Schumann, of whom he was a great admirer.

The *Impromptus*, *Op*. 20 and 37, and the *German Suite*, though containing here and there beautiful ideas, are over-elaborated and are not particularly convenient to play. Most of his work, however, shows considerable power of *characterization*, with refined poetical style but with no particular individuality. The beautiful *Nocturnes*, *Op*. 38 (R.F.), the lovely *Galatea* (*Erotiken*, Bos), and the *Dryads*, show the influence of Chopin. Of his short characteristic pieces, the *Romantic Studies* which, he says, are intended " to illustrate musically scenes from the life of a true friend," the *Songs and Dances*, *Op*. 33 (Aug.), and the *Wanderbilder* (Peters), rank almost with the best of their kind. Jensen wrote a good deal of Duet Music, of which probably the tuneful and spirited *Wedding Music*, *Op*. 45, is best known. On the whole, there is much in Jensen's music that one would not like to lose. In style he was bolder than Bennett or Kirchner, and in power of characterization almost the equal of Heller and Schumann.

We have coupled the names of Jensen and J. L. Nicodé (b. 1853, of Polish descent, trained in Berlin, settled in Dresden) as poets of the youthful emotions. Both portray the romantic passions and feelings of Youth, as may be seen from a comparison of the titles of their similar works ; for instance, in Nicodé's *Liebesleben* we have (1) First Meeting, (2) Ardent Longing, (3) Tête-à-tête, etc., and in Jensen's *Romantic Studies*, Bk. I, we have (1) Vow, (2) New Life, (5) Longing, etc.

Both belong to the Schumann characteristic school, but both have individuality combined with graphic description of passing emotions.

Nicodé is the more powerful and more modern, especially in the *Dreaming and Awakening*. His Schumannesque *Op*. 6, *Souvenir of Schumann*, his *Tarantella in G♯ minor*, and his useful Concert Study, *Elfin Dance*, are good music. The clever and interesting *Symphonic Variations*, as arranged by himself for Duet reflect the influence of Brahms to whom they are dedicated.

One of the best characteristic works descriptive of Youth, and a happy one on the whole, is the *Youthful Reminiscences* by Ferdinand Hiller (Forsyth), one of those later works in which he inclined towards Schumannesque Romanticism.

Gustave Merkel (1827–1885) may also be classed as one of the smaller characteristic poets. His piano works, though lacking modern harmonies, are melodious and effective, especially in modulatory effects ; and among them we may single out the *Frühlingslied, Op*. 18, the *Bagatelles, Op*. 149 (Ash), *Op*. 31 (No. 4), *Op*. 81 (Nos. 2 and 4, Jennings), *Op*. 108 (No. 2) and *Op*. 120 (Bos.) Merkel, who settled in Dresden, is best known as a writer of valuable organ works.

CHAPTER XII

THE REFLEX OF SCHUMANN

" The pianoforte is the confidant of our solitary and deepest thoughts."
—*Schumann.*

THE influence of Schumann on *style* in pianoforte composition has probably been more far-reaching than that of any other composer since the time of Beethoven. Both in spirit, in technique and in harmony his works formed a model which has been eagerly seized upon by composers in all styles and of all nationalities during the last half-century.

Schumann's contemporary and friend, Theodore Kirchner, was one of the most prominent apostles of his style. Born at Neukirchen in Saxony in 1824, he was trained as a boy at Leipzig, where he also became, like Bennett and Brahms, a special protégé of Schumann. Kirchner eventually settled in Leipzig. His works are practically all for piano ; and in his smaller pieces, which constitute the majority, he is almost as charming as his avowed model. The best known of these, the *Album Leaves*, as played by Madame Schumann, are not very characteristic of him : his best works are more difficult and, probably for that reason, less known. His share in the distinguishing *harmonic* richness of Schumann, his boldness in modulatory effect, his equal command of the " still and bewegt " (the peaceful and the agitated styles), together with his elusive, meditative melancholy (also characteristic of his model) make his works full of interest to the student. His *technique* is more natural—more suited to the instrument—than that of Schumann ; but in the composition of larger works requiring considerable thematic development Kirchner falls far short of his model. Another distinguishing characteristic is the *innig* feeling, or deep-brooding introspectiveness, which was exemplified sometimes to excess in Schumann and especially present in the later works of Beethoven and in Brahms.

Kirchner's best works may be summarized in his *Op.* 5
Grüsse), the *Im Zwielicht, Op.* 31 (R.B.), the *Op.* 24 (*Still und Bewegt*) and Selections from *Op.* 32 (*Aus trüben Tagen*).

Kirchner. "Still and Bewegt."

Kirchner, like others, wrote much that was mediocre and not
up to the standard of the above. His strength lay in the polished
style of the smaller pieces of original conception and not in the
flattering imitation of Schumann in his *Florestan and Eusebius*
and *Neue Davidsbündler Tänze*.

Carl Reinecke (b. 1824 ; d. 1909 or 1910) may also be included
in the Schumann group. His music is thoroughly imbued with
romantic and poetic feeling, modern and graceful in character,
and possessing those little harmonic traits which, as in Schumann,
give warmth of colouring and idea. He is especially charming
in smaller pieces, such as the *Chansons des jeunes filles* (Cranz),
and in the longer, purely characteristic pieces, *Op.* 86. *Pictures
from the South* (André Off.), *Pictures to Tennyson's " Enoch
Arden "* (Ditson), *Op.* 219 (B.F.W.), *Ländler, Op.* 152 (R.F.),
and the *Albumblätter, Op.* 243 (F.F.), Nos. 1 and 5.

Pleasant blending of the old with the new is seen in the
Op. 197 (B. and B.) and the *Gavotte in D* (Eu.), while the more

serious aspect is artistically displayed in the four clavier pieces, *Op*. 117 (C.S.), the *Op*. 215 *Ballade* (G.R.), and the classically-conceived and noble *Concertos*. Reinecke is also responsible for some interesting Transcriptions, and has a sympathetic eye to the needs of the younger generation, as may be seen in his *Kindergarten* and other educational works for the young. Until recently he was one of the " grand old men of music." A Concerto virtuoso from the age of twelve, he appeared in public as late as 1906 (at the age of eighty-two) in one of Mozart's Concertos ; and since 1860 he had occupied a leading position at Leipzig as Conductor of the Gewandhaus Concerts, Professor at the Conservatorium, etc.

In the works of Waldemar Bargiel (1828–1897) we have the best features of his model (Schumann) in the melodic invention and warmth of *harmonic* treatment, as well as in the characteristic *technique*—the groping in octaves in the bass while the right hand is engaged in mystifying devices. On the whole, however, the tone of Bargiel's music, as exemplified in his *Suite, Op*. 21 (Schles.) and in *Op*. 32 (8 Pieces) is more straightforward than that of his model or of Kirchner. It is well written and dignified. Bargiel was a step-brother of Madame Schumann, was trained at Leipzig and settled in Berlin.

Robert Volkman (1815–1883), like Schumann and Kirchner, was a Saxon. A composer of wide activities, he is known principally as a successful imitator of the *characteristic* style of Schumann as in the melodious *Grandmother's Songs, Wanderskizzen*, and some duets (*Musical Picture Book*, etc.). Volkman's strong point lay in his gift of melody, as in the *Op*. 17 (Cranz) and *Op*. 19 (Univ.) ; and, though lacking command of technique and variety of treatment, his works remain popular from their dignity and simplicity of style. Volkman was educated at Leipzig and ultimately settled in Pesth.

The Austrian Hugo Reinhold also shows the influence of Schumann, though in his essentially diatonic style he lacks the characteristic richness of harmony and modulation. His *Op*. 54 and 55 (Kistner), *Op*. 59 (D.C.), and *Op*. 45 (Jennings) deserve mention.

L. C. Wolf, in his attractive and virile *Op*. 16 (R.B.), *Op*. 21 and 25 (G.R.) is more Schumannesque in style.

C. I. Brambach (b. 1833), a pupil of Hiller and resident in Bonn, shows an attractive style in his *Op*. 34 *Fantasiestücke*, which is cast in classical mould, in the charming *Reigen*, *Op.* 50 (Schott) and in *Op.* 66 (Leuckart.).

The *Op.* 17 (Rahter) of Albert Gorter (b. 1862 in Munich), with its modern colouring, the spontaneous and refined *Op.* 23. 25 and 26 (Kistner) of Josef Zöhrer, the artistic *Op.* 47 (No. 1), *Op.* 69 (No. 1) (Kahnt) of Ed. Zillmann, the *Op.* 30 (No. 6) of Kufferath (Schott) and some of the compositions of Rud. Niemann (1837–1898), for example, the *Intermezzo* (Kistner), etc., likewise show the unmistakable influence of the greatest of the Romanticists—Schumann.

Richard Strauss (b. 1864 in Munich) is known principally for his orchestral programme works. His pianoforte works, *Op.* 3 (Five Pieces) and *Op.* 5 (*Sonata in B minor*) (Univ.) were written before the age of nineteen while he was still at school. The former are melodious and full of character and are mostly Schumannesque in style. The Sonata is somewhat halting in development, but is interesting on the whole. The humour in the *Burlesque* for piano and orchestra is apparently confined to the unexpected antics of the big drum, piccolo and bassoon. In the melodrama *Enoch Arden* Strauss seems to be in his element in artistic characterization on the piano of the musical background for the recitation of the poem.

Max Reger (b. 1873 in Bavaria) is another of the moderns in whose work Schumann's influence may be discerned. His music is discussed in Chapter **XIX**.

CHAPTER XIII

JOHANNES BRAHMS AND HIS FOLLOWERS

" He is come—a young blood by whose cradle Graces and Heroes kept watch."—*Schumann.*

Johannes Brahms (1833–97)

JOHANNES BRAHMS was the son of a double-bass player who officiated in the band of the Opera House at Hamburg.

Young Brahms made his appearance as a prodigy at the age of ten. Becoming a pupil of Marxsen, we find that he appeared both as composer and pianist when fifteen, and that later he was employed in the unenviable task of playing dance music and accompanying wretched singers at " Lokals " as well as occasionally arranging dances and marches for the garden orchestras. A meeting with the eccentric Hungarian violinist Remenyi was the cause of a joint concert tour undertaken in 1853, during which the shy-mannered, blond and youthful composer met Joachim. Brahms had already written his *F♯ minor Sonata* and *E♭ minor Scherzo* and the meeting is memorable as leading to his introduction to Schumann and Liszt. It is necessary to mention that at this time musical Germany was divided into three camps : (1) the Academical and Classic School of Mendelssohn ; (2) the Romantic School of Schumann who, while adhering to the old forms in the main, added to them new rhythmic and harmonic effects ; (3) the " New German " School of Liszt, who, with Berlioz, Wagner, Bülow, Raff and Cornelius championed the cause of programme music by advocating the expression of poetical ideas without regard to enveloping form. Near akin as they both were in character and genius, Schumann soon became enamoured of his young friend Brahms, and the famous article entitled *New Paths* appeared in Schumann's organ, *The New Musical Journal* (*Neue Zeitschrift für Musik*), written in Schumann's poetical and literary style, thus : " He is come—a young blood by whose

cradle graces and heroes kept watch. . . . He is called
Johannes Brahms, come from Hamburg, where he worked in
obscure tranquillity."

Brahms had been advised to go to Leipzig and introduce his
compositions himself. His adviser and publisher, Dr. Härtel,
wrote that " His playing belongs essentially to his music. I do
not remember to have heard such original tone effects before."

Schumann's criticisms on Brahms' early works are interesting.
The *Sonata in F minor* he described as " So profoundly grasped,
living, deep and warm throughout, and so closely woven
together. Of the *Ballades* (*Op.* 10) he wrote: " The first is
wonderful, quite new, the close beautiful—original. The
second, how different, how diversified, how suggestive to the
imagination ; magical tones are in it. The bass F♯ at the end
seems to lead to the 3rd Ballade. What shall we call this ?
Demoniacal—quite splendid, and becoming more and more
mysterious after the *pp* in the Trio, and the return and close! "
Schumann also spoke of the " splendid Variations " (on a theme
of his own), and of the " quite new " *F♯ minor Sonata.*

Dr. Pohl, however, on the other side, wrote that Brahms'
ideas were " indiscriminate, his work inconsistent and defective
in style," and that, like Schumann, he had " the subtle habit
of mind, the tendency to the indefinite and misty," but even
Pohl praised his diversity of harmony and rhythm and his
wealth and freedom of ideas.

The presentation at Leipzig of Brahms' *D minor Concerto*
in 1859 called forth anew a chorus of criticisms. The virtuoso
element, which the general public had always been led to expect,
was wanting ; and the Leipzig *Signale* described the work as
" Symphony with Pianoforte Obbligato."

Brahms then took the work to Hamburg, where it had a
triumphant reception ; but to-day conservative Leipzig is the
chief stronghold of Brahms in Germany.

Three years later Brahms left for Vienna, where he received
a favourable reception and where he ultimately settled for life.
The stream of criticism was resumed by Hanslick of Vienna,
who pointed out that Brahms was " best in the Variation
form," and that his themes were apparently chosen for the
most part " for their capacity for contrapuntal treatment
rather than for merit." Whether as the result of these criticisms,
or of his appointment as Conductor of the " Sing-Akademie,"

where he had the congenial task of conducting Bach's choral works, Brahms did not compose any more pianoforte music for twenty-five years, except the *Handel* and *Paganini Variations*.

After this long break appeared, in 1879, the *Op.* 76 for pianoforte, rapidly followed by others, notably the *B♭ Concerto* in 1882. One result of Brahms' residence in Vienna, and no doubt also of his early associations with Remenyi, was his contact with the Hungarian elements, which resulted in the presentation of the famous traditional *Hungarian Dances* for pianoforte in Duet form, with a further Transcription by Joachim for violin and piano. The first set appeared in 1869, the second in 1879.

The light-hearted *Viennese* and the atmosphere of the *Strauss Valse* showed their influence also in the attractive but simple, lieder-like strains of the *Liebeslieder Walzer*, *Op.* 52 and *Op.* 65, for piano Duet and four voices—*ad lib.*—compositions, by the by, plentifully endowed with diminished sevenths and of no great original artistic merit. In these the voice parts do not merely follow the melody but weave equally individual melodies from the concurrent harmonies.

Brahms' melody, we would say, possesses the qualities of his origin.

As a North-German, his sincerity and earnestness of purpose is represented in his music—especially in his love of Folk-song and his composition of characteristic German Lieder.

As regards what Mr. Fuller Maitland calls his " daring experiments " in *cross rhythms* and elaborate syncopations, many of these cross-grained effects are more comprehensible to the ear than to the eye, but it is certain, nevertheless, that they are overdone and give an impression of straining after originality.

Perhaps the most distinguished feature of Brahms as a composer in general is his power of structural development, *i.e.*, the proper organization of all the themes by means of the various technical devices, and their artistic presentation in the whole.

Whether the result with him is pleasing is another matter ; but the polyphonic weft of Brahms, derived, as it is, through Schumann and the later Beethoven, probably makes him the greatest technician in this branch of the art since the death of the Bonn master. It has been said that his smaller pieces, where there is not so much room for development, are the more pleasing, but here we are met by the objection that his naturally big *style* is best in the larger works, so that, perhaps, the best course is to take each work on its own merits.

Looking at the early *Sonata in C, Op.* 1, we see that the first movement opens in fine style, but that it is somewhat patchy in development.

The connective work is accomplished, not so much by actual *thematic development, i.e.,* the splitting up of a subject and the resulting discourse on the various heads—as by a favourite device (after the manner of Schubert) of Variations over a theme as a whole, which appears in various positions and keys. Especially is this so in the charming *Andante* on the theme of an old German Volkslied—a theme which appears also in the boisterous *Finale*. The *Op.* 2, the *F♯ minor Sonata*, impresses one as being artificial as well as abrupt and ponderous in style, though occasionally we catch a glimpse of the simple sincerity of the German lied-form.

The *Scherzo in E♭ minor, Op.* 4, is in a bold and fiery mood, to which the Schumannesque *Trio* comes as a grateful relief and contrast.

The *Sonata in F minor, Op.* 5, is one of the finest of his works. The extraordinarily fine 1st movement, with its song of triumph over fate in the 2nd theme—the poetical moonlight *Andante* with the motto—

> " Der Abend dämmert, das Mondlicht scheint,
> Da sind zwei Herzen in Liebe vereint
> Und halten sich selig umfangen."
> *(Sternau).*

the Henseltian *dolcissimo* section, the passionate " Love-Song " *Coda,* with its organ-like close, the conflicting *Scherzo* and calm, sustained *Intermezzo,* the fond " Retrospect " in the *Intermezzo* of the *Andante* theme, the Scherzo-like *Finale,* reminding one of Schumann's *Aufschwung* (" Soaring ")—all suggest that the work had been inspired by Beethoven's *Moonlight Sonata;* though whether any autobiographical interest attaches, as in the case of Beethoven, is uncertain. Over all is the inspiration of the Volkslied and an abysmal organ or double-bass-like profundity. Though breathing the spirit of Bach and of Beethoven, the development in these early works is not based so much on inversion of themes as in Beethoven, but is brought about rather by transformation effected through various modern technical forms of figuration.

What strikes one about the *Ballades*, *Op*. 10, is (1) the organ or double-bass effect continually present through the octave bass doublings—Brahms always appears to revel in the bottom octaves of the piano ; (2) the mysterious folk-lore element, a nocturnal and unearthly strain here naturally appropriate, though a Ballad is, of course, not always given over to the mysterious.   These two elements are present, moreover, in very much else of what he wrote, and both are derived, together with the obscurity of style (resulting from tangled rhythmic and contrapuntal effects), from Schumann and the later Beethoven. The pervading sense of fulness obtained from doubled octave melodies and from doubled and trebled massed harmonies is very different from the more truly pianistic style of Henselt, Chopin and the Russian School.   Relief from this in the Ballads is seen, however, in the Schumannesque *Intermezzo* in No. 3.

Brahms' one-sided cyclopean technique is specially shown in his *Variations*.   Those on an inspired theme of Schumann, *Op*. 9, and the Duet Variations, *Op*. 23, are better than the *Op*. 21 (on an original theme) both as regards effect and musicianship. The latter, though ingenious, seem to have been suggested by the masterly *Variations Sérieuses* of Mendelssohn, which, however, they quite fail to equal.   The result suggests that, craftsman as he was, Brahms was best in the Variation form when writing on a theme *not* of his own creation.   Mr. Huneker, in his literary rhapsody on the *Op*. 9, thus describes the *Variations* on the theme of Schumann : " The theme is never lost ; it lurks behind formidable ambushes of skips, double notes and octaves ; it woos, caresses, sighs, smiles, coquets and sneers—in a word, a modern magician weaves for you the most delightful stories imaginable."

Brahms' *technique* seems to have been derived mostly from Clementi with his primitive, bare and direct successions of 3rds, 6ths and octaves, but the massed chords and cross-rhythms are principally from Schumann.   The influence of both is to be seen in the *Paganini Variations* (which are announced as *Studies* and valuable as such, in Brahms' style) ; No. 1 of the First Book being based apparently on Schumann's *Toccata*, and the first of the Second Book on a *Study in 3rds* in Clementi's *Gradus*.

Brahms' Variations are all difficult and, perhaps, as a result of their very technical character, they are, as has been said, more interesting to the performer than to the listener. The Variations on a theme of Handel's, *Op.* 24 (excluding the Fugue) are less difficult in some respects and are the most popular. While we are on the subject of *technique*, we may mention the somewhat capricious arrangements exemplified in those on Chopin's *F minor Study* in which single notes become 6ths, the left-hand topsy-turvy version of Weber's *Moto Perpetuo*, the study-like transcription of Bach's violin *Chaconne* for left hand alone, and the 51 *Studies* which are based on some of his technical peculiarities.

The *D Minor Concerto, Op.* 15, was originally planned as a Symphony, but owing to orchestral difficulties, Brahms first thought of making it a Sonata for two pianos, and finally decided to make it a Concerto. The original conception was inspired by the tragedy of Schumann's attempted suicide, and the 4th movement—a Funeral March—was later incorporated in his German *Requiem*. The above incident, therefore, is the key to this rugged and stirring work. This Concerto, with its emotional, noble *Maestoso* and *Adagio* movements, is notable for the absence of bravura work and of that rhythmical obscurity appearing in his later works.

In the later *Concerto in B♭, Op.* 83, one is conscious of some striving after effect and of much more elaboration.

The virtuoso has to weave much ornamentation over a suave initial theme, and the counterfoil, the serious element, comes in the succeeding *Allegro Appassionato*, followed again by a dreamy 'cello solo in the Schumannesque *Andante* and a playful *Finale* in which thematic development is prominent.

With *Op.* 76 (Eight Pieces—*Capriccios* and *Intermezzi*) begin the sets of small pieces written after Brahms' twenty-five years' rest from composing for the piano, and they represent his matured style.

The No. 4 of these is a representative example with its linked and syncopated rhythms, the fluttering in the mystic regions of the bass and the unexpected modulation to the episode in the key of the flat 6th.

The first Rhapsody in *Op.* 79 depicts in sombre, rich colouring a wild, determined theme, broken by bold, massive chords conflictingly hurled together, and also a lovely, simple, expressive theme forming an effective foil to the principal subject.

The masterly second subject we can imagine to have been suggested by the ghostly legend of the " Erl King." In the *Op.* 116, *Fantasias*, is seen the true Brahms, spartanlike and full of inward broodings and wayward rhythmic subtleties. In No. 1 of the popular *Intermezzi, Op.* 117, founded on the slumber-song, *Schlafe sanft, mein Kind*, and in the *Romanze* of the six Pieces, *Op.* 118, we have a favourite and effective device of hiding away the melody in the inner parts and accompanying it by syncopated rhythms.

The mysterious wandering in the lower regions and bewildering rhythmical effects appear again in the *Intermezzi, Op.* 118, while the device of exchange of massive chords between the hands is seen in the popular *Ballad in G minor* of the same set.   Perhaps we may contrast the Schumannesque massiveness of the latter with the *Ballades* of Chopin and conclude that, though stern and cold, it is possibly on account of this a more healthy style. Brahms' best work, despite its intellectual and technical prolixities, may be described as a mental tonic.

A charming miniature is the first *Intermezzo* of the *Op.* 119 (four Pieces)—his last work for pianoforte. In the episode Brahms relaxes, and the listener yields to an attractive melody, only, however, to be pulled up later by the rhythmical change in the bass and the saddened feeling which resumes sway. Brahms has been declared " a Mystic," a profound thinker, and, above all, a " German," " the greatest tonal architect since Beethoven," " a master of the Variation form," a champion of absolute music (forgetting his *Moonlight Sonata*), and a kind of musical " Browning," whose frequent moments of obscurity are relieved by simplicity of idea.   These, together with peculiarities of technique, summarize for us in a manner the qualities of Brahms as a composer for the pianoforte.

Apart, however, from the peculiarities of technique and the masterly architectural ability, Brahms' music will live because it plumbs the depths of what is noble and enduring in human sentiment.   Grandeur, sublimity and earnestness of purpose will continue to be the anchor of very much that is best or really *classic* in pianoforte music—as in all branches of the art, and, indeed, in all art itself.

FOLLOWERS OF BRAHMS

Brahms, so far, does not seem to have had any lasting or deep influence on the present generation of pianoforte composers.

There are those who seem to be attracted by the peculiarities and obscurities of the North German Classic, but who do not possess his loftiness of purpose nor his simple *lied*-like melody, and the dangers of such a model are obvious. Brahms' style is more or less apparent in the Austrian composer Von Herzogenberg (b. 1843), who, in his *Op.* 3 *Variations* and *Op.* 4 *Fantasia* (B. and H.) shows a quiet meditative style, while the somewhat rhapsodic and chromatic *Op.* 69, 59 (5) of Fr. Gernsheim of Berlin (b. 1839) suffers from want of clearness. A brooding spirit appears also in the *Op.* 38, 41 (two pianos) and 43 (Kahnt) of Von Savenau. J. Erb, in his meditative *Op.* 39 (No. 2), is clearer in style ; but Herman Scholtz, though serious-minded, lacks melodic gifts, as, for instance, in his *Ballade, Op.* 78 (Leuckart). The virtuoso pedagogue Von Bülow (1830–1894) did not excel in composition. His well-written *Ballade, Op.* 11, is thoughtful in style, but the simple *Album Blatt* (Schott) is more attractive. His *Carnival* is mostly uninspired. The virtuoso D'Albert (b. 1864) excels in his early *Suite, Op.* 1 and *Concerto* (B. and B.), which were both written during his pupilage in London ; but his later works show the faults of Brahms without his merits.

CHAPTER XIV

THE BRAVURA SCHOOLS AND HENSELT

" Brilliancy of execution is valuable only when it serves higher purposes."—*Schumann*.

HAVING dilated on the Romantic movement in pianoforte music with its various side issues—a movement that is still in force—we must temporarily go back to consider the influence of the bravura virtuoso element as initiated by Weber, of the Romantics, and appearing in the Viennese and Parisian Schools of artist-composers. This attained a climax in Liszt, the Hungarian, and Henselt, the Bavarian, and afterwards blended with the virtuoso-romantic style of Rubinstein, the Russian Jew, and Raff, the Swiss disciple of Liszt.

At the time that Czerny (1791–1857), the initiator of the Viennese bravura style, was disseminating his style of execution through his pupils, there existed several styles or schools of composition. The earnest, dramatic, but formally developed School of Beethoven ; the blended Lyric, Classic and Romantic Schools of Schubert and Mendelssohn ; and the Romantic Schools of Chopin and Schumann.

The School of Czerny, as represented by his pupils Döhler, Th. Kullak and Liszt, was a kind of reaction against the unattainable thunderbolts of Beethoven—one that, while cultivating technical brilliancy, made its object, on the whole, not the pondering over life's problems, but the pleasing of the ear by disingenuous melody, graceful flourishes and somewhat superficial attractiveness. There is room, no doubt, for this class of composition, for music is an art which should appeal to all classes of hearers.

The compositions of this Viennese School may indeed be regarded as the better-class salon music of the period. Much of such music necessarily goes out of fashion as public taste advances, and it is remarkable that practically only those compositions which are technically interesting or useful now survive.

An exception must, however, be made in favour of Liszt, who brought himself more into touch with the best of his period, and, by virtue of his national characteristics and his success as a transcriber, or rather paraphraser, gained a position of some permanence in art.

The name of Carl Czerny (b. 1791 in Vienna), a Czech by nationality, is now known to us, not by his trivial *Rondos*, *Fantasias*, etc., but (1) by his *Studies* and indispensable educational works which, though *mentally* not so artistic as those of his senior Cramer (b. 1771), survey a much greater field, and are *technically* more useful ; (2) as the master of the virtuosi referred to elsewhere (Part IV, Chapter XVI).

Theodore Döhler (1814–56), born in Naples, was famous as an executant and travelled, like most other virtuosi, far and wide on the necessary concert tours.

Döhler was superior to Talexy, Plachy, Hünten and Rosellen of the Parisian School ; but unfortunately he was overshadowed by his more brilliant contemporary, Liszt. His works are mostly of a quiet *idyllic* character. Indeed, Döhler possessed the ideal temperament for a writer of *Nocturnes*. His dreamy, plaintive, almost melancholy nature comes out in his *Romance*, *Op*. 25, the *Souvenir de Florence*, *Op*. 34, and the delicately ornamented *Nocturne* in D♭, *Op*. 34. His *technique* is of the smooth and swift style of Thalberg, of which a good idea may be obtained from his bravura *Variations* and *Fantasia*, *Op*. 17, his *Tarantelle in G minor*, his useful Studies, and the pieces for left hand alone which, with those of Kalkbrenner, were the first to appear in that style (*Döhler Alb.*, Lit).

Döhler, though superior to Thalberg in lyrical interest, lacks, like him, warmth of feeling. After being ennobled by the Duke of Lucca, Döhler married a Russian Countess and after settling for a time in St. Petersburg ultimately died in Florence.

Theodore Kullak (1812–82) is now known mostly by his *School of Octaves* and his *Kinderleben* (child life), some numbers of which are still interesting.

His style is melodious but colourless, as in the pleasing Pastorales. *La Gazelle; Sylphides* and *Boléro* (Siegel) are technically interesting. Kullak settled in Berlin in 1843 and was much in request as a teacher. Bischoff, Moskowsky and the Schwarwenkas were among his pupils.

The pianoforte music of Thalberg (1812–71) is in advance of

that of Döhler and Kullak, being richer and more sonorous in style. Thalberg's scope, however, is very limited and lacks development of idea—the interest being generally sustained by the somewhat unvaried technical treatment of each Piece, as, for instance, in the *Thème Original et Etude* (repeated notes), *La Cadence* (alternate " turns " and staccato notes), and the *Andante in D♮* (short chromatic runs) (*Thalberg Album*, Aug.). His twelve *Grand Studies*, however, show more variety of technique and are useful, especially *La Trille* and *La Babillarde*. One technical device much exploited by Thalberg in his Pieces, and originally brought forward by Pollini, was that of utilizing the thumbs of both hands for the melody notes while the rest of the fingers spin around wide-spread and brilliant *arpeggio* figures.

As an executant Thalberg secured much fame in his wide world tours, and in 1836 he competed with Liszt in Paris (*See* next Chapter). Thalberg generally held his own as an interpreter of Salon music. His command of the keyboard caused Liszt to remark, " Thalberg is the only artist who can play the violin on the keyboard ; " his style being calm, clear, faultless and full of expression as compared with the frenzy and aplomb of Liszt. Chopin interestingly wrote, " Thalberg plays famously, but he is not my man. He is younger than me, pleases the ladies very much, makes *pot pourris* on *La Muette* (*Masaniello*), plays the *forte* and *piano* with the pedal but not with the hand, takes 10ths as easily as I do octaves, and wears studs with diamonds." Besides the compositions mentioned, the *Moïse* operatic Fantasia the Variations on *Home, Sweet Home* and the *Tarantelle* (Schott) are most widely known—the latter being one of the best of his works, which now, on the whole, would be classed as of the Salon-educational order.

Though he was not a pupil of Czerny, Thalberg's music is in the Viennese style and occupies an intermediate position both in sonority and technique between that of Döhler and Liszt, both of whom were Czerny's pupils. Born in Geneva, and educated in Vienna, his life was divided between concert touring and residence near Naples, where he died in 1871. The modern French Virtuoso School dates from the appointment, in 1797, of Louis Adam to the Conservatoire in Paris where he taught Fr. Kalkbrenner (1784-1883), who again had an important influence on the pianists of that day. Kalkbrenner was much in request as a fashionable teacher both in Paris and in London, where he resided from 1814 to 1823. As a technician he did much to develop the cultivation of the wrist, the independence of the fingers and of the left hand. His *Op.* 42 was a Sonata for left-hand solo.

In execution Marmontel says he had " a faultless neatness in the most difficult passages and a left hand of unparalleled bravura " ; and as a virtuoso he was most successful. Kalk-brenner's compositions, however, mostly belong to a low level. A *Concerto in D minor*, a few Studies, the Salon '*Femme de Marin*, and the educational *Rondo affettuoso* and *Rondo in C* (Ash) still survive.

The shallow compositions of the once fashionable Herz (1806–88), apart from a showy technique based on Weber, are likewise now forgotten ; though a few Etudes and the Variations on the so-called *Last Thought of Weber* (really by Reissiger) survive.

The compositions of J. Rosenhain (1813–94) are superior, as inclining to the Romantic Style, but this, as in his *Romance*, *Op.* 31 (No. 3) (Joubert), does not rise above mediocrity.

The music of Em. Prudent (1820–63), though colourless, is also of better class, as, for instance, in his *Le Ruisseau* (Joubert) and *L'Hirondelle* (Aug.). He somewhat resembles Döhler in lack of variety of technique as well as of warmth of feeling.

W. Krüger (1820–83), the most musicianly of the " Parisian " virtuosi (who were all of German origin, by the by, except Prudent and Goria), is known by his *Polonaise, Boléro, Caprices* and *Nocturnes*, which are modern and attractive.

Al. Goria's (1823–60) melodious and dignified *Etudes de Salon* and *Marcia* for two pianos (Lit.) deserve attention.

The compositions and flippant Variations of Hünten and Rosellen are now forgotten, except for a few Studies by the latter, which still survive.

HENSELT (1814–89)

The virtuoso Henselt stands alone. He has been called the " German Chopin." Born in Bavaria, he studied in the capital, Munich, and with Hummel at Weimar. A successful concert tour in 1837, at the age of twenty-three, was followed by his departure for St. Petersburg.

Previous to this his *Op.* 1, the *Ricordanza* Variations, showing a new style of technique, and the romantic and poetical *Studies* had already appeared. In these, eschewing the fashionable scale-embroidery of Thalberg, he specialised in the more sonorous spun-out *arpeggio* extensions of Weber, which may be said also to have formed the basis of Chopin's style. Henselt was of the same age as Döhler, two years younger than Thalberg, three than Liszt and five than Chopin, whose *La ci darem* Variations appeared in 1839. How much therefore of Henselt's original style was modelled on that of Chopin is difficult to determine but it would seem as if it was rather the result of his devotion to Weber (of whom he was particularly fond)—especially as his technique went in some respects beyond that of Chopin, so as to stand directly next to that of Liszt.

The features of Henselt's music are a refined but sonorous lyrical style, combined with a unique fulness of effect arising from original technique. Unfortunately he was of a retiring nature and did not compose very much : a standard *Concerto,* the poetical *Studies, Op.* 2 and 5, the Weber *Transcriptions* and Variante editions (Schles.), the charming but neglected *Romances Russes* (Schles.), a second piano part to a selection from Cramer's Studies, and a few small attractive romantic pieces such as the *Frühlingslied, Wiegenlied, Impromptu in C minor, La Gondola (Album,* Aug.), two *Valses, Op.* 28 (Siegel), 1st and 2nd *Nocturnes* (Ash). A collected edition is most desirable. In one sense Henselt carried the *arpeggio* extension technique to a cul-de-sac, *i.e.*, as far as the present keyboard is concerned.

Mendelssohn, in 1838, testified to this speciality of Henselt's, the " playing wide-spread chords," and said " that he went on all day stretching his fingers over *arpeggios* played *prestissimo.*" Lenz*, in the same year, heard Henselt play his *F♯ major Etude, Si oiseau j'etais,* and he says, " It was like an æolian harp hidden beneath garlands of sweetest flowers. An intoxicating perfume was crushed from the blossoms under his hands—soft, like falling rose-leaves—the alternating sixths, which, in one and the same octave, pursued, teased, embraced and enraptured ! " Lenz also dilates on Henselt's " charm of rich fulness of tone in *pianissimo,*" and his taking of the instrument

* " Great piano virtuosos."—*Schirmer.*

by storm in the *Minore*. In the combination of his ethereal
arpeggio work and the dramatic power and energy, which we
find in the *Heroic* and *Thanksgiving after a Storm* Etudes, we
must assign to Henselt an original and unique position as an
artist—the equal of Chopin on one side and of Liszt on the other.
Most important of all, however, Henselt is the true beginning of
the unique Russian School of Pianoforte Music. As Lenz
remarks, " Henselt's coming to us (1838) marked the obsolescence
of the Hummel-Field School and brought the piano into quite
another channel." Henceforth the Russian School, soon to
bring forth fruit in the remarkable works of Glazounow,
Scriabin and others, was based on the most pianistic of styles
those of Henselt and Chopin.   An example of Henselt's style is
here given, and the fingering should be noted.

Romances Russes (Nº1) Henselt.

CHAPTER XV

" The compositions of a virtuoso often reveal not only his peculiarities, but those of his instruments."—*Spohr.*

FRANZ (FERENCZ) LISZT was born in 1811 near Odenburg in Hungary. His father, a Hungarian, was an accountant to Prince Esterhazy ; his mother was a German. Young Franz began the piano at the age of six years and, making good progress, was very soon in request as a prodigy at local concerts. By the generosity of some of the nobility who were friends of the Esterhazys, young Liszt was placed under the noted teachers Czerny and Salieri in Vienna ; and though he rebelled somewhat against Czerny's systematic schooling, his eighteen months' instruction gave him a good foundation in technique. He then again appeared in public—once in Beethoven's presence, when the latter, after Liszt's improvisation, bestowed upon the young genius a kiss of benediction. A triumphal tour was made to Paris, where, however, Liszt was refused admission to the Conservatoire on account of his nationality. As a result of this the young virtuoso soon became the idol of the Parisian Salons. Liszt now came over at the age of twelve to England, and appeared with the greatest success at concerts at which Clementi, Cramer, Ries, and Kalkbrenner were present. The *Morning Post* of that time relates how " the little fellow " was handed the theme *Zitti, Zitti* for extemporization, and, " though not very well acquainted with the air, sat down and roved about the instrument, occasionally touching a few bars of the melody, then taking it as a subject for a transient fugue. But the best part of the performance was that wherein he introduced the air with his right hand while the left hand swept the keys chromatically ; then crossed over his right hand and played the subject with the left, while the right descended by semitones to the bottom ! It is needless to say that his efforts were crowned with the most brilliant success." At these " Recitals " —a term then new to London—Liszt would leave the instrument between the pieces and freely move among his friends,

until he felt disposed to return to the piano. Various other
tours to England, France and Switzerland followed, adding
further to his fame. The death of his father, in 1827, and an
illness turned his thoughts towards the Church, but, fortunately
for art, his inclination was not permanent. In 1830, after the
July Revolution, the news went round the Salons that " Liszt is
no longer devout " ; and he now became a member of the
literary circles and was captivated by the doctrines of the
St. Simonians.

The next influence—a far-reaching one—was the visit of
Paganini, after which Liszt retired for a time and then emerged
with a new technique. His attempts at imitation of Paganini's
effects widened the domain of the piano, and it became, so to
speak, almost an orchestra in itself. His contact with Berlioz
and sympathy with the ideals of that daring orchestral
romanticist led to his first notable Transcription, that of Berlioz's
Symphony *Episode in the Life of an Artist*.

The beautiful *Harmonies poétiques et religieuses*, appearing in
1835, were suggested by a collection of poems by Lamartine
which had been published in 1830. In these the freedom from
classical formula and the daring of the new Romantic movement
is apparent. Rhythm, expression and harmonies alike are
untrammelled.

Chopin now passed through Paris, and both were drawn
together—the poetic, spiritual and slightly-built Pole and the
energetic, tall and lion-hearted Hungarian. The poetic charm
of Chopin made itself felt in the impromptu-like *Apparitions*.

During Liszt's association with the Countess D'Agoult he
retired to Switzerland (1835–39), and during his sojourn by the
Lake of Como he originated the delightfully artistic and refined
Années de Pèlerinage. In his first year's *Pilgrimage* (in Switzerland) we see the influence ˙of nature in all its moods, as, for
instance, in the charming numbers, *Au Bord d'une Source* and
Les Cloches de Genève. In his " second year " impressions of
Italy we have pictures which reproduce the effect of plastic art,
as in the *Sposalizio* and *Il Penseroso*. In the former a picture
of Raphael, in the latter a statue, is represented, and beauty of
thought is transferred from the seeing eye to the hearing ear.
Other similar subjects represented are the *Sonnets of Petrarch*
and a *Reading of Dante*, in which a web of artistic ornamentation
is woven round a characteristic and expressive theme.

Liszt's visit to Italy and his association with Rossini led to the Rossini Transcriptions, and to this period also belong the important Transcriptions of Beethoven's Symphonies and the Transcriptions of Schubert's Songs.

An episode during this sojourn was the Thalberg-Liszt contest in Paris. The Parisians had been dazzled by Thalberg, who was championed by Fétis as the pianist of the future, in opposition to the dictum of Berlioz, who pronounced for Liszt. A contest was arranged in Princess Belgiojoso's Salon. The audience was apparently unable to form an opinion and time alone has pronounced in favour of Liszt. Liszt himself tells an amusing story of the value of public opinion in art matters. He says : " For instance, I played the same piece, now as a composition of Beethoven, now of Czerny, then again as my own. The day on which I introduced it as my own I won the most encouraging applause. ' It was not at all bad for my age ! ' they said. The day on which I played it as Czerny's they scarcely listened to me ; but if I played it under Beethoven's authority I was quite sure of the bravos of the whole assembly."

Liszt's recitals in Vienna in 1837 created a veritable furore.

A correspondent of Schumann's in the *Neue Zeitschrift für Musik* gives the following description of Liszt's appearance, " Imagine an extremely thin, narrow-shouldered, slender man, with hair falling over his face and neck, an uncommonly intellectual, lively, pale, highly interesting countenance, an extremely animated manner, an eye capable of every expression, beaming in conversation, a benevolent glance, strangely accentuated speech, and you have Liszt as he is in general.

This fantastic exterior is only the covering of an internal volcano, from which tones are hurled, like flames amid gigantic ruins, not caressing, but with the force of thunderbolts."

A virtuoso comparison is made : " In Liszt the most passionate declamation is conspicuous, in Thalberg the most delicate sensibility, in Clara Wieck natural enthusiasm, in Henselt genuine German lyricism."

What was most unique in Liszt's style was " high soaring mind and originality."

Liszt was unrivalled in his power of making the piano sing, and his performances of his truly artistic Transcriptions of Schubert's Songs were most successful. In these Liszt does not alter the melody or the harmonies, and practically all the artistic touches are introduced in the framework or form of the accompaniment—such Variations from the original being introduced to accentuate the mood or feeling of the original.

The delightful Caprices entitled *Soirées de Vienne*, founded on the Valses of Schubert and also written about this time, present Schubert's rich melodies and harmonies orchestrated, so to speak, under the deft fingers of Liszt—an ensemble that is altogether piquant and enchanting. In No. 3 of the charming, Nocturne-like *Consolations* and *Liebesträume* we discern the influence of Chopin, though in the latter the ornamental passages are Lisztian. In the unique, poetical *Etudes d'exécution transcendante*, ably edited by Dannreuther (Augener), we have Liszt's own style and technique alone.

It is notable that Liszt revised these *Etudes* over a considerable period of time (final Ed. 1852), as he " came to distinguish between proper pianoforte effects and mere dare-devil bravura."

Liszt had been through the Classics with Czerny, had studied and was *au fait* with the *legato* style of Chopin, but his style of technique was practically his own. Mention should be made of his manner of holding the hand high, with the fingers sloping down to the keys, thereby giving increased power. " His effects were always extremes. Thus his rattling octaves, his rapid chromatic scales of 3rds and 6ths, both major and minor, as well as of diminished 5ths, *i.e.*, of the diminished 7th divided between the two hands, owe their startling effect to *quasistaccato*."

Liszt, however, did not aim alone at pyrotechnics. His style included Bach-like Part-Playing, a new method of using the pedals, and, above all, a new increased sonority of style. It was this sonority of effect—increasingly cultivated by him—together with his symphonic style that put the piano on a footing with the orchestra. The *Mazeppa Etude*, in which tumultuous successions of 3rds are interpolated by alternate hands while the melody is hammered out in widespread, sonorous chords, is an example.

Previous to 1830 the prevailing style of performance had been mainly classical characterized by smoothness, rapidity and occasional *cantabile* passages. Liszt introduced, as a performer, " strong contrasts of feeling, as well as giving proper individualization to the part-playing and attention to the innermost depths of expression."

From 1839 to 1847 Liszt was occupied in concert tours as a virtuoso, after which he settled in Weimar for some twelve years

as conductor of the Court Theatre, where his sympathies with the romantic movement were the cause of his giving representations of the works of Wagner, Berlioz, Schubert and Schumann.

Weimar became an art centre and pupils flocked to Liszt from all parts of the world, but the maestro found time also for compositions in other forms—especially Oratorios, Songs and Symphonic works. His resignation of the Weimar position in 1861 led him to divide his time henceforward between Weimar, Budapest, where he was honoured by the Government of his native land, and Rome.

In 1879 his religious fervour came to the fore again and he was made an Honorary Canon (without the restrictions of the priesthood) and an Abbé of the Church of Rome.

A triumphal visit to England and a few continental cities in 1886 shortly preceded his lamented death, which took place at Bayreuth in the midst of the Wagner Festival.

Of the works belonging to the " more mature " period of Liszt's life as a composer we should mention the *Concertos*, of which the one in E♭ is called the *Triangle Concerto*, the five *Fantasias* for pianoforte and orchestra, the unorchestrated *Concerto Pathétique*, as it is now termed, and the somewhat rhapsodic *Sonata in B minor*, in which the movements are continuous, and thematic development is practically absent. Liszt's strength did not lie in thematic or orderly development of form. His method of composition consisted rather in the metamorphosis of the rhythm of harmonies of his theme or themes—a method which could be made effective for a short time, but which fails, through mere repetition, to sustain the interest in larger works.

The *Sonata* has been called a drama " full of nobility, a drastic intellectuality and sonorous brilliancy " (Huneker's *Mezzotints*). The slow movement is, perhaps, the best from the orthodox point of view.

Liszt's nationality stood him in good stead in the popular and brilliant Hungarian *Rhapsodies* (*see* Part IV, Chapter III), founded mostly on the traditional Magyar melodies, in which he has incorporated the unique dulcimer and other effects heard in the gipsy performances of the Hungarian national music.

Space does not suffice to mention all of Liszt's works of importance, but, of the Operatic Transcriptions, once so popular, the very difficult and showy *Don Giovanni Fantasia* and the Wagner-Liszt Transcriptions are very much played, as also are the *Campanella* from the Paganini Etudes (founded on Paganini's *Bell Rondo*), the Concert Etudes, *Waldesrauschen* and *Gnomenreigen*, *Spanish Rhapsody*, *Legend of St. Francis* (the impromptu, in which he preaches to the birds), Transcriptions of Mendelssohn's *Wedding March* and *Elfenreigen*, of Schubert's *Marches* and of Chopin's *Chant Polonais*, which are among his best works. We may here conclude in the words of Schumann's eulogy on Liszt : " A remarkable, variously gifted and most inspiring mind. His own life is to be found in his music."

CHAPTER XVI

TWO MODERN ROMANTICS—RUBINSTEIN AND RAFF

Rubinstein (1830–94)

An examination of the pianoforte compositions of Rubinstein, as a whole, forces one to the conclusion that they have, of late, been somewhat overlooked. Having on one side that " Backwash of Classicism," Mendelssohn, and on the other the apostle of modernism, Liszt, and seeking, as one might, for that romantic, impetuous virtuosity in his compositions which characterized his playing, the general public have settled down mostly to belief in the *Melody in F*, and the brilliant but trivially-inclined *Valse Caprice*.

The reality is that the strength of Rubinstein's essentially lyrical genius lay in the creation of simple, sincere melodies, like those of the *Melody in F*, the *Romance, Op.* 20, the languorous minor-mode *Barcarolles, Op.* 30 and 50, the *E♭ Romance, Op.* 44, and the expressive *Nocturne, Op.* 75, or else in the presentation of his ideas ornamented by attractive and varied modern technique. Regarding the latter, one need only compare him with the lyric romantic Mendelssohn and others of that class to see what a wonderful variety of attractive technical figuration he introduces.

A favourite plan with Rubinstein, as, for instance, in *La Mélancolie,* is to introduce in the process of development new and increasingly interesting technical figures ; in the example mentioned four different stages or varieties of technique are presented. The compositions showing this blend of technical and lyrical interest include the very effective and varied *Rêve Angélique* from the *Kamennoi Ostrow Album* (Schott), the brilliant *Tarantelle, Op.* 82, the *Valse Caprice* and the virtuoso *Polonaise in B♭*, the dreamy and delicately written 5th *Barcarolle* (Senff) in Lisztian style, the *Rêverie, Op.* 75, the melancholy *Op.* 51, the characteristic Etudes *L'Ondine* and *Près du Ruisseau*, a charming *Valse, Op.* 93, the dainty *Serenade, Op.* 22, its opposite the dream-awakening *Aubade, Op. 75*, and the *Duets, Op. 50* and *Bal Costumé*.

Many of his works, however, have merely technical interest and lack inspiration, and among these must be included the *Variations, Op. 88*, and the *Concertos* (Senff), of which the 3rd is the most popular. The *Concertos* do not approach those of Mendelssohn and Weber in ideas and general interest, though surpassing them in technical treatment. Rubinstein, moreover, did not seem to have any particular gift for the short characteristic pieces exploited by Heller and Schumann, but his Hunting Sketch *Hallali*, the *Hermite* in *Op. 93*, the *Caprice Russe* and the *Marche Orientale, Op. 93*, may be mentioned.

Unlike his Slavonic contemporary Tschaïkowsky (who, however, was somewhat deficient in the highest development of piano technique) he had no great feeling for rhythmical effects or music in national style.

On the whole the impression made by Rubinstein's best works is that the greater number require the utmost delicacy and expression to do them justice and that the few successful brilliant pieces are not by any means the most artistic. In technical style, utilizing the extensions of Henselt (then settled in St. Petersburg) and some of the airy flights of Liszt, Rubinstein combines the technical excellences of both, and it is owing to this technical brilliance (a feature of the Russian School then rising) that many of his pieces, in which lyrical inspiration falls short, are attractive.

Like Meyerbeer, Mendelssohn, Joachim and many others, Rubinstein was of Jewish descent. Born in 1829, he made his début as an artist at the age of ten and commenced his first European tour two years later, in 1841. In Paris, where he played before Liszt and Chopin, he was publicly embraced by the great virtuoso Liszt. Through the death of his father he was thrown on his own resources at the age of 16, but after five years of varying fortunes he found himself firmly established in St. Petersburg.

An early *Concerto in F*, a succession of operas and some Chamber Music proved his capacity as a composer, and by 1857 he had written four Concertos and four Symphonies.

Concert tours, composition and teaching at the great St. Petersburg Conservatorium, which he founded, occupied the rest of a busy life till he died in 1894.

RAFF (1822–82)

Raff's pianoforte music, like that of Rubinstein, is specially attractive on its technical side, but is not so lyrical nor so refined in style. The lyrical element, except in a few pieces such as the attractive *Fleurette*, *Op.* 75, the *Berceuse*, *Op.* 125, the *Abends* and the 1st *Fantasie*, is somewhat colourless and placid.

He was Swiss by birth, and one may find the key to this characteristic in the Swiss melodies on which he rhapsodizes in *Op.* 60 (J.S.). The element of triviality enters more largely into Raff's compositions than into those of Rubinstein, both in ideas and in style of technique, but this was probably owing to the demands of the publishers for whom he wrote.

Raff's associations with Liszt in the advocacy of the " new German " movement also bore fruit in the Lisztian technique which we find so much in evidence in his works.

In Raff's work there is less leaning towards Classical technique than in Rubinstein and more towards mere showy effect than in Liszt.

It is, however, the exceptions that determine Raff's position as a composer. In the serious style, the soundly written *E minor Suite*, the popular *Rigodon* (*G minor Suite*) (Metzler), the *Fugue in Op.* 17 (J.S.), the *Minuet*, *Op.* 126 (P. and M.), the *Gavotte*, *Op.* 125, and the well developed and melodious *Concerto*, *Op.* 185, show a brilliant combination of older style and modern technique.

Beside the above, the *Bolero*, *Op.* 111 (Lengnick), the light-winged *Tarantella de Procida* (Aug.) and *La Fileuse*, the showy *Polka de la Reine* (Peters), the *Serenade*, *Op.* 20 (Lit.) and *L'Espiègle*, *Op.* 125, are brilliant and attractive, especially from the point of view of pianoforte technique. Raff wrote a number of paraphrases, operatic and otherwise, besides a huge number of other, mostly inferior, piano works. His life was a struggle against adversity, and this probably accounts for the very uneven quality of his compositions. Born (1822) at Lachen in Switzerland, he followed the profession of a schoolmaster, but, encouraged by Liszt, Schumann and Mendelssohn, took to musical composition.

His symphonic and other works bring him almost into the front rank of composers in the modern Romantic style.

CHAPTER XVII

MODERN CLASSICISTS

Moscheles, Hiller, St. Saëns, etc.

" Regard the subject matter of a piece of music as of greater moment than its outward form."—*Mendelssohn.*

1794–1870. Moscheles.
1811–85. Hiller.
1833–97. Brahms.
1835. Saint-Saëns born.
1839–1902. Rheinberger.

1821. Moscheles' *G minor Concerto.*
1827. Beethoven died.
1833. Hummel died.
1847. Mendelssohn died.
1853. Brahms' first works published.
1862. Saint-Saëns' 1st *Concerto.*

THE greatest impetus which Classicism has received since the death of Beethoven in 1827 was undoubtedly given by Brahms (*see* Part III, Chapter XIII), whose first compositions did not appear till sixteen years afterwards.   Meanwhile, the Classical movement had been continued by Hummel (*see* Part III, Chapter II), pupil of Mozart and contemporary of Beethoven, who worked on for ten years after Beethoven's death, and by Moscheles, who was some sixteen years younger than Hummel.

Moscheles (1794–1870) seems to stand at the parting of the ways.

On one side we have the Classic School, ending with Beethoven and Hummel, on the other the more plastic School of Moscheles, Mendelssohn, Hiller, St. Saëns and others.   Moscheles seems to have led the life of a virtuoso for the ten years previous to his settling in London, where he resided from 1826 to 1846. *
In 1824 Moscheles had given Mendelssohn lessons and the latter, as head of the Conservatorium at Leipzig, later offered his old Tutor the principal Professorship of the piano in 1846, a post which he accepted and held till his death in 1870.

* *See* Moscheles' interesting Autobiography.

Moscheles is now known for his *Concertos* (Chapter XXII), which are models in their balance of the bravura element, and in mastery of form, for the polished *Studies*, *Op.* 70, and the characteristic *Studies*, *Op.* 25 (*see also* Part IV, Chapter XVI), for his *Duet Sonatas* and the *Duo for two Pianos, Hommage à Handel*. His music shows his fondness for the past, and, while not deep in sentiment, is refined and dignified. Moscheles did not sympathize with modern art (except Mendelssohn and, in part, Schumann), while his own work shows the influence of Weber and Mozart. As a virtuoso Moscheles played octaves in the old style with a stiff wrist, but improved upon his predecessor Hummel by greater use of the now indispensable sustaining pedal.

Ferdinand Hiller (1811–85) resembled Mendelssohn in his Jewish descent, and in ease of circumstances ; his earlier works, too, have a Mendelssohnian cast.

But association with Liszt, Chopin and others gave his later works an inclination to the Romantic, so that musically he stands as a Cosmopolitan, though with Classical leanings.

Like Moscheles, Hiller commenced as a virtuoso, and like him also he formed a link with the past. As a pupil of Hummel he witnessed the death-bed of Beethoven, and was the friend of Mendelssohn and Schumann, as well as of most modern artists. From 1853 Hiller, who was also accomplished as a clever litterateur and conductor, settled at Cologne.

His pianoforte works are well written and are notable for rhythmical effect, but mostly lack inspiration. His *F♯ minor Concerto* remains a Classic (*see* Chapter XXII) while, of miscellaneous pieces which survive, there are a Mendelssohnian *Bolero, Op.* 29 (Hof.), a Chopinesque *Impromptu, Op.* 40, (J. Sch.), a cosmopolitan *Suite, Op.* 144 (Novello), and, probably the most acceptable, the *Youthful Reminiscences* (Forsyth), in which Schumann's influence is noticeable.

A few of his not particularly graceful *Studies* also survive.

Fr. Kiel (b. 1821) is not only a classicist and a contrapuntist but is also capable of instilling modern style into modern forms, as, for example, in his *Melodies, Humoresques, Caprices* and *Valses*, in the Chopinesque *Impromptu, Op.* 19 (Schles.) and the *Bolero* (Harris).

W. Taubert (1811–91) in his six *Scherzos* (B. and H.) leaned towards Beethoven. In his other works, such as *Le Printemps*,

Lays of Love and *La Campanella*, he wrote in a graceful, lyrical style but without individuality.

Julius Röntgen, who was born in Leipzig in 1855 of Dutch descent and settled in Amsterdam, also takes the Classics as his models, though his work is modern in technique and feeling. His virile *Sonata, Op. 2*, the interesting *Fantasiestücke, Op. 5*, in which the influence of Schumann is apparent, the *Variations, Op. 11*, the *Passacaglia, Op. 7*, and the *Ballad in D minor* (B. and H.) are all worthy of attention.

Hans von Bronsart (b. 1830), a pupil of Liszt, who has resided mostly in Hanover and Berlin, has written two noble *Fantasias* (B. and H.), in which symmetrical balance of ideas is not neglected, and also a standard *Concerto*.

A *Concerto* and a romantic and rhapsodic *Sonata* by Felix Draeseke (b. 1835) of Dresden, some pleasing and sound, though not brilliant, *Variations* (B. and H.) by Van Bruyck (b. 1828), a writer on clavier music, and a fresh and vigorous *Chaconne* and *Polonaise* (Schles.) by Richard Franck also deserve mention.

Clara Schumann is known as the wife of the celebrated composer whose marriage in 1840, after the surmounting of many difficulties, is one of the romances of musical history. Her piano works are characterized by dignity and show the influence of Beethoven. Of these the 3rd *Romance, Op. 21*, written partly in the style of Chopin, is the best.

Classic influence in France has been continued mainly through the works of Saint Saëns and, to some extent, through César Franck (the latter a Belgian) (*see* Part IV, Chapter IX) ; in Italy through Sgambati (Part IV, Chapter XII), and in England through Parry and Stanford (Part IV, Chapter XIV).

CONCERNING SAINT SAËNS

One of the most versatile composers of the present era, Tschaïkowsky aptly pointed out (in 1875) that, while he represented the advanced School, he united Classical methods with modern feeling ; combining " the style of Sebastian Bach, for whom he has evident affection, with the national French elements, of which the characteristic piquant rhythm makes itself clearly felt."

Born at Paris in 1835 of a Norman family, he lived to become one of the " grand old men " of the musical world. His first *Symphony*, showing the influence of Mendelssohn and Beethoven, was performed when he was eighteen, and his first *Concerto* for piano, which caters much for the virtuoso and evinces no distinctive style, was published nine years later. About this time Saint-Saëns appeared as a successful interpreter of Mozart's piano Concertos and as one of the best organists in Paris. The 2nd and 3rd of his five important *Concertos*, showing the influence of Schumann, appeared about 1868. Following the siege of Paris in 1870, Saint Saëns took part in a patriotic art movement, which resulted in *La Rhapsodie D'Auvergne* for Piano and Orchestra, in which Auvergnate folk melodies are developed for the piano with remarkable vigour, the orchestral part being unimportant. *Le Rouet d'Omphale*, in which Saint Saëns essays programme music after the manner of Liszt's *Symphonic Poems*, was originally written as a *Rondo for Two Pianos* and as such performed in 1872. The piquant themes and strange rhythm of the Fantasia *Africa* for Piano and Orchestra also suggest local colouring. The *Polonaise* and the *Scherzo*, both *for two Pianos* (1892), the artistic and attractive *Thème Varié* (1894), on a theme of Beethoven's—also for two Pianos—together with various pieces suggestive of travel, *i.e.*, the *Souvenir d'Italie, Feuillet d'Album* for Duet, *Valse Canariote, Caprice Arabe* (two Pianos) and *Souvenir d'Ismailia* complete the list of his principal works for Piano. Saint-Saëns is an exception to the all-absorbing passion with composers in France for the opera, his dramatic instincts having mostly found vent in the depicting of " programme " and national- or local-colour characteristics in works of more or less classical conception.

In workmanship and powers of development Saint-Saëns stands in the front rank, and, though he lapses occasionally, his work is not infrequently inspired, as, for instance, in his well-known melody *Le Cygne*.

He has done much also towards the acclimatization in France of the rhythmic and melodic features of Schumann and Liszt, as, for example, in his valuable *Concertos*, and towards raising the level of French musical art generally.

On the whole, Classicism, as represented by that dignity, repose, thematic and formal development which is characteristic of the best models, is somewhat at a discount at the present time, when orchestral programme work holds the field.   Possibly at a later time, when hazy impressionism and orchestral colouring have had their day, a return may be made to more normal conditions, when the logical sequence and development of ideas may again be considered as a *sine qua non* for the *best* forms of the art. The reader is further referred to the Chapter on the most popular form of pianistic Classic compositions— the Concerto (Part III, Chapter XXIII) and to that on the one next in favour, the modern Sonata (Part III, Chapter XXI).

CHAPTER XVIII

THE MODERN CONTRAPUNTAL ELEMENT: RHEINBERGER, ETC.

" Practise industriously the Fugues of good masters."—*Schumann.*

MUSIC, as we understand it, was primarily intended to be beautiful. Its function is to move the emotions, feelings and passions of the heart, to stir up deeds of chivalry and to inspire deeds of kindness. Music is, indeed, a solace in distress, a mental stimulant in health, and a joy to all. Unorganized music, however, falls into a mere rabble of sound, and before it can appeal to the ordinary mind, the intellectual element must be taken into consideration. The necessary element of " the beautiful " must be controlled ; effects of contrast, balance of ideas and of emotions must be secured ; and, in short, music as generally understood must possess all the attributes of an art. For instance, one theme may be set against another for contrast's sake, and ideas may be repeated, dissected and commented upon in many different ways. In this setting of chains, however, this fashioning and controlling of the emotional element, there is always a danger lest the fleeting inspiration should be lost sight of or smothered in constructive technique.

This perpetual struggle between the emotions and their architectural framework is typified in music by the nineteenth-century Romantic movement, led by Schumann ; and by the " New German " School of Programme music headed by Liszt, the reactive tendency of which is to make the form of the musical structure quite a secondary matter (Part III, Chapter I).

In no other branch of the art do we find the inspiration or the emotional element so shackled as in the Canon and Fugue ; and consequently it is proportionately rare to find examples, which are inwardly as well as outwardly satisfying. Notwithstanding this, the Fugue should, and can, satisfy all moods. It can, as Schumann says, be " the organ of cheerfulness and gaiety, as well as of dignity," and it may even be soul-inspiring, interpreting faithfully Browning's lines—

"Such a Fugue would catch
Soul heavenwards up."

In these forms of art—" cribbed, cabined and confined " as they are—the work of Sebastian Bach, though speaking to us in what would nowadays be termed a North-German dialect, is still pre-eminent. His immortal 48 *Preludes* and *Fugues* and other similar compositions survive to-day, not because of his wonderful and unsurpassed technique, but because he was able to subdue the form and to infuse into it his own sincere and honest, well-balanced emotions (*see also* Part I, Chapter X).

Looking at the technical figuration employed in contrapuntal works, not only in Bach, but in his successors down to the present day, we must note the influence of the organ.

Bach was, above all, an organist, and the organ style pervades all his works. Moreover, he was imitated as a model by Mendelssohn, Schumann, Brahms, Rheinberger, Reger and others, and the organ style is also undoubtedly apparent in their contrapuntal compositions.

Handel, in his separate clavier *Fugues* and in those belonging to the *Suites* sinks the North-German style in the Italian model, and consequently they usually lack great emotional depth ; but owing to their warmth of feeling, noble style, and effectiveness, they may be said to approach closely to those of Sebastian Bach.

Handel's style is, in addition somewhat freer in keyboard technique than that of Bach, suggesting rather the influence of the orchestra than of the organ, as in Bach's case.

Mention may be now made of masters whose works are interesting only from an educational point of view, as, for instance, the *Fugues* and contrapuntal *Studies* of Clementi, and the 48 *Canons* and *Fugues* of Clementi's pupil Klengel (1784–1852). " Papa " Haydn excelled in effective contrapuntal writing, but he wrote comparatively little pianoforte music beyond the *Sonatas*.

Mozart essayed all forms with success. His *C major Fantasia* and *Fugue*, the *Duet Fugue in G minor* and the *C minor Fugue* for two pianos are not only masterly in style, but breathe forth his characteristic sweetness and nobility of expression.   In style of technique, like Handel, he shows the influence of the orchestra rather than of the organ.

The *Fugues* of Beethoven do not impress one as being of his best.   His style was essentially an orchestral one, while the contrapuntal fugal structure is, in its essence, vocal or organ-like. It is, therefore, perhaps not difficult to discern why Beethoven's Fugue in his *Op*. 35 *Variations* and those in the later *Sonatas*, *Op*. 106, etc., are somewhat stilted in style.

Mendelssohn approaches most nearly to Bach and Handel in his mastery of the fugal style.   His 1st, 2nd, 5th and 6th Preludes to his *Fugues, Op*. 35, remind one of the *Songs without Words*; the 3rd being an airy caprice and the 4th a *lied*-like Duetto in Canon form ; while the *Fugues* are distinguished by melodic inspiration and variety of style in which the expressive and emotional element plays quite a large part.   The 2nd *Fugue in D* might, indeed, be taken by some people for one of his *Lieder ohne Worte.*

Schumann comes next to Mendelssohn in mastery of the fugal style.   Both composers were strongly influenced by Bach and the organ.   Mendelssohn was an eminent organist and organ composer, while Schumann, among his " maxims " advises the student to " try your little fingers at the organ bench and wonder at this great musical power," as well as to " lose no opportunity of practising on the organ."

In the best of his *Fugues, Op*. 72, No. 1 and the *Fughettes, Op*. 32, No. 4, *Op*. 126 (2 and 3), we have the peculiarities of Schumann's style, his massiveness combined with a lack of fluency (as compared, for instance, with Mendelssohn) and of variety of figuration, but full of rich harmonic charm and noble sentiment.

In the works of Brahms generally the organ profundity of Bach is easily apparent.   His one *Fugue in B♭*, at the end of the *Handel Variations*, is masculine in style and fertile in device, but the technical imitation of Schumann's somewhat ungainly style becomes in Brahms something akin to clumsiness. With him the subject is early enveloped in 6ths, a counter-subject is run in double 3rds, and the working-out is done by means of abrupt passages of 6ths, 3rds and octaves.

To pass from Brahms to Rheinberger is like passing from a stern and rugged mountainous pass to a broad smiling valley.

Rheinberger (1839–1902), the greatest contrapuntist since Mendelssohn, is pre-eminently an organist and organ composer, and organ style is reflected in his pianoforte *Fugues*. He is a member of the Mendelssohn-Schumann School, but unfortunately his work lacks individuality.

His Pieces in this style are *Op*. 39, No. 1, the whole of the 2nd set of *Op*. 68 (especially 1 and 2), and the *Elégie* and *Ermahnung* (*Op*. 183), both of which are in Canon form. In these we have the thorough mastery of all the artificial devices used in the most artificial of musical forms, combined with a quiet grace and meditativeness. Brilliancy and the virtuoso element are wanting, but artistic charm is present to those who look for it. The *Op*. 68, No. 1, is a good example of mastery in the use of some of the ordinary devices, here exemplified in the inversion of themes combined with stretto, canonic imitation, and augmentation of subject. Moreover, what is most important, the whole is interesting and artistic. The fine *Toccatas* of Rheinberger, it should be noted, differ much from the well-known Etude-like examples of Clementi, Pollini, Onslow, Czerny, Mayer and Schumann, and follow those of Bach, which are in free fugal style and, in addition to the development of a set subject, deal with various subsidiary themes. The *Op*. 12 (Aug.) is the more closely knit and is more in organ style, while the *Op*. 115 (R.F.) is somewhat modern in feeling.

Rheinberger did not confine himself to a past age, but his versatility is shown in pieces which are modern and pleasing. The popular *Die Jagd* and four-hand *Tarantella*, *Op*. 122, the *Aus Italien, Pièces de Concert, Impromptu*, *Op*. 6, *Jagdscene*, and modern Romantic *Sonata*, *Op*. 184 (Ks.) deserve attention.

Rheinberger was organist at the village parish church of Vadioz, near Lake Constance, at the early age of seven. He was educated at Munich Conservatorium, becoming Professor there at a later time. His *Wallenstein Symphony* and *E♭ Piano Quartette* are well known.

The late Leipzig Professor Jadassohn has also proved, in his 2nd *Serenade* (R.F.), consisting of 12 Canons with free accompaniment, (especially in Nos. 1, 5, 7, 8, 9 and 11) that it is possible to write attractively and in modern style within the narrow limits of canon form.

Max Reger has written two *Fugues* in his *Op*. 81 and 86 (L. and K.) and also the one for two pianos on a theme of

Beethoven. The latter is the most straightforward and is worthy of study. One will note the organ-like fulness of effect and the final working together of the Beethoven theme and Fugue subject.

Of other noteworthy compositions, in this style, we might mention a pianistic *Fugue*, *Op.* 89 (No. 1) by W. Berger (K.), the smooth and expressive Nos. 5 and 10 of 10 *Fugues* of Robert Fuchs (Rc.), the *Op.* 1, 2 and 3 of E. Hutchison, the *Op.* 41 of Kroeger, the *Preludes* and *Fugues* and *Toccata* of J. Vogt, the Röntgen *Op.* 28, Glazounow *Op.* 62, Raff *Op.* 91 and 72, Saint-Saëns *Op.* 111, Martucci *Op.* 28, the Fugues of Samuel Wesley, of Sgambati, *Op.* 6, and of Curtis (Belgium).

CHAPTER XIX

THE music of Max Reger (b. 1873) bears the direct impress of a powerful personality, which, in spirit and development of style, is closely related to that of Schumann. Reger has, indeed, imitated the technical characteristics of Brahms and has attempted the inimitable contrapuntal style of Bach, but both without any great artistic success. His most successful works are decidedly in the style of Schumann, and yet they have an individuality of their own. The manifest influence of Bach in these is undoubtedly Bach as filtered through Schumann.

Generally speaking, these successful works are found in the slow movements, some of which are beautiful ; but, on the other hand, the energetic and burlesque element (following the weakness of Schumann) is exaggerated and frequently elephantine in aspect. Among his later works, the *Sonatinas, Op.* 89 (L. and K.), which are Miniature Sonatas rather than educational works, are more attractive, especially the *No. 2 in D.* His more elaborate Schumannesque *Reveries*, entitled *Aus meinem Tagebuch* (From My Diary) suggest also the influence of Brahms and are full of subtle romantic interest. One feature is the frequent use of unrelated phrases, following each other in startlingly unrelated keys and yet leading back to sanity in the appearance of the principal theme. Where this device is less used the effect is beautiful, as in No. 10.

Like the impressionist Debussy, Reger requires some apprenticeship, so that, taking the principal early works in order, the best of the *Six Pieces, Op.* 24 (1 and 5) (R.F.), we note that the elegant No. 1 (*Valse Impromptu*) is quite clear in design and that the No. 5, a *Chant de la Nuit* with its groping octaves in the base, is nocturnal and mystic in the Schumannesque-Brahms style. Brahms' technique is also apparent in the similar rugged *Northern Ballad*, from the interesting *Aquarellen, Op.* 25 (Aug.).

The sad *Elégie*, the profound depth of the *Resignation* of
Op. 26, the Chopinesque *Rêverie* of the *Fantasiestücke, Op.* 24
(R.F.), the tuneful and lightly treated four-hand *Picturesque*

Pieces (Univ. Ed.), the *Intermezzo* No. 4, and the wild *Impromptu*
of the seven *Characterstücke, Op.* 32 (Univ. Ed.) are amongst the
best of his works.   With the *Intermezzi, Op.* 45 (Univ. Ed.).

Reger begins to wield the thunderbolts of Jove. In these interesting Sketches there are some powerful passages, marred, unfortunately, by characteristic incoherence.

We note the cross-grained No. 1, the will-o'-the-wisp No. 2, the quasi-Liszt-Wagnerian Rhapsody No. 3. No. 4 (referred to above) is a wild Lisztian Caprice, and No. 5 an aimless Rhapsody. No. 6 is more coherent than the latter, but its interest centres in its secondary theme and subsequent treatment. The rhapsodic characteristics of the *Intermezzi* are also in evidence in the charming impressionist *Silhouettes*, *Op*. 53 (Un. Ed.), which should come next as inclining to the clearer style of his later works already described.

In his *Träume am Kamin, Op*. 143 (Simrock) we have intimate Schumannesque sketches written in an erudite and somewhat chromatic style.

Reger's work is undoubtedly the problem of the pianoforte music of to-day. The special difficulties and peculiarities require study, and much depends on the interpretation ; but at the same time the straining after effect and lack of homogeneity are defects which may disappear in the later works. As in the case of Debussy, one can learn to appreciate the charm of his virtues without losing sight of features which mar and perhaps serve as a foil to them.

The same drawbacks are present in the *Variations and Fugue on a Theme of Bach, Op*. 81 (L. and K.), the *Variations and Fugue for two Pianos on a Theme of Beethoven, Op*. 86 (L. and K.), and the technically interesting *Variations and Fugue, Op*. 134 (Simrock) ; but in these there is also much complication and over-elaboration. (*See further* Chapter XXIV.)

Max Reger hailed from Bavaria and, while still a young man, was a prolific composer of organ music, chamber music, songs (two hundred) and choral music. He was a pupil of Professor Riemann at Leipzig and lived at Munich.

CHAPTER XX

WE now come to the minor composers of German nationality in the modern Romantic style, who have been more or less influenced by Mendelssohn, whose polished lyric style has been, and still is, a powerful factor with smaller composers and in the smaller genre of piece. Combined with this lyrical aspect, however, there is usually found some reminiscence of Schumann in the harmonic treatment in which Mendelssohn was somewhat behind his contemporaries. Of these minor composers we may first mention Heinrich Hofmann (b. 1842), a prolific composer in almost all branches of composition, but of no great individuality or depth of feeling. A graceful and finished style characterizes his piano works, of which his best known are in Duet form (Chapter XXIII), as, for instance, the *Italian Love Tale* and *Hungarian Dances*.

Hofmann seems best in *Elf and Fairy Music, Op.* 122, No. 4 (Hammond). His characteristic Solo sketch, *The Trumpeter of Säckingen*, is well-known.

Hofmann was a pupil of Kullak and later was known as a virtuoso and resident in Berlin.

Franz Bendel was born in 1833 in Bohemia. He was a pupil of Liszt and from 1862 a teacher in Berlin. His pretty, descriptive German *Fairy Tales* (Lit.) and *By Lake Geneva*, the *Hommage à Chopin*, *Tarantella* and well-known *Cascade* are in good style and popular, as are also his Salon works.

The name of A. Löschorn (1819–1905) is connected with educational works. His pieces are modern in style, melodious and pleasant though not deep. His effective *La Belle Amazone* (Hammond), *Op.* 172 and 173, 161 and 162, 152 and 154 (R.F.), and the artistic *Op.* 199 (2 and 3), 200 (No. 4) (B. and B.) are commendable. Löschorn was a pupil of Berger and also resident in Berlin.

The works of Fr. Spindler (b. 1817) are similar to those of Löschorn, but more transparent and simple. Though a writer of Symphonies and Chamber Music, he is best known for his Piano Salon Music. His *Op.* 11 (Brauer), *Op.* 186 (S.L.) and

Op. 392 (R.F.) may be mentioned. Spindler settled in Dresden as a teacher in 1841. The name of Ernst Pauer (b. 1826 in Vienna, d. 1905) is known for his *Cascade* (Schott) and educational Collections, which give him also a place among the composers in the above style.

Following the Lyric Romantic style, but with no particular individuality or leaning to any one composer, we may classify the following :—

Hugo Kaun, in his charmingly modulated *Nocturne*, *Op.* 56 and *Op.* 42, No. 7.

The *Capriccio* and *Transcriptions* of R. Burmeister (b. 1860), a pupil of Liszt who settled in America.

Robert Klein, in the well-written and artistically varied Harmonies of the *Mazurkas*, *Op.* 19 and 24.

The bright and dainty *Miniatures*, *Op.* 25 and 31 (Rahter) of Paul Zilcher.

The dignified and refined *Op.* 27 (Kahnt) of Emil Büchner (b. 1826).

Josef Weiss, who shows ability and serious purpose in his *Op.* 18 (Challier), *Op.* 27 and 32 (Kahnt).

The very characteristic *Gipsy Dances* (F.S.) of Aug. Weiss.

The very melodious *Op.* 32 and 36 (B. and B.) of Karl Zuschneid.

Constantin Sternberg (settled in America) in the interesting *Op.* 49, No. 1, *Op.* 50, No. 2 (F.S.).

Oscar Klein (b. 1858) in his well-written sentimental pieces, *Op.* 40 (2 and 3), *Op.* 43 (No. 8) (A.P.S.).

Max Meyer Olbersleben (b. 1850), a pupil of Liszt and active in many branches of composition, writes in a refined and meditative style. His *Ballad*, *Op.* 8 (F.S.) and *Sketchbook*, *Op.* 20 (1 and 3) (R.F.) deserve attention.

Max Fiedler shows freedom of style in his *Impromptu in A♭* (B. and H.), while W. Junker has written transparent lyrical pieces, *Op.* 5 and 7 and a *Barcarolle* (B. and H.).

We may also mention individual works in this style by composers of various nationalities:—Emil Liebling's *Op.* 34 (Sr.) ; Georg Liebling's elegant *Op.* 9 and 11 (Schles.) ; M. Pery's *Romanze*, *Op.* 15 and 25 (St.) ; A. Staeger's fresh and modern *Op.* 3 (R.F.) ; Leon Erdstein's original *Op.* 2 and 3 (Bos) ; W. Berger's *Op.* 2 (1) (P. and M.) and *Op.* 43 (Sm.) ; Arnold Krug's *Op.* 31 (1, 2 and 6) ;

Henschel's two *Nocturnes* (R. and E.) ; L. Schotte's *Idylle* and *Allegro* (Laudy) ; C. Schäfer's artistic *Op.* 21 (Laudy) ; Al. Gorter's *Stimmungsbilder* (Rahter) ; E. Gayrhos' *Op.* 23 (3) and 35 (Janin) ; and various pieces by Ad. Frey (Ditson).

The twentieth century has opened with the domination of the orchestra in matters musical. The spirit of the orchestra is in the air. Wagner made the orchestra the musical link of his opera mechanism, the means by which characterization was secured ; while Liszt, on his part, strove to make the piano, what it can never become, a second orchestra. Liszt, however, wisely confined his efforts to emulating the fulness of effect obtained in an orchestra by more or less brilliant technical devices—often of the showy order, and left alone the imitation of effects, melodic and harmonic, which are only effective when interpreted through the medium of certain orchestral colouring or timbre. This, however, has not always been kept in mind by pianoforte composers who affect an orchestral style, with consequent loss of effect.

Wagner could not in any way be styled a pianoforte composer. What he did write for the piano was characteristic of him, but quite orchestral in style and ineffective, as in his *Ankunft bei den Schwarzen Schwänen* (Siegel).

One of the principal writers given to orchestral diction is Karg-Elert, who is best approached in his four clavier pieces, *Op.* 23, and the Scandinavian Airs (Hofmeister). The wayward *Walzer Scenen, Op.* 45 (Kistner), inspired by Schumann, requires previous study, but the Swabian Cycle, *Op.* 38 (No. 1, 2 and 6) (Simon) and *Bagatelles* (No. 2) (Kistner) possess the breezy traits of folksong combined with the modern tendences of Schumann and Brahms. Karg-Elert may be almost called the German Grieg.

Felix Weingärtner (b. 1863) was a pupil of Liszt. He is an ultra-modern apostle of daydreams, as seen in his *Cycles*:—in Bk. II of the *Op.* 2 and in *Op.* 3 (*Aus vergangener Zeit*) (Fr. Schubert).

Wil. Kienzl (b. 1857), of Austrian origin, reaches a high level of poetic characterization in the 1st Book of his *Op.* 46 (B. and B.) ; while the *Harzbilder* of Georg Schumann (B. and B.), who possesses vigour and powers of characterization, the *Wood Fantasies* of Rich. Franck (Schles.), the vague *Op.* 41 of Schulz-Beuthen (Reinecke) and the *Op.* 54 of Ad. Coerne all deserve notice as belonging to this style.

CHAPTER XXI

THE SONATA SINCE BEETHOVEN

WITH Beethoven, as we have seen, was reached the climax of thematic and formal development of the Sonata.

Beethoven's contemporaries, Weber (Chapter III) and Schubert (Chapter IV) especially, developed the Romantic element in the Sonata by emphasizing the dramatic and lyrical elements respectively.

Schubert also combined specially attractive and frequent modulations with the lyric element.

Schumann's Sonatas include the so-called *Concert sans Orchestre*, and two others written in 1835 (seven years after Schubert's death). In these we have charming lyrical slow movements, but the quicker movements are more broken up while the technique is often massive, fulness of effect being sought by chords and by the doubling of the bass part. Both the technical and actual development of ideas is much more homogeneous than in Weber and Schubert.

Schumann does not surpass Schubert in his modulations, but the constant transitions introduced are kept in better balance. The movements also are connected by related subject matter. The subjects are not so suited to thematic development as those of Beethoven, and, to compensate for this, more subordinate themes are introduced ; these, combined with allusions to the chief theme, fill up the gap. This subordination of actual treatment to the ideas themselves is not the only sign of the Romantic movement in the Sonata form ; it is illustrated in equal measure by the new, glowing, harmonic colouration introduced, the neutral tints of the past yielding to more gorgeous rays. All three of Schumann's *Sonatas* are fine works. The first, *in F♯ minor*, with its stirring 1st movement, entrancing *Aria* and humorous carnival-like *Scherzo* and *Finale*, is richer in feeling and interest than the 2nd or *G minor Sonata* which, though energetic, is more technical and less poetical in interest.

The interesting and lyrical 3rd or "*Concerto*" *Sonata*, with its characteristic Scherzo (omitted in the first two Editions) has more unity of style than the former.

183

Chopin's Sonatas are interesting for his characteristic technique, but, in *form*, luxuriant detail is preferred to concise balance of ideas, and therefore organic unity is lacking.   In the *Bb minor Sonata* the fascinating *Scherzo*, the popular *Funeral March*, with its haunting *cantabile* episode and the weird *Finale*, stand out prominently.

This work, and the freer style of the *B minor Sonata*, with its characteristic *Scherzo*, poetical slow movement and bravura *Finale*, form a retrograde progression from Schumann, so that, to get the next link in the evolution of the Sonata we must consider the work in *B minor* by Liszt which, in a way, secures unity of purpose by linking the movements together, and by deriving the theme for the slow movement from that of the Introduction.   Liszt's development, however, was that of the " transformation " type and the contents of the *Sonata* do not place it on a high level as regards formal structure.

The Sonatas of Brahms discussed in Chapter XIII appeal to us next.   Both as regards general style and technique, they are influenced by Schumann, as well as in the transient use of subordinate transitions of key, but any actual connection of movements is lacking.

As early works his *Sonatas, Op.* 1, 2 and 5 do not represent Brahms' thematic work at its best, since in these it is mostly limited to sequential imitation of whole phrases.   The working out, therefore, is not minute, as it is in Beethoven.

The lyrical moments in all three Sonatas, and especially in the *Op.* 5, suggest the influence of Schubert towards whom Brahms seems to have had a special leaning.

No special attempt at development is made in the Sonatas of Heller, and the same may be said of the poetically-inclined Raff and Rubinstein ; while, curious to relate, the Sonatas of Mendelssohn, a Classicist by nature and a successful composer of Chamber Music and Concertos, are very free in style and of little value.

Josef Rheinberger's well-written and dignified *Romantic Sonata* (Ks.), with an effective first movement, and his attractive four-hand *Sonata, Op.* 122 (R.F.), are more or less in organ style.

There is also an attractive poetical but somewhat rhapsodical *Op.* 6 of Draeseke (Rz.).

It has been said that the Sonata, as built upon the Beethoven model, has been on the decline ever since Beethoven's time, and this, especially as regards structural work, may be taken as correct.

Modern composers do not work so minutely ; they are content to work on models initiated by Schubert, Schumann and Brahms, to make the development on broader lines and to substitute for close thematic interest the attractions of modern tone-colouring. After all, the actual contents of the *form* are of more importance than the form itself.

Effectiveness, as a whole, combined with artistic feeling, form the subject of the picture ; disposition of outline *and* colouring are necessarily of secondary consideration. An artistically-woven texture and well-balanced structure are, of course, necessary, but they do not make a work of art by themselves.

From this standpoint, therefore, it is possible to look on the Sonatas of Schumann in *form*, but not necessarily in *technique* or *style*, as an evolution of the fittest—as, in short, the model for the twentieth-century Sonata.

We have already spoken of Schumann's own Sonatas. We have now to enumerate the most successful works since those of Schumann, Brahms and Liszt, in which Romanticism takes so bold a stand. Of these we first note the striking and original *Op*. 7 of Grieg, in which new rhythmical and harmonic effects, the result of the new national element, stand out conspicuously.

The *Sonata in F, Op.* 12, of Sibelius, the Finnish composer (*see* Part IV, Chapter XIII), is equally striking and Scandinavian in style ; a fine work, though lacking (as regards the 1st movement at least) in homogeneity.

The works of Ed. MacDowell appeal to us next in his tragic and heroic *Sonatas*—two of the finest though intensely modern works—deep, reflective, distinctly genre pieces of rich romantic character. The *Norse* and *Keltic Sonatas* are also impressive, the former from its successful local colouring. The latter has been termed " colossal " (*see* Part IV, Chapter XV). Mr. Gilman, in his *Biography*, speaks of it as portraying " the heroic Gaelic world, . . . that miraculous world of stupendous passions and aspirations, of bards and heroes and sublime adventure."

Coming to the remarkable Russian School, we have the important *Op*. 74 and 75 of Glazounow, displaying mastery of thematic and contrapuntal development (*see* Part IV, Chapter

VI). The *Op.* 74 is over-elaborated, but the 2nd Sonata (*Op.* 75) is one of the best since Schumann, whose influence is so apparent in the 1st and and final movements. A sparkling Henseltian *Scherzo* and the combination of fugal work with a chorale theme are special features.

Scriabin, in his three *Sonatas* and *Sonata Fantasie*, combines free style with poetical rhapsody, cross-rhythms and a glittering technique founded on that of Chopin. These Sonatas stand as a class almost by themselves. Difficult as they are, much depends on the interpretation given to them in performance.

Jos. Wihtol's well-written and artistic *Op.* 1 shows national feeling. The two attractive Sonatas, *Op.* 4 of B. Kalafati, and *Op.* 10 of B. Solotarjow are Schumannesque in spirit but Lisztian in technique, and, like those of Wihtol, more regular in form.

An elegant *Sonata in C* by Lack, in characteristic style, stands out among works by modern French composers (Part IV, Chapter VIII).

Of works by English composers (*see also* Part IV, Chapter XIV) the *Op.* 2, by Onslow (Part II, Chapter V), which is good in its way, belongs to the Beethoven-Clementi School; the programme Sonata of Sterndale Bennett entitled *The Maid of Orleans*, lacks development and must be considered principally as a poetical composition.

The first of two *Sonatas* by Sir Hubert Parry, though an early work, is grateful, refined, lyric and idyllic in style and shows the influence of Heller. It has a delightful *Scherzo* with a Schumannesque episode.

A pleasant Mendelssohnian *Sonata* by J. F. Barnett may be mentioned, and a remarkable *Sonata in D minor* by B. J. Dale, full of dramatic feeling and melody, though somewhat over-elaborated, also claims attention. The clever *fin-de-siècle Variations*, of which the Schumannesque 4th is the most effective, and the brilliant Lisztian *Finale* are noteworthy. An early work of the gifted W. Y. Hurlstone and a dignified, impressive and musicianly work by J. B. McEwen deserve special attention.

The *Op.* 37 of Tschaïkowsky, the *Op.* 12 of Steinhammer, the *Op.* 10 of Röntgen and the recent *Sonatinas* by Reger should also be included among noteworthy modern works of the kind.

CHAPTER XXII

THE CONCERTO AND THE VIRTUOSO

" The greatest merit of a virtuoso will always consist in a pure and perfect rendering of the composer's ideas."—*Wagner.*

THE term Concerto (German, *Concert*) was originally applied to any vocal, and later to any instrumental, concerted or ensemble compositions *without* solo parts, as in the Italian *Concerto Ecclesiastico* or *Concerto da Chiesa.*

As regards *form*, the present Concerto, constructed, as it is, in modified Sonata form, may be said to have originated in a *Concerto da Camera* for two violins and bass by Torelli, published in 1686.

In *style*, however, the early *Concerti da Camera* are composed after the manner of a Symphony : they do not consist for the most part of a solo work with orchestral accompaniment, as in the modern Concerto, but are fully orchestral, or practically so, throughout. The germ of the *solo* idea came from the *Concerto Grosso*, initiated by Torelli in 1709, in which a combination of solo instruments was accompanied by the rest of the orchestra, as in Handel's 12 Concertos for two violini and violoncelli soli with accompaniment of stringed orchestra.

Opportunities for the *Cadenza*, a distinguishing feature of the modern Concerto, consisting of a brilliant technical display by the soloist, were probably first provided by Handel in his organ Concertos.

Generally speaking, the Concerto before Mozart, as represented by those of Handel, Rameau, Seb. Bach, W. F. Bach and Em. Bach (Steingräber, Ed.), bears little resemblance to the present form. The solo instrument or instruments usually enter and keep with the accompanying instruments and do not show any particular individuality, though in the Concertos of Seb. Bach, and of his son Emmanuel Bach, more enterprise is shown in this way. The form also is not defined and the number of movements varies very much. The *D major Clavier-Concerto* of J. S. Bach consists of an Allegro in $\frac{4}{4}$ time, Larghetto, and Allegro in $\frac{6}{8}$ time ; the five-movement *E minor Concerto* of Handel contains a Polonaise, while the *C minor* of Em. Bach is practically in one well-knit movement, with subsidiary Adagio and Minuet sections.

This form of Concerto therefore may be classified as *concerted* works in the style of the old Sonatas and Overtures of the Bach and Handel period ending with Em. Bach about 1772. Of these older models, those for two and three claviers by J. Seb. Bach stand out as the most prominent. The celebrated *Triple Concerto in D minor* by J. S. Bach was composed about 1730, and was probably performed by him and his two sons Friedemann and Emmanuel at the Concerts of the Leipzig University Musical Society.

In the preface to the *Concerto*, which was not published till 1845, there is a copy of the instructions from Bach's son Friedemann as to its performance : " The executants of this Concerto should remember that thumping and loudness is not the true interpretation of this work, for the composer was a true poet as much as a great contrapuntist and he wanted the instrument to sing and not to groan in the hands of the players. The music should therefore be played with absolute neatness and delicacy and in a singing style without much assistance from the pedal. The accompaniment of the strings should not be too prominent and it should always take the subordinate part in the rendering of this glorious masterpiece." An historic performance of this Concerto was given in London in 1844 by Moscheles, Mendelssohn and Thalberg, when Moscheles unexpectedly interpolated a Cadenza where provision is not made for one and Mendelssohn, in friendly rivalry, followed suit.

The melodious *Italian Concerto* (St) of Bach was written in the style of one of the Italian violin Concertos, but for one clavier alone. It has been suggested that the *p* and *f* marks indicate, as it were, solo and accompaniment portions.

The modern Concerto form is the result, with added modifications, of the work of Mozart, who wrote nearly fifty Concertos for various instruments. Em. Bach's last clavier Concertos were published in 1772 and next year, in 1773, appeared the first Concerto of importance by Mozart, No. 5 *in D*, as scored for strings, oboes, horns, trumpets and drums.   The *Concerto for Three Pianos in F* and that *for Two Pianos in E♭*, recently revived, were published in 1776 and 1780 respectively.

It must be remembered, however, that Concertos in the old style appeared later, as, for instance, the best of Haydn's *in D*, which was published in 1782.

Of the many examples of Mozart's genius in this class, with their simple melody and delightfully modern modulations, the *D minor* (1785), with its beautiful *Romanze* (*see* Ex.) is regarded as the finest. This work was probably publicly performed in 1796 by Beethoven, who is known to have deeply studied Mozart's works.

Romanze.. Mozart.

The last three Concertos, including the *Coronation Concerto in D* (1788), which created a sensation on its performance in Vienna, and the last, *in B♭*, require special mention as anticipating much of Beethoven.

The technique of Mozart's Concertos belongs to a past age and it is this fact that has probably caused their disuse for a time ; but their manifold artistic beauty has recently caused a desirable revival, desirable if for nothing else, for the triumph, of art over technical display.   The advance on those of the Bach period consists in (1) the individuality of the solo part ; (2) the orchestral accompaniment, which, by means of instrumental colouring and thematic development of ideas, adds to the interest of the whole ; (3) the unity of the whole ; and (4) the evolution of modern Concerto form. The latter, as ultimately developed by Mozart and adopted by Beethoven, differs from strict Sonata form in having a double exposition—the first for the orchestra, the second for the solo with orchestral accompaniment. The double exposition also made it necessary that the 2nd subject, when given first by the orchestra, should appear in the key of the Tonic. The solo exposition also is more florid and contains additional matter (as with Mozart) or development (as with Beethoven).

Later developments following the early use of Mozart—who uses a short Introduction in place of the orchestral exposition— as well as the tentative use in the later works of both Mozart and Beethoven of fragmentary openings with the solo instrument, led to the praiseworthy and more concise Sonata form adopted by Mendelssohn and most later composers. This more modern form consists of a single exposition only, by the solo instrument with the orchestra.

A characteristic of the Concerto (though not confined to it) is the introduction of a Cadenza, or a brilliant improvisation, generally introduced (at least by Mozart and Beethoven) on a $\frac{6}{4}$ chord of the Tonic in the final orchestral *tutti* of the recapitulation.

Not trusting, however, to the improvisatory powers of the executant, both Beethoven and Mozart, as well as later composers, have written out the Cadenzas in full.

Moscheles, Busoni, Reinecke, Winding, Röntgen and others have also written Cadenzas for Beethoven's Concertos, while Beethoven, Hummel, Reinecke, Rudorff and others have done similar service for those of Mozart. A further development has been the omission of the customary Cadenza, as in Beethoven's E♭ *Concerto*, those of Mendelssohn, the *D minor* of Brahms and others.

The finest of Beethoven's *Concertos* is probably the one in E♭, *Op.* 73—one of those works which show his genius at its ripest stage—though the *G major* and *C minor* are, perhaps, more often performed. At the commencement Beethoven begins, not with the orchestra only, as in other Concertos, but with the solo instrument, and such is the brilliance of the

introductory passages that " no one can forget that he is listening
to a Concerto for the pianoforte " (Analysis, Grove. *See* Ex. A).

The orchestra now takes in hand the enunciation of the 1st and
2nd Themes of the movement (*see* Exs. B and C), and the pianoforte, after a brilliant two-octave chromatic scale, introduces
the principal subject in massed chords for both hands.

The development section gives a good idea of Beethoven's

method of breaking up his subjects into small sections or
motives, and using them over and over again as accompaniment,
bass, melody, or ornament, until the movement is homogeneous
throughout. The various ideas, such as the turn on the broken
chord in the 1st subject, are tossed about from pianoforte to
wind or string instruments and *vice versa*, first in one key and
then in another, until almost a kaleidoscopic effect is obtained,
or else new subsidiary melodies are introduced, as in the
following :—

In this *Concerto*, contrary to the usual previous custom,
Beethoven substitutes a written Cadenza for the customary
extemporization and provides an accompaniment for the latter
portion. We have not space to quote from the lovely hymn-
like *Adagio* and the gay and energetic *Finale*, but the student
might profitably refer to the score for his own pleasure and
instruction.

Of Concertos by the contemporaries of Beethoven those in
A minor and *B minor* by Hummel call for notice. These,
though containing much merely mechanical passage work, also
exemplify Hummel's genius for effective modulation.

The once popular Concertos of Dussek (1760–1812) have now
fallen into disuse. Though pleasing and melodious, their
slight structure, strictly lyrical style and lack of variety and
scope of technique have rendered them practically obsolete.

Written in a somewhat mechanical imitation of the style of
Beethoven, the *C♯ minor Concerto* of Ries is still used for
educational purposes.

The same may be said of Kalkbrenner's (1784–1849) more
technical *Concerto in D minor*.

With Field (1782–1837) we come to purely lyrical style,
combined with romantic feeling but evincing the same weaknesses
as Dussek, whom he resembled in some respects.

Field is educationally represented by his *E♭* and *A♭ Concertos.*
Schumann, speaking of the poetical *7th Concerto in C minor*,

describes the middle *Notturno* as " woven from the odour of roses and lily's snow," and rhapsodizes over the last movement thus : " Thy divine tedium, thy charm, thy delightful awkwardness, thy soulful beauty, bewitching enough to kiss from beginning to end."

The *E♭ Concerto* is wonderfully fresh and modern in harmonic feeling ; Field being, indeed, a direct link with modern Romance. His style of development shows the influence of Mozart, but in the *cantabile* portions one is reminded of his own Nocturnes.

Weber's Concertos show rich harmonies, interesting rhythms and attractive, brilliant technique. The popular *Concertstück* is scarcely in Concerto form, but the *C* and *E♭ Concertos* are both standard works.

The polished style of Moscheles' Concertos makes them educationally valuable. The Weberish *G minor* and the 7th (*Pathétique*) *Concertos* have been the most popular, but the former is somewhat unequal in style. The *E♭, Op.* 56 (Klemm) is more dignified and spontaneous.

The *E major, Op.* 64 has an interesting *Finale* built up on *The British Grenadiers* while the *Souvenir d'Irlande, Op.* 69, is constructed in free style on Irish airs, two of which are ingeniously combined together in the *Finale*. Both works may be considered as departing somewhat from the dignity of the usual type.

Conservative Mendelssohn (the pupil of Moscheles), with his somewhat limited though brilliant technique, put some of his best work into his Concertos.

The sincerity of purpose and more artistic atmosphere of the early *G minor Concerto* at once placed it ahead of the Concertos of Hummel, which at the time were the battle-horse of every budding virtuoso. The unique fairy scherzo element in the *Andante* and the youthful gaiety of the *Finale* render the work attractive. The 2nd *Concerto* (1837) is, perhaps, too reflective and not very spontaneous in style.

The *F minor Concerto* (1840) of Sterndale Bennett is brilliant and individual in style, but, like Mendelssohn's, shows a somewhat limited variety of technique. Apart from the absence of a really contrasted final movement, Bennett, in his larger works, evinces some of the weaknesses of those other composers in the earlier lyric style, Dussek and Field, *viz.*, the persistent use of stand-still basses and a lack of effective modulations.

The main attraction is Bennett's fount of idyllic melody, specially exemplified in the beautiful *Barcarolle* movement.

The lyrical and dignified *F♯ minor Concerto* of Ferd. Hiller is always interesting though more classical in style than Mendelssohn (Part III, Chapter XVII). The romantic style is now continued in Chopin, who resembles Field in his lyrical nature and his weakness in structure and management of the orchestra. Chopin, however, excelled in his delightful modern and unique technical figuration.

His Concertos were both early works, being written at the age of 20 and 21 (Part IV, Chapter II).

The orchestral portions have been re-scored by Klindworth, Tausig and others, and both works have been much criticized from a structural point of view.

The rambling *tutti*, for instance, in the 1st movement of the *E minor*, lacks balance and sense of key relationship, etc., but one would say that the poetical charm is really of more importance than the enveloping form, and both have become standard works. As Schumann pointed out, it was " the *spirit* of Beethoven " which Chopin led " into the Concert Hall."

Chopin, he says, was " the pupil of the first masters—Beethoven, Schubert and Field. The first formed his mind in boldness, the second in tenderness, the third his hand to its flexibility."

Chopin's genius lay, indeed, in lyricism rather than in thematic formalism. This is borne out by the beautiful *Cantilena Adagio* in the *F minor Concerto*, of which Schumann says, " What are ten editorial crowns compared to one such Adagio ! "

Coming to the ardent apostle of Romanticism himself, it looks as if Schumann had been strongly influenced by his own analyses of the Concertos of Field and Chopin, for his own *Concerto in A minor* (*Allegro*, 1841; *Intermezzo* and *Finale*, 1845) is one of the most delightful of his works, full of warm, romantic feeling, intensely lyrical and technically attractive. The 1st movement is thoroughly homogeneous, though the development is of the Transformation type, as, for instance, in the reappearance of the chief theme given out with clarinets and bassoons, as in Ex. A and B (here in relative major).

A delightful touch is the Rondo-like re-appearance of the 1st theme in the key of A♭ leading to the development section

which commences in that key. Both the 1st movement and
charming Intermezzo, with the beautiful 'cello solo responded to
by violin and clarinet, prove, with the continual dialogue or

interchange of ideas between the soloist and the orchestra,
that the Concerto is no mere Symphony with Pianoforte
Obbligato.

Schumann shows the best side of his technique in this work,
while it is also free from the ineffective subtleties characteristic
of him.

The one-movement *Concertstück, Op.* 92, and the *Concert
Allegro* are both in Concerto style, but inspiration and romantic
feeling are less apparent. The *Concert sans Orchestre* of
Schumann is really a Sonata, of which the title was altered by
the publisher.

Henselt's *Concerto* (*c.* 1838) written before that of Schumann
is more in the style of those by Chopin (1829-30). Founded on
quasi-Folk-song melodies, the development proceeds mostly in
Variation form, in which Chopinesque technique appears
diversified by those peculiarly wide-spread figures of which he
made special use. (*See* Ex. from the *Concerto.*)

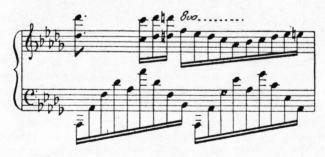

The somewhat grandiose and rhapsodical *Eb Concerto* of Liszt (Schles.) serves in a way as the starting point for the next generation of Concerto writers, both in technique, and in form—or the want of it. The Hungarian national style is depicted in the piquant *Allegretto*, which, with its frequent use of the Triangle, has given the name of *Triangle Concerto* to the work.

Rubinstein's Concertos have more variety of technique than those of Mendelssohn, which they otherwise resemble, though they are not so interesting. The 3rd is the most popular.

The versatile Raff wrote also a melodious Concerto.

A straightforward tuneful Schumannesque work by Ig. Brüll (B. and B.) ; the Lisztian and florid work by D'Albert, written when he was a student in England ; a romantic modern work by the American Hy. Holden Huss (Schirmer) ; the very melodious and Weberish *Op.* 63 by Ravina (Leduc), and the dramatic and dignified *Op.* 31 by B. Godard should be mentioned as some of the most effective modern Concertos in romantic style.

Of recent modern works with a classic leaning we have the dignified *F♯ minor Concerto* of Reinecke (B. and H.), endued with poetical feeling, and modern in style and technique ; and the interesting one in *Ab* by Rheinberger, which is masculine and well worked out, with a *penchant* for fugal (always appropriate) work.

The Concertos of Saint-Saëns (*see* Chapter XVII), a master of classical form—and the *Op.* 10 of Bronsart are also important modern works.

The Concertos of Brahms (*see* Chapter XIII) have been described (and actually classified) as Symphonies with pianoforte accompaniment. The rugged *D minor* was, indeed, planned originally as a Symphony.

Nobility and seriousness of purpose distinguish the *Maestoso* and *Adagio* movements, while the whole work is notable for (1) the absence of his later rhythmical obscurity ; (2) its emotional effects ; (3) the absence of the bravura element. In the *Bb Concerto*, however, the virtuoso is set to work from the outset weaving highly elaborate and clever ornamentation over a suave initial theme, after which the serious *Allegro Appassionato* appears somewhat at a disadvantage. The interesting dreamy and wayward 'cello solo in the Andante, with the Schumannesque pianoforte elaborations, present a grateful contrast and prepare the way for the Scherzo-like *Finale* in which thematic development is more prominent.

National colour has been a powerful influence in the modern Concerto. The very attractive *A minor Concerto* of Grieg stands out prominently as portraying the characteristic rhythms and melodic figures of Norwegian music.

A notable work of this class is the *Scottish Concerto* of Sir Alex Mackenzie founded on Scottish airs (*see* Part IV, Chapter XIV).

The poetical Pole (Part IV, Chapter II) is represented by an effective work by Paderewski (B. and B.), the refined *Op*. 12 of Zarzycki (B. and B.), and the brilliant *Op*. 20 by Jos. Wieniawski (Cranz) ; while the neatly written and recently revived *Concerto Hollandais* by Litolff is built on Dutch airs.

Of the Russian School there are the nationalistic work by Rimsky-Korsakow (Belaiew) (Part IV, Chapter VI), the *Op*. 20 of the poetical Scriabin (Belaiew), the Lisztian and nationally coloured *Op*. 4 of Liapounow (B. and B.), a successful *Concerto* by Rachmaninoff, and works by Arensky, Glazounow (*Op*. 92) and the popular Tschaïkowsky in *Bb minor*.

Jules Major's stirring and brilliant *Op*. 12 (Leuckart), like the *Eb Concerto* of Liszt, shows its Hungarian origin.

OTHER WORKS WITH ORCHESTRA

Other modern Concertos there are that are worthy of attention, as, for instance, the *Concerto, Op*. 9 by G. Mingcozzi (C. and J.), an attractive work with dramatic feeling, melodious and practical, and *Concertos* by Arthur Hinton (Fischer). The following have been performed at Queen's Hall Concerts : one by K. Bruckshaw, 1914 ; Delius, *C minor*, 1907 ; H. Farjeon, *in D*, 1903 ; Josef Holbrooke, *Concerto Dramatique*, 1903 ; Ed. Isaacs, *C♯ minor*, 1907 ; York Bowen, No. 3, 1920 ; Lenormand, *in F minor*, 1903 ; Ed. Schütt, *G minor*, 1904 ; L. Schytte, *Op*. 28, 1902 ; Sinding, *in Db*, 1904 ; Stenhammer, *Op*. 23, 1920 ; Palmgren, *Op*. 33, 1920 ; also the American works : J. A. Carpenter's *Concertino, Maria Zucca No. 2*, and Jno. Powell's *Negro Concerto*.

The less formal *Concertstück* has not attracted the ambition of the composer generally so much as the Concerto.

The most important are, the attractive Hummel *Rondo Brilliant, Op*. 56 (Ash. St.), the favourite Mendelssohn, *Op. 22, Capriccio Brillant*, the characteristic Chopin, *Op. 2, La ci darem Variations* (St.), and the well-known Weber *Concertstück*.

These four form a valuable educational quasi-Concerto course. To these may be added the Moscheles-like *E♭ Rondo* of Mendelssohn (St.), the brilliant and nationally characteristic Polish *Fantasia* and *Krakowiak* of Chopin (St.), the *Caprice Russe* and *Fantasie in C minor* of Rubinstein (Senff), the bright *Allegro de Concert* by Blumenfeld (Blf.), the melodious and classically inclined *Rhapsodie* of Brüll (Doblinger), the interesting Chopinesque *Concertstück* of Brandt Buys, the pleasing and well-written *Scene Veneziane* of Pirani, Saint-Saëns' *Africa Fantasia*, and the *Rouet d'Omphale* and César Franck's Symphonic poem *Les Eolides* (Lit.), *Variations Symphoniques* and *Les Djinns*. The Beethoven *G minor Fantasia*, which includes a part for Chorus, is in Variation form.

We may also mention the *Concertstück* by Charles Trew (J.W.), a well-written and attractive work. The following have also been performed at Queen's Hall, London.

Crowther, *Concertstück*, 1899 ;   Walford Davies, *Conversations* 1914 ; N. Gatty, *Allegro*, 1903 ; F. Matthay, *Concert Piece*,1909 ; Louis Aubert, *Fantasia*, 1911 ; Gabriel Fauré, *Ballade*, 1913 ; *Fantasy*, 1920 ; Egon Petri, *Concertstück*, 1906 ; Poldowski's *Pat Malone's Wake*, 1919 ; Busoni, *Indian Fantasy*, 1921 ; R. Strauss, *Burlesque*, 1920 ; Liszt, *Todten Tanz*, 1921 ; *Hungarian Fantasia*, 1920 ; *Rhapsodie Espagnole*, 1920 ; Schubert-Liszt, *Wanderer Fantasia*, 1920 ; Vincent D'Indy, *Symphonie Montagnarde*, 1901 and E. Schelling's *Suite Fantastique*.

" If a virtuoso chances to astonish me for a moment, the wonder is immediately replaced by involuntary repugnance." " No rope-dancing for me."—*Schumann*.

THE VIRTUOSO ELEMENT

By the Italian word *virtuoso* was originally understood " A man who loves the noble arts and is a critic of them." Nowadays we understand the word to mean, not an *artistic critic* but an *artistic executant* with a leaning towards the phenomenal.

Unfortunately, from the prevalence of mere technical display on the part of some so-called virtuosi, the word and its substantive virtuosity have become allied with empty musical sensationalism.

The Concerto itself, as the vehicle for exceptional technical powers combined with artistic musical form, has also suffered from the same misassociation of ideas : hence the amusing incident in Paris in 1904 when a *claque* objected to and whistled down the Beethoven *Concerto in G* as an inartistic composition. The opinions ventured, on this occasion, by leading French composers are most instructive. M. Saint-Saëns championed virtuosity as triumphing " in all arts, in literature, and especially in poetry."   As " the foundation of the picturesque in music, it gives wings to the artist by means of which he escapes from the commonplace of the world and its dulness."

M. Fauré agreed that " many mediocre Concertos exist . . . for mere technical display," while M. Vincent D'Indy was of the very conservative opinion that the present form " is a very degenerate descendant " of the Italian form as used by Bach.

Nevertheless, as was pointed out by others, virtuosity *is* indispensable for the interpretation of many master-works of the great composers, of which the Concerto is only one form.

No work can be considered as a master-work that subordinates musical ideas to mere technique, or even to matters of form. Inspiration must come first. If, therefore, the work is a masterly one and inspired, and the interpretation is conscientiously artistic, the laws of art are satisfied and the virtuoso truly justified.

The following Table is intended to illustrate the development of the modern Concerto as dating from Mozart.

The Concerto

MOZART.	SUBORDINATE.
1785. *D minor*.	1783–1812. Dussek (*G minor*).
1791. B♭ (last).	1784–1849. Kalkbrenner (*D minor*).
BEETHOVEN.	1784-1838. Ries in *C♯ minor*.
1809. E♭, *Op*. 73.	1778–1837. Hummel in *A minor*.
	in *B minor*.
EARLY ROMANTIC.	MODERN CLASSIC.
1782–1837. Field, *E♭* and *A♭*.	1821. Moscheles, *G minor*.
1786–1826. Weber in C 1810 ;	1831. Mendelssohn, *G minor*.
in E♭ 1812.	1840. Bennett, *F minor*.
	1811– Hiller, *F♯ minor*.
MODERN ROMANTIC.	Brahms, *Op.* 15, *D minor*.
1830-1. Chopin, *Two Concertos*.	*Op.* 83, *B♭*.
1838. Henselt, *F minor*.	St. Saëns, *E♭*.
1841. Schumann, *A minor*.	Rheinberger, *A♭*.
Liszt, *E♭*.	Reinecke, *F♯ minor*.
Rubinstein, 3rd.	

Nationalistic

Grieg in *A minor*.
McKenzie, Scottish.
Major, *Op.* 12.
Paderewski.

Rimsky-Korsakow.
Liapounow.
Rachmaninoff.

Study of the Concerto

The study of the Concerto has the double advantage of cultivating the bravura style and ensemble work at one and the same time.

If the student has already acquired a satisfactory foundation equal in grade to the *Studies, Op.* 70 of Moscheles (including special double-note and octave work) he may at once commence with the attractive Weber *in C,* Hiller *in F♯* (no double 3rds), or Ravina, *Op.* 65 (Leduc) ; and taking next the light Moscheles *in G minor* or the more comprehensive Moscheles *in E♭ minor* proceed through the brilliant Mendelssohn *in G minor* to the *Concertos* of Schumann, Chopin and others on the romantic side, or to the *chefs d'œuvre* of Beethoven and modern Classicists.

CHAPTER XXIII

FOUR-HAND MUSIC AND WORKS FOR THE LEFT HAND

" Lose no opportunity of playing music Duos, Trios, etc., with others. This will make your playing broader and more flowing."—*Schumann*.

To the modern player of Duets it is interesting to know that early four-hand music was written for two separate instruments. No doubt this was owing to the limited compass of the harpsichords then used. All such four-hand works, up to the time of the first *Duet Sonata*, which is said to have been composed by Mozart in 1765, were for two harpsichords or clavichords, as, for example, the *C major* and *C minor Concertos* of J. S. Bach and those of Friedemann Bach.

That such disposition (*i.e.*, for two claviers) continued to be a favourite mode of exposition is apparent from the *Sonatas* of Clementi, Dussek and Haydn, the *Concertos* and the *Sonata and Fugue* of Mozart, and the compositions by Hummel, Moscheles and others mentioned later.

Following the first *Duet Sonata* of Mozart, early examples of *Duets* appeared in compositions by J. C. Bach (the third son of Sebastian) and by Haydn in the *Master and Scholar Variations*, 1783. Mozart's own compositions in the *Duet Sonatas* (B. and H.), *Variations, Fantasias, Fugues*, and the *Adagio and Allegro* (1780–91) are the most important of that time. Then followed Clementi's noteworthy seven *Duet Sonatas* (B. and H.), those of Dussek, the brilliant *Ab Sonata* of Hummel, and Beethoven's interesting but unimportant *Marches* and *Variations* (Lit.). The romantic element enters with the *Duets* of Weber, exemplified in the educational series, *Op.* 3 and 10 (the latter written on popular airs) and in his characteristically bright eight *Pieces, Op.* 60 (Lit.). In the most important and voluminous *Duets* of Schubert we have also the lyric element combined with romantic feeling and a talent for charming modulations.

Schubert himself was very fond of Duet playing and put very much of his best work into that form.

The brilliant and interesting *Variations*, the stirring *Heroic*, *Military* and *Hungarian* Marches, the popularly-written *Polonaises* and *Rondos*, the fine *Fantasia*, the brilliant *Divertissement à la Hongroise*—made much of by Liszt—a Mozartian *Sonata*, a naïve *Allegro* (*Les Orages de la Vie*) and the *Grand Duo in C* (all Lit.) influenced by Beethoven and thought by Schumann to have been originally planned as a Symphony—all rank as Classics in this form. Regarding the Symphonic movements of the latter, Schumann, as critic, says that " Schubert is a maidenly character compared with Beethoven—far more talkative, softer and broader," though " compared with others he is man enough." Schubert, he says, " brings in his powerful passages and works in masses ; but there is always a masculine and feminine contrast ; one commands, and one teaches and persuades."

Schumann added harmonic richness and polyphonic interest to Duet Literature. One notes, also, the increasing interest in young people shown in the charming, yet lightly written *Twelve Pieces for Young and Old*, and in the *Children's Ball*. The *Eastern Pictures*, *Op*. 66, are characteristic and somewhat subtle in style, but the later *Ball Scenes*, *Op*. 109 (Lit.) are very happily appropriate. Since Schumann died, half a century has produced a profusion of all classes of works for four hands, and yet Duet-playing is much less popular than it was.

Possibly the great advance in technical execution has brought about the greater preference for solo work.

The characteristic sketch style was continued, after Schumann, in Volkmann's *Musical Picture Book* and *Tageszeiten*, in Jensen's attractive *Hochzeitsmusik* (Bos.), and in Reinecke's *Marschvorspiele ;* as well as in Rubinstein's *Charakterbilder*, Nicodé's *Pictures from the South*, Hiller's *Operetta without Words*, Huber's *Op*. 56 and 108, Schytte's *Op*. 112, the very melodious *Kermesse* of Hoffmann, and the distinctive *Six Pieces* (P.) of Sinding.

Duets in more or less classical form seem to be dwindling in number. The *Sonatas*, *Rondos* and *Op*. 142 of Moscheles, the *Op*. 1 of R. Fuchs, Brahms' *Op*. 23 *Variations*, a *Scherzo* of Ferd. Hummel, and Rheinberger's *Grosse Sonate*, *Op*. 122, with an attractive *Tarantella*, stand out prominently. (For other works, *see* Ruthardt.)

The National Dance and National Music in general seem to be specially suitable for four-handed playing. The popular arrangement of Hungarian Dances for two performers by Brahms may be said to have led the way, and was followed by the arrangements of Gobbi, Chovan and H. Hoffmann.

These have been succeeded by the attractive and artistic *Slavische* (Bohemian) *Tänze* and the *Op.* 59 and 69 of Dvorák, the ever-popular *Spanish Dances* (Sm.) and the attractive New *Spanish Dances* and *Polish Dances* by Moskowski, the invigorating *Danses Galiciennes* by Zarembski (Sm.), the *Norwegian Dances* by Grieg (P.), the *Nordisches* (or Norsk melodies) by Xaver Scharwenka (Sm.) and H. Hoffmann (Nov.), the *English*, *Scotch* and *Irish Dances* by Ashton, the popular Danish *Volkstänze* by Emil Hartman (Sm.), the *Italian Songs* by Pirani, the *Swiss Suite* and *Russian Op.* 76 by Wilm, and the *Roumanian Dances* by Chovan. Each of these portrays in an agreeable manner the characteristics of the various nationalities. Of the more cosmopolitan *Waltz* or *Ländler* there are artistic examples of the simple *Ländler* in the *Op.* 23 of Wrede (Sl.), in Grünberger, *Op.* 57 (G.R.) and Raif, *Op.* 4, 7 and 9 (J.). In the more modern Waltz form Witte, *Op.* 7 (P. and M.), Hille, *Op.* 10 (Sg.) and Kiel, *Op.* 73 and 78 (B. and B.) may serve as examples.

In four-hand Suites, Goldner, in his melodious *Waldscenen*, in the *Suites*, *Op.* 59, 61, 63 and 64, and in the six *Suites Modernes* (F.S.) leads the way. There are also the attractive *Baltic Shore Suite* and *Op.* 180 (No. 5) of Wilm (R.F.), the *Op.* 24 of F. Mann (F.), the poetical *Op.* 129 (*Atalante*) of H. Hoffmann (Ch.) ; as well as the *Serenades* of Wrede (Sl.) and Fuchs (Un. Ed.), the *Op.* 8 of E. E. Taubert and *Op.* 12 of Schuler, which are written on the model of the *Suites for Strings* which go by that name.

In the poetical style the name of Heinrich Hoffmann and his . graceful and pleasing series, the *Italian Love Tale*, and *Op.* 29 (Nov.) and *Genrebilder*, *Op.* 102 and 108 (Ch.) are well known. The modern and effective *Waltz-Caprices* by Karg-Elert (Hf.), the agreeable *Op.* 38 of Kleffel (R.F.) and *Op.* 25 of Olbersleben (R.F.), the Kündiger *Gnomenreigen* (R.), Sharpe's *Romance*, *Op.* 24 (Wl.), Kaun, *Op.* 18 (Ed. S.), Kiel, *Op.* 74 (Educational), (B. and B.), Asantschewsky, *Op.* 8 and Rudorff, *Op.* 4 may be also included in this style.

Instructive Duets

These date, as already mentioned, from the *Duets* of Haydn (*Master and Pupil*), Mozart and Beethoven, etc., down to our own day. It is not long ago that the tuneful *Sonatinas* of Diabelli held the field, notably the one *in D*, but these are now out of date. The average Sonatina is not advisable for early instructive work, either for two or four hands ; the National Airs and Dances are much more encouraging, besides providing a more healthy foundation. Such works as C. H. H. Parry's *Popular Tunes of the British Isles* are admirable as a beginning, leading to the easily arranged Classics as in Hartung's *Op*. 33 (Kaun), *Classics for the Young* (Litolff), and Löw's *Four-Hand School Book*, II (Litolff).

Transcriptions.—Perhaps in no way is the Duet form more useful than in Transcriptions of standard orchestral works which, as originally laid out, demand breadth of scope and effect. The Overtures and Symphonies of the great masters thus presented help us in a sense to realize the magnitude of conception of such works as compared with Chamber Music or the humbler Piano (*see* Chapter on " Transcriptions ").

For Two Pianos

Of this form of composition, already spoken of, the Bach *Concertos* (for two pianos), Mozart's fine *Concerto in E♭* and *Sonata and Fugue* (P.), Schumann's *Andante and Variations*, Moscheles' *Hommage à Handel*, Chopin's *Rondo*, and Saint-Saëns' *Variations, Op*. 35, stand out as Classics. To these we may add an effective *Concertstück* by Al. Schmitt (Sl.), Grieg's *Op*. 51, Wilm's *Prelude and Saraband* and *Waltzes*, the solid Kirchner's *Polonaise* (Hf.), the *March* by Goria (Lit.), Parry's masculine and Bach-like *Duo in E minor* (B. and H.), the *Variations* of Sinding, the piquant and elegant *Andante* and *Scherzettino* and *Duo Symphoniques* by Chaminade (En.), and the three *Valses Romantiques* by Chabrier (En.).

Variations by Somervell, Fischoff and Eymien, the *Prelude and Double Fugue* by Julius Harrison, the *Variations Artistiques* by Pfeiffer (Jb.), the *Variations, Op*. 13 of Herzogenberg, the expressive *Phantasiestücke* by Von Savenau (K.) and the attractive *Suites* of Arensky, Rachmaninoff and Longo also deserve attention.

The composition of works for two pianos seems to be increasing. This increase probably arises from the more artistic presentation of ensemble works in this form and from the convenience of using a second piano, in practice, to represent the part of the orchestra in a Concerto.

A full list of such arrangements as the latter can be seen in Ruthardt's *Guide*.

The stentorian and not very artistic effect of the once fashionable arrangements for six and eight pianos is fortunately now somewhat out of date.

Practically speaking, the repertoire for three or more pianos is confined to the Concertos of Bach and Mozart ; the *D minor Concerto* of Bach being the principal representative of this class.

WORKS FOR LEFT HAND

The limited scope of pieces for left hand alone confines their interest to the educational or purely virtuoso aspect. Left-hand playing received an impetus from the performances of Count Zichy (b. 1849), the son of an Hungarian nobleman, who, having the misfortune to lose his right arm at the age of seventeen, gave all his energy to playing solos with his left hand and subsequently was able to astound and delight the critics.

In addition to the left-hand technical foundation mentioned elsewhere the following pieces may be mentioned as forming a good course : Hollander, *Intermezzi, Op.* 31, Bk. I (Sl.) ; Niemann, *Op.* 40, No. 2 (Ks.), *Left-Hand Album* (Peters), Pauer's *Culture of the Left-Hand*, Pt. IV (Aug.), Reinecke, *Op.* 179 (Peters), and the Bach-Philipp *Transcriptions* (Fm.). A pleasant short course consists of Germer's *Op.* 41, followed by Graue's melodic *Op.* 25 (S. and H.) (two vols.) or Niemann's *Valse, Op.* 36 (Lit.), Hoffmann's *Op.* 32 (Dk.) and Vantyn, *Op.* 16, Bk. II. Instead of the latter, Rheinberger's *Op.* 113 or the more difficult Reger *Studies* (Univ. Ed.) may be taken.

CHAPTER XXIV

VARIATIONS FOR PIANOFORTE

THE Variation form has played an exceedingly important part in the evolution of pianoforte music, especially in its technical aspect.

The composers of early clavier music were not content with the ordinary Dance and Song tunes which they put into their *Suites*, but felt they must stimulate interest by inserting ornamental passages of grace-notes, runs, etc. Many ways of doing this were gradually found out, such as, by Variations on the form of the melody, or by the technical breaking up of the chords, etc., in the Bass; or by the alteration of the harmonies. The transposition of the melody into the various parts, as well as the insertion of passages constructed in imitation of part of, or the whole of, the theme, were devices frequently used. In the cultivation of brilliancy of the Variations used, as in the early Variations of the Elizabethan composers, technique was remarkably developed, while from one of their devices—that of inserting new themes between the Variations probably arose the Round or Rondo form. Byrd (1546–1623) and Bull (1563–1628), especially the former (*see* Part I, Chapter II), were past-masters of the Variation form of the period. Byrd's Variations on *Pavans* and *Galliards*, including those on the well-known air, the *Carman's Whistle*, though full of points of imitation, are mainly melodically varied. In some of the *Variations* of Bull the harmonies alone remain as the connecting link with the original, the rest being freely disposed.

Alternation of rhythm was early adopted as an interesting device. In the *Aria detta da Frescobaldi* the 4/2 time theme emerges as a 3/2 Galliard and a 6/4 Courante. The Variations (published in 1616) in Frescobaldi's *Partita* (Suite) *Sopra Folia* (a ground bass or Chaconne dance theme not usually quoted in its original form) are more florid. Both examples are canonic or imitative and show strongly the influence of the organ; they do not, however, equal the earlier English Virginal compositions. Frescobaldi's influence is seen in his successors Froberger (1600–1667) and Pasquini (1637–1710). We might note that Froberger precedes Purcell (who died in 1695) while Pasquini

(*Suites* written about 1697), whom Purcell surpasses in freedom of style, was a contemporary.

In the remarkable *Auf die Mayerin* Suite by Froberger (*Frobergiana*, Senff), composed after the manner of the *Canzoni Francesi* on a popular air, the common-time Theme appears as a 12/8 Gigue, 3/2 Courante, and 3/2 time Sarabande. In the interesting and probably unique *Chromatica* Variation chromatic progressions and altered harmony appear throughout over the usual bass.

Pasquini, with whom the Variation form was a favourite, wrote two sets on the usual theme *La Follia*, also " capricious " Variations and Variations " of invention," besides the usual Partita or Suite Variations. Both in Froberger's and Pasquini's Variations (*c.* 1697–1702) the technique is much freer, comparatively modern, and with less use of canonic imitation. The Suite Variations were usually called " Doubles."

A favourite form of the Variation was the " ground " or continuous " ground bass " or " basso ostinato," in which the Theme is put in the bass and repeated several times with ever-varying melody and harmony. Excellent examples can be found in Purcell (*Eighth Suite*, etc.) and Blow, and a good modern example of the basso ostinato is that by Arensky. Occasionally we find that the bass itself, especially in Italian composers, begins to be varied. In the practically identical forms of the Chaconne and Passacaglia the bass theme in the latter usually dissolves sooner or later into figuration and, appearing in other parts, is treated by imitation or in other ways. Originally the Chaconne, like the Passacaglia, was used as a Dance form :—

> " Jadis c'était la chaconne
> Qui couronnait un long bal,
> Ressuscitait, dans sa verve gasconne,
> Danseuses aux abois et danseurs mis-à-mal."   (E.D.)

The *Passecaille* and *Chaconne Variations* of Bach and Handel should be mentioned, as well as some striking and modern examples to be found in the *Passacaglias* by Dohnanyi and Nawratil and *La Chaconne* by R. Franke.

The masterly Bach 32 *Variations on an Aria* (Sarabande) *in G major*, for a harpsichord with two rows of keys, are contrapuntal in style but are contained throughout in similar harmonies and the Theme is variously presented in Canon form, Fughetta,

Overture (French style) and as a *Quodlibet*, in which fragments of German Volkslieder are introduced.

Handel, in the popular *Harmonious Blacksmith* Variations, the Passacaglia in the *G minor Suite*, and the 60 Variations-Chaconne, like his contemporary Rameau and the Italian School, anticipated his successors by largely putting aside contrapuntal devices and thinking more of the melody and effectiveness as opposed to scholastic ingenuity.

Mozart took up the same style and, by using grace-notes, shakes, broken octaves, repeated notes, and the insertion of showy Cadenzas, brought the Variation form into the forefront of popular favour. One speciality with Mozart was the ante-final *Adagio*, a movement always floridly ornamental.

Haydn took a more serious view of the form again and anticipated Beethoven by frequently building on the harmonic basis as compared with the general melodic style of Mozart, who, however, in his Sonatas cultivated more the harmonic style. A good example of Haydn's procedure is his artistic double-themed *F minor Variations*.

Beethoven builds *mainly* on the harmonic basis and uses less of the ornamented-melody style of Mozart. The remarkable 32 Variations in *C minor*, which form really a kind of Chaconne, are almost entirely harmonic in style. The Variations are only identified with the theme by means of its sequential character. Imitation is seen in the 17th and 22nd Variations, but the rest are brilliantly technical. Equally remarkable, from an analytical and artistic point of view, are the poetical Variations in the Sonata, *Op.* 109, and the very brilliant ones in *Op.* 111.

Beethoven's originality is seen in all that he wrote. In the *Op.* 34, written on a theme *in F*, most of the Variations are in different keys, while in the masterly *Diabelli Variations* (the last pianoforte work of Beethoven) (Part II, Chapter VII), which are also of special technical interest, the more correct term would be *Transformations*.

In these the connecting link is haphazardly harmonic, melodic or rhythmic, sometimes merely by analogy, leaving but a cadence or similar rhythmic periods for purposes of recognition, as in the mazy 20th. The work has been somewhat neglected recently at Recitals. Bülow, when performing it at Leipzig in 1857, suggested various titles such as I *March*, II *Ländler*, III *Duet*, IX *War March*, XVIII *Idyll*.

No student should be content until he knows the best Variations by Beethoven and Mozart. Bülow's annotated edition of three works of the former (Univ. Ed.) is useful.

The lyric Schubert and Mendelssohn, as was only to be expected, followed generally the melodic *Arabesques* of Mozart.

Schubert's *Impromptu in B♭*, and the very attractive *Duet Variations in A♭, Op.* 35, together with the *Variations Sérieuses* of Mendelssohn, are masterly examples of this style, both showing also unity of the earlier classic style with the spirit of Romance. Schubert was very fond of the Variation form, using it frequently and especially in the bass as a kind of thematic development. His *Impromptus* are mostly in Variation form.

Weber's *Variations* are distinguished by their thoroughly melodic (as opposed to harmonic) character. They are all bright and dramatic in style. Weber generally shows a decided leaning to chromatic harmony. His later sets, the *Op.* 28, 37 and 55, tend to the bravura style.

Schumann's *Abegg Variations* (1833), the *Etudes Symphoniques* and the *Variations* for two pianos are a direct continuation of Beethoven's method. They are decidedly harmonic in character and very freely interpreted through his characteristic technique. In the *Abegg Variations*, the bass of the theme appears first of all and, besides serving as a connecting link, forms the subject of a final Fugue.

Brahms stamped his intellectuality and masterly analytical power on his *Variations*. In method they are a continuation of Beethoven and Schumann. We note, for instance, the very free use of the harmonic style, in frequent cases forsaking the usual clues in order to carry out an idea in sequence, and the Schubert-like feature of the frequent appearance of the theme in the bass, together with the use of Canon form, as in the Handel Variations. Their distinguishing characteristic, however, is that of more advanced technique and some lack of poetry of sentiment as compared with Schumann. Brahms' *Paganini Variations* (like Schumann's *Etudes Symphoniques*) are avowedly laid out as Studies.

These and his Handel Variations give the key to his technical style (*see* Chapter XIII). The influence of Liszt, however, is also seen in some of his works and the *Op.* 21 (1 and 2) are more lightly spun out.

In the evolution of technique and style the Variation form has always played an important part.

The *La ci darem* Variations of Chopin (1830) and the *Ricordanza* Variations of Henselt (1836) both heralded new styles. Thalberg's smooth-fingered Variations on *Home, Sweet Home*, together with the trivial ones of Herz on Reissiger's so-called *Last Thought* of Weber, also show the fashions of a past age.

Coming to the Variation form of recent times, there are, in the more or less Classic style, the following noteworthy works : Lachner, *Op.* 42 ; Reinecke, *Op.* 235 (Zm.), Mandyczevski, *Op.* 5 (Un. Ed.) ; the difficult *Op.* 88 of Rubinstein ; those from Raff's *Op.* 91 and the fine *Op.* 48 of Xaver Scharwenka, which is technically modern and useful.

An interesting short set by F. Kiel, *Op.* 71 (1) (B. and B.) in contrapuntal style ; the resourceful and pianistic *Op.* 91 by W. Berger (K.) ; the ingenious and modern 19 *Variations* of Sir Hubert Parry, in form continuous, and set in various keys ; and the fine *Ballade* of Grieg are important.

Other outstanding works are the complicated *Op.* 81 (on a theme by Bach) by Reger, the *Op.* 13 of Fuchs, the *Elegy* of D. G. Mason (Srm.), *Op.* 14 of J. Cros. Hoffmann and a virtuoso work of Rosenthal. The piquant and elegant *Op.* 89 of Chaminade, the *Variations Capricieuses* of Frugatta, *Op.* 23 of Galeotti and works by Alnaes and Th. Holland require mention.

Those of the important Russian School (Part IV, Chapter VI) deserve special notice, as, for instance, in the masterly *Op.* 72 of Glazounow, the Chopinesque *Op.* 35 and 51 of Liadov, the *Op.* 8 of Blumenfeld, the effective Variations on a Lettish theme by Wihtol, the *Op.* 19 of Tschaïkowsky and effective works by Rachmaninoff, Amani, Alenew, Antipov and Bleichmann.

Of important Variations for two pianos there are the *Op.* 86 by Max Reger, the work of Saint-Saëns on a theme of Beethoven, those by Norman O'Neill on an Irish theme, the *Op.* 45 of Eymieu (In.) and those by Longo.

For pianoforte and orchestra we have the advanced modern symphonic *Variations* of César Franck (Part IV, Chapter IX) which are Schumannesque in spirit but Lisztian in technique.

In conclusion we may make mention of one peculiar form, and that is the Symphonic Variations of Vincent D'Indy, which begin with the most difficult and end with the simplest.

CHAPTER XXV

MODERN DANCE FORMS FOR PIANOFORTE

WE have seen the influence of the old Dance forms in the evolution of the Suite and Sonata. The modern Dance also had an important influence on modern music, especially on that written for the piano.

Taking what may be called the Round Dances—the Waltz, Polka and Galop, we find that they emanate from the Austrian Empire. The Waltz was the outcome of the Ländler dance hailing from the " Landel " of Alpine Austria, including Styria, Salzburg and the Tyrol. The Polka comes from Bohemia and the Galop from Upper Austria. The ancient Landel or Ländler (really the Tyrolese country dance) was a slow whirling dance.

In France it became known as *L'Autrichienne* (The Austrian Dance) and *Tyrolienne*.

In Germany the Landel took the title of *Deutscher* (German) *Tanz*. In Switzerland it took the French title of *Allemande* (German Dance). The latter should be distinguished from the Prelude-like movement in 4/4 time taken from the old French Suite. *Dreher* or *Drehtanz* (Turning Dance) was also an old German name. In Italy *Tedesco* (German Dance) was the version. The term *Styrienne* was applied by Lanner, the Waltz composer, to examples with the unusual grouping of four bars of 9/4 followed by four bars of 6/4 time. It is necessary to mention these varying titles expressive of the same thing—the ancient slow waltz—in order to avoid confusion.

The masters of the Beethoven era disdained not to write *Deutsche Tänze* for the ballroom ; Dances which, though simple, were works of art both for orchestra and for piano. At this time the Salon or artistic form of the Waltz had scarcely arisen. Collections of *Deutsche Tänze* by Haydn (1792), Beethoven (1795-9 and 1802), Mozart (about 50 Waltzes dating from 1787), Weber, Schubert (over 200), Hummel, Gryowetz and others, appeared at various times.   So far the Waltz was modelled in the very simple form of two eight-bar sentences followed by a similar *trio* and *da capo* and used in sets of six to twelve numbers. Schubert, however, introduced more feeling into his *Valses Sentimentales, Valses Nobles,* etc., more modulation and some expansion of form.

This, together with Weber's popular *Invitation to the Valse,* using an Introduction and reminiscent Coda, prepared the way both for the modern artistic Dance Waltz of Strauss and Lanner and for the poetic *Valses de Salon* of Chopin, and for innumerable other composers' works not intended for dancing but as absolute music of the most artistic *genre.*

The developed modern Waltz thus dates from Vienna about the beginning of the nineteenth century.   The charming compositions of Joseph Lanner (1801-43) and Johann Strauss (1804-49) sent the gay Vienna into ecstasies of delight and set the model for the rest of the artistic world.   It should be noted that Brahms, Dvorák, Kiel and a few other modern composers have shown a tendency to go back to the simpler form.

The German Galop, anciently *Hopser Rutscher* or Hop Dance, has not been drawn on very largely as a Salon composition. Schüloff's *Galop di Bravura* and Liszt's *Galop Chromatique* are examples.

Of the Polka, a modern Bohemian dance (*see* Part IV, Chapter IV), perhaps the best known artistic, though free, example, is the *Polka de la Reine* by Raff.

The Polish *Mazurka,* with its accented weak beats has been, especially developed in its art form by Chopin, as also has the national *Polonaise* (*see* Part IV, Chapter II) with the characteristic deferred or weak Cadences.   The *Duet Polonaises* of Schubert and the solo numbers by Weber are prominent examples.   The similar form of the Spanish *Bolero* (*see* Part IV, Chapter II) but provided with ordinary cadence—has been used by Chopin and others, the rapid whirling Neapolitan *Tarantella* by Chopin, Heller and others.

Besides those principal forms generally in use with composers for piano, there are the less-known National Dances dealt with in the various Chapters on National Music.

The Ballet, a Dance movement usually in piquant French style, and of operatic origin, is frequently used by lighter composers.   The orchestral *Ballets* of Delibes and other French composers form excellent models. (The term *Balletto* refers to a movement in Suites by Italian composers.)

The March, as an art form, has been illustrated by the best masters, especially in four-hand form. Those by Beethoven and Schubert are well known. The buoyant quick-step march seems to have found a congenial home in the United States of America, where it is in special favour.

CHAPTER XXVI

TRANSCRIPTIONS—PRELUDES AND INDEFINITE FORMS

THE pianoforte Transcription is one of the most valuable forms of composition from a practical point of view. As the " maid-of-all-work "—as the universal piano has been called—it brings within our reach artistic compositions for orchestra, chorus, organ, voice, etc., which it might be difficult to hear in their original form.

The modern Transcription, with its frequent crowded orchestral indications, differs much from the old figured bass and super-imposed melody, which the cembalist of that day filled up to the the best of his ability, aided by the octave couplers in use on the harpsichord.

The most artistic method of Transcription or arrangement is that of Liszt, whereby a *reconstruction* of the composition is made, bringing out the essential leads, voice parts and general effects of the score.

The drawback in the Liszt model is that, as in the case of its originator, mere cultivation of the difficult or exuberance of technique is apt to find a place. Another drawback is that the piano cannot really produce or imitate varieties of orchestral tone, and thus compositions like those of R. Strauss and Berlioz—which depend on orchestral colouring and its resulting orchestral harmony-effects—are unsuccessful. Moreover, despite all brilliant technical devices, the arrangements of Bach's organ compositions can never give more than a weak reflection of the stupendous body of tone of the organ, though the two-piano (four-hand) arrangement by Philipp (Ric.) should be more effective. Similar objections must apply in varying degree to Transcriptions of compositions for the solo voice, violin, etc., which imagination or past associations must necessarily amplify; so that, after all, Transcription must, generally speaking, be considered to be more utilitarian than artistic, though, of course, it may be both. Perhaps those instances in which a composer makes a Transcription of his own compositions are among the most successful.

With regard to the Transcription of the combined orchestral and vocal score of an opera, much depends on the arranger.

Of the *Clavier Extractors*, as Wagner called them, Mr. Dannreuther has said (*Mus. Times*, Aug. 98) : " It is interesting to compare the method and the effect of Klindworth's pianoforte scores of the *Ring* with Bülow's version of the score of *Tristan*, Tausig's of the *Meistersinger*, and Joseph Rubinstein's of *Parsifal*. Klindworth's version is, perhaps, even harder to play than any other, but it is more efficient ; it reflects the orchestral score as closely as do Liszt's Transcriptions of Weber's *Overtures* or of Berlioz's and Beethoven's *Symphonies* and *Concertos* Liszt's Transcriptions are Klindworth's models." Mr. Dannreuther knew of " no better practice for pianists who are up to Liszt's technique than Klindworth's *Nibelungen*."

The art of transcribing from the organ has been dealt with in a masterly way by Busoni in the Supplement to Vol. I of his Edition of Bach's *Forty-Eight* (Schirmer).

Interesting comparisons may be made between the pianistic versions of Busoni, the two piano arrangements by Philipp, the ponderous versions of Reger, the sound and concert-like arrangements of D'Albert, the practical and effective arrangements of Sandor-Laszlo (Brd.), and those of Szanto, Goé, Ansorge, Emile R. Blanche (F.F.), Zadora (Simrock) and others. For an enumeration of the many other important Transcriptions the reader must be referred to the Ruthardt *Guide*, and it must suffice here to mention the prominent examples of the various kinds, such as :

Chamber Music—Martucci, Schultze, etc.

Symphonies—Beethoven by Liszt, Brahms by Reger (Sim.) and by Klengel (Sim.).

Overtures—*Tannhäuser* by Liszt.

Orchestral Suites—Tschaïkowsky's *Casse-Noisette* (Bos.), German's *Gipsy Suite* (Nov.) and Cowen's *Old English Suite* (Nov.).

Concert—Schubert's *Marches* by Tausig and Liszt ; Schubert's *Waltzes* by Liszt ; Weber by Godowsky.

Older Piano Works—Scarlatti, etc., by Sandor Laszlo (Brd.).

Opera Extracts—Schubert's *Rosamunde* by Fischoff ; Gluck's *Gavotte* by Brahms.

Classic Transcriptions—*Early Classic Masters*, trans. by A. M. Henderson (B. & F.).

Songs—Schubert, Mendelssohn, etc., by Liszt, Heller etc.

Operatic—Wagner by Liszt, Brassin's *Wagner Fire Music*, Jaell's *Wagner Preislied*, etc.

Solos as Duets—Weber by Kleinmichel, Cramer by Henselt.

Two Pianos—Most Concertos; Philipp's Organ Transcriptions.

The Transcriptions of orchestral compositions made by the composers themselves stand out as a special class, *e.g.*, those by A. Ricci Signorini (C. and J.) of his musical poems, *Il Viaggio di Maria Egiziana, La Caccia di Veruccio, Papiol, Troll, Dafne e Cloe, Guida di Kerioth*, and the Suite *Stati d'Anima*. In these interesting orchestral works we may see the modern impressionist with his striking harmonic colouring after the manner of Debussy.

MODERN SUITES

The old Dance forms are still cultivated by modern composers in Suite form, though perhaps not so much is made of these interesting old movements as might be. A fine *Suite* by Martin Grabert, *Op.* 15 (S. and H.) and attractive ones by D'Albert, *Op.* 1; Reinecke, *Op.* 197; Longo, *Op.* 13 and 31; Falconi, *Op.* 26; Sinding, B. Godard, P. Lacombe, D. Fleuret, Niemann (Lit.), Hoth, *Op.* 6 (R.); Ferd. Hummel (four hands) (J.), A. Backer Gröndahl, J. A. Hagg and Smith-Hald. (*Op.* 5) (F.F.), should be mentioned.

The word Suite is also applied to collections of Pieces of various kinds; some of which, like those of Raff, resemble partly the old Suites. His *Op.* 91 has a Fantasia and Fugue, Gigue, Cavatina and March. Other examples are Reinecke, *Op.* 157, Hiller, *Op.* 144, and Brüll, 2nd Suite. Those by Bargiel and Schytte make some use of Sonata form. There are Suites also of Modern Dances (Gurlitt), of National Dances or pieces (*African Suite*, Coleridge-Taylor; *Suites Italiennes, Valle de Paz*) and of poetical Pieces, such as Raff's *Suite for Small Hands* and other *Suites* by Esposito, *Op.* 34; Whiting's *Op.* 15; York Bowen's, Hoffmann's *Ballet-Suite* (Un.) and Goldner's *Four-hand Suites*. Of Suites for two pianos there are fine examples by Arensky, Longo and Rachmaninoff.

INDEFINITE FORMS

The words *Prelude* and *Introduction* have the same general meaning. In pianoforte music, however, an *Introduction* is generally understood as being of a grave, dignified character—practically formless—and is used to lead the way in a set composition like a Sonata. The *Prelude*, on the other hand, is usually a separate composition, often in more or less definite form and worked out, like the *Etude*, on some particular technical figure. The *Prelude*, however, varies much in style (*see specially* Part IV, Chapter VI). The *Preludes* of Bach, often written in imitative style, differ from the poetical but *mixed Preludes* of Chopin, many of which are purely in *Etude* style ; while these again differ from the perfect little works of Heller. The *Modern Toccata* is practically an elaborated *Etude*, and is developed like the *Prelude* on some particular figure, but written more in *bravura* style. Besides the Augener Collection, with examples of Clementi, Pollini, Onslow, Czerny, Mayer and Schumann, there are notable examples by Bennett, Leschetitzky, Stanford, O'Leary, Alb. Jonas and Wm. Mason.

The *Old Toccata* form, exemplified in compositions by Bach and Rheinberger, is written in free fugal style.

The *Caprice, Scherzo, Impromptu* and the modern *Fantasia* resemble each other in indefiniteness of form, but can be distinguished as a rule by the style or mode in which they are written. One has only to compare the dainty and fairy-like *Capriccios* of Mendelssohn with the more robust and energetic, yet playful, *Scherzos* of Beethoven to discern the difference between the two generally. The running figuration usually developed, as it were, unpremeditatively, as a certain accompanimental bass, is characteristic of the *Impromptus* of Chopin and Schubert, while we distinguish the *Fantasias* of Mozart, Schumann and Mendelssohn by their more pretentious style. The *Fantasia*, it should be noted, is written (1) on an original Theme like those mentioned, or (2) on popular airs, as in Moscheles' composition on Irish Airs (Ash), in which, at the close, two airs are worked in together at the same time.

As illustrating differences in form, some movements in Mendelssohn's *Fantasias* are more or less in *Sonata* form, while those of Liszt and Thalberg are practically *potpourris*.

The *Intermezzo*—generally a middle movement—is very indefinite in form. It is used by Schumann, in the *Novelettes*, in the sense of a *Trio* or *Episode*.

CHAPTER XXVII

SALON MUSIC

THE difference between the best Salon music and good music of the Romantic type is often difficult to define. Equally difficult is it to show in what the essence of Salon music consists. Admittedly it is not of the *highest* type, intellectually speaking, nor, on the other hand, is it necessarily shallow. Salon music may serve its purpose to while away a leisure hour, though it may not elevate.

Music, like literature and the other arts, is many-sided. Recreation, study, amusement, and elevation of the emotions are some of the various aspects, so that if we speak of Salon music as recreative in the best sense we shall not be far from the truth. In our selection here made we shall, of course, treat only of the best.

Since the ideas of various nationalities differ as to what constitutes amusement or recreation, we must expect to find different national ideals of Salon music. German Salon music often reminds one of the open-air Tyrolean *Lied* and the *Zither-klang;* but French Salon music is of the real atmosphere of the Salon, with its Sentimental Valse and showy, brilliant style. Austrian Vienna, with its Strauss Valse atmosphere, also believes in a light style ; while hustling America is devoted to the energetic Quick-step March. Other nations, again, have founded their styles, more or less, on the foregoing.

The principal defect in Salon music is its harmonic aspect which, in many compositions, hovers perpetually between tonic and dominant ; and to this may be added a shallow sameness of technique which is often flippant in style.

Concerning deficiencies in general, we all know the sentimental uninspired Valse *à la* Chopin, the piece with left-hand melody and very much repeated *arpeggio* in the right-hand above;

as well as the threadbare melody of the *Galop de Salon* and the snippety *Mazurka*, with snatches of melody interspersed by sudden runs and *arpeggios*.

The best Salon music is, however, not devoid of poetry and romantic feeling. It may likewise, perhaps, be brilliant but not shallow ; while it may also be valuable from the *educational* point of view.

We may now direct attention to the best composers coming under this head, at the same time mentioning representative works by each.

German Composers

Charles Godard writes in elegant French style, educational and melodious, *Op.* 109, 116, 140–1 (R.F.). Nurnberg, similar style (*Comp*. No. 1, 3, 9, 11 (R.F.). Gustave Lange, well-known works in expressive style : *Blumenlied*, etc., also *Op*. 218 and 219 (Frs.). H. Wenzel, light and pleasing educational works : *Op*. 21, 85, 287, 258 (Portius). Gänschals, similar style, mostly in octaves ; also with bell and zither effects, *Op*. 346 (R.F.), *Op*. 80 (Portius). Bohms writes in popular and varied style—four Pieces (Hammond ; also Schott). F. Behr (*known also as* Wm. Cooper, Chas. Morley, Fr. D'Orso) is energetic and tuneful, *Op*. 406, 626 (R.F.), *Gitanelle* (St. Lucas), *Pomponette* (D'Orso) (Schott). Carl Hein is light and pleasing, *Op*. 239, 147 (R.F.), but lacks harmonic variety. F. Baumfelder, best in slow movements, *Op*. 192, 28 (Hof.). Schiffmacher, shows influence of Schubert and Chopin, *Op*. 95 and 53 (Choudens), *Aletter* and *Translateur*, piquant Dance movements (Bos.). Hans Mayer, poetic and modern style (Bos.). Winterberger is contemplative and artistic, *Op*. 80, 81 and 84 (J.S.). Goldner, refined style, *Op*. 47 (F.S. jr.). Grützmacher, brilliant and well written, *Op*. 17, 21, 55 (Kahnt). Goldbeck, superior romantic style, also Lisztian technique, *Op*. 51, 47, 44, 52 (J.S.). Handrock is the German Sydney Smith, *Op*. 39, 41, 42 and 57 (Kahnt). Von Walden, idyllic, *Op*. 61, 84 (Zm.). Golde, refined, *Op*. 62 (Ch.). Fr. Kirchner, prolific educational works, some well written. Oesten, best in Operatic Fantasias, Salon, *Op*. 75 (Gl. R.). Jos. Löw, better educational style, *Op*. 372, 360 (Fischer). K. Kölling, educational, *Op*. 303 (Cranz). Val. Armand, fresh and interesting, *Op*. 63, 62, etc. (R.F.).

Jungmann, poetic but unequal style, *Op.* 29, 31 (Bos.) (Lit. Alb.). Wollenhaupt, settled in New York and died there ; vigorous, rhythmical and melodious, *The Gazelle*, *Le Ruisseau* and others are good practice (two vols. Kahnt, Lit. Alb. and Aug. Selection). Louis Köhler (the Etude-writer), interesting and brilliant, *Op.* 54, 55, etc. (J.S.). Ch. Voss, technically interesting, *Op.* 95, 161 (Joubert), 1st *Valse* (Ash). Abesser, concert style, *Op.* 38, 87 (Kahnt). Gutman, the friend of Chopin, *Op.* 39 and 8, in romantic style. W. Krüger, the romantic *Harpe Ossianique* (Brandus) and *Polonaise Bolero*. Braungardt, favourite *Waldesrauschen* (Foetisch). Zumpe, Brinkman, Acton, write in sentimental style. Fesca (Lit. Alb.), technically interesting only. Jos. Ascher (Alb. Lit.), effective, though superficial in melody and harmony, *Fanfare Militaire*, *Mazurka des Tra ncaux*, etc. De Grau, light, brilliant ; *Pluie de Corail*, etc. Aug. Nolck, refined, educational, *Op.* 58, etc. (Aug.). Espen (Eul.) and Blattermann (Bos.), attractive, easy ed. pieces. St. Essipoff, prolific writer (real name Burnand), refined elegant style, *Op.* 17 (4), *Leonard*, etc., etc. Blumenthal (b. 1829, settled in London), melodious ; *La Source*, *Le Dévouement* (Ash), *Chant de Cygne* (Chappell). Oscar Strauss, fresh and light, *Harlequinade* (Ch.). Gustave Merkel, some good Salon music, *Waltzes*, *Op.* 95, etc. D. Krug, prolific composer, *Op.* 285 (Siegel). Fritz Spindler, well-written and tuneful easy Pieces (Leonard, Albums Lit. and Nov.). Jaell, graceful romantic works, *La Sylphide*, *Le Carillon* (Senff). Franz Bendel (1833–74 ; Bohemian), wrote in good style ; *La Cascade* (Aug.), *La Gondola* (Album Lit.), *Souvenir de Prague*, etc.

The modern French School shows more of the real atmosphere of the Salons, and French composers show the influence of Chopin where the German School leans to Hummel and the Tyrolean Lied.

J. Leybach (b. 1817 in Alsace) shows brilliancy and elegance ; 1st and 2nd *Boleros*, *Les Vendangeurs* (Schott), *Puritani Fantasia* (Bos.). Ch. Delioux (b. 1830) superior style, well-written and effective ; *Caprice Nocturne* (Benoit), *Op.* 27, 82 and 3 (Choudens), *Les Bohémiens*, *Les Matelots* (Gregh), *Carnaval Espagnol* and *Mandoline* (Schott). Louis Brasson (1836–84), German style, interesting ; *Op.* 17 (Schott) and *Barcarolle* (Kahnt). Al. Goria (1823–60), artistic works ; Chopinesque 1st *Caprice Nocturne*, interesting *Op.* 19, and 1st four of six

Etudes de Salon (Choudens). Kowalski (b. 1841), refined, modern harmonies ; 2nd *Élégie, Danse des Dryades* (Schott), *Op.* 89, 87, 93 and 30 (Sulzbach). F. Lemaire, *Op.* 29 and 54 (Lemoine) and V. Dolmetsch (Leduc), piquant Ballet music. Paul Wachs (b. 1851), light but spontaneous and artistic ; *Ballerine* (Leduc), *Madrilena* and *Rose du Poète* (Laudy). Gabriel Marie, sincere and artistic ; *Tendre Œil* (Bos.), *Impromptu Valse* (Costellat). Ernest Gillet, light, refined Pieces ; *Le Rouet* (Album Cranz, Bos.). Ed. Chavagnat, delicate and piquant ; *Le Sylphe* (Hamelle), *Les Ailes* (Gregh). E. Anthoine (b. 1836), elegant Pieces (Leduc). The compositions of A. Elterlen, *Op.* 21-4 (Clot Fils), Gast. Lemaire, 21 and 26 (Cranz), P. Rougnon, *Op.* 122 (Hamelle), F. Garnier (Ash) and E. Nollet, *Op.* 31 (Ash), are more Teutonic in style. C. Neustadt (b. 1838), elegant educ. works (Hammond). G. Bachmann (1848–98), very light, brilliant Pieces, but better style in *Chanson Légende, Chanson des Bois* (Clot Fils). Lebierre, brilliant ; *Tarantelle, Op.* 62 (Schott). A. Tellier, very tuneful but light Pieces (Bos.). A. Laudry, elegant ; *Op.* 212, etc. (Leduc). Louis Gregh, light and piquant, *Papillon, Les Spirales*, etc. The brilliant *Le Réveil* (Schott) of Godefroid, useful *Étude L'Arabesque* by Brisson, *Concert-Études* of Goria and *Spinnlied* of Litolff also deserve mention.

The Swiss Raff (*Polka Glissando*) and Gastone Bernheimer, original *Op.* 10 and 12 (Schott) ; Gayrhos, *Op.* 48 and 49 (Foetisch) ; Lysberg, in his refined *La Fontaine, Balladine* (Aug.), *Op.* 48, 94 (Hof.) ; Fr. Hitz, light Romances (Leduc) ; the Russian Meyer Helmund, pretty sentimental pieces (Laudy), and pieces by F. Borowski (Laudy) are also attractive.

ENGLISH SALON MUSIC

The Irishman, Wm. V. Wallace, composer of *Maritana*, etc., wrote a good deal of piano music in somewhat commonplace style. The *Polkas de Concert* and Paganini *Hexentanz* are still heard.

Brinley Richards (a Welshman), wrote melodious and transparent pieces (four vols. Hofmeister) which were once very popular. The Salon works of Ed. Harmston's composition (Coll. St. Ed.) are clear and melodious ; they are much occupied with Alpine bells, zither, harp and bird effects. The above

three writers are better known on the Continent than here.
S. B. Mills (1838–98), who settled in America, contributed some
very well written and attractive pieces : *Tarantellas, Recollections of Home* (Paul), etc.   Ed. Cutler's works are characterized
by harmonic and melodic freshness (*Op.* 28, 31, 33, etc. ;
Brauer).

Sydney Smith's (1839–89) music is always brilliant and
effective.   The *Harpe Eolienne, Jet d'Eau, Pas Redoublé* (Ash),
Arlequin (Aschenberg) are instances ;   and his well-written
Operatic Transcriptions and easy Pieces (under the *nom-de-plume*
of Paul Beaumont) are interesting.

George Aitken has written piquant Ballet music, *Les Sylphes*
(Schott) in French style.

" Anton Strelezki " (cousin of Sir Francis Burnand, writing
also under the name of Essipoff), is well known.   His Salon
pieces such as *La Caressante* (Ditson), *La Fileuse* (Vincent) and
La Coquette (Ash) are cast in refined, romantic mould.

The elegant pieces of the Dutch Van Westerhout, Sieveking,
Hageman and P. Raina should not be forgotten.

Belgian Salon music is mostly in very light style.   J. L.
Gobbaerts (1835–86) wrote over 1,200 pieces, many of them
educational, under the *nom-de-plumes* of Streabog, Ludovic and
Levi ;   most are now out of date ;   *L'Hirondelle* (Bos.).

Van Gael, superior, well-written and effective ;   *Air de Ballet,
Op.* 39 (Jennings), *Op.* 15, 28 (Katto).   C. de Wulf, *Op.* 17, 18
(Katto) are in similar style.   A. D'Haenens, brilliant and
graceful, *Op.* 56, 20 (Gregh), *Op.* 11 (Maison Beethoven), *Op.* 9
(Katto).   Justin Clerice, elegant and distinguished ;   *Serenade,*
etc. (Cranz).   Dupont, well written ;   *Chanson Hongroise* and
Gavotte (Schott).   Gustave Katto, melodious and fresh *Bergerie,
Valse Caprice*, etc. (Katto).   Alex Ermel, piquant and varied
Airs de Ballet (Bertram).   Hy. Weyts, tuneful *Serenade* and
works by Marius Carman (Cranz) should be noted.

Alfonso Cipollone is known for his clear and melodious pieces
(Cranz, etc.).   R. Sudessi is equally attractive.   Tito Mattei
(settled in London) well-known composer in brilliant style.
Melodious and effective ;   *Le Tourbillon*, the well-known Waltz
Une Perle, L'Aimant, etc. (Ash).   A. Sartorio, refined Pieces ;
Hortensia (S. and H.) and J. Romano, Pieces in lyrical style.

Czibulka (Album Bos. and *Op.* 230, R.F.) writes mostly in
light Viennese style.   The Pole De Konkski, who settled in

Paris, writes effective works but limited in capacity; the realistic *Réveil du Lion* and *Grande Polonaise* (Schott). Hustling America does not yet, apparently, revel in the luxuriant atmosphere of Salon music. The compositions of the Creole Gottschalk (b. New Orleans), who studied in Paris under Halle and toured extensively as a virtuoso, are of a refined sentimental style; *The Last Hope*, *La Jeunesse* and other pieces are well known. Wm. Mason's *Silberquelle* and *Op*. 20 (Schirmer) and W. G. Smith's refined and well-written *Op*. 87 (Schirmer) claim mention.

The following are refined Salon works: St. Essipoff, *Alla Minuetto;* Frederick Cowen, *Polka Gracieuse;* Fr. Mullen, *Air de Ballet;* Hubert Bath, *Miranda;* Reg. King, *Cynthia;* Gl. Hope, *Graceful Dance;* Ivy Herbert, *Danse de Ballet* (all Joseph Williams).

PART IV

———

THE ERA OF NATIONAL MUSIC

CHAPTER I

NATIONAL MUSIC

" Listen attentively to all folk-songs ; these are a treasure of lovely melodies and will teach you the character of different nations."—*Schumann.*

NATIONAL music represents " what is composed in the peculiar taste of the nation to whom it appertains, and appeals more powerfully than other music to the feelings of that nation." To obtain this music in all its purity we have to go back to the traditional Folk-Songs and Dance-Tunes obtaining among the people of the rural districts. Its characteristics vary according to the influence of climate and scenery, and, more directly, according to the particular instruments and form of scale in use. We note, for instance, the frequent use of augmented intervals in Polish and Eastern music and their presence in Chopin's Mazurkas and in the music of Mendelssohn, who was of Jewish descent.

Haydn was probably the first composer of note to make use of national idioms, displaying, as he does, the characteristics of Croatian folk melodies in much of his music (Hadow, *Haydn as a Croatian Composer*). The use of strongly-marked rhythm is also a distinguishing feature, and especially developed in Magyar (Hungarian) and in Spanish music.

The general tendency of all music for the last century and a half until recent years has been to follow that of German composers. Previous to that, however, Italy obtained the lead, though England had more or less of a National School, especially in music for the virginal and in vocal music, before the arrival of Handel with the Italian Opera.

Now, however, different nations, led by Norway, Sweden and Hungary, are encouraging their own particular cult to the undoubted enrichment of musical art. The martial glamour and melancholy of the Pole, the vigorous rhythms and breezy airs of the Scandinavian, the grace and piquancy of the French, the sunny voluptuousness of Italy, the philosophic German, the

227

Hungarian with his wild gipsy rhythms, the stately Spaniard in his march-like Bolero, the curiously morbid, half-Eastern, half-Norse characteristics of Holy Russia, and lastly, the frank, easy-going character and spasmodical features of the Composite Anglo-Dano-Celtic-Saxon are all truly mirrored in the pianoforte music of the various nationalities.

An interesting problem will have to be considered when the musical art culture of the Eastern and black races takes root. Already we have by Coleridge Taylor—the son of an African negro doctor, educated in England—highly interesting and artistic works pervaded by appropriate tone-colour and rhythms.

Possibly the Japanese may next appear on the musical horizon. Who can tell? Schumann's words, written at the dawn of the national movement, must indeed appear to us as prophetically inspired. He says, " Until now we have had three principal schools of music—Italian, French and German. How will it be when other nations step in, even from Patagonia ? "

The term *Slavonic* is generally applied to the Polish, Bohemian, Russian and Hungarian peoples. Of these the national musical style of each is quite individual and distinctive. We shall treat of the pianoforte music of each of these nationalities in succession.

Polish national music, like that of Hungary, is distinguished by its use of augmented intervals and accented weak beats as well as by varying length of phrase and of *tempo*. These common characteristics are partly owing to gipsy influence. Before treating of the music of Chopin, the leading Polish composer, we may mention Collections in which the characteristics of Polish music may be studied. These may be seen in the four-hand melodies, *Ruthéniennes,* and *Op.* 31 and 23 (Aug.) of Noskowski (b. 1848), in the *Schoumkas Ukrainiennes* by Zawadski (Eberle), in Noskowski's *Cracoviennes* (K.) and in Statkowski's *Polonica Album* (Obereks, Krakowiaks, Mazurkas) (R. and E.) ; also in the twelve Slavish folk melodies by E. I. Wolf (S.D.) and in the *Slavonic Dances* (Laudy) of Zawadski. It should be noted that the Polish Mazurka and Polonaise have become common property of all nations.

CHAPTER II

" In every piece we find, in his own refined hand, written on pearls:
' This is by Frederic Chopin.' "—*Schumann.*

THE position of Poland, as a kingdom bordered on all sides by
more powerful neighbours, favoured, in days of old, the
prevalence of internecine wars and strife. This state of affairs
did not encourage the best interests of the art. The cause of
music, however, improved very much in the reigns of the
Kings of Saxony (1697–1763) as Kings of Poland, and Polish
music began to be much heard. The national opera—a sign
of national interest in music, as in the similar case of Bohemia—
was inaugurated in 1778, and from that time, though reared in
times of terror and military oppression, the cause of Polish
music went forward.

Frederic Chopin, the son of Nicolas Chopin—a teacher of the
French language and himself of partial French extraction—was
born near Warsaw in 1810.

Frederic's mother was a Polish lady, Justina Kryzanowska.
Frederic's father having established a school in Warsaw which
was patronized by the Polish nobility, young Frederic, as a
prodigy, was made much of by his protégés.

At the age of eight, as a pupil of Elsner and Zwyny, young
Chopin made his début in the aristocratic salons of Warsaw.
He entered the Warsaw Lyceum when fourteen, but meanwhile
did not forget his composition and practice. At this time
he had the honour of extemporizing before the Emperor
Alexander and of seeing his *Op.* 1 (1825), a *Rondo in C minor*,
in all the glory of print. Leaving the Lyceum in 1827, he had,
by the autumn, already written *Three Polonaises, Op.* 7 in
individual style, the 1st *Nocturne*, showing the simple lyrical
style of Field, the interesting but somewhat immature *Sonatas*,
and the *Rondo for Two Pianos.*

By 1830 appeared the *La ci darem Variations* (written five
years before) which Schumann, as critic, hailed with the
exclamation, " Hats off, gentlemen ! A genius ! " Two other
early works were written when eighteen years of age, and are
of special interest—the nationalistic *Fantasia of Polish Airs* and
the *Krakowiak, Op.* 14 with their original " loose-textured,
wide-meshed " and " serpentine " technique. Chopin, meanwhile, had begun his travels. First to Berlin, then to Vienna,
Prague, Dresden, etc., he went, giving concerts and becoming
acquainted with several celebrities, as well as earning the
highest encomiums as a performer, though while in Vienna his
" modest " and " feebleness of tone " was commented on. The
latter he excused by saying, " this is my manner of playing which
pleases the ladies so much." It is interesting to note that at
this time these early Polish works referred to later met with
appreciation and drew forth this side-reference to Polish music :
" There is something in the Slavonic songs which almost never
fails in its effect, the cause of which, however, is difficult to
explain, for it is not only the rhythm and the quick change
from minor to major which produces the charm."

Other important compositions were now written, but the next
principal event in Chopin's life was his arrival in the congenial
sphere of Paris—a city then swarming with Polish refugees—
where he soon made a host of friends, among whom were Liszt,
Berlioz, Heine, Ernst, and others. Kalkbrenner, then at the
height of his fame, as a teacher was applied to for lessons, but
no arrangement was come to.

Chopin's first Concert in Paris took place in the spring of
1832, and he shortly found himself much sought after both as a
virtuoso and as a teacher. In 1835 occurred a memorable visit
to Leipzig, where he met Schumann, Mendelssohn and Clara
Wieck. Schumann thus describes Chopin's playing of his *Etude
in A♭* from the *Op.* 25. " Imagine an æolian harp that had all
the scales and that they were jumbled together by the hands of
an artist into all sorts of fantastic ornaments, but in such a
manner that a deeper fundamental tone and a softly-singing
higher part were always audible, and you have an approximate
idea of his playing."

In 1836 Chopin was introduced to " George Sand," the lady
novelist who has been described on the one hand as a " coarse-
fibred woman of the world," and on the other as " a great soul,

simple and affectionate." Her influence on the tone poet has been much debated. Older than Chopin, she described her affection for him as " une sorte d'affection maternelle," and for ten years she acted as a good angel by encouraging him in work and tending him in times of sickness. In the autumn of 1838 Chopin contracted the disease of consumption after a severe attack of bronchitis and much of his time had to be spent in the warmer South, with visits in the concert season to Paris. Notwithstanding rapidly failing health, he visited England and Scotland in 1848 and 1849, when he was presented to Queen Victoria, and gave concerts from which he returned quite " worn out."

The end was not far off and in October of the latter year he passed away and was buried in the Musicians' Corner of the Père Lachaise Cemetery in Paris—where, sad to relate, his tomb (in common with others) does not seem to be particularly well cared for.

For the proper study of Polish music we must look to the character of the Polish race with its traditions of chivalry, its courage and pride, love of finery and alternate fits of enthusiasm and depression.

Polish folk-song, with its hovering 'twixt major and Dorian mode is distinguished generally by its sense of melancholy, while the dances of its aristocracy favour somewhat oriental pomp and richness of style. It is interesting to note how Chopin, in his music interprets in spirit all these characteristics, together with the melodic and rhythmic peculiarities identified with it. The most characteristic of his compositions in this sense are the Mazurkas and the Polonaises. The Mazurka, as derived from the Krakowiak, exists in several different styles—martial, historical, village, wedding, etc. Reference to the many examples by Chopin will give an idea of the possible variety in this art form—the playful, pathetic, sad, defiant and chivalrous emotions are all represented. The usual rhythm is

The Polonaises also vary very much in character; the comparatively early work, *Op.* 22, for instance, at which the

Nocturne character of the *Andante Spianato* gives the key to the whole—with the exception of the virtuoso episodes which might have been written for a Concerto. The use of the orchestra with this composition, though scanty, may have suggested the Concerto style of treatment.

There are also the explosive one in *C♯ minor* with the tender and pathetic *meno mosso ;* the one in *E♭ minor*, telling of despair mingled with thunder and lightning ; the martial pomp and conflict of the *A major* and *A♭ major, Op.* 13 ; the latter with its ceaseless energy thundering out the call to arms in the reiterated bass motive.

On the other hand, the *Polonaise Fantasie in A♭, Op.* 61, breathing more of the Fantasia than of the Polonaise, is essentially a lyrical composition—a song of hope. Possibly the finest *Polonaise* is that in *F♯ minor* which mirrors in gorgeous tints the ancient feudal chivalry of Poland. Beginning, as it were, with stately gathering steps, it ushers in the grand ceremonial march past the throne prior to the opening of the Court festivities.

The music, however, soon begins to be expectant of the more sprightly measures to follow, and the result of this, after harking back once more to the theme of the stately procession, now appears in the opening *Mazurka*. At the conclusion of the latter, the stately pompous measure once more comes to the front—this time with renewed energy and emphasis until near the end, when it dies away. Finally, the March Past expires with an explosive *ff* on the last note.

Chopin wrote only one Krakowiak—an early work—and that also required the orchestra. This dance, originated in Cracovia and represents a kind of simplified Polonaise, the rhythm of which runs thus in 2/4 time :—

In this *Krakowiak, Op.* 4, and the *Op.* 13 *Fantasia on Polish Airs for Pianoforte and Orchestra*, the national element is very strong and scarcely as artistically assimilated as in his later works.

The most popular of Chopin's works, the *Waltzes*, are indeed " dance poems "—art forms in which the sport of the dance has been blended with poetry and romance.

We may single out the one in *A minor*, Chopin's own favourite, the popular one *in Db*—a whirling cloud of butterflies, the tender despairing *C♯ minor*, the quaintly simple *B minor*, the pathetic and meditative *F minor*, the cheerful one *in Ab* (*Op.* 64, No. 3), and the songlike, conflicting *Valse à deux temps;* the remainder of those best known being of the brilliant type.

Of the universally favourite *Studies*—beautiful from an æsthetic and indispensable from a technical point of view—it were difficult to speak too enthusiastically (*see* Chapter XVI).

The *Scherzos* of Chopin stand by themselves, as do those of Beethoven and Mendelssohn.

If Beethoven's *Scherzos* express spirit and true humour, and Mendelssohn's depict a world of fairies and sprites, those of Chopin curiously suggest a contradiction (since *Scherzo* implies playfulness) and embody passion, caprice and melancholy. For instance, we note the stormy music of the *Eb minor*, the ironic *B minor*—or " life tragedy," as it has been called, the dramatic *C♯ minor*, and the elegant and capricious *E major*.

The *Preludes* of Chopin are now so esteemed that one or more of them is rarely absent from the virtuoso's programme.

They have been curiously described by Schumann as " Sketches, commencements of Studies or, if you will, Ruins, single eagle wings all mixed together," and as containing " morbid, feverish, repellent matter." George Sand accounts for this *minor* element by stating her belief that they were composed during the depressing period of his illness and retreat to one of the cells of the monastery of Valdemosa, while Prof. Niecks says they remind him of an artist's portfolio filled with drawings in all stages of advancement—finished and unfinished.

If, however, one makes an analysis of the collection, it is possible to find some evidences of design on the part of the composer. We find (1) that the 24 *Preludes* represent all the keys in succession, each major being followed—not by its tonic minor, as in Bach's *Forty-Eight*—but by its relative minor key.

(2) (*a*) That each *Prelude* has a definite *technical* aim ; (*b*) that none overlaps in this respect or is redundant ; (*c*) that the length of each *Prelude*, considering the size of the technical figure, is a fairly average one.

(3) That they are, to a certain extent, examples of the bygone custom of preluding before a certain composition.

(4) That the stated element of morbidity is somewhat

apocryphal—there are two rather gloomy items, those in *A minor* and *E♭ minor*, and the key of the latter would suggest some such tone-colour.   Very few of the others are pathetic or sad, though it would be somewhat strange if, out of twelve Preludes in minor keys, some were not so.   Two favourites of the Series are : the one *in D♭*, with its " heaven-sent " melody, and the " thunder-riven vision," as it has been termed, of the one in *B♭ minor*.

As a whole they are full of technical interest.   There is the left-hand 'cello melody of No. 6 ; No. 15 exemplifies the difficult art of bringing out a two-part song against repeated notes ; interlacing of hands is shown in No. 17 ; the two-part left-hand obbligato against the right-hand melody in No. 21, and so on.

Both from a poetical and technical point of view the *Preludes* are most valuable.   Though in miniature form, their artistic merit is such that they deserve the closest study.

The unique *Impromptus* are freer in style.   The well-known 1st in *A♭* interprets its name in a natural manner ; it sounds really like an improvisation.

The *F♯ major* is in similar vein, opening with a two-part *Rêverie*, or crooning *Lullaby* ; then martial music approaches and the knight rides away leaving his lady to sing the lullaby in a sadder key (F major).   Soon, however, the original key returns, and brighter hopes and gay visions are expressed by a lovely variation of the original melody.

The *G♭ Impromptu*—which, by the way, requires the *main désossée* of a Thalberg—interprets the languorous gambolling of a violin and 'cello on a hot summer's day, interrupted here and there by strains of a Polish chant from a neighbouring church.   The 'cello solo, in the Trio, is very attractive.

Finally, there is the beautiful, emotional *Fantasie-Impromptu* —one of Chopin's posthumous works—a treasure which one would not willingly lose.

The *Fantasia in F minor, Op*. 49, is one of the very finest works of Chopin.   It reminds one of an elegy on the death of a hero, including memories of the conflict, strains in honour of the hero, and a recurring *requiescat in pace*.   The *Fantasia*, far from being structureless, displays features of recapitulation and transposition in tonic and related keys of secondary themes.

The *Nocturnes*, next to the *Valses*, are perhaps the most popular of Chopin's works.   The early *Op*. 9, No. 3, inspired by

Field, the 2nd *Op*. 55, the 1st of *Op*. 62 and the *Op*. 22 are not equal to his better work ; but there is much that is fine, including the one *in G* (a duet by song-birds) ; the *C minor Op*. 48, No. 1, in which we hear a lament, patriot's hymn, and again the conflict ; and the one in *E major*, reminding us of a violin solo, with imitation and a meditative dialogue in the bass.

Of the *Rondos*, the *Op*. 1 and 5 are early, immature works ; the *Op*. 16 is a weak imitation of Weber and may be classed with those posthumous works which, for the better reputation of the composer, should have been kept back and not published.

The *Ballades* are held by some to be the finest of Chopin's works.

In the first we can imagine a quaint old legend in which the moving phases are interpreted by dramatic changes of key and the *ff* climaxes are a joyous song of triumph.   No. 2 is a quaint pastoral romance interspersed with strange unearthly episodes. No. 3 is a happy and joyous love-song with a Schumannesque fervour about it.   No. 4 has the true legendary atmosphere and is consistently developed ; it offers little contrasted episode, but the pastoral effect is thereby enhanced, while the little touches of imitation, after the manner of Schumann, are noteworthy.   The fresh and vigorous *Allegro de Concert, Op*. 46, bears every sign of being composed at an early period ; probably it was revised before being published in 1841.

Much of it is in orchestral style, and shows the influence of Field, Hummel and Weber ; and, from various accounts, it was probably intended as part of a Concerto.

Quite a contrast to the above is the languorous *Barcarolle*, which we may imagine to be a love-song on a summer eve, while we are always sensible of the gentle rocking of the gondola in ever-swaying movement.   The *Berceuse* is akin to the *Barcarolle*, with its unvarying and undulating soothing burden, upon which is constructed the lovely duet theme, and which is charmingly presented in varied form later on.   Both partake somewhat of the character of Nocturnes.

The youthful *Bolero*, in which the introduction shows something of national colour, is unequal and patchy in style.

The A♭ section would appear to be inspired by Field.   The *Tarantelle* does not display much local colour but is spirited in style and effective.   It requires great clarity of execution.

We must now refer to Chopin's *Concerto* (*see also* Part III,

Chapter XXII). Chopin did not excel in the Sonata form, but his *Concertos*, which are in the style of Hummel, are better worked out, though the necessary scoring for the orchestra was not a strong point of his. The virtuoso element evidently appealed to Chopin, but it is in the beautiful lyrical portions that he is most successful.

As regards Chopin's technique, there is no doubt that he was much influenced by Bach. Madame Streicher speaks of his playing to her fourteen *Preludes* and *Fugues* by Bach from memory, and he avowed that he always practised Bach before appearing in public. Chopin was practically the founder of modern pianoforte technique. Liszt adorned it and added fripperies. Schumann and Rubinstein borrowed from him, while the Russian School is practically built on his style of technical figuration.

When the aide-de-camp of King Louis Philippe asked Chopin why he did not compose an opera, he modestly replied, " Ah, M. le Comte, let me compose piano music ; it's all I know how to do." Chopin's mastery of this branch of the art was apparently not sufficient, however, for the virtuoso Tausig, who must needs add fireworks to the piano part of the *E minor Concerto*—chromatic scales being put into doubled passages and interlocking octaves introduced for single notes !

As a teacher (most of his pupils were amateurs) Chopin showed much irritation of manner. He always insisted on suppleness of hand and easiness of position, with special attention to five-finger work on the black keys, a singing tone, a supple wrist for octave work and generally keeping the elbow low. His originality in fingering involving the frequent use of the thumb on the black keys was the outcome of the unique technical style of his compositions.

Liszt explains the *tempo rubato*, so noted a feature in the interpretation of Chopin's works, thus: " Look at these trees, the wind plays in the leaves, stirs up life among them, but the tree remains the same." The meaning of this is more apparent in Chopin's own *dictum* that the rubato should be generally confined to the melodic part or right hand. He is quoted as having said: " Let your left hand be your conductor and always keep time."

In personal appearance Chopin was refined and apparently of delicate constitution. A finely-cut face, high forehead and thin lips were characteristic features. He was, it appears, somewhat difficult of access to brother artists, owing, no doubt, to reserve and shyness, since, according to Liszt, he was most sociable, especially in the Salons, where he willingly yielded to the little stratagems to which the fashionable ladies of the day had recourse in order to get him to play to them.

Chopin, apart from his inauguration of modern pianoforte technique, and that delightful part of it directly associated with his name, is to us the pioneer of patriotism in music, that noblest of all phases of the noblest of arts. From this standpoint alone his name should endure ; and as long as the beautiful in art stands out pre-eminent, so long will his works remain as a model for the cult of nationalism in music allied to the superlatively beautiful.

THE POLISH SCHOOL

The leading Polish composer of the present day is Xaver Scharwenka (b. 1850), who is resident in Berlin and, apart from nationality, one of the most distinguished composers of pianoforte music. His works are characterized by that dignity and nobility of style, tinged with romantic sadness, which seems to be inherent in Polish composers. They are replete with natural and often inspired melody, virile harmony and a strong sense of rhythm. His *Theme and Variations* (Aug.) closely approaches Mendelssohn's *Variations Sérieuses* as one of the most masterly examples of this form. His *Polish Dances* (Aug.) especially Nos. 1, 10 and 19 are famous, as are also the *Four Mazurkas, Polonaise in C♯ minor, Tarantella* (No. 1), *Two Minuets, Op.* 49 (No. 1). We might mention also the massive and brilliant *Minuet, Op.* 18 (Aug.), the popular *Valse Caprice, Op.* 31 and *Valse Impromptu, Op.* 30 (P. and M.), the serious *Noveletten* and four-movement *Romanze* (P. and M.) and the attractive and characteristic four-hand works such as *Nordisches* (Simon)— founded on Northern folk-melodies, *Pictures from the South* (Aug.), and the *Op.* 24 (P. and M.), the *Sonata, Op.* 6 and *Ballade, Op.* 8, which are worthy of attention.

The works of his brother Philip Scharwenka (b. 1847) are more cosmopolitan in tone, excelling in the light rhythmical tuneful style, as, for instance, in the attractive 2nd and 3rd *Dance Caprice, Op.* 66, the *Dance Impromptu* and *Scherzino, Op.* 67,

and the 2nd and 3rd *Book of the Duets, Polnische Tanzweisen,*
Op. 38 (P. and M.).   The interesting *Op.* 36, *Bk.* I and *Op.* 12,
are attractive and in characteristic style.

Jos. Wieniawski, the virtuoso pianist (b. 1837), trained in
Paris, and pupil of Liszt) is known for his fine *Ballade, Op.* 31
(Cz.), mingling fire with melancholy, dignity with virtuosity of
style.   His *Barcarolle* (Cz.) is remarkable for its characteristic
chromatic harmony, while the original *Impromptu* (Senff)
virtuoso *Polonaises, Op.* 13 (Katto), *Op.* 27 (K.) and the
Mazurkas (Katto) are worthy of note.

Maurice Moskowski (b. 1854 in Breslau and educated in
Germany) is a leading composer.   He became known through
his tuneful Duet *Spanish Dances, Op.* 12 (Simon) and *Serenata,*
Op. 15.   Cosmopolitan as he is in style, it is through his gift of
melody and a sense of the *characteristic* element that he has
become popular.   Dignified, elegant, always technically effective,
he nevertheless is but rarely inspired.   The most distinctive of
his works may be said to be *Op.* 37 and 41, and the *Duets, Op.* 43,
55, 65 (Peters), *Op.* 38 (No. 1) (Bos.) and *Op.* 23 (Aug.).   From
the point of view of the budding virtuoso the *Op.* 34 and 36
(3, 4, 6), *Op.* 73 (3) (Bos.), *Op.* 32 (3) (B. and B.), *Op.* 27 (1)
(Aug.), and *Op.* 50 (3) are interesting and useful.

An original and gifted composer is Stojowski (b. 1870) (Pupil
of Zelenski and Paderewski), who is settled in New York.   His
works are distinctly Polish in character, piquant, fresh and
interesting.   The *Danses Humoresques* (Aug.) make striking use
of modern harmonic resources.   His *Mazurkas, Op.* 8 (No. 2)
(Scht.), No. 3 of the *Op.* 24 (Peters), *Op.* 30 (No. 3) (A.P.S.),
and the striking *Concerto* deserve notice.

The *Études* and *Concertos* (Scht.) of Jules Zarembski, a
Russian Pole (b. 1854, pupil of Liszt) are full of characteristic
and bizarre effects.   His *Polish Suite, Op.* 16 [*Polonaise, Dumka*
(*Complainte*) *Mazurka, Cracovienne* and *Kujawiak*] has also
the national element strongly depicted.

The *Duet Rêverie* and *Passion* and *Mazurkas, Op.* 4 (Scht.)
are interesting, as well as the *Solo Polonaise, Op.* 6 (Simon),
Mazurka de Concert (Scht.) and the *Duet Danses Galiciennes*
(Simon).

An indefinable charm and melancholy pervades the beautiful
and well-written *Mazurka, Op.* 20 (No. 2), *Serenade, Op.* 24 and
the *Op.* 34 (No. 5) (B. and B.) of A. Zarzycki (b. 1831 in

Austrian Poland), his *Op.* 18 and 19 and *Op.* 6 being also noteworthy.

The works of Th. Leschetitzki (b. 1830 in Austrian Poland and pupil of Czerny) are not particularly national in style, but they are technically effective. The *Souvenirs d'Italie* (B. and B.) (Nos. 1, 4 and 5) are interesting and educationally valuable from the virtuoso standpoint. Nos. 4, 6 and 9 of the *Contes de Jeunesse* (B. and B.) and the *Étude Caprice, Op.* 20 are also commendable.

Adolf Barjanski, in his nationalistic *Op.* 7 and 11 *Sonatas* (B. and H.) lacks development but shows good harmonic and *cantabile* effects. Jos. Wielhorski is best in a very pretty original Nocturne-like 3rd *Impromptu* (*Op.* 14) (B. and H.) with Chopinesque technique.

The fresh and individual *Op.* 13 *Polonaise* and *Krakowiak* of St. Niewiadomski, the virtuoso *Prelude, Papillon* and *Variations* (Fr.) of M. Rosenthal, the *Cracovienne, Op.* 14, No. 6 and *Concerto* (B. and B.) of Paderewski, as well as the national dances of Noskowski, *Variations* by Mandicewski (Un. Ed.) and *Mazurka, Op.* 33 (No. 1) (K.) by Czerwenski are interesting.

Jean Nicodé and Josef Hoffmann, whose compositions are noted elsewhere, are also of Polish nationality.

Last but not least should be mentioned Al. von Fielitz (b. 1860 at Leipzig), a Russian Pole by descent, a graceful writer whose charming and delicate *Nocturne, Op.* 5 (Rap.), *Op.* 22, No. 1 (Hus.), Character Pieces, *Children of the South* and *Preludes, Fantasia, Op.* 27 and better-class Salon Pieces, *Op.* 48 and 49 (B. and H.), are worthy of distinction.

CHAPTER III

OF all national music that of Hungary may be said to be the most individual.

This individuality arises doubtless from the Oriental origin of the Huns or Magyars, descended, as they are, from the Turanian race, which is closely allied to the people of Persia.

It is little more than three centuries ago that the original Magyar music began to be known generally, and at that time it is said to have been devoid of the *fioritura* or ornamental embroidery since added to it by the gipsies (also of Oriental origin) who appeared in Hungary about that time.

It is the pride of the Magyar, who abandoned his national art to the lawless but technically clever gipsy dependents, that is responsible for the extraordinary individuality of the present-day music of the Magyar. The gipsy violinists of Hungary play the Magyar folk-songs and patriotic melodies from memory to the improvised and highly ornamental accompaniment of the *zimbalon* (a kind of dulcimer, four octaves in compass), making their appeal to the sympathies of their patrons with strenuous zeal and frenetic excitement.

Magyar music may be classified into (1) the Folk-Songs; (2) National Dances; (3) the *Hallgatok* (" to listen to ") music— a Rhapsody of both song and dance, and, as such, forming the model for the *Rhapsodies* of Liszt and others. No special form is used in the latter.

The characteristic of Magyar music, with its abrupt rhythms and bold changes of key, are exemplified in the *Csardas*, a Dance form which is usually ushered in by a sad and pathetic *Lassan* movement succeeded by, or alternating with, the wild impassioned *Friska*. It may be said that the national Hungarian motto, " Weepingly Rejoices the Magyar," interprets, in a manner, the alternate pathetic and fiery movements so characteristic of its music.

241

The strange harmonic features of Magyar music are occasioned by the use of the sharpened 4th in addition to the notes of the harmonic minor scale. The rhythmical features lie in the periods of varying length, in the practically invariable 2/4 or 4/4 time in which it is written, and the frequent occurrence of syncopation, *i.e.*, of strong accents placed on naturally weak beats, as in the following *Example* :

Regarding Hungarian music in general*, the following are some who have done much to give it prominence in the art world. Cornelius Abranyi (1822–1903), pupil of Kalkbrenner and Chopin. As essayist, critic and historian, Abranyi did much to further the national art. His style in composition, however, shows a blend of the Magyar with the prevailing type. His *Rhapsodies*, *Sonata* and four-hand *Palotas Dances* may be mentioned. Charles Agghazy (b. 1855), a pupil of Liszt and Volkman. His numerous piano compositions are very attractive, the poetical pieces being quite national in style. They include the *Soirées Hongroises*, *Fantasiestücke*, *Impromptus*, four-hand *Hungarian Suite* and *Poems*. Geza Allaga (b. 1841) has written much for the zimbalon, also *Rhapsodies* and *Salon Pieces* for the piano. Stephen Bartalus (b. 1821), critic and historian of Magyar music, *Variations for Piano*. Ed. Bartay (1825–91) wrote Salon and orchestral music. Béla Bártók, rising composer of rhapsodies, a very characteristic *Rhapsodie for Orchestra and Piano* (Roz.), etc. Alex. Bertha (b. 1843) (lives in Paris), National Dances and Rhapsodies. Kálmàn Chován (b. 1852), Head of Training School of Music of Vienna ; well-written and attractive Pieces in national and poetic style. Francis Gaal (b. 1860), somewhat cosmopolitan *Rhapsodies* and poetical works. Henri Gobbi (b. 1842), shows the influence of Liszt in his Transcriptions of classic works for two pianos, the *Hungarian Suites* and smaller pieces. Gyula Kaldy (1838–1901), editor of Collections of National Music. Gyula J. Major (b. 1859), a leading composer, pupil of Erkel and Volkmann ; known for

* Information for this section was expressly supplied by the Principal of the Royal Academy of Music, Budapest.

his striking *Concerto*, *Magyar Sonata*, *Rhapsodies*, etc. Michel Mosonyi (1814–70), *Rhapsodies* and *Transcriptions*. Anthony Liposs (b. 1839), miscellaneous Pieces in national style. Imre Szekely (1823–87), eminent pianist, lived some years in London ; effective *Rhapsodies* (40), *Preludes* and *Fugues* and *Salon Music*. A. Szendy (b. 1863), distinguished performer, pupil of Liszt ; *Sonatas* and *Rhapsodies*. Charles Thern (1817–86), artistic romantic pieces and *Rhapsodies*. L. Zimay (1833–1900), characteristic pieces in national style. Smaller Pieces by Lamzi (b. 1861). The names of Ed. Mihalovich (b. 1865), Head of the R.A.M. at Budapest, and of Ed. Farkas and V. Herzfeld should also be mentioned.

Hungarian Music in general may be divided into :—

(1) " Original " *Hungarian Dances* and *Airs*.

(2) Compositions (*Rhapsodies*, *Paraphrases*, *Fantasias*, etc.) " built upon " Magyar Themes.

(3) Works showing " influence of " Hungarian style.

(4) Works in " Cosmopolitan " style by Hungarian composers.

(1) Treating of the original Folk-songs and Dances, we may mention the Historical Collection made by Julius (Gyula) Kaldy (Roz.) ranging from 1672 to 1838 and comprising the compositions of Czinka, Lavotta, Bihari, Czermak, Boka, Markus Rozsavolgyi and Szerdahelyi. Another, edited by Ede Bartay (Roz.) contains compositions by Gyorgy, Bihari, Czermak, Labotta, and Rozsavolgyi. Then there is also the well-known Collection by Keler Béla (André, Roz.) ; Béla himself having written many tuneful pieces in cosmopolitan style.

We may also mention Magy Zoltan's collection of *Czardas*, mostly original (Roz.) ; the *Exhibition Album of* 1885 (Roz.), containing works of various classes ; the popular arrangement by Brahms for four hands (and later for two), of well-known *Hungarian Dances* (Simrock), and the Collection by Schwalm (St.) for two and four hands. The *Carpathian Dances* (Augener) from the border range 'twixt Austrian Poland and Hungary show little of the real Hungarian element, while the *Ungarische Weisen* (S. and H.) contain an example apparently taken from the Styrian border.

(2) Of compositions built on Hungarian Airs we may particularize a very florid and effective 1st *Fantasia, Op.* 25, the 7th *Ábránd* or *Rhapsody* and the simpler *Bucsuhangok* by E. Szekely; the *Fantasie Hongroise* by Polonyi, *Op.* 14; the brilliant *Rhapsody, Op.* 28 by L. Zimay, and a short *Rhapsody* by Ig. Mihaly—a good specimen of the florid ornamentation used. Also the *Magyar Serenade* by G. Allega and *A Merengo* by J. Kirch. Carl Thern has a *Fantasie* (in Variation form), *Op.* 68, on two Hungarian Songs and an artistic and interesting *Rhapsody, Hegy Algah* (all Roz.). The well-written *Mélodies Tziganes* of Ed. Potzes (Kt.) show the zimbalon effects.

The *Op.* 11 of C. Agghazy gives very able and interesting presentations of the *Palotas* (Court Dance), *Tobozzo* and *Munkácsy Nota* Dances (Kn.); and the *Studies* in Hungarian style of M. Mosonyi give a good idea of the genuine gipsy *fioritura* (Roz.). The *Rhapsodies Hongroises* (Schott) of F. Korbay are very characteristic and in true rhapsodic style— full of varying rhythms, fitful changes of tempo and style, as are also the four *Morceaux* of Béla Bártók (Brd.). The artistic *Kleine Rhapsodien* and *Phantasiestücke* (Kn.) of C. Agghazy likewise give much of the jingle of the dulcimer mingled with the flourish of the violin; while of the short characteristic *Hungarian Intermezzi* and *Improvisations* of Vavrinecz (J.S.), No. 4 of the former shows the extraordinary harmonic and melodic effects which are possible in the Hungarian mode.

(3) Of works showing *Hungarian influence* we have the harmonically attractive and well-written *In den Csardas* for four hands and the poetical *Hungarian Pictures, Op.* 5 (Doblinger) by Kálmán Chován.

Goldmark's *Magyar Fantasia in B* and the *Op.* 12 (Duet) are developed on conventional lines, while the well-written *Hateredeti*, a series of Tone Poems by K. Abranyi, show a blend of Magyar and cosmopolitan styles. A series of Tone Poems by Gobbi, a *Zenek Ctemeny* by Al. Juhaz, *Ellentetek* by Major, *Vigasztalo Hosi alagya* by Agghazzi and *Sello* by Atilla Horvath are developed from more or less conventional Themes.

(4) Of works by Magyar composers in *Cosmopolitan style*, we may mention the freshly-written four-handed *Bagatelles* and *Bolcsodal* by Fr. Gaal, as well as his *Sixth Rhapsody*, from which we miss the *tremolo* passages, repeated notes and florid ornamentation of the true Magyar Rhapsody. Also there are the so-

called *Hungarian Sketches* of Volkmann, who settled in Hungary, and the *Pastorale, Op.* 17, of Chován, which shows effective and pleasing imitation. The following also are Hungarian composers whose compositions in the prevailing Germanic style may be touched upon. The ultra modern virtuoso Dohnanyi (b. 1877) and Szanto, both write in the elaborated modern style. A masterly *Passacaglia* (Db.), a characteristic *Concerto* and a well-written *Suite* in the ancient style (Simrock) by the former, and a rhapsodical but suggestive *Dramatic Elegy* (Kn.) by the latter deserve attention. Carl Goldmark (b. 1832) has achieved distinction by his successful *Concerto, Characteristic Pieces* and *Four-Hand Op.* 12. In attractive romantic style we have the well-known *Staccato Caprice* of Max Vogrich (b. 1852) ; settled in New York), together with his meritorious *Romancero* and *Valse Brillante* (Sr.), also the useful *Studies* of Joseffy (b. 1853) and Ed. Wolff (1816–80). The agreeable educational *Salon* (*Op.* 34 (1) (B.S.), *Op.* 60 (Brd.), *Op.* 63 (2) (Aug.) of Geza Horvath and *Pieces* of Louis Toth (Brd.) are commendable, while we may mention the representative *Ballade* of Adler (Sf.), *Nocturnes* by C. Abranyi (Kn.), the *Op.* 20 (Hf.) of Attila Horvath, the pleasant Chopinesque *Op.* 15 and 19 (By.) of Stephany, the attractive *Habanera* (Ld.) of Ketten, the refined and fresh *Valse Op.* 9 (2), *Mazurka, Op.* 12 (Aug.), and original *Impromptus* and *Nocturnes* of Jámbor (Aug.) and an impressionist *Op.* 7 of Rubin Goldmark (Dt.).

We have left the *Rhapsodies* of Liszt, as the most prominent of all Hungarian music, till the last. These effective compositions present various styles of treatment. As a rule a fragment of a Theme—generally a traditional one—is worked up as an introduction to the *Lassan* or slow movement. The latter is sometimes treated in Sequence, Imitation or Variation form with the addition of short original connecting Themes. The 3rd *Rhapsody* is, perhaps, the simplest in form and here the melody appears twice (each time both in Bass and Treble), followed by ornamental Fantasia work founded on simple form, containing repeated notes. The most popular is doubtless the *Second*, the finest, perhaps, the *Twelfth*. In both of these, and in some others, we find the imitation of the *Figura* or Trio, which appears in the Collections of *Csardas*, a passage written generally in the style of an Interlude and appearing between the *Lassan* and the *Friska*. This *Figura* is usually built in somewhat commonplace, improvisatory style, and mostly on the chord of the dominant 7th. In the *2nd Rhapsody* this begins after the *Friska* with " *Tempo giusto vivace,*" and from this *quasi-Figura* is developed the rest of the *Rhapsody*. In the *12th Rhapsody* four Themes are used, and after the appearance of the fourth Theme below the trill on the A♭, various fragments are combined to make up the *Figura* work. Finally, the *Allegro Zingaresca* appears at the close, with magical effect in the top octave.

In all the *Rhapsodies*, more or less, will be found the tinkling zimbalon or *quasi-campanella* dulcimer effects embodied in the rapid, repeated notes, passages played by alternate and inter-locking hands, together with the rapid skips and trills that became such a feature, not only of the *Rhapsodies* but of Liszt's most popular Transcriptions and original works. In short, much of the effectiveness of the new *technique*, as inspired by Liszt, must have been suggested by the attempts to reproduce the music of the Magyar.

Other technical features appearing are the cataracts of octaves in the bass ; showers of pearly Cadenzas in the treble and other highly pianistic devices.

It should be mentioned that portions of the *Rhapsodies* were originally brought out as *Hungarian Melodies*. Ten sets of these, entitled *Mélodies Hongroises*, date from 1839 to 1847 ; the 15 *Rhapsodies* appeared some six years later. We should not forget the interesting Transcriptions of Hungarian Songs appearing in Liszt's *Bilder aus Ungarn*.

Finally, it must be remembered that Hungarian music has had some influence on the Great Masters, as may be seen in the *Gipsy Rondo* of Haydn and in some of his Symphonies, in Brahms, and, above all, in Schubert's Duet works and the *Divertissement à la Hongroise, Op.* 54, a version of which was produced and performed *con amore* by Liszt in public. Hungarian influence is also prominent in works by Heller and many other composers.

CHAPTER IV

MUSIC IN BOHEMIA

THE appearance of Bohemia upon the musical horizon of Europe seems to date from the connection of Mozart in 1787, with its art centre, Prague, where he wrote *Don Giovanni* for its Opera House. The formation of the present National School of Composers did not commence until some sixty years later, when Smêtana began writing National Opera and Pianoforte works in the National style.

Previous to this, most works of artistic pretensions by Bohemian composers had been in the prevailing Germanic style. The individuality of the native Czech had, however, been kept alive from the earliest times by means of Czech literature, Folk-Song and National Dances. Prior to the time of John Huss the reformer, the Latin Church, together with prevailing French, German and Italian influence at Court, had been antagonistic to the nature of Folk-Song.

The reformation of 1402 brought about the regeneration of National Song and Church Music. The Guild of Meister-singers, the Church Society of *Literati*, the Collegium Musicum founded in 1616, the Court Orchestras and the establishment of National Opera in Prague in 1723 all helped in the development of the art.

The early composers, Benda (died 1795), Kotzeluch (1752–1818), and Gryowetz (1763–1850), who wrote fashionable pianoforte works of the period, are now forgotten ; but Dussek (1761–1812) the composer and pianist (*see* Part II, Chapter V) and Czerny the pedagogue, may be mentioned as instances of artists connected with the early period of Bohemian pianoforte music.

The purely national or Pan-Slavic movement in Bohemia began through the Opera. In 1807 opera in Italian was abolished and in 1862 the Bohemian Theatre was opened. Operas by the native composers Sebor, Karel Bendl, and Rozkoszny led the way for the appearance of Fredk. Smêtana (1824–84), the " Father of the Bohemian School."

As a pupil of Liszt, Smêtana began as a composer of Symphonic poems for orchestra and works for piano, and it was not until after 1866 that he initiated the series of operas in the National style which culminated in European recognition of the Bohemian School. As with Chopin and Liszt, so with Smêtana, the initiation of the National style began with works for the pianoforte.

Regarding the Bohemian style, it may be said that it has not the rhythmic or melodic interest of Hungarian music. Its principal features are a kind of breezy, untrammelled vigour, with, in some cases, alternating varieties of tempo.

In *Volkslieder* in the minor key we find strongly-marked rhythm and decisive character, but those in the major are in simple rhythm and pleasing tuneful style. No doubt the Slavonic, German and Gipsy elements are all represented in the music of the Czechs.

Of the many National Dances we have the well-known *Polka* [*pulka*=half(step)] in 2/4 time, dating from about 1830, the *Furiant*, a quick dance with sharp accents and alternating time, the *beseda dudik, hulan, trinozka, sedlak*, etc. Specimens of these dance forms were written by Dvořák, Smêtana and others. [*See* Smêtana, *Bohemian Dances* (Urbanek) and Malat, *Forty Tcheques Melodies* (Urbanek)].

The *Dumka*, as used by Dvořák, is a kind of *Rêverie* or *Élégie* and is probably related to the *Douma*—a narrative song form from the Ukraine district.

Smêtana's best work is in his Symphonic Poems and Operas. His piano works, however, though less interesting, show the vigour and masculinity of the National style, his melodies being mostly set in abrupt two-bar sections. Smêtana's pianoforte style is somewhat difficult and not always grateful to the performer. Of his characteristic pieces, *Op.* 1, No. 3 and 6, are the most attractive, and the *Bohemian Dances, Op.* 17 and some of the *Polkas* are worthy of study.

Zdenko Fibich (1850–1900) wrote a good deal of piano music, mostly in short pieces as, for instance, his *Fancies, Impressions* and *Recollections* (*Op.* 41, 44, 47, 57 (Ur.)]. These are original and in National style, but, apart from that, not very interesting, Neither Fibich nor Smêtana, as pioneers of Bohemian music, compare with Dvořák for general interest as far as pianoforte music is concerned.

Like the music of the Magyar, the pianoforte music of the Czech may be divided into (1) that written in direct National style ; (2) that showing influence of the National style ; (3) that which is Cosmopolitan in style.

(1) In these are included National Dances, some works by Dvořák referred to separately (next Chapter), the well-written and interesting *Op. 7* (*Polka* and *Furiant*) of Beda Kridlo, and the *Husitska Rhapsodie, Op.* 29 of Fr. Picka (Ur.), the latter founded on a chorale-like theme.

(2) Those showing influence of the National idiom reach a high level of excellence. Their technique is modern and the harmonic style fresh. In the clavier compositions of Jos. Suk and Oskar Nedbal—both members of the famous Bohemian String Quartet—there is in the Six Pieces of *Op.* 7 of Suk much that is attractive, sympathetic and characteristic. The *Op.* 1, 7 and 8 of Nedbal, who is also a prominent composer of opera, are, except the *Variation on a Theme* by Dvořák, mostly in lighter style. The *Rondo* of Em. Chvála, a composer of Chamber music and eminent critic, is an interesting example of modern nationalistic style in an old form—of, indeed, " new wine in old bottles." The interesting *Poetical Pieces, Op.* 20, with specimens in alternating tempo and 5/4 time ; the powerful Lisztian *Ballade, Op.* 2 by Vitezslav Novak, a leading composer of Chamber music and Songs, as well as the less Nationalistic, but very effective *Impromptu* of the *Op.* 15 of Alois Joranek and the dainty Chopinesque *Four Pieces, Op.* 2 by Hanuse Trnecka, deserve attention (all Ur.).

The works of Ed. Napravnik (b. 1839), who has lived much in Russia, are Slavonic in cast. His *Op.* 61 (1 and 2) (R.) are *educationally* valuable (db. 3rds and alt.· hands). The choral writers, Jos. Nesvera and Jos. Forster, have written some smaller *Pieces*, and a *Tarantelle, Op.* 56 (B.S.), by Charles Wehle (1825–83) and the *Valse, Op.* 44 by Louis Marek (Sl.) deserve mention.

(3) For Bohemian composers who have written in cosmopolitan style, we must go back to the times of Dussek and his contemporaries, Gelnick, Gryowetz and Kotzeluch, who indulged in fashionable trivialities.

The true successor of Dussek was Tomaschek (1774–1850), who wrote in a more serious style. His *Rhapsodies* (Hf.), published in 1812, attracted attention by their native wayward

vigour and are of historical value as a step in the evolution of
the National style. In the virtuoso *L'Inquiétude* (St.) and *Op.* 96
(B.S.) by Alex. Dreyschock, a pupil of Tomaschek, and a
brilliant pianist, who created a sensation by his left-hand solos,
may be discerned a trace of native style. Other pupils of
Tomaschek were Tedesco (1817–82), the " Hannibal of Octaves,"
known for his Bohemian *Op.* 22 and 24 ; and Schulhoff (b. 1825),
also a public performer.

The compositions of the latter became exceedingly popular
for their melodious, elegant and brilliant style. His best works
are the *Bohemian Airs*, the *Op.* 25, *Chanson* and *Polka*, *Op.* 33,
in national style, and the characteristic *Dances*, *Mazurkas*,
Op. 30 and 5, *Styrienne* (Lit.) and *Galop di Bravoura*.

Felix Dreyschock (b. 1860), the nephew of Alex. Dreyschock
is more cosmopolitan and shows something of the elegance of
the French style combined with technical and educational
value, as, for instance, in *Op.* 17, 21, 22, 24 and 37 No. 2 (Fr.)
and *Op.* 25 and 27 (J.). Alfred Grünfeld writes in a similar
but more serious style, his *Op.* 49, 50, 51 (B. and B.), *Op.* 17, 20,
21 (Ch.) being examples.

The Chopin-like *Valses* and *Polonaises* (Hf.) of Johann
Slunicko are attractive and effectively written.

For the rest, we may mention the melodious and elegant
Three Pieces, *Op.* 24 (Db.) and *Op.* 14 (Eu.) of Hansa Cesek ;
the original and attractive *Mazurkas*, *Op.* 15 (R.B.), the artistic
Schilflieder, *Op.* 11 and the useful *Studies* (Sl.) of Hans Seeling
(1828–62) ; Wenzel Plachy's (1785–1858) educational *Rondos*
and *Transcriptions* (Ash.) ; Hans. Schmitt's (b. 1835) *Studies*
and freshly-written *Fantasias*, *Op.* 66 (Db.) ; and the names
of A. F. Becvarosky, F. Z. Chotek (educational), J. Drechsler,
H. Kaan, Kafka (Salon Pieces), Jos. Low (educational),
Proksch (*Concertos*, three pianos), and Bernard Rie (*Études*).

CHAPTER V

ANTONIN DVOŘÁK (1841–1904)

ANTONIN DVOŘÁK (pronounced Dvorshak) was born in 1841 at Mülhausen, a small village near Prague. His father occupied the village inn. As a boy Dvořák was taught singing and the violin by the village schoolmaster; and subsequently, on removing to schools at Zeonitz and Kainnitz, he learnt the organ, piano and something of harmony. After much debate young Dvořák was allowed to prepare for the musical profession, and he entered Prague Organ School at the age of sixteen. In order to eke out his small allowance he joined one of the small local bands as a violinist.

In 1860—after a three-years' course Dvořák graduated at his school and, fortunately for him, became a violin player in the orchestra at the Bohemian Theatre of which Smêtana was the conductor. It was not until eleven years later, in 1873, that an organist's position lifted Dvořák into a more independent position, but, undaunted by adverse circumstances, Dvořák was the whole of this intervening period diligently at work on Symphonies, Chamber music and Piano music. It was in this same year (1873) that he became known as a composer by his patriotic hymn for Chorus and Orchestra, *The Heirs of the White Mountain*. Two years previously he had written his first Opera in the Wagnerian style, which, being rejected, was rewritten in the National style and thereupon accepted. Dvořák's career was now one continual success. Liszt procured him Concert hearings and Brahms got his works published.

His *Slavonic Dances*, written in 1878, became popular in Germany; other works, the *Stabat Mater*, Orchestral and Chamber music closely followed and were successfully produced —some of these making their first appearance in this country. From 1892 to 1895 Dvořák was Director of the New York National Conservatoire, where he made the mistaken effort of attempting through the " New World " Symphony and other works, to found a National American School on purely Negro melodies.

His subsequent life at Prague was devoted to Opera, of which nine were composed, orchestral and other works—strongly imbued with Bohemian and other idioms in the National style. The death of Dvořák in 1904 will be remembered for the general and universal expression of regret that so great a master of all that is best in the music of his country should have passed away.

Dvořák does not seem to have written very much piano music and a good portion of it, inspired, perhaps, by the four-hand Brahms arrangements of Hungarian music, is also laid out for four hands.

We may take the Bohemian National *Furiantes in D* and *F*, *Op*. 42 (B. and B.) and the *Rhapsodies*, *Op*. 45 (Sr.)—as arranged by Kirchner—as reflecting the peculiarities of Bohemian music, with its simplicity of character mostly expressed in Waltz time with occasional irregular (quasi-Gipsy) rhythms.

The *Slavisch Dances* for four hands, *Op*. 46 and 72 are more vigorous, and using more the 2/4 rhythm are interesting as presenting some points of resemblance to Scotch music.

The *Poetische Stimmungsbilder*, *Op*. 85 (Sr.) have no distinguishing feature, but, on the other hand, the duet *Legends*, *Op*. 59 (Sr.) are amongst the best and most characteristic of his works. Dvořák seems to be most original where he can indulge in mystery and is not limited in the interpretative means at his disposal—as, for example, in his well-known *Spectre's Bride*; and hence it is in the mysterious depths of the Bohemian Forests, as in the four-hand *Böhmerwald*, that we meet with his most original and characteristic pianoforte work.

The interesting Sketches, *Silhouetten*, *Op*. 8 (Hf.) are of special interest as showing Dvořák's use of chromatic tonality, *i.e.*, the sudden transition to chromatically related keys and the return to the original tonality.

Of the *Op*. 52 (Hf.) the *Impromptu, Intermezzo and Gigue* are imitations of more or less Classic style, but are not particularly successful ; the *Eclogue*, however, is more characteristic of him.

Dvořák's *Dumka* (*Élégie*), *Op*. 35 (B. and B.) is musicianly, characteristic and National, but not very inspired. The *Suite*, *Op*. 98 (Sr.) is interesting, attractive, musicianly and subtly reminiscent of the technique of Chopin ; rhythmically speaking, it again suggests Scottish music. The *Humoresken, Op*. 101 (Sr.) which are mostly in lyrical form, show also National feeling and Caprice—but alas, no humour. One of the set has become deservedly popular as arranged for the violin, but, strange to say, its features are not those of humour but of delightful grace alternating with truly lyrical fervour. The diatonic *Polonaise for Four Hands* (Aug.), the abrupt *Furiant* of the *Op.* 12 (Aug.), *Minuets*, *Mazurkas* and *Waltzes* also claim attention, as well as the *Scottish Dances*, *Op.* 41 (B. and B.) which, however, are *not* particularly Scottish in style.

The success of Dvořák's compositions may be attributed to (1) the nuances of Bohemian melody; (2) the use of modern harmonies; and (3) the Dance rhythms of the Czechs. New forms of expression of musical ideas were created and their novelty, no less than the sterling genius which evolved highly artistic works out of comparatively crude material, helped to set forth a new individuality in the musical world. With regard to musical form, Dvořák, while not extending its resources, sometimes used the *Dumka* (*Élégie*) for the slow movement, and the *Furiant* for the *Scherzo* in set compositions. As regards technical style, his works are grateful to play, while the varying combination of rhythms and new harmonic modulatory effects always tend to make them interesting and attractive.

CHAPTER VI

RUSSIAN PIANOFORTE MUSIC

As in the case of other European countries, the key to the distinctive national style of Russia lies in the traditional folk-song, aided by the rich heritage of imaginative literature, exemplified in the National Poetry and Folk-Tale.

These folk-songs may be divided into such as Ritual or Mythic songs, Ceremonial, Epic or Historic. Freely metrical and expressive in style, they are sung in harmony and mostly in the minor mode. The Dance-Songs showing Gipsy influence, as in Bohemia and Hungary, are in the major mode. Those of Great Russia are brighter than the poetic ones of Little Russia.

The improvised epic *Doumas* of the Ukraine and somewhat monotonous *Dainos* of Lithuania form another class, while modal or ecclesiastical influence is generally apparent. The National characteristics can be studied in the following interesting Collections for pianoforte: *Russian Folk-Songs and Dances* (Kleinmichel) (B.S.), showing the characteristic three-bar sections; Wilm's arrangement of *Russian Folk-Songs*, and Wihtol's Transcriptions of *Lettish Melodies* (Blf.). Granville Bantock has utilized Russian Themes in his *Russian Scenes* (Bos.).

Generally speaking, their principal characteristics may be said to lie in the peculiar rhythm, original melody, ornamental embroideries, and strange cadences showing modal influence.

The prevailing minor key and a rugged kind of gloom seems to dominate much Russian music, and this no doubt accounts for much of the so-called pessimism of the Russian School.

Apart from National Song and Dance, music in Russia seems to have been imported up to the time of Glinka (1804–57), who studied with Field in St. Petersburg and also in Berlin. Glinka wrote National Operas in which the National Folk-Song appears as well as in his Symphonies and Chamber music.

His pianoforte works, while showing touches, both harmonic and melodious, of the Slav temperament, are not quite in

National style. His modern and artistically attractive *Barcarolle*, *Tarantella* and *Souvenir d'un Mazurka* have something of the artistic meditative character of his teacher, Field.

Dargomisky and Seroff are classified as representing the transition from Glinka to the Modern School. Dargomisky (1813–69) wrote Operas and Orchestral works and a three-hand *Tarantelle Slave for Piano*. Seroff (1820–71) was chiefly an Opera composer.

The originator of the Modern Russian School is Mili Balakirew, who, with César Cui, Modest Moussorgsky, Alexander Borodin, and Rimsky-Korsakow set himself to establish it on the basis of Russian folk-song.

Balakirew (b. 1836) first gained fame as a pianist and later as a composer—chiefly of Songs and Pianoforte works. His individuality is seen in the quaint, murmuring, chromatic under-current of sweet discontent in his charming *Dumka* (complaint) (Zim), *1st Nocturne* (St.) and *Idylle-Étude* (Bos.).

César Cui, the historian of Russian music, says, with some show of reason, that his works are " distinguished by broad and limpid melody and elegance of accompaniment, also by passion and *abandon*."

His *harmonies* and *technique* are founded on Liszt and Chopin, and the virtuoso element is considerable, whether in the poetical Pieces or in the more technical *Toccata*, the *3rd Scherzo* and *Valse di Bravura* (Zim), the artistic, somewhat Lisztian *Transcriptions*, *L'Alouette* on a Glinka Theme (Eu. or St.), or the *Fantasia* on *A Life for the Czar* (Zm.). The *Humoresque Tyrolienne* and *Oriental Fantasia Islamey* may be mentioned, the latter for its true descriptive colouring.

N. Rimsky-Korsakow (b. 1844) is an admiral by profession. In musical art he is chiefly a symphonist after the highly-coloured style of Berlioz. His works are distinguished by good taste and self-restraint combined with sonority of style and the use of National idiom and Folk-Song melody.

His pianoforte *Concerto* is founded on the characteristic theme :—

from which its continuous movements are developed.

The work is pervaded by National feeling and is somewhat ornamental in style, the technique and development being after the manner of Liszt.

In the pianoforte *Op.* 11 of the four Pieces showing successively Chopin, Schumann, Henselt and Chopin as models, the *Second* is attractive and the best ; the Variations on the notes B, A, C, H show skill but, like other similar compositions, are pointless.

A. Borodin (1834–87), apart from his share in the National movement, is known mostly for his Songs, Symphonies and Chamber music. His best pianoforte work, the *Petite Suite* (Bos.), though poetical in feeling, lacks inspiration.

Moussorgsky (1839–81) excels in the national style. His characteristic vigour and emotional realism are seen to some extent in his *Exposition Tableaux* (Bl.) and in the *Kinderscherz* and *Intermezzo* (Bl.), but otherwise he has no distinctive message.

César Cui (b. 1835) is of partial French descent and is by profession a military engineer. Cui excels in the Song form and his Piano works do not specially exemplify Russian style. The *Miniatures* (Fr.) are obviously inspired by Schumann, as also are his best works, the *Petit Caprice* (*Op.* 25) and *Romanzetta, Op.* 39 (Bos.). These are graceful and pleasing, though not distinguished in manner.

Leaving the founders of the Russian School, we come to Alexander Glazounow (b. 1865), one of the most eminent European composers of the present time. Born at St. Petersberg, where his father was a bookseller, he appeared as a Symphonist at the age of sixteen, in 1881. In this country Glazounow is known mostly by his Symphonies, which are remarkable for their logical treatment, clever technical and contrapuntal manipulation and fluent style.

His Pianoforte compositions, on the other hand, though equally remarkable and effective, would seem to be almost unknown in this country.

Combining as they do, in large measure, the *technique* of a Liszt, the development of a Brahms and the romantic feeling of a Chopin, it is hardly an exaggeration to say that a new pianistic world opens to us in the compositions of Glazounow and in the works of the new Russian composers for pianoforte generally.

It may be said of Glazounow's works that they are, at first

sight, not distinguished by more than occasional leanings to the National style, and that they are sometimes complex and uninspired. Their outstanding feature is, no doubt, their remarkable technical effect resulting in a combination of sonority and sweetness.

The widespread material and frequent sustained pedal notes make the piano hum like an orchestra, sparkling awhile with Chopinesque broken and combined 3rds and 6ths heard in the highest treble register. For technical disposition of harmonic material securing luxuriant beauty of sound the works of Glazounow are difficult to equal. As an example, there is the *Petite Valse*, *Op*. 36 (Blf.), in which, though the Themes in themselves are not distinguished, the effect of the whole is charming : it reminds one of a Turner sunset, aglow with beauty of colour. Such work represents the prevailing tendency towards impressionism and idealization of technique. Another phase of Glazounow's work is his power of development, as in the *Barcarolle, Novellette, Op*. 22, *Prelude, Op*. 25 and *Nocturne, Op*. 37, which open somewhat unpromisingly, but, by means of variation, combination of Themes and effective technique lying well under the hands, attain a most interesting climax. In the *Fugue, Op*. 62, a masterly one on two subjects, and the *Variations, Op*. 72, the latest developments of modern technique combined with contrapuntal genius are displayed. The *Sonatas Op*. 74 and 75 also display mastery of contrapuntal work combined with thematic development, but with a resulting tendency towards over-elaboration. The *2nd Sonata* is mostly in the style of Schumann and is technically effective.

National feeling is noticeable in some of the higher *Opus* numbers of Glazounow's works, and a vein of idyllic discontent runs through the chromatic *Caprice, Impromptu Op*. 49, and *Prelude and Fugue, Op*. 62, while the very interesting *Mazurkas, Op*. 35, are National in tone and effective. The masterly *Variations, Op*. 72 (fourteen in number) are built on a Nationalistic Theme commencing

and exemplify various styles from the Handelian to the Liszt *quasi-campanella*.

As regards direct tunefulness, there are the noble *Prelude* and cheerful *Gavotte* in *Op*. 49, the *Pastorale*, the sparkling *Polka*, the simple *Valse* of the *Op*. 42 and the effective *Salon* and *Concert Valses*, *Op*. 43 and 41. The poetical and brilliant *Impromptus*, *Op*. 54 and the melodious *2nd Étude*, *Op*. 31, deserve special mention. With the exception of the ingenious but pointless *Suite*, *Op*. 2 on *Sascha* (S representing E♭), and the similar but more effective *Waltz*, *Op*. 23, on the Theme *Sabela*, the works of Glazounow (Blf.), stand as prominent representatives of the unique Russian School.

It is, perhaps, not a very remarkable feature in the Russian School of Composers for pianoforte, founded as it is on the efforts of Field, Henselt (the German Chopin), the two Rubinsteins and Balakirew, that in forming their National style, they should have followed to so large an extent the spirit and technique of the most genuinely pianistic of all styles—that of Chopin: but it is remarkable that they should not only have attained superiority in that style, but have suggested, in addition, through the works of Scriabin and Blumenfeld a further development of it. This style is mostly in evidence in the form of the *Prelude*—a form akin to the *Étude*, but distinctly poetical in spirit. Russian composers have made this form their own and, basing it on the *Preludes* and *Impromptus* of Chopin, have elaborated it, making it generally longer and more difficult, while keeping the fleeting, iridescent artistic touch.

Generally speaking, we may distinguish the *Preludes* of Blumenfeld as elaborate, those of Liadoff as idyllic, those of Scriabin as mystic, while those of Wihtol are poetical but less Slavonic than the others.

Much of the voluminous work of Alexander Scriabin will probably remain a sealed book to the average pianist.

We find in them the virtuoso instinct combined with poetical feeling, but rhapsodically expressed through excessive use of rhythmical complications. The cross rhythms and combination of rhythms are used even in Dance forms, such as the *Mazurkas*, *Polonaise* and *Valse*.

General complication is present also in the more pretentious works, such as the *Sonatas*, *Allegro Passionata*, *Allegro de Concert*, the *Tragödie* and many of the *Preludes* and *Etudes*, relieved only by the usual glittering, artistic, technical figuration, which is characteristically Russian.

His style, built almost entirely on Chopin, both in feeling and technique (but *not* in melodic inspiration) usually presents widespread Henseltian-Chopin figures, in which the left hand frequently passes beyond the right. They are probably the most difficult of all works to read and interpret.

The redeeming features are the National atmosphere and the highly interesting smaller works, as, for instance, some of the *Preludes* and *Impromptus*, in which his delicate style appears full of *rêverie* and waywardness, as of a breath among leaves. In these his style would seem to be in direct succession to that of Chopin. The best of these works are the following, the beautiful six *Preludes*, *Op.* 13, No. 1 and 3 of *Op.* 17, *Op.* 16 (No. 1), *Op.* 22 (No. 3), and the specially Schumannish *Op.* 35 (No. 3) and *Op.* 27 (No. 1). There is also the same delicate filagree work in the *Impromptus*, *Op.* 14 and *Op.* 10, while turgid Slavonic force is expressed in the interesting two *Poems*, *Op.* 32, and the *Fantasie*, *Op.* 28.

The one successful large work is the *Concerto in F♯ minor*, *Op.* 20, a delicately-wrought work, full of elegiac poetical feeling, in which the slow movement consists of brilliant yet restrained and artistic variations on an expressive Theme written in National style.

Scriabin was born in Moscow in 1872. He studied at Moscow Conservatoire and thence made Concert Tours in Europe as a virtuoso, introducing his own compositions.

The Example given on p. 260 is from the first *Prelude* in *Op.* 17 (Blf.).

Anatole Liadow (b. 1850 at St. Petersburg) is the senior of the younger Russian School which has sprung up on the foundation of Rimsky-Korsakow. He was educated at the Conservatoire of St. Petersburg and has been Professor there since 1878.

Liadow may be termed the Russian Chopin. He resembles the Polish Composer both in technique and style, though possessing individuality. Some of his earlier works, however, such as the pretty *Valse*, *Op.* 9 and *Impromptu*, *Op.* 6 (Bos.), the light *Intermezzo*, *Op.* 7 (Fr.) and the more forceful *Novelette*, *Op.* 20 (Blf.), are evidently formed on the Schumann model.

Though Slavonic in feeling, Liadow's compositions are usually idyllic in style. The *Ballade*, *Op.* 21 and *On the Prairie*, *Op.* 23,

the most National of his works, have practically none of the
passion and turgidity of other Russian composers.

Liadow, again, has little of the fitful wayward moods of
Scriabin and has much more lyrical feeling, while in technical
figuration he is similar to the latter but has more variety, and
is not so difficult.   His works are, moreover, more interesting
to the average student.   We may divide Liadow's works into
the light-winged and melodious *Preludes, Op.* 10 (No. 2) (Bos.),
Op. 36, 39, 41 and 42, the *Bagatelles, Op.* 53, the similar and
Étude-like *Preludes, Op.* 27 and *Étude, Op.* 48, the interesting
and characteristic *Mazurkas, Op.* 38 and 31, the artistic
Barcarolle, Berceuse, Idylle, Canzonetta and *Bagatelle, Op.* 7, the
light but artistic *Op.* 52, 29 and 32.

The *Variations, Op.* 51 and 35 are also specially interesting
for the artistic Chopin-like technical treatment.

The fragment given on p. 261 is from the *Idylle Andante Rubato.*
Like Scriabin and others, Liadow requires only the gift of
inspired melody to insure him a place in the front rank of
pianoforte composers.

Nicholas de Stcherbatchew (b. 1853) reveals himself to us
chiefly in two aspects : (1) as a brilliant technician in Romantic
style ; (2) as a poet and impressionist.

The former aspect is illustrated by the fine *Fantasies-Études*, *Op.* 26, which are in Suite form, the interesting *Preludes, Op.* 21,

Andante Rubato

virtuoso *Op.* 19, and *Impromptu Étude, Op.* 22, modelled on Schumann, the Chopinesque *Villanelle, Op.* 38, and Nos. 4, 6, 9 and 14 of the brilliant and attractive *Pantomimes, Op.* 8. The technical style of the other compositions inclines to that of Liszt and Chopin. The impressionist compositions of Stcherbatchew, dating from about 1886, are of historical importance as being the probable forerunners of the works of Debussy and others of the French School. The younger composer, Scriabin, has also shown some tendency to this style.

Of the compositions in this style we may mention the languorous *Barcarolle, Op.* 35, *Son d'Été* and *Clair de Lune, Op.* 25.

In the remarkable Example quoted from the latter on p. 262, the accompanying chords, like echoing harmonies, should be extremely lightly played, in order that the necessary " eerie " effect may be realized. There are also *L'Étoile du Berger, Op.* 23, with its pastoral atmosphere, the interesting and artistic effects of running water and song of birds in the other *Idylls, Op.* 23, the fall of leaves in the *Étude, Op.* 30, and the enigmatical garden and fairy scenes in *Op*. 8 (No. 2 and 7). The Valses *Pages Intimes* incline likewise to this impressionist style.

Stcherbatchew is more successful in his light compositions in the French style—the *Valse, Op*. 39, *New Marionettes, Op*. 41, *Guitarre, Op*. 15, and his own Transcription of the pretty *Serenade for Strings*—than in his best lyrical poetical Pieces *Adieux, Canzone* and *Souvenance*. We notice some slight Slavonic flavour in the melancholy of the quieter Pieces and in the *Mazurkas, Op*. 42 and 16 (No. 3), but, on the whole, the composer's merit lies on the technical side and in some of the impressionist Pieces rather than in the National vein ; in short, in the combination of beautiful harmonies and modulations with attractive technique.

There is an attractive vigour and National element, together with lyrical feeling about the *Mazurkas* [*Op*. 35, 11, 22 and 2 (No. 3 and 4)] and the *Suites Polonaises* of Felix Blumenfeld (b. 1863), the chief of the South Russian group.

The Chopinesque technique which is so highly developed in Russian composers appears in the Étude-like *Impromptus, Op*. 28 and 3, the *Valse Étude, Op*. 4 and the poetical Sketches, *Le Soir, Op*. 21 (No. 2), from which the following is taken :—

Une Course, Op. 21 (No. 3) and *Op.* 16. The latter, a *Valse Impromptu,* is also a notable example of technical effect developed on the harmonic theme :—

The *Poetical Études Fantasies* and *Sur Mer,* cast in the bravura mould, are also well worthy of attention. The remarkable collection of *Preludes, Op.* 12 and 17) the latter numbering twenty-four in all the keys, are based on the style of Chopin, but are much more elaborate and ambitious, constituting, as it were, a further development of that form.

Compared with the mystical quasi-impressionist *Preludes* of Scriabin and the idyllic ones of Liadow, they are more masculine and straightforwardly lyrical in style and lack something of their delicacy of touch. Nevertheless, they are full of poetical feeling and represent a great variety of effective technical treatment. The lyrical, romantic and technically effective are combined in the interesting *Nocturne Fantasie, Op.* 6 ; in (No. 3) of the *Moments Lyriques* and the *Suite Lyrique,* while the technically resourceful *Variations,* a *Ballade* and a *Valse, Op.* 22, deserve mention.

Coming to the *Preludes* of Joseph Wihtol (b. 1863 and educated at St. Petersburg Conservatoire) we are again confronted with an *embarras de richesses.* His *other* compositions, the artistic and expressive *Berceuses, Op.* 18 and 8, the *Meditation* and *Impromptu, Op.* 20, the well-written *Sonata, Op.* 1, in National style, consisting of *Allegro, Variations* and *Scherzando,* the clever *Variations* on a Lettish Theme, *Op.* 6, the original *Mazurka* and *Valse, Op.* 6, the *Valse Caprice, Op.* 24, and the realistic *Humoresque* are attractive ; but he excels in his *Preludes,* in which the hand of the artist is everywhere apparent.

The distinguishing features, apart from those already mentioned here, are the leaning to the chromatic style, the charming modulation, and the greater variety in vigour and delicacy of style ; but the Slavonic element is not so prominent, as may possibly be expected from a Lett of the Baltic Provinces, where the population is largely Germanic.   The best of the *Preludes* are *Op.* 13 (in 3rds), 19, 16, 23, 10 and 25.   The latter is represented in the following Example :—

There are also excellent poetical *Études, Op.* 26 (3) and single numbers in *Op.* 22, 19, 25.

S. M. Liapounow (b. 1859), who writes in the Liszt-Chopin style, is best known for his *Études Transcendantes*, for a fine *Concerto, Op.* 4 which is full of romantic poetical feeling, and for an *Étude* and *Valse* in *Op.* 1 (Blf.).

Mention may here be made of the humorous *Paraphrases* of *Variations* on a one-fingered Theme jointly contributed by

Borodin, Cui, Liadow, and Korsakow (Blf.) in pursuance of a once fashionable plan (*see* Part II, Chapter VII, on Beethoven's *Diabelli Variations*).

We have postponed consideration of Tschaïkowsky, Rachmaninoff and Arensky till now because, though their works are popular from an expressive point of view, they are inferior to the foregoing as regards genuine pianoforte style.

Tschaïkowsky, although a leading Russian composer, is not essentially a writer of pianoforte music, his domain lying in his considerable powers of characterization through the medium of orchestral colour. Of his piano music, much of which is somewhat inferior in interest, as such, to that of other Russian composers—both on the score of National feeling and through lack of suitable technical expression—we find that his most successful Pieces are those in which his gift of the " characteristic " is combined with melodic inspiration, as in the *Barcarolle* (June), *Troika Fahrt* (Sleigh Ride) (November) and *Snowdrops* (April) from the *Seasons* (Bos.). Though written in conventional style, the melodic feeling in these is fresh and, to some extent, Slavonic, as in the *Chant sans Paroles* (*Op.* 2), *Chanson Triste* of the *Op.* 40, *Feuillet d'Album* of the *Op.* 19, and the *Mazurka de Salon*, *Op.* 9, No. 3 (Album Lit.).

Tschaïkowsky has a keen feeling for *rhythmic* effects and these, as in his *Capriccioso* (*Op.* 19), the *Polka de Salon*, the very Slavonic *Danse Russe* (*Op.* 40), and the *Valse de Salon*, *Op.* 51, are attractive where otherwise the melodic inspiration is wanting. For his principal pianoforte work we must look to the *Concerto* (*Op.* 23) *in* B♭ *minor* with its gorgeous orchestration, Slavonic style and pompous leading Theme, the Schumannish *Poco Meno*, the Nocturne-like *Andantino* with the fairy *Prestissimo*, the capricious *Allegro con Fuoco*, with the suave second subject and thundering *Finale*. The B♭ *minor Concerto* was written in 1874-5 and first played by Bülow in Boston, U.S.A. The pianoforte part was rewritten in 1889, probably as the result of the criticism of the technique by Nicolai Rubinstein. Of the other two *Concertos*, that *in* G is more developed, but is somewhat symphonic in style, while the one *in* E♭ is fantastic and vigorous. The masculine, but very difficult and long *Fantasia with Orchestra*, *Op.* 56, a conventional *Sonata* and somewhat unattractive *Variations* may be also mentioned.

Here we shall say that Tschaïkowsky (1840-93), like Cui, was partly of French descent.

He fortunately came early under the influence of Anton Rubinstein, by whom he was induced to take up music seriously.

He was appointed Teacher of Harmony at the Conservatoire in Moscow in 1866, holding that position till 1877.

Generally speaking, Tschaïkowsky is known principally by his emotional *Pathetic Symphony*, the popular (and noisy) 1812 *Overture*, the light *Nutcracker Suite* and the orchestral *Italian Capriccio*.   In the future, however, it is possible he will be known as the composer of the last four *Symphonies*, the *A minor Trio*, the *String Quartet*, his *Songs* and the 1st *Pianoforte Concerto*.   The merit of Tschaïkoswky's piano music lies in his sense of melody, in which he surpasses his confrères, enhanced by piquant rhythm but affected somewhat adversely by lack of modern technique.

Sergei Rachmaninoff (b. 1873; educated at the Conservatoires of St. Petersburg and Moscow) surpasses his senior Arensky in dignity of style.   His works show decided tone colour, manifested through daring harmonies and modulations, characteristic rhythm effects, modern technique and expressive melodic style. The best-known are the fatalistic *C♯ minor Prelude*, a beautiful *Melody in E*, a very original *Serenade* and a fine *Élégie* (Bos.), while the rare sense of humour is ably depicted in the *Polichinelle* and *Humoresque*.   Of less known works there are the first *Concerto*, with graceful slow movement and brilliant *Finale*, an effective and better developed 2nd *Concerto*, a clever *Suite for Two Pianos* and some effective *Variations*.

Taking next the works of Anton Arensky (1861–1906), we find that their characteristics, in brief, are tunefulness and talent for the scholastic.

Arensky was educated at the St. Petersburg Conservatoire. Of his pianoforte works probably the best is the sparkling *Suite, Op* 15 *for Two Pianos* (*Romance, Valse* and *Polonaise*) (Bos.), which is mostly written in Variation form.   Of the smaller pieces, the *Consolation, Op*. 36, is probably the best.

The Pieces in Canon form, *Op*. 1 (R.) and the *Basso Ostinato* on a subject in 5/4 time are exceptionally ingenious and tuneful. In the latter the recurring bass presents a different figure in each bar, while, as Tschaïkowsky pointed out, the Piece, or rather the accompaniment to the bass, is really in 3/4 time. Arensky's partially Slavonic style is rather similar to that of Tschaïkowsky. It is more pianistic on the one hand, but lacks the rhythmic interest of the former.   Attention may be drawn to his *Concerto, Op.* 2 and *Fantasia with Orchestra* on Russian folksongs.

Of composers of small Pieces in more or less National style there is first : W. Rebikow, whose powers of characterization are principally seen in the clever dramatic *Melonique Sketches*, of which *Les Rêves* is set in the old modes. His *Autumn Reveries* (Jr.), which are mostly in National style, are also interesting. L. Aloiz wrote a melodious and artistically treated *Barcarolle, Op.* 4 (Jr.) and *Mazurka, Op.* 35 (Bos.).

A. Gretchaninow, refined and characteristic *Pastels* (*Chant d'Antonine, Nocturne*, etc.). The *Op.* 13 (*Doumka*, etc.) and *Esquisses Orientales* of W. Kotschetow are very Russian in style. A. Ilynsky, pretty *Cradle Song* (Jennings) and *Op.* 7 (Jr.). N. Artibouchew, two *Mazurkas, Op.* 3 (Blf.). A. Zatayewitsch, *4th Mazurka* (Jr.). S. Scepanowski, well-written and interesting *Barcarolle* and *Eclogue*, and also *L'Insouciance*, which is very Slavonic in style.

The compositions of the South Russian School of composers, while National in style, are distinguished by a more luxuriant style of melody. We may mention briefly H. Amany, whose best works are delicate and artistic in manner, *Souvenir* and *Élégie, Op.* 7, *Prelude*, No. 3 of *Op.* 8 and the effective *Variations*. E. Alenew's works are allied to those of Chopin and Schumann in technique. There is a pretty set of pieces, *Op.* 7 and the more elaborate but effective *Op.* 10, with attractive and well-written *Variations, Valse*, and the Schumannesque *Intermezzo* and *Canzona*.

The *2nd Sonata* (*Op.* 4), and *2nd Novelette, Op.* 6, of B. Kalafaty, are a welcome addition to musical literature in the massive and richly harmonised style of Schumann, in which Lisztian technique is present. The *Nocturne, Op.* 5 is Nationalistic.

The characteristic Russian *Sérénade Levantine, Mazurkas, Op.* 27 and an *Étude, Op.* 30 of A. Alpheraky may be mentioned ; as well as the melodious *Op.* 16 (3 Pieces) and two *Mazurkas, Op.* 6 by Sigismund Blumenfeld.

Of the South Russian composers who have no partial leanings towards National or Individual style there are A. Korestchenko, who has written dainty poetic Pieces in modern harmonic style, *Op.* 19 (1, 2, 3 and 5)(Bes.) and the *Rhapsodies Georgiennes*, founded on Caucasian melodies, and Genari Kargenow, composer of small melodious Pieces showing the influence of Schubert, e.g., *Impromptu, Op.* 10 (No. 6), *Album Lyrique* (No. 3 and 4) (R.) as well as some educational Pieces.

A. Kopylow, in the pretty sympathetic *Miniature Pieces, Op.* 20, vies with Schumann, his model, in warmth and treatment of idea. The poetical and melodious *Album Leaves, Op.* 26 and *Pieces, Op.* 13, the Slavonic *Mazurkas, Op.* 3 and 8 (Bl.) and the pretty *Petit Ruisseau* (Zm.), are worthy of note, and a scholastic composition consisting of three fluently written Fugues is of interest. C. Antipow leans to Chopin in the attractive *Impromptu* and *Valse, Op.* 13, the poetical *Étude, Op.* 1 (No. 3), and the *Nocturne, Op.* 6, tinged with Slavonic colour.

A. Koptiaiew, Schumannish *Bal Masqué* (Jr.). J. Bleichman, daintily written *Miscellanies* (Jr.). A. Winkler, brightly written *Étude-Humoreske* (Bl.). B. Grodzky, popular *Valse Mélodique.* The pianoforte music of Meyer Helmund (b. St. Petersburg, 1861), the Song writer, is mostly in light Salon style, but his *Op.* 72 (Hs.) and *Petit Serenade* may be mentioned. Felix Borowski is known for his well written, elegant and artistic Pieces (Ld.). His *Mazurka Russe* (Wh.) and *Sonata Russe* are Nationalistic. M. Ladoukhine, *Miniatures* in simple lyrical style (Jr.). N. Terestchenko, Schumannish *Intermezzi* and *L'Oiseau Voltige* (Jr.). W. Sapellinkow, finely written *Pieces, Op.* 6 and 7, and *Concert Étude, Op.* 3 (J.A.). A. Goedicke, attractive *Duetto* and *Valse* (Jr.). O. Gabrilowitsch, *Caprice Burlesque* (B. and B.). Basile Wrangell, tuneful *Op.* 1 and 13 (Srm.).

Of Russian composers in the prevailing Germanic or European style the most prominent are Ed. Schütt (b. St. Petersburg, 1856 ; studied at Leipzig, settled in Vienna) and Nicolai von Wilm (b. 1834) ; studied in Leipzig, resident in St. Petersburg and Wiesbaden).

Ed. Schütt writes in artistically refined, meditative and somewhat chromatic style and his best efforts are simple conceptions in the expressive style, as in *Tendre Aveu, Op.* 47, *Valse Mignonne Op.* 16, the charming slow movements of the *Carnaval Mignon* and the *Poésies, Op.* 58 (Lg.). The *Op.* 28 and 45, the *Scènes de Bal*, written in popular style, the interesting 4-hand *Scènes Champêtres* (Lg.), the *Danse Caractéristique* (Jn.), the *Romance Op.* 38 (St.), and Nos. 1 and 5 of the *Silhouettes* (B. and B.) are also attractive. The artistic but somewhat meditative *Concert*

Caprices on the themes of Strauss *Valses* (Cz.), the dignified *Preludes*, and the richly harmonic *Concerto* claim notice, while the Slavonic element is present in the *Caprice Slave*, the 4th *Prelude, Op.* 35 in 7/4 time, the *Rococo, Op.* 17, and the *Mazurka, Op.* 40 (Jn.).

Schütt's style shows the influence of Chopin and Schumann.

Von Wilm is known as a prolific writer of excellent educational works, the earlier of which are in the style of Heller (Fs.), the latter in that of Mendelssohn and Schumann. Of general interest are the *Op.* 2, *Op.* 107 (1 and 7) (Bos.), *Op.* 138, 149 (Ld.), *Op.* 173 (No. 3), the interesting *Duets, Op.* 169 (R.F.) and the *Ball Suite* for two pianos. S. Barmotin's technically interesting *Variations* (Blk.) must also be noticed.

CHAPTER VII

AUSTRIAN OR SOUTH GERMAN COMPOSERS

MUSICALLY speaking, Austria has always differed from the more austere North Germany, as represented, for instance, by the Saxons, Bach and Handel, and the Hamburger, Brahms, in the more intensely *lyrical* character of its composers. Schubert, the song-writer, Haydn, the light-hearted Croatian, and Mozart from Salzburg prove the contrast. It was Vienna which took the musical supremacy from Italy and passed it on to Leipzig and Berlin in the North. Up to 1914 Vienna was looked upon as the Paris of the South, the centre of all that is light and gay-hearted, and it is still the home of the Strauss Waltz and Viennese Opera, though no doubt it would be wrong to judge Vienna in an *artistic* sense entirely from this point of view.

The musicianly works of Ignaz Brüll (born at Prosnitz, Moravia, in 1846) show the characteristic prominence of melody. His noteworthy second *Sonata* (A.P.S.) shows the influence of Folk-Song, as also do the attractive *Tanzweisen*, *Op*. 89, No. 1 (Bos.) and *Op*. 69 (1 and 3) (G.R.) ; while the pleasant *Idylle, Op*. 37 (Bk.), *Op*. 72 (1 and 4) (A.P.S.) and the *Romance, Op*. 38 (1) (Ash.) are in lyrical style. The *Prelude* and *Quasi-Variazione* of the *2nd Suite* (A.P.S.) are worthy of attention. Brüll wrote also a *Sonata* for two pianos.

The compositions of Hugo Reinhold (b. 1854 at Vienna) (*see* Part III, Chapter XII), Heinr. von Herzogenberg (b. at Graz, Styria, 1843) (*see* Part III, Chapter XIII), Wilhelm Kienzl (b. 1857 in Upper Austria), (Part III, Chapter XX), and Ernst Pauer (b. at Vienna, 1826) (Part III, Chapter XX) are treated of in the Chapters indicated. Ferdinand Hummel, though born in Berlin (1855), may be classed as South German. His works are noted for their *melodiousness*, their bold harmonic style and the energy one associates with Hungarian music. The *Skizzen, Op*. 13, the E♭ *Polonaise*, the four-hand *Suite* and the *Scherzo* (Jn.) are worthy of attention.

The *Passacaglia* and *3rd Ballad*, by the serious-minded Carl Navratil (b. 1836 at Vienna), and Robert Fischoff's (b. 1804) pleasing and melodious *Impromptus* (Cz.), " *Melusine* " *Étude* (Db.) and *Variations* for two pianos can be commended. The light, tuneful pieces of Roderick Bass, *Fête Champêtre* (Bos.), etc. ; F. de Gernerth's brilliant and melodious *Caprice, Op.* 62 and *Valse, Op.* 63 (Eb.) ; B. Schönberg's *Ungarische Tänze* (St.) and Baron le Baillon's poetical *Stimmungsbilder* (Eb.) may be mentioned.

Other Austrian composers dealt with elsewhere are Wagenseil (d. 1777), Eberl (d. 1807), Woelfl (d. 1812), Czerny, Diabelli, Herz, Neukom, Egghard, Czerwinski and Pacher.

Of composers from the Southern kingdom of Bavaria we might mention Burgmüller, Eckard, Henselt, Kessler, Kunz, Lachner, Reger, Aloys Schmitt and Richard Strauss.

CHAPTER VIII

To the lover of pianoforte music the French School is somewhat disappointing.

No doubt the whole genius of the French people is dramatic, and the love of effect and theatrical pose leads their composers to give their best energies to the Opera to the detriment of the less sensational art. This tendency, however, is balanced to some extent by the innate national feeling for the artistic, so that, whether any inspiration is reserved for the humble pianoforte or not, what does appear is at least generally artistic in style. It goes without saying that the French do not excel in the *Sonata*, and it is difficult to mention any one French composer who has written universally acknowledged successful examples of this form, unless we include the *Concertos* as coming under this head. On the other hand, the influence of the Opera makes them unequalled in the light *Ballet* forms and in the elegant, piquant style allied thereto.

The studied love of effect also leads to some almost National peculiarities of style, as, for instance, the intensified depicting of light and shade, the persistent and repeated accentuation of somewhat ugly chromatic dissonances (augmented 5ths, etc.), in order that the ensuing diatonic progressions may appear beautiful by contrast.

Lavoix, in an effusion on *La Musique Française*, says, " Our musical imagination does not rise into the sphere of ecstasy and absolute music as with the German masters. . . . It has, moreover, less lyricism than with the Germans, less sensuousness than with the Italians ; but it excels in precious qualities of expression ; of correctness, of sober and profound emotion."

The emancipation from the Opera and the desired devotion to National Music will doubtless be accomplished in good time, as in other countries, through the National Folk-Song and Dance. The study of the simple, natural and engaging National element is exemplified in the four-hand *Danses Populaires Françaises* by Tiersot (Lm.), the *Vieux Airs* and *Basque Airs* by Paul Lacombe (Cs.) and the *Ballet en Forme de Danses Anciennes* by Bergé (B.P.).

The *Chansons* and *Pastorales* of the Troubadours of Provence and Northern France in the twelfth and thirteenth centuries, the later tender *Romances* and gay *Vaudevilles*, the *Chansons-Ballades* (Dance Songs mostly in 6/8 time), the *Bourrée Songs* of Aubergne, the *Noëls* and *Drinking Songs* of Burgundy and the pathetic songs of the Béarnais in their simple, unsophisticated style, give the key to the National feeling; as do also the *National Dances* of the old set *Branles* and *Minuets*, the gayer *Passepied*, the lively *Tambourin* and the *Rigodon*. Apart from the National movement, however, French instrumental music has made wonderful strides in the last twenty years.

Emancipating itself from the Kalkbrenner and Herz trivialities on the one hand, and the absorbing Opera on the other, it has, under the leadership of Saint-Saëns (Part III, Chapter XVII) approached more nearly to the level attained by other nations. We may now give a brief account of the leading composers of Pianoforte music.

The individuality of Benjamin Godard appears, as in his *2nd Romance* (Hl.), in passages of great beauty and tenderness which are nevertheless marred by certain dissonant melodic or harmonic passages persistently repeated. His individuality is best seen in small Pieces such as the *1st Mazurka* (L.G.), *Redowa*, *Op. 141*, *Serenade Op. 138* (No. 2) (Hl.), *Suite Op. 103* (Jb.) and *Scherzo Op. 107*. Instances of dissonant persistent figures can be seen in the *2nd Nocturne* (Cz.), the *Valse Villageoise*, the *4th* and *8th Valses*, and the *Op. 58* (Lc.), the effect sometimes verging on impressionism. His powers of development are seen in the movement *La Fée d'Amour* from the *Sonate Fantastique* (Hl.), in which the climaxes are well worked up. He essayed the diatonic manner successfully in *Collections* in the " Style Ancien " (L.G.). His *Études de Concert Op. 149* are useful and interesting for variety of technical treatment. Paul Lacombe is one of the few French composers who seem to have got away to a large extent from the influence of the " Ballet " and the excruciating augmented 5th, as, for example, in his masculine *3rd Suite* (Lc.), the noteworthy *Suite with Orchestra*, the refined *Sketches, Souvenirs, Airs de Ballet, Intermède et Lied, Toccatina*, etc.

The Piano works of Gabriel Fauré are generally characterized by broad melody and elevated style, as in his *Nocturnes*, etc., but a bizarre habit of plunging into disconnected and extraneous keys frequently makes its appearance. There is commendable freedom from this in the *3rd Romance* (Hl.) and in the original and poetic *Mazurka*.

Theodore Lack (b. 1846 at Finisterre) is one of the principal composers in what is eminently the French elegant style. His *Sonata in C* (1904) is interesting on the whole, though thematic development is not conspicuous. Generally speaking, his works are characterized by melodiousness and piquancy unmarred by the usual French weakness of triviality. His *Moment de Caprice* (Lc.), *Calabraise* and *Au Gré des Flots* (Hl.) are in his best style. The *Polonaise for Two Pianos* should be mentioned.

Ch. M. Widor (b. 1845), the distinguished organist, has written two *Concertos*, a *Fantasia with Orchestra*, *Suites* and interesting *Miniatures*, *Dans les Bois*. His *Waltzes* are melodious but lack distinction.

Mme. Chaminade (b. 1861 in Paris) is the leading French lady composer. Showing signs of ability at an early age she became a pupil of Le Couppey (piano) and Savard (theory), and she has since won fame both as a composer and as a performer. Mme. Chaminade excels in the dainty and charming inspirations of the Ballet type, the *Pas des Amphores*, *Air de Ballet*, *Valse Ballet*, *Pas de Cymbales* and the pretty *Callirrhoë Transcription*.

Those of her compositions of the Romance type, as, for instance, the pretty *Sérénade*, the elegant, though not deep, *Élégie*, the *Valse Romantique*, the *Mélancolie*, and the *Romance en Ré*, are almost equally successful. The artistic *Divertissement Pastoral* and *Tristesse*, as well as the four-hand *Andante* and *Scherzettino* and the striking *Duo Symphonique* for three pianos show to some extent classical influence. These are attractive, always clear-cut, piquant and melodious, and the same may be said of the *Caprice Humoristique*, the *4th Valse*, *Op.* 91, the *Thème Varié* and the *Novelette* (En.). Distinction and elegance are the features of the one type, inspired piquancy and charm combined with clever artistic writing are those of the other. The pianistic world would be the poorer if it were to lose the lighter compositions of Mme. Chaminade. Other works are a *Concertstück* with orchestra, besides an *Orchestral Suite*, *Symphony*, *Trios*, many *Songs*, and her *Romanesca* and *Air à Danser* (Enoch).

Massenet is a clever but somewhat uninspired composer of orchestral and operatic music, where he excels in orchestral colouring.

In the words of a compatriot, " He has written little for piano and his pianoforte music is not very characteristic : one finds in it reminiscences of Chopin and the influence of Stephen Heller. Nevertheless, there are some pretty things in his *Scènes de Bal* for four hands (Hartmann), written in an aggravating style (*d'un style tourmenté*) and very difficult in execution, and in his 7 *Improvisations* (Hartmann)."

Of French composers in the Romantic style we have Henri Ravina (b. 1818 at Bordeaux), formerly known as a virtuoso, whose simple and artistic style is seen in his four-hand *Pièces Intimes* (Lc.), *Nocturne, Op.* 55, *Petit Bolero, Op.* 62 (Lc.) and refined *Studies* (*see* Chapter XVI).

Mel. Bonis has written his *Pensées d'Automne* and *Méditation* (Lc.) in a dignified, refined and superior style. Gabriel Pierné is best known by the Transcription of his charming *Serenade Op.* 7 and graceful 1st *Nocturne*. His fairy-like touch is seen also in the *Fantasinagorie* and *Coquetterie* in the *Op.* 3 (Lc.).

Theodore Ritter (real name Bennet, b. 1841 in Paris, d. 1886) was a pupil of Liszt and wrote popular pieces, technically effective and transparently melodious, such as *Les Courriers, Le Tourbillon*, etc. The pianoforte works of the orchestral writer and symphonist *D'Indy* (b. 1852) are of slight academic interest only. As a pupil of César Franck he has a similar tendency to impressionism. Louis Lacombe's (b. 1818) piano works are similarly uninspired. We may mention *Le Torrent* (*Harmonies de Nature*) and the *Transcription, Op.* 39 as perhaps the most attractive.

Henri Litolff (b. London, 1818, of Alsatian parents ; died 1891), wrote the well-known effective *Chant de la Fileuse* (Lit.) and the *Chanson du Rouet* (Jb.). He is known to posterity principally as the founder of the Publishing House of Litolff.

His 1st and 2nd *Études de Concert* (Sl.) are highly useful and his *Concerto Hollandais* on Dutch airs is occasionally performed.

L. Würmser has written a very modern and effective *Impromptu* as well as an interesting *Idylle* and *Feuillet d'Album* (Cs.).

The works of Ch. V. Alkan (1813–88) are principally of technical interest. His *Études Mineures, Prières* and *Benedictus* for two pianos (Cs.) are well written but, though showing French facility for extraneous modulation, they lack modern harmonic effects and, above all, inspiration.

Geo. Pfeiffer (b. 1835) has composed some excellent *Studies*, an effective and original *Bolero* (L.G.) and some *Concertos*. F. Peru's unaffected and charming 6 *Pieces* (Lc.) are French and artistic. Fernand le Borne, like Würmser, depicts with the utmost delicacy and charm of refinement his *Scènes Fantastiques* (Lessarague), while Ch. Lefèbre, in his dreamy *Ballade* (B.P.), shows most artistic modulatory effects. Henri Lutz's 5 *Pieces* (2 and 4) (B.P.) are poetical. The early works of Réné Lenormand are of academic interest only, but his later works, such as the *Novelette Op*. 60 (J.W.), are poetical, though somewhat uninspired. Henri Eymieu (b. 1860) may be mentioned as composer of a well-written and attractive *Andante with Variations* for two pianos. (Jn.). J. Jemain's best work is a very modern *Berceuse Op*. 10 (Ct.).

Francis Thomé (b. 1850 ; Mauritius) is best in broad flowing compositions of the type of his *Simple Aveu*. He is happy also in the dainty little improvised *Preludes*, Bks. 528 and 539 (Lm.) and *Papillons* (Hl.). Léon Delafosse is known for his showy and melodious *Fantasia with Orchestra*.

Ch. de S. Delioux (b. 1830) may be mentioned for the tone-colouring of his *Carnaval Espagnol Op*. 38 and *Mandoline Op*. 28 (St.): *Prudent* for his *Études de Genre* (No. 6, *Feu Follet* on black keys) (St.), which are well written and effective. Auguste Durand's light and unhackneyed Pieces, *Air de Ballet Op*. 77 and *Kermesse Op*. 71 ; the fine *Variations* by Chevillard ; the *Sonata* and *Variations* on a Theme of Rameau by Dukas ; the Concert and Poetical *Studies* of Ravel ; the delicate *Tone Pictures* of Lacroix and the " heroic " Pieces of Vanzande deserve notice.

Claude Debussy (b. 1862), the impressionist and designer of " atmosphere," has come very much to the front of late. M. Calvocoressi points out that the inclination of the younger French composers is towards impressionism, as is also the case to some extent in Great Britain. (*See* Chapter XIV).

He avers that the quasi-classical *Suite Bergamesque* (Fromont), *Pavane* and *Minuet Antique* of Debussy and the *Sonatine* of Ravel are " full of really picturesque colour and of extreme modernism in style ; " and he dilates on the daring harmonic experiments of " picturesque and expressive music " of Ravel and " the thrilling sense of colour " in works by De Sévérac (b. 1873).

In playing over the compositions of Debussy the question occurs to one—does their charming picturesque character suggest the beautiful in nature, or does it remind us of the languorous sentimentality which is often characteristic of Chopin, and which one would associate with glamour of the Salon and the artificialities of the relaxations of Society? As it happens, the Selection played may possibly suggest the latter atmosphere, coupled with abrupt effects which challenge acutely the sense of contrast. Can it be that this phase represents the real Debussy? Perhaps not !

An examination of the whole of his Piano works reveals to us that there are, as it were, two Debussys, or shall we say, two phases of Debussy—an earlier (and, incidentally, an easier) phase, and a later phase, which is more mystical, more individual, less understood, yet, on the whole, a charming companion of the keyboard. And thus it occurs to one that it would be best for the student to approach the later phase through the earlier, and, in any case, for the ordinary pupil to attempt first the easier pieces in progressive order, and thus gain an insight into those which are more difficult of comprehension. To do this, suppose we take first the piquant 2nd Arabesque. An engaging melodic sense pervades the whole with various little asides or sudden incursions into unexpected keys. The effect is charming and the piece is technically useful.

We next attack the Album " de moyenne force " (of medium difficulty) and the melodious smoothly-flowing Le Bateau claims our attention. The 1st Arabesque, with its refreshing harmonies and pleasant rippling character appeals to us next. These form three valuable educational Pieces in the earlier refined Salon style. The other items of the Album do not, at present, especially claim our interest. Other items in the earlier style which may be referred to are the Cortége et Air de Danse from L'Enfant Prodigue and the arranged Ballet from the Petite Suite for four hands ; also the Prélude from La Demoiselle Élue and the Prélude, Danseuses de Delphe. The next to be noticed as introducing the higher technical work might be the Prélude Sarabande and Toccata (Fromont). There is no mistaking the individuality of the 'Prélude, the scintillating, rich but

bizarre harmonies of the *Sarabande*, and the attractiveness of
the *Toccata*, which reminds us of Heller but with added harmonic
richness. The engaging *Suite Bergamesque* would naturally
follow. In this the *Prelude* will appeal to all—its modulations
of key are not so brusque as in the ensuing old-world *Minuet*,
with its archaic atmosphere, which contrasts strongly with the
popular and beautiful *Clair de Lune*—and the still more impressionistic *La Terrasse des Audiences du Clair de Lune* of the
Preludes. Compare the former with the *Moonlight Sonatas* of
Beethoven and Brahms and realize the progress music has
made in the creation of atmosphere. After this the melodious
but antique *Passepied* comes somewhat as an anti-climax, so
that we long for the atmosphere which we find, for instance, in
the *Cathédrale Engloutie* (Buried Cathedral) with its long-
drawn-out, swelling harmonies.

But we are almost getting along too quickly, for the later
style of Debussy needs an apprenticeship in order fully to
appreciate its effect. Three Pieces may serve for this : the
Valse la plus que Lente (*Album de majeure force*), in which we
have the languorous, sentimental element of the heavy-laden
Air of the Salon, and the *Mazurka* and *Valse Romantique*
(Fromont). In each case we have vague, cloying harmonies
leading as a strong relief into a beautiful gleam of sunlight or
fascinating technical passage as in the *Valse Romantique*. The
former Piece will probably be found the more attractive. Other
works in this stage and claiming more technique are the
interesting *Danse* (Fromont) with its perverse *Valse-à-deux-
temps* rhythm, and the *Ballade*, a well-defined melody with an
antique and varied setting.

In the remaining works we are well into the later style.
Incursions into it have been already mentioned, as in the
Cathédrale Engloutie, with its " fifthy " chain of harmonies and
linked mysteries, and the *Terrasse des Audiences*, " in which
apparently unrelated series of harmonies seem to float in from
an outer world."

We have the same barbaric " fifthiness " in the *Danse
Profane*, in its subdued opening Theme. The thoroughly
Eastern atmosphere, which has become so popular through
Miss Amy Woodeford Finden's *Indian Lyrics*, is in evidence,
with swirling accompaniments, alternating chords and Indian
tom-tom effects—an effective though mystical work. One

imagines, in the *Danse Sacve*, the presence of the whirling dervish. Both need the orchestral accompaniment to realize fully all the effects.

The *Pagodas* of the *Estampes* next claims our attention as a masterpiece of impressionist Eastern scenes and unaccustomed sounds, the native chant and the tinkling of Pagoda bells.

It is the undoubted drawback of all purely Impressionistic or Programme music that its various phases have often to be denoted to be intelligible. How many of us who did not know the title of the *Chaos* in Haydn's *Creation* could correctly name it? Indeed, unless such music has interesting melody and harmony, apart from its Programme, its existence can hardly be qualified.

Something of this might be laid to Debussy's charge. Of the books of *Preludes*, for instance, we might mention *Des Pas sur la Neige* and the *Sérénade Interrompue*, of which we have only the background in the *quasi guitarre*. There are also those wild flights which are possibly suggestive with a title, but incomprehensible without—as in the *Hommage à Haydn*, *Voiles*, *Le Vent dans la Plaine*, *Brouillards*, *Cloches à travers les Feuilles*, *Les Fées*, *Ondine*, *Hommage à Pickwick*, *Canopé*, *Feuilles Mortes*, *L'Ile joyeuse*, that picture of desolation *La Lune descend sur le Temple qui fut*, and the dirge-like *Berceuse Héroïque*.

In *Masques* and the other Sketches of the Children's Corner we have little beyond rhythm and the vague harmonic background, with the exception of *Ad Parnassum*, which would make an excellent study.

In surveying the various styles we encounter in Debussy, one cannot help forming the opinion that he is not only an idealistic impressionist, but also a realist. We get the former phase in the *Clair de Lune*, and the latter, with its mixture of extraneous and out-of-tune noises breaking in from the outer world, in the *Terrasse des Audiences*—a feature more developed in other works. As in actual nature, we hear a jumble of sounds, the rustling of leaves, the chirp of birds, the striking of bells and of chimes in various dissonant keys. There is room in Music, as in other Arts, for these phases of Nature, but we must not mistake the importance of the phase; realism is not always beautiful. After all, the idealist, with his beautiful vision, is to be preferred to the realist. But we can learn from both. Let us take, for example, the well-known realistic *Jardins sous la Pluie*. We hear the realistic drip, drip of the rain, a melody floats out and the shower grows intermittent, but soon the pelting rain resumes sway and that is all.   One can hardly say that we receive an impression of beautiful flowers and of the scents of the garden. In the *Poissons d'Or* we have no sounds for interpretation: nothing but the gleam of a bevy of goldfish and a shimmering, graceful movement, and yet Debussy has built up a more elaborate composition of some thirteen pages in length, full of flights of *arpeggio*, whirling *tremolo* and quick alternating chords. The idealist here depicts a mental emotion—that experienced by a sight of the goldfish—and endeavours to communicate the sense of novelty and delight to his hearers : and the worth of the picture depends on the sense of enjoyment experienced, and its individuality of effect.   There is again the popular *Reflets dans l'Eau*, in which the case is similar.   A soundless picture is interpreted in sound waves of rippling *arpeggios*, across which comes apparently the chime of a distant steeple (an auxiliary effect, with a *pianissimo* Coda dying away at the close.   In this more homogeneous of Debussy's works, the chime motive acts as a connecting link.   In the remarkable *Hommage à Rameau*, the great harmonist of the musically primitive past is approached through an orgy of modern harmony which would probably make the ancient shade of Rameau flee in dismay.

Of those works in which the atmosphere is more definite we can instance the *Mouvement de Habanera* in the attractive *La Soirée dans Grenade* (Estampes) and the *La Puerta del Vino* (Preludes) with their Spanish quasi-Eastern half-lights ; also *Général Lavine* (Preludes) and *Golliwog* (Children's Corner), both devoted to the rhythm of the cake-walk and endowed also with melody—a feature not always present in the impressionist picture, with its lack of outline.

In conclusion it might be interesting to note what are the typical features of Debussy's later style.   Let us take his well-known *Reflets dans l'Eau*.   Here we have (1) a pretty, scintillating accompaniment of secondary harmonies against a short theme *in D* (page 1, lines 3 and 4).   (2) Sudden extraneous modulations (page 1, etc.).   (3) Remote modal or tonal effects from use of whole-tone scale, etc. (pages 2 and 4).   (4) The use of *cacophony* followed by a grateful burst of *euphony*, typically French (change to E♭, page 5).   Debussy, like Wagner, does not invent new harmonic combinations, but makes daring use of extraneous concords against discords (*see* page 1, bar 9 ; page 6, bar 10), or against other concords. As to the *form* of his works, Debussy uses no more than is necessary to connect his ideas, and, after all, the contents of a work are more important than its form. In the work described above a short Theme appears thrice with varied treatment and serves to unify the work. Finally, let me advise the student not only to try the above course, but to analyse and find out how Debussy produces those charming effects which appeal to so many admirers.

Maurice Ravel (b. 1875) claims attention as a post-Debussyist not through impressionism but through his refined simplicity of style combined with Lisztian technique. He is best known by his brilliant *Jet d'Eau*, and beautiful *Sonatine*.

Of other composers we can recommend A. Fleury—*Intermezzo-Valse* of elusive charm (L.G.) ; Ch. de Bériot, *L'Amazone (Salon Étude)* (L.G.) ; D. Fleury, *Prélude (Suite Ancienne)* (Jn.) ; Em. Bernard, *Rêverie Caprice* (Jn.) ; A. P. F. Boely, *Danse Villageoise* (Cs.) ; Em. Passard, *Op.* 121 (L.H.) ; Lef. Wély (1817–70), the well-known Salon Pieces *Les Cloches du Monastère* and *Bolero* (L.G.) ; L. Diemer, a fresh *Petite Valse* (Hl.) ; Luc. Vieuxtemps, *Barcarolle* (L.G.) ; M. Dubois, dainty and modern *Petite Valse* (Lc.) ; Fr. Brisson (b. 1821), refined and technically interesting Pieces, as *L'Arabesque* (Lc.) and *La Volière* (L.G.) ; Paul Paget, *Minuet* and *Dix Pièces* (Fm.) in tasteful style with modern harmonies ; E. Nollet, a Thalbergian *Les Perles ;* Barbadette (b. 1827), *Sonatas, Scènes d'Enfants*, etc. ; *Pieces* by P. H. Barbara (1823–63) and F. Bentayoux (b. 1840) ; Bizet— composer of *Carmen*—pleasing *Chants du Rhin ;* Gounod, com poser of *Faust, Various Pieces* in the sentimental style (Aug.) ; Ch. Chaulieu (1788–1849), *Pièces* and *Studies ;* Hy. and L. E. Jadin, *Concertos* and *Sonatas ;* J. A. Ladurner (1766–1839), two- and four-hand *Sonatas ;* and G. Louchet (b. 1840), popular small *Pièces*.

CHAPTER IX

THE MUSIC OF THE NETHERLANDS

César Franck, etc.

IN considering the Pianoforte music of Belgium we must not lose sight of the dual individuality of the people. There is the fair-haired, reflective Fleming, akin to the Dutch and first-cousin to ourselves, famous in earlier times for his superiority in the pictorial art, and there is also the dark, lively Celtic Walloon, akin to, and speaking a dialect of, the French people, and noted from early times for his enthusiastic devotion to, and excellence in, the more emotional art of music.

Going back to the great school of Netherlandish choral composers, commencing in the fifteenth century, we find the names of the Walloons Dufay, Josquin des Prés, Roland de Lattre (Orlando di Lasso) and others. In the eighteenth century we find Grétry (1741–1813), who incorporated the pathetic simplicity of the Walloon Folk-Song into his Operas. He wrote also some (for that period) interesting *Pianoforte Sonatas*. Later times have witnessed the devotion of the Belgians generally and especially of the Walloons to the violin, as represented in the composers and virtuosos Vieuxtemps, De Bériot, Léonard, Prume, Ysaye, César Thomson and Musin, as well as the 'cellist Gerardy. Other branches of the art have been represented, however, in the eminent César Franck, whom we treat of later on, and in Lekeu, Paul Gilson and the eminent Flemish Opera composer, Jan Blockh (b. 1851).

The characteristic qualities of Walloon and Flemish Folk Music—as evinced in the following pianoforte scores, *Noël Walloons* (Mu.), *Danses Anciennes de Liége* (Mu.) and the eighteenth-century music of Ghent (By.), *Popular Flemish Airs* (Berghs) (Ko.) and Arthur de Greef's *Transcriptions de Chansons Flamandes*, are cheerful simplicity and tunefulness, regularity of tempo, mostly in 6/8 time, and a striking likeness to Old English

Songs and Dances.   In the Liége Dances is one number, *Les Maclottes*, which is practically identical with a well-known English Hornpipe, and one Flemish Air is entitled, *Hip, hip, hoera.*

Since the Flemish are first-cousins of the Anglo-Saxons, the resemblance is to some extent explained.   Some of the *Cramignons*, as sung and danced at the fêtes in the district of Liége (the *Farandoles* of Liége) and old Netherlandish airs are very irregular in time, and this feature is reflected in the music of Lekeu, the promising Walloon composer who died at an early age. The general features of Belgian music, owing to the prominence of the Walloon element, may be said to be light-hearted tunefulness tending sometimes to the trivial.

Among those composers showing classical influence are S. Curtis, in his 10 *Poetical Pieces* (1, 3, 5, 6 and 9) and effective *Prelude* and *Fugue* (By.) ; Daniel van Goen's well-written *Au Bords de Loing* (Hm.) and *Legend* (Ff.) ; and Adolphe Samuel's attractive series of Characteristic Pieces in Schumann's style, *Op.* 52 (3 to 6, 9, 11, 12) (By.).

Of the piano compositions of Guillaume Lekeu (already referred to) there are 3 Pieces—a tender Wagnerian *Chansonnette*, a *Valse Oubliée* and a wild Nationalistic *Danse Joyeuse*—all displaying irregular phrase lengths after the manner of the Walloon folk-melodies.   In this division we may include the two *Scherzi* of Philippe Rufer (Ch.) and a *Minuet* by A. Chesneau (Bm.).

In the Romantic and Lyric styles we have the composer Paul Gilson (b. in Brussels, 1869), whose charming Impressionist *Paysages* and *Nocturne* (G.O.) show the influence of Wagner ; also the pretty *Sérénade Nocturne* (G.O.) of Aug. de Brock, and the quaint impressionist *Album de Croquis* of Eugène Samuel. P. L. L. Benoit (b. 1834), who is also a writer on Flemish music, has written an interesting and melodious 1st *Caprice* and 2 *Mazurkas* (Cs.).   Franz de Vos writes in Chopin's style.   His 6 *Feuillets d'Album, Mal du Pays, Moments du Piano* (By.) are sympathetic, artistic and *recherché*.   We may mention also P. Crets, *La Cascade* (Bm.) ; Ad. Wouters, *Moments de Musique* (Bm.) ; Léon Pagnion, *Mélancolie* (Ks.) ; the *Petite Histoire* by Ch. Grellinger, the *Ballade* of Th. Mége (By.) ; the 3rd *Nocturne* of J. Eykens (Ks.) ; the *Impromptu* and *Méditation* by van B. Douglas (Fb.) ; as well as J. F. de Coninck (1791–1866), *Concertos, Sonatas*, etc.

Composers of note are Carl Smulders, whose dignified and modern *Concerto* (Mu.) may be mentioned, and *Sylvain Dupuis*, whose *Op.* 23 (6 *Pieces*) (Ks.) is poetical and artistic.   Also there is Maurice Koettlitz, modern and melodious *Op.* 9, 12, 23, 24, 25 ; Xavier Carlier, represented by an attractive *Scherzo* and *Chant de Soir* (Cz.) ; Ch. Melant, pretty and artistic *Romance* and *Bluette* (Ks.) ; Van Avermaete, *Sarabande Op.* 59 (By.) ; Magnus Désiré (b. 1828), mainly Salon music ; Dupont, *Op.* 37, 27 (St.) and 1st *Rondo Ardenne* for four hands (Cz.) ; Alf. Mailly, 1st *Esquisse* (Cz.) ; J. L. Gobbaerts (1836–86), an educational writer under noms de plume of Streabog, Ludovic, etc., and J. M. Gregoir (1817–72), *Concerto, Studies*, etc.

CÉSAR FRANCK

César Franck (1822–90), the greatest of the Belgian School, is a mediæval Mystic and Romantic, known principally through his sacred choral and descriptive orchestral works.   Franck was born at Liége, whence he removed to Paris at the age of fifteen, to remain there until his death in 1890.   Having obtained the *Grand Prix* for Piano at the Conservatoire he was apparently intended for a virtuoso, and his youthful works, *Op.* 3 (*Eclogue*), *Op.* 4 *Duet on God Save the King, Op.* 5, *Caprice* and *Op.* 7. *Fantasias* on Polish Airs were written for Piano.   An unsuccessful attempt at Opera, however, turned him into other channels, and he wrote Masses, Motets, Oratorios (*The Beatitudes*), Organ, Orchestral and Chamber Music.   Five years before his death he wrote some works for Piano and Orchestra : the Symphonic Poem *Les Djinns*, in the descriptive supernatural element of which the orchestra appears to most advantage ; the clever *Variations Symphoniques* (Lit.) employing brilliant modern technique and delicate orchestral manipulation, and the poetical *Les Éolides* (Lit.), which is the most directly melodious of his works.   In the previous year (1884) Franck had written his well-known *Prélude, Chorales* and *Fugue*, which, in dignity and style, shows the influence of Bach and the organ. and the clever *Prélude, Aria* and *Finale* (Hl.) which forms a kind of sequel to the former.

Notwithstanding a certain nobility of style there are drawbacks to Franck's art.   A Mystic and Impressionist by nature, it is rarely that, from the atmosphere of technical figuration and short-lived imitation, he produces anything in the nature of a melodic idea. If it were not for the lack of lyrical style, he might be called the Belgian Schumann, whom Franck resembles in subtle and mystic Romantic feeling. His strength lies in his ability to create an atmosphere, as in the supernatural *Les Djinns* and other works. For the rest, his vague outline and freedom of form, the restless chromatic harmonies and quasi-contrapuntal structure require intellectual penetration for the due appreciation of what lies beyond. Franck's position in the story of Pianoforte music is, in a word, that of an impressionist influenced by Bach, writing for the combined forces of Piano and Orchestra.

PIANOFORTE MUSIC OF HOLLAND

The people of Holland are closely akin to their neighbours, the Flemings of North Belgium and, like them, are reflective in temperament. Attaining, like them, great eminence in painting, and sharing with them, to some extent, the honours of the early Polyphonic Choral Age, they have not, as yet, become prominent in the realms of modern instrumental music. Their music does not seem to possess any very distinctive traits and it resembles to some extent their Folk-Songs, which are meditative and sincere in character, but lacking somewhat in strong feelings and vigour.

Little need be said historically of Dutch music here, except that, as in other countries, instrumental music first appeared in vocal or polyphonic style. Compositions were written for voices *or* instruments and *Om te singen op te spielen* corresponded to the usual Italian *Da cantare e suonare* (To be sung or played). In the pre-clavier period the lute was the universal instrument.

The clavier became fashionable at the end of the seventeenth century, but no Dutch Harpsichord or Pianoforte music seems to have become prominent till the present century.

Jan Brandts Buys has made some interesting attempts in Pianoforte music in the interpretation of the *National Folk-Song*. In his interesting *Aus dem Lande Rembrandt's* (Cohen) he has artistically treated some of the Dutch *Volkslieder* [*see also Altniederländsche Volkslieder*, arranged by Kremser (Lk.)]. In these and the *Tänze und Weisen* (Cz.) he occasionally, however, introduces an ultra-modern style. Holland, musically speaking, is somewhat conservative and the music is of the universal rather than of the distinctive type, but the efforts of Brandts Buys are in the right direction.

Litolff's *Concerto Hollandais*, as founded on Dutch Airs, is another instance of what is possible. A promising composer is Ulfert Schults, though he is as yet given to restless changes of key. His *Op.* 5 *Papillons* (A.M.) and an attractive *Tambourin Op.* 14 show originality and masterly grip. One of the most important Dutch composers is Julius Röntgen (b. 1855 in Leipzig of Dutch descent and settled in Amsterdam) who blends both Classical and Romantic elements in his works (*see* Part III, Chapter XVII). Louis Saar (b. in Rotterdam, 1868), who settled in America in 1892, was a pupil of Rheinberger and spent a winter with Brahms whose influence is seen in the two *Ballads* (Srm.), the rugged *D minor* with a characteristic Nocturnal episode, and the dignified one in *F major*. A *Valse Noble* and *Berceuse Op.* 24 (Srm.) and a book of *Duets Op.* 21 (E.S.) are very attractive.

Leander Schlegel in his 3 *Pieces Op.* 10 (R.), 6 *Fantasias, Op.* 15 (B. and H.) and *Adagio* (*Suite, Op.* 14) (Fritzsch) has the brooding meditative spirit of Schumann and Brahms and the linked, syncopated orchestral diction of Wagner, specially manifested in the interesting Sketch *Gretchen vor der Mater Dolorosa*. The *Phantasie Walzer*, despite its restless modulatory spirit, is attractive. The dreamy *Nachruf* is technically interesting and melodically so, as far as the Impressionist nature of the Sketch allows it to be.

Dirk Schäfer, in his richly harmonized and Schumannesque 4 *Petits Morceaux* (S.D.), strikes a pathetic note, while Von Brucker Fock excels in his *Moments Musicaux* (A.M.), which are ably written in a refined and poetic vein.

The *Preludes* of Joh. Wijsman (A.M.) show elemental force and originality of idea.

Van Tetterode is a fluent writer, but lacking in ideas, his *Op.* 3 *Étude Caprice* being the best.

Henri Tibbe has written an artistically modern *Walzer Op.* 10 (A.M.). Ed. Silas (born 1827 in Amsterdam and settled in London) has written much for Piano. His tuneful and well-written *Romance* and *Barcarolle* may be mentioned.

J. H. Oushoorn's *Impromptu, Op.* 10, *Serenade, Op.* 22 (Lange) and *Minuetto* (Lht.) are modern and melodious. The 6 *Character*

Sketches of Philip Toots (A.S.), depicting F. W. Weber's *Dreizehn Lieder* show promise, modern style and disciplined power.

James Kwast (b. 1852) writes in melodious, solid but somewhat uninspired style, *Op.* 8 *Widmung* (B. and F.) being among his best.   M. van de Sandt's (b. 1863) 4 *Pieces* (A.S.) are lyrical and Mendelssohnian.

The 8 *Scènes Lyriques Op.* 61 (J.A.) and *Op.* 17 (Lht.) of Alex Heyblom are interesting, well written and tuneful.   The Piano works of S. de Lange (b. 1840), the organ virtuoso, who is settled in Stuttgart, are organistic.   We may mention his *Op.* 29 (Wernthal).   Of prominent Dutch composers of partial German descent there are M. van Leeuwen, whose praiseworthy *Op.* 3, *Marionetten Hochzeitsscenen* (Lht.) is after the style of Schumann's *Carnival.*

Joz. Schravesande's *Three Pieces* (Lht.) are in melodious and transparent style, and the *Bagatelles, Op.* 12 (1 and 5) can be commended.

The following modern works also are worthy of mention :—

J. G. Litzau, *Lyric Pieces* (Lht.) ;   Jan Morks, *Op.* 80, *Miniatures* (Lht.) ;   Richard Hol (b. 1825), *Sonatas ;* K. Kuiler, *Bagatelles* (Noske) ;   von Groningen (b. 1851), *Suite for Two Pianos ; Pieces* by W. de Haan ;   M. L. Hageman ;   Berthold Tours (who settled in London), *Gavottes,* etc. ;   G. H. Witte, *Characteristic Pieces ;* A. J. Ackerman, *Duets ;* von Boom, *Duets* and *Studies ;* A. Fodom (1759–1849), *Concertos, Sonatas ;* Karl Heymann (b. 1853), *Elfenspiel,* etc. ;   D. Koning, *Studies* and *Sonatas ;* C. M. Mansuy, *Sonatas* and *Fugues ;* L. Coenen (b. 1828), *Octave Studies ;* Ten Have, *Romance* (Ct.) ;   M. J. Bouman, 2 *Pieces* (Lht.).

We may judge from the above that little Holland does not lack Pianoforte composers.

CHAPTER X

SWISS COMPOSERS FOR PIANOFORTE

No very distinctive style attaches to music by Swiss composers, but the National melodies have been set forth in four-hand Swiss *Lieder und Tänze* (R.F.) by Hans Huber and in Fantasia form by Bern, *Aus Berg und Thal* (Hug) ; while of the compositions inspired by Swiss associations in the favourite Styrienne and Tyrolienne rhythms may be mentioned the four-hand *Swiss Suite* by Wilm (Hug).

One of the leading Swiss composers is E. Jacques Dalcroze, who writes effectively in modern style despite a tendency to a somewhat French feeling for ineffective extraneous modulation. His 6 *Danses Romandes* (S.J.), the *Op.* 8 (Jn.), an effective *Arabesque* and *Valse Caprice*, a Wagnerian *Nocturne* (B.P.) and the *Ballade, Op.* 46 may be specially mentioned.

Paul Juon is of Swiss parentage. He was brought up in Russia, but is resident in Berlin. Most of his music is in the prevailing complicated Lisztian orchestral style and shows some instinct for melody. His simpler and most attractive Pieces are *Op.* 1 (5 and 6), *Satyr und Nymphen* (1 and 3) and an effective *Ballad* (Sl.). Russian influence is seen in the more complicated *Preludes* (1 and 2) and *Caprices, Op.* 26 and in the four-hand *Dance Rhythms, Op.* 14. The *New Dance Rhythms, Op.* 24, are remarkable for their rhapsodical tempo ; scarcely two bars are in the same tempo. Various times, such as 1/4, 2/4, 3/4, 4/4, 5/4 alternate, and the result is interesting though not very dance-like in some instances.

The genius of Hans Huber (b. 1852, educated in Leipzig, resident in Basle), shows best in those works of his which are modelled on Schumann. His music descriptive of nine Scenes from Heller's *Nadlaub* (A.P.S.) is one of the most interesting modern characteristic works, dignified and not without distinction in style. Other attractive works in similar style are *Op.* 86 (No. 2) (Sg.) ; 3 *Pieces* (No. 3) (A.P.S.) ; 3 *Pieces* (J.S.), *Op.* 77 (No. 4) ; *Op.* 85 (1 and 5) (R.F.) ; the *Skizzen, Op.* 51 (Hg.), and

6 *Romances* (2, 3 and 4) (Ff.). The descriptive four-hand *Ländliche Suite, Op.* 73 (B. and B.) is attractive. Huber has also written a *Concerto* (B. and H.).

C. J. Lysberg *or* Bovy (1821–73) is now known principally as a composer of better-class Salon music. His pleasing *Idylle* and *Romance, Op.* 46 are in romantic style.

The following composers are Swiss :—J. Vogel (b. 1850), agreeable *Papillons* (Ff.) ; Justin Bischoff (b. 1845), *Chanson du Printemps* (Ff.) ; W. Rehberg, poetic *Barcarolle* (Fritzsch) ; Geo. Pantillon, *Op.* 28, Nos. 2 and 3 (Ff.).

It is quite appropriate that Switzerland, the holiday ground of Europe, should excel in pleasantly-written instructive works. Of these are the graceful *Seven Pieces* of A. Lambert Gentil ; Joseph Lauber's *Op.* 13, No. 3, *Op.* 14, No. 2, *Op.* 23, No. 1, *Op.* 25, No. 1, and *Chaconne ;* Eugene Gayrhos' *Aquarelles* and numerous other works built upon good models, as well as the easy pieces by Angelo d'Arosa (Foetisch), Gustave Sandré, E. Rostek, W. Grünberg, J. Hanson, A. Roth, Ch. Grellinger (all Ff.) and P. Hahnemann (*Op.* 7–9 and 14).

A deeper note prevails in the Pieces by Hy. Reymond—*Pièces Intimes* (Nos. 1, 2 and 5) and the *Prelude* and *Fugue.*

Switzerland has its advanced disciple of Debussy in Emile R. Blanchet, and just as Debussy requires an introduction, so the student should try first his *Barcarolles, Serenade Op.* 25, No. 2, *Prelude, Op.* 26, No. 2, and that striking Impressionist Eastern Sketch *Adrianople, Op.* 18 (Ff.).

The leading composer of Swiss nationality, Raff, has been dealt with elsewhere.

CHAPTER XI

THE people of Spain are a people unto themselves. Reputedly proud and reserved in manner, they are also, in matters of musical art, somewhat isolated and retrograde. At present the dominion of Italian Opera is still felt, as it has been until recently in other countries, and this hinders the development of what would probably be one of the most individual of National styles in musical art. In the past Spain has had prominent composers in Morales, Guerrero, Vittoria, and the organists Cabezon and Selmas, as well as clever theorists.

Early instrumental music was, as in other countries, mostly written for the lute, and as such showed the contrapuntal style of the period and the influence of the Netherlandish composers.

The hope of Spain's musical future is in its rich store of unique *Songs* and *Dances* with their oriental flavour. Professor Felipe Pedrell of Barcelona, the author and critic, has said that " every country should establish its system of music on the basis of National Song." No doubt, the National Dance is also intended, since the two are always bound up together, as in the

stately old Spanish *Sarabande* with its $\frac{3}{4}$

the *Jota Aragonesa* and the *Jota Navarresa*.

These two latter are in 3/4 time, mostly in two-bar sections

to the rhythm and in the *minor* mode.

They are danced to the accompaniment of castanets, with a vocal refrain in 3rds, while the melody is played by a mandoline.

In the 3/8 *Fandango* or *Malagueña Rondeña,* with its guitar accompaniment and castanet rhythm of

the vocal refrain or *copla* (couplet) alternates with the instrumental *ritornel.*

Spanish Songs and Dances derive their names from the various provinces.

The *Bolero*, with its | 𝄽 | rhythm and more or less elaborated castanet accompaniment, and the various kinds of Sequidillas (written in 3/4 or 3/8 time in the *minor*)with their quick changes of movement and of key are similarly performed and belong to the provinces of Galicia and old Castile.

The music of Andalusia or Southern Spain shows most of all the Eastern element, and is of a languorous, dreamy type with a highly-ornamented voice-part, and to this belong the graceful *Tirana* in 6/8 time, *Fandango* and *Habañera* types. The *Guajiras* and *Tango* are akin to the latter and belong to Cuba. The Andalusian *Cachuca* in 3/4 time resembles the *Bolero.* Mention of these is necessary as showing the lines on which much Spanish Pianoforte music is written. With these and the 5/8 and 7/4 Basque melodies, the traditional *Ballads,* the peasant *Villancicos* and the ancient *Romanceros,* Spain has ample material for artistic development of National style. Spanish music reflects the proud and pompous, yet fiery and vivacious elements of the Spanish character.

Don Pedro Albeniz (1795–1830) has been called the founder of the modern Spanish Pianoforte School. A pupil of Herz and Kalkbrenner, he wrote some 70 Pianoforte works, such as Rondos, Variations, etc., and a Method for the Madrid Conservatoire.

His grand-nephew Don Isaac Albeniz (1861–1909), the composer of 220 published Pieces, was resident in London. His *Concerto Fantastique,* interesting *Sevillana Dances, Barcarolle Catalane, Cadiz Gaditana, Caprice Créole* (J.W.) and *Suites*

Espagnoles (especially the *Suite Iberia*, 1905) are artistic compositions and fully reflect the Spanish style.

Gonzalo de J. Nuñez has written a characteristic *Aragonese* and .cosmopolitan *Doux Songe* (St.). Oscar de la Cinna has written his tuneful *Jota Aragonesa, Chanson Andalouse,* and *Moment Joyeux* (St.) in National style. His *Moorish War Scenes* and *Album of 6 Pieces* (W.A.), particularly the former, are in similar vein.

The *Jota Navarresa, Habañera* and *Zapateado* (after Sarasate) by Berthe Marx (St.) are also interesting. Alberto Jonas' (b. 1868 at Madrid and settled in America) artistic and attractive *Northern Dances* and poetical *Valse, Op.* 18 and *Mazurka* (Srm.) are not in Spanish idiom, nor are the beautiful and original six *Caprices Nocturnes* by Rafael de Aceves (Lm.), though he has written several Pieces in Spanish rhythm.

Essentially Spanish are the *Malagueña Serenade* and *Jota Aragonesa* of J. Mulder (Jm.). The artistic *Rapsodia Aragonesa* of E. Granados and his attractive *Danzas Españolas* and *Goyescas* are well known, as is the *Jota Aragonesa* of A. Nogues (U.L.) ; while the Eastern colouring of the *Rapsodia Andaluzia* of Costa Noguerras is very apparent. In the impressionistic Gabriel Grovlez's *Child's Garden* a quasi-Eastern atmosphere is produced by simple means. The lighter *Dances* of Alberto Cota (U.L.) are pleasing, and we may also mention the pleasant *Serenata Española* of S. Lanrich (St.) and a *Zapateado* by Sant Esteban (Lm.).

Spanish Dances and Rhythms have inspired composers of all nationalities. We need only mention the *Rhapsodie Espagnole* of Liszt, which is built upon two or three Spanish tunes—the much-exploited *Les Folies d'Espagne* and *La Jota Aragonesa;* also *Grenada* by Delioux (Sh.), *Fantasie* by Gevaert (Ks.), *Spanish Dances* by Moskowski (Aug.), *Boleros* by Nuchirez (Ash) and Geo. Matthias (Lc.), and the *Alborada* by Colomer (Jn.). Lastly reference may be made to the *Spanish Dances and Romances* (Aug.) arranged by Pauer.

Other Spanish composers claiming attention are Zabalza (1833–94), *Studies,* etc. ; J. M. Echeverria (b. 1855), *Mazurka, Serenata,* etc. ; Guelbeuza (1819–86) ; and the young Anda-lusians J. Turina, in his *Sonata Romantique* and *Suites,* and Manuel de Falla, in his imaginative Spanish Pieces.

In the absence of information as to the works of the following, which are very difficult to procure, we must merely mention the names of Chapi, Malati, Saldoni (1807–90), Eslava (1807–78), Breton, Morera, Rogelis Vellar, Bartolomé Casas and Conrado de Campo.

PORTUGUESE PIANOFORTE MUSIC

The music of Portugal does not bulk largely on the artistic horizon, so it is with some surprise that one finds Portuguese Piano music reaching so high a standard as it does. Simple melodiousness inclining to the sentimental, refinement, modern technique and freedom from pessimism are its general characteristics. The easeful and pensive melancholy of the people is reflected in their art and one finds oneself comparing their Pianoforte compositions with those of Chopin. The National Dance Songs are the *Fados* with the rhythm

the *Malhao, Fandango*, etc.

The best-known Portuguese composer is José Vianna da Motta, whose *Fantasiestück* (Cohen) and *4th Portuguese Rhapsody* on *Cracão da Tarde* are attractive compositions, the latter especially so with its modern technique and skilful and varied artistic treatment.

An *Idyllio* on a melody from Antigua by A. P. Lima, Jr. (Nu.) is in similar style, but inclined to be sentimental.

A. Kiel has the melodic gift and has written some tuneful and artistically-wrought short works in *Papillon*, the *4th* Book of the *Recueil*, *Douze Mélodies* and the 2nd and 3rd Books of the *Impressions Poétiques*. Em. Lami writes in Chopinesque style, as, for instance, in his well-written and elaborated Nocturnes *La Charmeuse* and *Gentilesse* (Nu.) ; while J. G. Daddi approximates to Liszt's style in his *Andante Cantabile* and *La Mélan colie* (Nu.).

The attractive and piquant *Arlequin* and *Entr'acte* of Th. del Negro (Nu.) are somewhat after the French style.

J. Neuparth delights in dramatic contrast and daring harmonies, as in his *Rêverie, Op. 5, Vision, Minuet* and *Charme* (Nu.).

G. Ribeiro has written a very tuneful *Idylle* and *Tarantelle* (Nu.) and F. Bahia two artistic and individual Pieces, *Barcarolle* and *A Briza* (Nu.). We may also mention D. R. Silva—a Chopinesque *Nocturne Op.* 24 and *Rondo de Concert* (Nu.) ; Vargas, Jr., a *Scherzo* ; E. Viera, *Caprice Mazurka ;* F. Gazul, *Grace* (Nu.), and Arthur Napoléon, the pianist (b. 1843), some effective Pieces. Leoncavello's *Spanish Album* (Asch.) is a welcome addition to this category.

CHAPTER XII

MODERN ITALIAN PIANOFORTE MUSIC

SINCE the decease of D. Scarlatti (d. 1757) Italy would seem to have been almost entirely taken up with the pursuit of Opera, while young Italian composers appear to be immersed in Wagner.

The devotion to the mental and technical subtleties of the modern German School has apparently been the means of young Italy losing sight of the glorious heritage of inspired melody which has been associated in the past with Italian Art.

Wagner's many-coloured Orchestral style transferred to the piano becomes of non-effect, hence the ineffectiveness of most modern Italian pianoforte music. The hope of the young Italian School seems to lie in the increasing devotion to the ancient *Suite*, to which some of their number have a distinct leaning.

The revivification of old Italian melody in this form with modern harmonies may go far to form a modern and true National School.

To the transition period from Scarlatti to the present day may be assigned :—

Th. Dohler (1814–56) (*see* Part III, Chapter XIV).

G. Giordani (b. 1753) ; *Concertos, Sonatas*, etc.

S. Golinelli (b. 1818) ; once popular *Sonatas, Fantasias*, etc.

B. Asioli (1769–1832) ; *Sonatas, Four-Hand Capriccios*, etc.

G. Concone (1810–61) ; interesting *Characteristic Studies*.

Italy's modern writers for Piano may be summarized as follows, taking first those who have been influenced by Classical models :—

Cesare Galeotti has written an attractive *Sonata, Op.* 32 (Lm.), full of dignity and well developed, and an interesting *Nocturne*. The technique suggests the influence of Liszt and Brahms. The three *Pieces, Op.* 118, 122, 214 (Hm.), the *Theme and Variations*,

Op. 23, and the *Étude de Concert, Op.* 19, though not inspired, are interesting.

Alfonso Falconi, a promising writer, is vigorous and masculine in his *Suite* (R.), in which the old Italian style peeps out, and in the interesting and characteristic *Canti dell' Allia* (R.) and the *Serenata, Op.* 39 (Hg.).

Alessandro Longo is one of those who point to the future of Italy: he excels in the ancient style. His *Prelude* (Rc.), *Capriccio* (R.), *Toccata* and *Fugue* (Hg.) and *Variations for Two Pianos* are effective and well written. Of Pieces in the modern style those most instructive are *Op.* 16 (2 and 6) (A.P.S.). Ed. Poldini, on the other hand, is, in one sense, a kind of modern Italian Mendelssohn—a poet of fun, witchery and caprice combined with a masterly modern style and clever modulatory effects as in *Fêtes Galantes* (Fr.), *Op.* 30 (1 and 3) and *Op.* 20 (No. 7) (E.S.). *See also* his *Suite, Op.* 90 (Chester).

Michele Esposito (educated in Naples—now Prof. A.I.A.M., Dublin) possesses modern technique and style with pleasing melody. His *1st Nocturne, Op.* 13, an attractive *Op.* 26 (No. 2), and a well-written modern poetical *Suite* (7 Pieces) (B. and H.) are worthy of interest. A refined writer is D'Ambrosio, whose characteristic *Chanson Napolitaine* and tasteful French *Valse, Op.* 37 (3) (J.W.) deserve mention. Of the brothers Fumagalli, Adolphe (b. 1828) composes tasteful French Salon music (*Papillon* and *Rêverie*) (Chd.), while Luca (b. 1837) writes a refined modern style in his 2 *Pieces* (Jn.) and 2 *Sketches* (Hg.). Another and separate Fumagalli, Benito, has also composed some well-written works (R.B.). Frank Alfano is a most promising composer with an ultra-refined, almost cloying Romantic style. Owing to his ultra-modern style, his strength is harmonic rather than melodic. His best works are *Op.* 11 (1 and 4) and *Op.* 8 (2 and 4) (Hg.), while other interesting Pieces are *Op.* 24 (1 and 3) and *Op.* 16 (1, 2 and 3) (B. and B.). Carlo Albanesi (b. 1856 at Naples) is Professor at the R.A.M., London. He possesses an elegant, somewhat French style combined with warm-hearted Italian melody. We may mention his *Aveu, 2nd Ballet, Berceuse* and *2nd Gavotte* (Ch.) and also a well-written *Sonata in B♭ minor* (B. and H.).

Eugenio Pirani (b. 1852, settled in Berlin) has written artistic *Impromptus* on *Chansons Populaires Italiennes* (R.) His *Valse, Op.* 30 and *Feux Follets* (Sl.) are in French style.

G. Andreoli (1835–60) wrote a poetic *Barcarolle* and *Serenade* (Hg.), and the following also deserve mention :—

Al. Cajani, tasteful *Barcarolle* (Srm.). Da Crescenzo, *Ricordi da Napoli* (Aug.). Al. Luigini, *Rêverie* (Ct.). Foschini, *Capricciosetta* (M.C.). Marchisio, *Preludio* (M.C.). Leoncavallo, *Gagliardo* (Bk.). Fr. Cilea, *Op.* 28 (1 and 2) (B. and B.). S. Lazzari, *2nd Miniature* (B.P.). G. B. Polleri, *Capriccio* and *Op.* 12 (F.S.). P. Floridia (b. 1860), *Op.* 15, *Epithalme* (Hg.). Busoni, *Op.* 9 (Rc.). E. Wolf Ferrari, *2nd Impromptu*, *Op.* 13 (R.). F. Luzzato (b. 1857), distinguished and melodious *Op.* 35 (Hm.). Del Valle de Paz (b. 1861), graceful *Pieces* (Aug.) and a *Pianoforte School*.

We may now set apart those composers who write strongly in the modern Germanic style. G. Sgambati (1843–1914), whose mother was English), above all his compatriots, has the air of Classic repose. This and some feeling for melody renders him at his best in small lyrical works, as in the refined *Romance*, *Op.* 23 (No. 1) (St.) and *Op.* 36 (P.). His *5th Nocturne, Op.* 14 *Gavotte*, and *Étude Mélodique, Op.* 21, deserve mention, but his works as a rule lack distinction in melody and harmony.

L. Sinigaglia has a somewhat bizarre and chromatic style, as seen in his *Capriccio* (St.). G. Frugatta's (b. 1860) rich chromatic style is characterized by a pessimistic undertone and lack of melodic spontaneity. His most straightforward works probably are the Chopinesque *Croquis de Valses* (St.), the most attractive, very characteristic *Gondolina*, and *Andalousienne* (St.), the 3 *Caprices* (Jn.) and the *Variations, Op.* 36. F. da Venezia shows also modern German influence, with the usual technical fluency, lack of charm and National feeling. His most attractive works are the Brahms-Chopinesque *Intermezzo, Op.* 5, and *Scherzo, Op.* 2 (Hg.). G. Martucci (1856–1909) is imbued with mysterious pessimism and orchestral Wagnerian diction. His 4 *Pieces, Op.* 74 (R.) and a *Concerto* show him at his best.

M. E. Bossi (b. 1861) is best in the Wagnerian *Ultimo Canto, Op.* 109 (R.B.), the *Prelude, Op.* 101 (Hg.) and a French *Papillon* (Hs.). His *Satire Musicale* (R.B.)—a piece of musical fooling—has one piece in ninths, the next in consecutive fifths, another in the key of C, but only remotely touching that key, and the last in two keys at once ; a *Satire* indeed which explains itself. Bossi is a fluent and promising composer, but somewhat lacking in inspiration.

One notable branch of activity in the present period, and a sign of good promise, is the production of *educational* works. The Italians Busoni (for Bach), Buonamici (for Beethoven), Mugellini (for Bach) and Valle de Paz, are doing good work in the preparation of Critical Editions and Educational Collections ; while the National Collection of Old Italian Masters for Piano by the Societá Anonima Notari (Chester) keeps before the student the glories of the old Italian School.

CHAPTER XIII

SCANDINAVIAN PIANOFORTE MUSIC

UNDER the designation of Scandinavian we may include Denmark, Sweden, Norway, Iceland, and Finland. The music-loving people inhabiting these countries are noted for their rich store of traditional Song and Dance, which was, until a century ago, perpetuated by ear alone. Of Scandinavian music as a whole, the distinguishing features are the heroic epic element, and the peculiarities due to the use of certain instruments, such as the Norwegian harp-like " Langleike," and the " Hardanger Fiddle," with its extra vibrating sympathetic strings, an instrument used for Dances and Marches only; also the wooden Horn called the " Lur," used in the Highlands, the Swedish " Nycel-harpe," which resembles the " Langleike," and the Finnish " Kantele," which has five strings tuned to the scale of G, A, B♭, C, D. The influence of the latter instrument is particularly reflected in the musical setting of the national *Runos*, or Finnish Ballads.

One feature of Scandinavian Folk-Songs is that the majority are in the minor mode. Some begin in the major and end in the minor, and *vice versa*, while some show the influence of the old modes. Generally, also, they are in duple or 2/4 time. The Norwegian, North Swedish, and Danish melodies (except Jutland) are usually in 8-bar rhythm, while those of North Denmark and the opposite district of Norway are free as regards rhythm, and are more declamatory in style.

We have mentioned the Epic Songs, or *Kampevise*, as they are termed, as being characteristic of Scandinavia. There are also the pastoral or Herdman's Songs, in which the " Lur " or Shepherd's Horn is used. Coming to the National Dances, we find that the *Polska*, and the *Halling*, which is danced to the accompaniment of the Hardanger Fiddle, are the principal. The *Halling* is mostly in 2/4 time, major mode, and generally taken *allegretto*. We are familiar with examples of the *Halling* and of the triple-time Spring Dances in the works of Grieg. For instance, the simple *Halling* in his *Op.* 71 occurs in a slightly different and more developed form in the well-known *Bridal Dance*.

The people of our own country, who are largely, at least in the northern half, of Scandinavian origin, should not fail to be interested in Scandinavian Song and Dance melodies, since some at least of these are practically identical with British melodies.

The national movement in Scandinavian music is comparatively recent. Formerly, like the music of this and other countries, it was in foreign hands, and foreign models prevailed. The movement bringing forward Northern Music and Song which resulted in the foundation of what was called the Gothic Union, with its Collection of Swedish, Danish, and Norwegian Songs, proved to be the stimulus which was required to bring the National Schools of Composition to life.

DANISH PIANOFORTE MUSIC

Denmark has its heroic or historic ballads, Scherzlieder, children's songs, love songs, sailor songs, street ballads, and sacred songs. A recent Danish authority, Hjalman Thuren, has said that " a greater part of the Norwegian and Swedish Folk-Songs have the same rhythm and the same tonality as the Danish."

In speaking of Danish music, the prominent name of Gade springs to one's mind.

The master of Gade, by name A. P. Berggreen, the compiler of the best Selection of Danish Folk-Songs, has expressed the opinion that the characteristics of Norwegian, Swedish, and Danish Folk-Song progress, as it were, from the pointed and springing outline of Norwegian melody to the more quiescent form of Swedish and Danish melody. There is no doubt something to be said for this comparison, though it apparently does not seem to apply to Pianoforte music, for if we listen to the delightful *Nordische Volkstänze* of Emil Hartmann (1836–89), the son of John Hartmann, the " Father of the National Danish School," who was born in 1805, we find breezy and melodious movements which are certainly vigorous and pointed enough.

The *Volkstänze* were originally written for orchestra, and then transcribed by the composer for the piano. (1) First we

have a *Scherzo* which would seem to anticipate Grieg, except in the important qualification of modern harmonic effects, in which Grieg was certainly one of, if not the foremost of all composers. (2) There is also a *Minuet,* and (3) a *Halling,* both of which contain the characteristic Scottish snap. In this connection it is interesting to note that both our Scottish Reel and English Hornpipe are probably of Scandinavian origin.

The elder Johann Hartmann, the " Father of Danish Music," who was born in 1805 and died in 1899 at the age of ninety-four, and whose daughter married Gade, the composer, was the first Danish composer of note who portrayed National characteristics in his works. His *Studies (Op.* 53) and *Kleine Noveletten, (Op.* 53) are fairly well known. The third of the *Noveletten,* written in Minuet form, contains Scandinavian features which seem to foreshadow Grieg. In other numbers Johann Hartmann seems also to anticipate Gade. It is interesting now to note how that Emil Hornemann (1841–1906), who is known for his melodious easy *Studies, Piano Caprices,* and Collection of *Folk-Songs,* was living in Copenhagen in 1863, along with the Norwegians

Grieg and Nordraak, and that these were making history in
their efforts to revolutionize the " old conservative côterie," as
Grieg termed musical Europe.   Before we leave Emil Hartmann
I should mention that, besides his popular *Volkstänze*, he wrote,
among other things, some attractive *Ball Scenes* (Litolff), a
Sonata, Op. 17, a *Concerto*, some *Suites* (Duet, *Carnival, Op.* 32),
some *Mazurkas*, an *Arabesque*, and *Caprice*.   The latter is in
brilliant style, showing the influence of Weber and Mendelssohn
as regards technique, and to some extent as regards style,
but is lacking somewhat in individuality and National feeling.
The second theme is interesting and inclines to Schumann.

We now come to Gade (1817–90), the chief Danish composer
for the Pianoforte, who, apart from his Nationality, deserves
distinction as one of the best poetical and characteristic
composers for that instrument.

Gade has been somewhat unthinkingly classed by critics as
Mendelssohnian.   With the exception, however, of a few
cantabile movements, such as the *Barcarolle* of the *Aquarelles*,
his individuality, clothed as it is in a light, rhythmical, piquant
and refined style, can easily be discerned.   If we go back to
Johann Hartmann's *Noveletten* we may note the origin of some
of these features.   I am inclined to think that the long, tripping
staccato passages of the *Canzonette* and *Humoreske*, and the
marked lilting rhytm of the *Capriccio*, of the *Aquarelles*, the
Ring Dance, and *Weihnachtsmarsch*, from the *Children's
Christmas Eve*, are, rhythmically speaking, of Scandinavian
origin, while the light-flowing figures in alternate hands, such as
occur in *Im Walde* (*Fantasiestücke*), and the homely melodies,
such as that in the *Canzonetta*, from the *Albumblätter*, betoken
also an individuality apart from considerations of nationality.
Gade, we may say, excelled in the fairy-elf style as represented
in the small *Poetical Sketch*, and as compared with Mendelssohn's
pre-eminence in his larger *Scherzos*, which are designed on a
larger scale.   Something of the light tripping style may be seen
in the elder Hartmann's *Noveletten, Nos.* 6 and 2, and it is very
likely, as I have hinted, that Gade may have formed something
of his style from that of his father-in-law.   Gade's larger works
do not chain the interest so well as his small dainty pieces, such
as the *Aquarellen, Idyllen*, and *Albumblätter*.   It is these smaller
works that Gade will, in all probability, be known by in the
future, though his *Sonata, Op.* 28, a little-known work, and the

Volkstänze, Op. 31 (Br. and Härtel), deserve special mention. Of his other works the *Northern Tone Pictures, Op.* 4, *Frühlingsblumen, Op.* 2, *Op.* 27 *Arabesque* (Br. & Härtel), and the four-hand *Marches, Op.* 18 and the thirty *Scandinavian Volkslieder*, published by Peters, may be mentioned.

Gade was taught by Berggreen in Copenhagen and at Leipzig, where he was a friend of the Lyric Romantic composers, Mendelssohn and Schumann; and at a period when these two composers were recognized, as they are to-day, as models of style, it is no mean thing that Gade preserved his own individuality. We always find his childlike and simple nature reproduced in his compositions. In the Idyllic element he resembles our own Sterndale Bennett; in dainty power of characterization, Schumann and Heller; while, as regards National feeling, though to some extent overshadowed by the Leipzig element, there is much we can point to in his works as a continuance of the work of the Hartmanns.

Aug. Winding, who was born 1825, died 1900, and was but eight years younger than Gade, was also a pupil of his, as well as of Reinecke and others. Winding represents a kind of combined Danish Schumann and Heller. Though he is at home in the virtuoso element, as may be seen in his effective *Toccata*, he is best known in the charming *Characteristic Sketch* which was perfected and made so artistic by Heller and Schumann. Messrs. Steingräber have published a number of his later works, which deserve the attention of all who appreciate characteristic music for the piano. Winding's *Toccata, No.* 2, *in E minor, Op.* 43, will give an idea of his technical style. The work is evidently founded on the usual Schumann and Czerny model (a kind of poetical study in double notes), and is distinguished by an interesting meditative melancholy combined with fire and energy.

It is difficult, in the space allowed, to give an idea of Winding's characteristic talent, but, taking the *Recollections of Home, Op.* 44, we may note a lively Piece entitled *The Spinning Wheel* —a well-worn theme, but here artistically treated. A simple but pretty *Ländler* in the same book deserves mention also. The *Travel* sketches from *Far and Near* represent a succession of movements such as *Hungarian Reitermarsch, Styrian Waltzer, Tarantella, Gondoliera*, representations of different climes. The most interesting and the best, from the point of Nationality,

are the two entitled *Nordische Tanzweise* and *Auf Bergshöhe*
(On the Mountains). These speak for themselves, with their

" Auf Bergshohe" Winding, Op. 45

characteristic rhythm and plaintive melody. Of the *Albumblätter*, perhaps the best are a very Scandinavian *Im Volkston*,
with its harmonies something after the Grieg style, and a
charming little Waltz.

Of the interesting book entitled *Aus der Kinderwelt*, one may
particularly recognize the inspiration of Schumann in both of
the Pieces entitled *In Sunshine* and *A Fatal Story*.

These grateful Sketches of Windings, together with those
of his Swedish contemporary Ad. Hägg, may be fitly ranged

along with the world-wide popular *Kinderscenen* of Schumann, whom we may term the leading poet of the child's musical world.

Winding was for some years both the Director and the Professor in the Copenhagen Conservatoire. Besides a *Concerto* and *Concert Allegro* of his own, he wrote well-known cadenzas for the Concertos of Beethoven and Mozart. Besides the above, *Op.* 43–44, 45, 46–51, there are the *Reisebilder, Op.* 3, *Genrebilder, Op.* 15, some interesting Pieces in the form of *Studies* (*Op.* 25), *Preludes* in all keys, *Op.* 26, *Duet* (*Op.* 32), *In Youthful Days,* also *Op.* 30 (*Songs for Klavier*), *Op.* 33 (*Album Leaves*), and (*Bagatelles*), *Op.* 40.

Julius Bechgaard, born 1843 in Copenhagen, where he now lives, was a pupil at Leipzig, and also of Gade at Copenhagen. His *Poésies Musicales* (27 numbers) are written in a poetical and unhackneyed style. The shorter numbers are the best. Bechgaard seems to have something of the daintiness of Gade. An illustration of this is seen in the *Arabesque* from the first book.

Perhaps the best-known Danish composer of pianoforte of the present day is Ludvig Schytte (born 1850), who was also a pupil of Gade. He now resides in Vienna, and is mostly known by refined and elegant pieces of the salon style, which I need not describe, as they are well known, but he has also done a good deal of work of a higher class.

His *Naturstimmungen*, of which No. 3, *On the Mountain*, is the most Scandinavian in character, and the *Improvisations* (3 and 4) are well written and attractive, and we note the Scandinavian style of the *Minuetto* in the latter piece.

His *Modern Suites*, written in educational style, show also the influence of Folk-Song melodies in their short rhythmical periods and artless and vigorous style.

Some of Schytte's excellent Studies (most of which are published by Hansen), lean to the brilliant style of Liszt, of whom he was a pupil. Especially is this so in his *Caprices and Fantasies*, while his admirably written pieces for the young also deserve special mention. His musical illustrations to *Andersen's Fairy Tales* are dainty and fresh characterizations, melodious and attractive. A successful *Concerto*, *Duet* arrangements of Danish and Swedish melodies, and a *Sonata in B♭* should be kept in mind.

The *Idylls* of Alfred Tofft (Augener) deserve attention for their elegiac character. His other works are refined, but not always distinctive in style.

It is interesting to note that in the land of Hans Andersen, the world-renowned writer of fairy tales, so much music descriptive of the pranks of elves and fairies should be found in Danish Pianoforte music. Possibly the idea began with Johann Hartmann, whose *Op*. 50 consists of small characteristic Sketches with introductory poetry by Hans Andersen. We mentioned its presence in Gade's works, and we find the same element in the three books of dramatic Sketches by P. A. D. Steenfeldt depicted in a simple but vivid manner, and showing Scandinavian influence as in the numbers entitled severally *The Gnome King's Bride, The Fairy Queen, The Brownies*.

F. L. Wiel-Lange, a clergyman, pupil of Gade and Hartmann, in his four books of *Fairy Tales*, illustrating those made famous by Andersen, has exploited the same sphere. Ludvig Schytte and Adolf Hägg, the Swede, have also done something in the same way. Of other works by Wiel-Lange, we may mention *Skovblomster* (Forest Flowers), *Ved Löwfald* (At Löwfald), *Stimmungsbilder* (Summer Idylls), *I Skumringen* (In the Twilight), etc. The latter are agreeable little Sketches.

We are all acquainted with the *Wanderstunden* and other Sketches of Stephen Heller, depicting noonday reveries in the forest and his sympathies with nature in its every mood. It may be said also that Sinding's more concertized *Frühlings-rauschen* appeals to us in the same way as a popular nature study.

In P. T. Lange-Müller's poetical Reveries, the *Skovstykker* (Forest Pieces) we have Nature similarly revealed to us, both in the gloomy depths of the forest and in its lighter, more breezy aspect. Scandinavian atmosphere prevails, and the second book is perhaps the best. The last number, *Op.* 13, partakes of both aspects of the *Forest Reverie*. Other works are his *Op.* 66, *Fantasie*, and *Op.* 26, *Meraner Reigen*, for Duet.

The elusive spirit of reverie must be sought in the similarly interesting *Daempede* melodies. Perhaps the first number is the easiest to interpret. One wonders, in music of this kind, how much would have been possible without the brooding spirit of Schumann, the chief of the Romanticists.

Of other Danish composers we may mention *Otto Malling*, the organ composer, who has written sets of *Humoreskes*, *Fantasies, Op.* 16, *Rhapsodies, Op.* 21, and especially Aug. Enna, born 1860, the brilliant opera composer, whose life reads like a romance. Enna has written some very agreeable

Pianoforte Pieces, though they are lacking, perhaps, in distinctive style. The numbers of the first book, however, of his *Eight Pieces* (Bote & Bock) are very melodious. The *Barcarolle* will suffice as an example. Two sets of *Characteristic Pieces* and a set of other *Five Pieces* by him are published.

Enna's grandfather was an Italian soldier in Napoleon's army, who married a German girl ; his father was a poor shoemaker. The composer himself, after a chequered career, was enabled to study in Germany through the help of Gade. Other Danish composers there are whose works may be said to be agreeable, but without any particular individuality, such as those of Anton Ree (1820-66), the *Album Leaves* of C. Rübner, the solid but tuneful compositions of Victor Bendix, Conductor of the Danish Concert Society (b. 1851), including a *Sonata, Op.* 26, *Stimmungsbilder (Op.* 9), and *Five Pieces (Op.* 2). An effective *Concerto in G minor* by Bendix was produced in London, December 6th, 1907.

We would finally speak of Fini Henriques, who is known for his well-written Children's Pieces. Of his Variations and Lyric Pieces *Op.* 11, 15, 19, two former works have been well spoken of. Louis Glass is known for some *Sonatas (Op.* 25 *in A♭*, etc.), composed in the Brahmsian manner. His *Op.* 20 *I det Fri* (six Characteristic Sketches, *Out in the Open*), shows originality in a style somewhat elaborated and combines with rich modern harmonies power of characterization, but lacks any particular message. The *Sketches, Op.* 21, a *Children's Album, Op.* 24, and *Lyric Bagatelles, Op.* 25, are by his pen. Of C. H. Glass the sets of Pieces *Op.* 56, 57, 58 deserve mention. The Fairy Sketches, *Fra Nissernes Verden*, taken from the *Op.* 56, show originality, modern harmonies, and ability to portray the Characteristic. There are also the *Salon* composers, Hitz and H. C. Lumbye, to be mentioned.

E. F. Weyse, known for his Studies, I take to be German, as he was born near Hamburg, and I suppose of German parents, though he is generally reckoned as Danish. Similar circumstances attend Friedrich Kuhlau, the composer of educational *Sonatas*, who, like Weyse, settled in Copenhagen.

It will be seen that for such a small country as Denmark there are quite a number of reputable composers for piano. If we summarize the foregoing we may say, though forecasting what is to follow, that the National element, on the whole, is not quite so frequently found in Danish music as in Swedish, and especially in Norwegian music.

I would suggest that the contrast is not so much of melody of outline, as was opined by Berggreen, *i.e.*, not so much in lack in the *quality* of distinctive features, but rather the lack of *quantity* of music designedly National in feeling. One might say that National feeling manifested itself in different stages in the three countries, Denmark, Sweden, and Norway, and that there is more room for the leaven of Nationality to work in Denmark than in Norway. Time alone will alter this and show what are the possibilities of Danish music, as manifested through the pianoforte.

SWEDISH PIANOFORTE MUSIC.

For a long time, as in other countries, imported or foreign art held sway in Sweden, and it is only of recent years that Swedish composers have begun to build on its foundation of natural Folk-Song and Dance melodies.

I do not intend to do more than mention the names of the older composers, Johann Agrell (1707–65), the pianoforte composer of the Dussek-Haydn period, the vocal composers Bellman, Ohlstrom, Otto Lindblad, Wennerberg, Josephson, and Adolf Lindblad, the Swedish Schubert; the orchestral composers, Albert Rubenson, Franz Berwald, and Södermann; and Ivar Hallström, the founder of Swedish opera, who all, more or less, wrote in the prevailing European mode.

As regards the *younger* Swedish composers, it is now interesting to note that, though they are followers, to a certain extent, of Liszt, Berlioz, Wagner, and Schumann, they are still uplifted in their aim of building upon the plaintive sweetness of their own Native Song.

Before treating of these younger Swedish composers, however, we might say that Swedish Folk-Song and Dance music, upon which they have built, resembles that of Norway to some extent, except that it perhaps shows somewhat less vigour and variety of rhythm.

The *Halling Dance* in 2/4 time and the *Spring Dances*, as in Norway, are in use; and if there is any distinctive form, it is the *Polska*, which is mostly written in the *minor* mode and in 3/4 time. The *Polska*, we should mention, was originally an

importation from Poland 'in the seventeenth century.   There
is little doubt, indeed, that the *March* or Processional-like
Polonaise, gave rise to the Swedish *Polska*, which, taking root in
West Gothland in the seventeenth century, took on its present
form and character.   In the Collection of twenty Gothland
Polskas, collected by Ad. Hägg, we find still the old Polonaise
character.   They are mostly in the *major* mode, and have the
familiar divided or six half-beats in the 3-time bar.

In Nos. 17 and 18 of these *Polskas* we note that there is the

West Gothland Polkas

Orsa Polska.

usual rhythm, but they show also the tendency to a florid or, shall we say, Scotch-reel like character. In other parts of Sweden the *Polska* has become indued with the plaintive *minor* mode and the simplicity of character distinctive of Swedish music, though the Polonaise character is still strictly retained in the *Fackeltanz*, or *Torch Dance* (*Svenska Toner*, p. 10). One may show the transition to the more characteristically Swedish form through two examples in the *minor* from West Gothland (*Svenska Volkviser*, 1, and *Fifty Melodies*, 13.) In the next example the quasi-Waltz or Mazurka rhythm in the *minor* mode (most characteristic of the real Swedish *Polska*) becomes very apparent. Perhaps we may say that many of the *Polskas* have taken on something of the character of the Swedish ballad [No. 10 (50 *Melodies*)], assimilating something of their dreamy *minor* mode and lyrical form.

On the other hand, many of the *Polskas* seem to have taken on the character of the quicker 2/4 time *Halling*, which resembles much the Scottish reel, and which again, as I have said, is most probably of Norwegian origin.

In No. 25 of the 50 *Melodies* we notice the halting syncopated character present in the *Halling* as well as the *Polska*. In both cases the accentuation of weak beats probably comes from the original Polish dance. Those further interested in Swedish Dances I can refer to the interesting and skilful arrangements made for Concert use by Richard Andersen in something after the style of Brahms' *Hungarian Dances* and the Duet, *Swedish Dances*, of Schytte.

I have gone into the question of the Swedish Dance forms because it is in these, as in other countries, that we note the distinguishing features of National music. Turning to the older of the Cosmopolitan School of Swedish composers, and putting on one side those of the Classical era, such as Agrell, etc., we come to L. Adolf Hägg, born 1850, the composer of a meritorious *Nordische Symphonie*, and who, as a pupil of Gade, wrote somewhat in his master's style, also to Ludvig Normann (1831–85), who became known as the husband of Madame Neruda, who later again was known as Lady Hallé.

A quiet idyllic restful strain runs through the compositions of Normann. Of his *Op.* 2, 5 and 14, a *Vivace con fuoco* from the *Op.* 2 deserves perpetuation, and when the therapeutic influence of music comes to be more practically considered in the neurasthenic atmosphere of to-day, the soothing and attractive *Concertstücke*, with Orchestra, *Op.* 54 (R. Forberg), will assuredly have a place.

Vivace con fuoco.   *Ludvig Normann, Op. 2, No. 3.*

Hägg's compositions may not at once commend themselves to the present-day hearer, imbued as he is probably with the hurry and bustle of the twentieth century. Like much of Schumann's music, that of Hägg is introspective, and requires a quiet, meditative hour for its appreciation. He has a good deal of the quiet artlessness of Gade, of whom he was a great admirer, and like him also he is best in smaller Pieces, though, on the other hand, unlike Gade, he has little of the sparkling and dainty passages typical of the Danish composer, and even in his more energetic and brilliant compositions there is always, one will notice, an underlying idyllic element ; especially is it so in the sweet *Blumenlieder*. These unassuming but artistic little Pieces merit, I think, a place in the front rank of works of that *genre*. The *Characterstücke* and *Balletstücke* are in a similar vein, but are somewhat larger and more developed. One of the former is entitled *Greeting to Frau Matilde Gåde*, and is exceedingly pretty. The Epilogue to the otherwise very solid five *Fantasies* also deserves special mention. The *Blumenstück* is a charmingly simple little Piece, with a weakness, however (as in some of his other Pieces), and that is in the connecting episode. Needless to say, Hägg's Pieces, as in the

case of most modern pianoforte composers, show the influence
of Schumann.   The *Blumenstück* and *Balletstücke* especially
recall this influence.

We know how the supernatural element plays a large part
in Scandinavian composition.   Hägg's *Kobolde und Nixen*
recalls to us at once the elves, sprites, nymphs, and goblins with
which we are familiar through the fairy tales of our youth.
No. 1, here instanced, I would name *Dance of Sprites*, and a lover's
song.   No. 2, *Hall of the Gnomes or Mountain Kings*, with a
second Theme illustrating *Happiness*, or the lovers' meeting,
the last remarkable for its almost orchestral fulness of tone and
its harmonic richness.   No. 3 recalls the elves' mad revels or
rejoicings, during which the Theme of the gnomes is thundered
out.   This exciting last movement reminds one of the supernatural element depicted in Wagner's *Tannhäuser*, and Grieg's
Hall of the Mountain Kings.

On the whole, Hägg's nationality is not very prominent, but
it is certainly noticeable in the fresh and artless melodies of his
short movements, as in the *Volkstänze* from the *Characterstücke*,

Humoresk.—Gustaf Hägg. Op. 18

the *Kobolde und Nixen*, and others.   Hägg, we think, deserves
some attention on this side of the water.   His characteristic
small Pieces take a prominent place, and their attractiveness
is increased to some extent by the flavour and individuality of
the nationality to which he belongs.   Hägg, who was a fairly
voluminous composer, wrote also a *Sonata in F minor*, a *Suite*

Sentimentale, three *Kleine Suiten* in the old style, a *Ballade*, *Waltzes*, *Impromptus*, and other smaller works. I should mention, by-the-by, that Hägg's name is not mentioned in English dictionaries of music.

Other Swedish pianoforte composers more Cosmopolitan are Gustav Hägg, Hugo Sedström, Valborg Aulin, V. P. Vretblad, and others.

Gustav Hägg, who is organist at the Klara Kirche, at Stockholm, in general shows a strongly ultra-modern tendency, as in the Collections of Pieces *Op*. 18 and 21. His quick movements are best, as in the *Humoreske*, taken from the five Pieces *Op*. 18, which is both vivacious and interesting. Most Humoreskes are nothing more, so to speak, than capricious Caprices. Hägg seems to have something of genuine humour.

Adolf Wiklund, who has written a popular *Concerto*, is a clever writer in the Schumann-Brahms style. Rich harmonies and easy-flowing melody characterize the noteworthy *Fantasia* of the *Op.* 3.

Hugo Sedström happily combines the rich harmonic effect with a gift for melody, and is one of the most promising of the younger composers. We note the attractive Pieces entitled *Mystik*, with its Scandinavian atmosphere, and the sentimental *Idyll* of the *Op.* 16. His *Op.* 15 (Five Pieces), Four Pieces *Op.* 13, and Four Pieces *Op.* 12, are similarly interesting.

In the Sketches, *Op.* 3, of Patrick Vretblad we may notice particularly the influence of Schumann, who, above all others, has become a model for modern composers of the Pianoforte. This influence is seen in the rich, glowing harmonies and broad-flowing melodies of the *Album Leaf* and *Canzona*, which are particularly attractive. The *Op.* 12 is also refined in style.

W. Berwald—whose works, by-the-by, are published by Ditson, of New York, and whom I take to be a Swede—writes also in a very refined modern style. A *Canzonetta* is a good example of his attractive manner.

Adrian Dahl writes with technical fluency and a command of melody. His tuneful *Valse de Concert* is interesting.

The strength of Miss Valborg Aulin's Pieces lies in their modern attractive harmonies. They are generally dainty, agreeable, but perhaps not distinctive in style. A *Caprice* from the *Collection of Pieces Op.* 5 will serve as an example.

Ed. Rendahl writes in a very melodious though cosmopolitan style. A pretty *Serenade* from the Eight Pieces is an instance, Some of his *Collection of Seven Pieces*, however, are in National style, and attractive. The *Valse Arabeske* by Gustav Brink may be mentioned.

Richard Andersen, the teacher of Stenhammar and Wiklund, is the composer of twenty-one freshly written short Sketches. which form useful studies in style. His *Pieces, Op.* 14, and the seven *Sketches* also are attractive.

Emil Anjou has written light and refined six Sketches or *Fantasies*, which are not lacking in Scandinavian atmosphere.

Tuneful, attractive, but not very individual are the four *Album Leaves* by Nina Wahlström, the six Pieces of the *Sketches* of A. N. Myreberg, and the Collection of *Sketches* of *Op.* 20 and 27 by Torsten Petre.

Miscellaneous items by Albert Rubensen and August Korling, and a meritorious *Idyll* by Jacobson, may also be mentioned.

The leading Swedish Pianoforte composers of the Wagner and Liszt *régime* are Emil Sjögren, who was born in 1853, and educated in Berlin ; W. Peterson Berger (b. 1867, educated in Stockholm and Dresden), the Swedish virtuoso Wilhelm Stenhammar (b. 1871, educated in Stockholm and Berlin), and others to be mentioned later. These younger composers are not only more modern, but are also, I might say, imbued to a greater extent with National feeling.

Sjögren, it should be said, is principally a Song and Violin composer. His Pianoforte works are somewhat orchestral in style, and lean toward Impressionism, thus exemplifying the modern tendency to rich *recherché* harmonies (in which, of all composers, he approaches more closely to Grieg) and of the oft accompanying lack of melodic inspiration.

His naturally big style appears to advantage in his *Nuptial March* and the energetic and festive Sketch, *The Village Inn or Village Fête*, from his interesting six Fantasies entitled *Wandering*. These are well worthy of inspection. The rich harmonic colouring and skilful working out of what sometimes are insignificant ideas makes them attractive. An instance of this may be shown in a Sketch from one of the three lyric poems entitled *A Rower's Song*.

The harmonic aspect of Sjögren's music comes out strongly in the *Prélude Funèbre* and the *March of the Three Holy Kings*. His *Op.* 20 (*Moods*), *Op.* 14, *Novelettes*, and the *Erotikon*, consisting of expressive Sketches in the modern style, though showing Scandinavian atmosphere, deserve attention. Sjögren, since 1891, has been organist at the Johannis Kirche in Stockholm. Sjögren's work is distinctly National in tone. This Nationality, with increased definiteness, comes out specially in his beautiful vocal *Romances* as arranged by Peterson-Berger.

Peterson-Berger, the opera composer, we may say at once, is not as richly harmonic as Sjögren, but is more Scandinavian in style. His Lisztian *Norlandsk Rapsodie,* and the charming Sketches *In the Highlands* and *Memories,* from the *Six Pieces,* and the new Collection of *Frösoblömster* (Fröso Flowers) are poetical, fresh, and vigorous both in harmonies and melody. His first Collection of *Frösoblömster* is not as individual or interesting, while the attractive *Dance Poems* again are Cosmopolitan. The Sketches in the *Ladies' Album (Damernas Album)* are, however, interesting, dignified, and refined. The idyllic, dreamy Reveries entitled *Last Summer* are also remarkable for their Scandinavian and realistic or Impressionist tendency.

Quite similar in spirit are the somewhat rhapsodic *Barcarolle* and *Legend* of the *Op.* 7 of Lennart Lundberg (b. 1870), a teacher at the Stockholm Conservatoire.

Stenhammar, as I have said, is the principal Swedish pianist. He is now Conductor of the Musical Union at Gothenburg, and has composed Wagnerian Operas and Choral Works. His *Concerto, Op.* 1, is poetical and very interesting. Like his other works, it is pervaded by an idyllic pensiveness throughout. It is well written and technically attractive. The fluctuating moods of the *Moderato,* the fairy-like *Vivacissimo,* the Folk-Song melody of the *Andante,* and the animated *Finale,* all go to make up an attractive work. The *Sonate, Op.* 12, is a dignified, high-souled work which gains in re-hearing ; while the solidly

written three *Fantasies Op.* 11, are meditative and introspective.

National style comes again to the front in Bror. Beckman's
Strangaspel (or string music). Like the last-mentioned
composer, Beckman also combines with National feeling
modern harmonies and a leaning to Impressionism. A quaint
number of this work is one entitled *The Scythe-Grinder Sings,* in
which you have the squeaking three-note accompaniment of
the revolving grindstone with the Song melody. The beautiful
Nature Sketch No. 5, entitled *Sunset in the Blue Mountains,* is
thoroughly Scandinavian and interesting.

The *Yuletide Sketches* of Otto Olsen (not to be confused with
Ole Olsen, the Norwegian) are also interesting (especially No. 5,

Gnomes) for their rhythmical and National traits. A Sketch by Wilhelm Svedström, entitled *Pa Fjellet* (On the Mountains) is similarly of interest.

We shall conclude with compositions of one of the youngest Swedish composers, Karl Wohlfart—a coming man, say my Swedish friends—and of Andreas Hallen (b. 1846), a noted choral, symphonic, and operatic composer, who was Conductor at the Opera House at Stockholm. Wohlfart's *Bilder Fran Landet, Op.* 7 (Country Sketches), are fresh and charming, thoroughly Scandinavian, and contain some of the harmonic beauty one always looks for in Grieg. The Folk-Song melody in the *Ballad* by Hallen is fittingly clothed in rich and artistic harmonies, interpreting the words of the well-known ballad entitled, *There was an old King*, or in the German :—

Es war ein alter König
Sein Herz war schwer, sein Haupt war grau.

This is an instance of the Swedish National spirit allied to modern harmonies and methods. The result is artistic, but no such technical display is endeavoured, as might have been expected at the hands of a Liszt.

In summarizing the foregoing, I would say that Denmark is apparently the least advanced in asserting its musical Nationality, but that, speaking generally, it has two eminent composers also of Characteristic Pianoforte Music in Gade and Winding. We noted also the devotion of the Danish composers to the Fairy World, as exploited by their countryman, Hans Andersen.

As regards Sweden, its adopted Dance form of the *Polska* reflects to some extent its National style. Adolff Hägg, with his Danish compatriot Winding, shares with Schumann and Jensen pre-eminence in the characterization of the Children's World ; while Sweden's Pianoforte composers in the Cosmopolitan style, such as Gustav Hägg, Hugo Sedström, Valborg Aulin, and Rendahl, have written much of interest. The more eminent Emil Sjögren, Peterson-Berger, Stenhammar, and Bror. Beckman, in their more modern style, have not only much more of the rich modern harmonic style, but also much more National feeling. Left in the hands of such as Sjögren, Peterson-Berger, Stenhammar, and Bror. Beckman, the musical future of Sweden has little to fear.

Norwegian Pianoforte Music

Norway, the land of the mountain, fiord and forest, has a distinctive musical culture of its own quaint, traditional Folk-Melodies. These, as has been mentioned, show the influence of the old modes and the various old-fashioned instruments in use. [See *Album of Norwegian National Music*, English Edition (Hals.) and *Scandinavian Album* (Aug.)] Musical history in Norway seems to commence with O. O. Lindemann, the noted compiler of its *National Song*, and one of its first composers ; after whom Ole Bull (b. 1810), the eccentric violinist, attracted attention.

The first prominent name, however, is that of Halfdan Kjerulf (1815–68), whose artistic Songs are universally popular. His freshly-written Pianoforte music. abounding, as it does, in distinctive National colour, led the way for that of Grieg. Kjerulf and Grieg are, indeed, the mainstays of the Norwegian National movement as manifested in Pianoforte music. Kjerulf first made his mark with his Songs, and by Government aid he was enabled to study at Leipzig, whence he returned to settle down as a Teacher in his native town of Christiania.

Of his most prominent Pieces we may point out the sprightly and vigorous National characteristics of the *Caprice* and *Humoreske* of the *Op.* 12, the *Frühlingswehen* of the *Op.* 24, and *Spring Dance, Op.* 27.

Since, however, these were, at a later time, eclipsed in some measure by those of Grieg, it is not surprising that the charming Mendelssohnian *Frühlingslied*, the Henseltian *Wiegenlied*, the original and beautiful *Berceuse, Op.* 12 and the *Élégie* (Hals) should be more popular, expressing, as they do, the suave, artistic charm which made his Songs so popular.

The most capable composer of this period next to Kjerulf is Christian Capellen, whose music, though not Nationalistic, is broad and melodious in style. The artistic *Album Leaves, Op.* 10 and *Nocturne, Op.* 12, the pretty *Foraarshilsen,* the expressive *Impromptu, Op.* 16, and *Élégie, Op.* 22 (Wa.), together with the Nationally energetic and attractive *Mazurka Caprice, Op.* 15, and *Scherzo* (Wa.)—all in Mendelssohn-Schumann style —are specially worthy of note.

Thomas Dyke Ackland Tellefsen (1823–74), a native of Trondhjem and one of the youngest of the pre-Grieg School should not be forgotten. He was a pupil of Chopin, and his teacher's influence is visible in his compositions, as, for instance, in the energetic and dignified *Impromptu, Op.* 38, and the refined and well-written *Nocturne, Op.* 39 (Cs.) ; but the National element also is strong in the *Huldredansen* (National Dance) and *Mazurkas, Op.* 1 (Wa.).

O. Winter Hjelm (b. 1837) was trained at Leipzig. His tuneful *Danse Burlesque* (Wa.), after the model of Schumann and Chopin, as well as the *Bravura Étude,* in Henselt-Chopin style, and the *Flying Sketches* (Hs.) of Ed. Neupert should be mentioned. Neupert was an excellent pianist who, after several Concert Tours, settled in New York in 1888.

Leading lights at this time also were Johann Selmer, composer of ambitious Orchestral and Choral works and successful Songs ; and Richard Nordraak (1842–66), a talented Song composer, who was the means of turning Grieg from the " effeminate Mendelssohn-Gade Scandinavianism " into the sphere of Northern Folk-Song.

Ed. Hagerup Grieg (b. 1843) is partly of Scotch ancestry, being descended from the Greigs of Peterhead (a branch of the clan Macgregor), his great-grandfather Alexander Greig having migrated to Norway after the rising of 1715. At the instance of Ole Bull, young Grieg was sent to Leipzig at the age of fifteen (in 1858). In 1863, when residing in Copenhagen, he received encouragement from Gade and Hartmann, the then representatives of the Scandinavian School, and in the next year, meeting the patriotic Richard Nordraak and Ole Bull, he was again inspired by them to eschew the prevailing Germanic style and compose on the lines of his own native strains the *Norwegian Folk-Song* and *Dance.* Previous to the latter incident Grieg had written his since-popular *Poetische Tonbilder,*

Op. 3, which are in the Schumann–Mendelssohn style—
characteristic little Sketches, not unlike those of Gade, but
already full of little energetic syncopations and short characteristic Norwegian melodic figures, as in No. 3, as well as of the
individual chromatic progressions and bustling little dramatic
episodes. In his next much more National work, (*Op.* 6), the
Humoresken dedicated to Nordraak, we find that the first number
is really a *Spring Dance* under the title of *Tempo di Valse.*
Nos. 3 and 4 are thoroughly in Norwegian Dance style and the
Schumann-Mendelssohn element is kept in the background.
The next work, (*Op.* 7), the *Sonata in G minor*, presents decided
features of originality as compared with other *Sonatas* in the
modern Romantic style. The figuration and rhythmical
effects, both due to the National element, distinguish the work
as unique of its kind. In the next *Op.* 12, the 1st Book of
Lyric Pieces, four numbers are Norwegian Songs and Dances
(one, a *Norsk* or *Spring Dance*), three are in National style, and
one (the 1st) shows the interesting influence of Schumann, as it
appears in his later works, giving rise to new and attractive
harmonic combinations and a more Lyrical style.

Op. 16 is the fine *Concerto in A minor*, one of his most
characteristic works, though not strong in thematic development. It is based on the leading Theme, commencing (*a*), and

continued through the interesting augmented interval progression as in (*b*) and the 2nd Theme (*c*). Both are first intro-

duced by the Orchestra in the usual way (*see* Part III, Chapter XXII). In the *Op*. 19, *From the People's Life*, we meet with the vigorous Nationalistic *Auf den Bergen*, the *Carnival*, with its rousing " snap " and the well-known *Bridal Procession*, which is based on the Theme of a *Halling Dance*, with its lilting rhythm and characteristic persistent dominant progression, as in (*a*), (*b*), (*c*).

Of the remaining most prominent works there is first the four-hand 1st *Peer Gynt Suite*, *Op*. 23, with the rhythmically interesting *Troldans* and *Anitra's Dance*, the harmonically rich *Death of Åse* and the charming tone-sketch *Morning*.

The fine and effective *Ballade*, *Op*. 24, consists of rhapsodical *Variations* on a Folk-Song melody, *The Nordland Peasantry*, showing masterly and original harmony effects and modern technique. The Theme is as follows :—

The 2nd, 3rd and 10th Book of *Lyric Pieces* deserve special attention.   The 2nd Book has three numbers in direct National form : a *Folk Tune*, an elaborated *Halling* and a simple *Spring Dance* ; two show Norwegian style, while two—the *Waltz* and *Canon*, as well as most of the 3rd Book, are distinctly Schumannish, especially the *Papillon*, *Vöglein* and *Erotik*.

The 3rd Book is notable also for its harmonic and modulatory charm.   The 10th Book is mostly Norwegian in tone.   We must refer our readers to the various works in order that they may see for themselves their many beauties.   Grieg's originality consisted of certain melodic and rhythmic figures common to the National Song and Dance ; suave figures such as

energetic ones such as

combined with an unusual gift for harmonic effects and artistic style.   The latter alone would probably have ensured Grieg's prominence as a composer.

It is a mistake, we think, to judge of Grieg's works, on the whole, either as " Norwegian Folk-Music sublimated " or as having " much more of Grieg in them than of Norway."   The right classification is, as we have shown : (1) Those directly transcribed from or inspired by the National music; (2) those combining both Grieg and the National element; (3) those poetical Pieces modelled on the Romantic style of Schumann.

Our composer, after settling for some years in Christiania, retired to his villa near Bergen, where he was enabled, by a Government pension, to devote himself to composition.

Those who know only the graceful and popular *Frühlingsrauschen* of Christian Sinding will not recognize the massive Schumannesque technique and straightforward diatonic style in which most of his pieces are written.

It may suffice to mention the *Caprices* (Nos. 3, 5 and 12 (Hs.),

No. 7 of the *Intermezzi, Op.* 65 (P.) and the lighter *Duets, Op.* 71 (P.)   Also *Op.* 52, No. 3, and *Op.* 59, No. 3 (Wood edn.).

Sinding generally lacks individuality and often inspiration, as well as the variety of rhythm and melodic figuration, which are associated with Norwegian music, and he is best in the Song-without-Words style.   Besides the above, we may refer the student to the *Mélodies Mignonnes, Op.* 52, *Études, Impromptus,* the early *Variations for Two Pianos,* and the *Concerto in D♭.*

Sinding was born in 1856.   He studied in Leipzig and resides in Christiania.   His Songs and Chamber Music are highly esteemed.   The *Capriccioso* (Norsk Jubilee Album) (Wa.) gives a good idea of Sinding's style.

Written in Norwegian style is Frederick Mullen's bracing and melodious *Norway Revisited* (Swan).

Capriccioso—Sinding.

Agathe Backer-Gröndahl (1847–1907) probably ranks next to Sinding as a Norse composer.   As a pianist pupil of Kullak and Liszt she made many Concert Tours in Europe, and her *Études, Op.* 22, and *Idylls* (Wa.) are of technical importance.   Her compositions show various styles, including the energetic *Humoreske* (Wa.) and *Caprice* (Hals) ; but the most individual and interesting may be classified as (1) the artistic and poetical

characteristic *Sketches*, *Op.* 36 (No. 47), *Op.* 39 (Bk. I), *Op.* 49
(No. 3), *Op.* 53 (No. 3) and *Op.* 59 (No. 3) (Wa.), which somewhat
resemble those of Grieg in refinement of style, but are practically
without the Norwegian characteristics ; (2) those pre-eminently
in National style—the arrangement of *Norsk Airs*, *Op.* 30 and 33,
the *Spring Dance* and *Swedish Polska* in *Op.* 55, the *Huldreslaat*
(Slatt Dance), the rugged *Ballade*, *Op.* 36 and above all the
interesting *Fairy Suite, In The Blue Mountains* (Wa.), in which
she approaches closely to Grieg.

The best works of Ole Olson (b. 1851) have a specially rugged
National character and wayward individuality.   The attractive
characteristic *Dances*, *Op.* 66, and especially the wild *Tarantelle*
(Wa.), the savage *Fanitul* from the Pieces put together to form
the *Petite Suite* (Cz.), the rugged *Sagn, Stampestubben, Opritt-
schnicken* (2nd Album Comp. Hals), *Brurslaat* (Dance) (Wa.),
and *Festforspiel*, *Op.* 58 (Hals) are all interesting.

Olsen lived for some time in Paris, and his popular light Pieces
show French influence.

Johann Backer Lunde, like Sinding, seems to have formed his
style on the model of Schumann, as manifested in his *Papillons*.
His earliest works are capriciously National and bizarre, the
later ones preserving the Norwegian masculinity of style and

rhythm, and though they are not always melodically inspired, they are interesting. Of these we note specially those in the light, capricious style, the *Impromptu* in *Op*. 12 (Hals), *Scherzino* and *Valse*, *Op*. 13, the *Papillons*, *Mazurka* and *Caprice*, *Op*. 19, the *Pastorale* of *Op*. 18 and the 1st *Valse*, *Op*. 20.

In the expressive style there are the *Arabesque*, *Op*. 13 and *Romances*, *Op*. 13 and 19.

In the three *Ballades* of *Op*. 18 Lunde returns to the rugged Norwegian style and the powerful *Ballade in D minor* is specially noteworthy.

Signe Lund Skabo writes only occasionally in Norwegian style; he has the gift of melody and makes use of modern harmonies.

The *Norsk Pieces*, *Op*. 15 (Zp.) and the light, almost French, *Op*. 16 are very attractive. No. 2 of *Op*. 17 and No. 1 of *Op*. 24 are more Nationalistic, while *Op*. 19 and 24 (2 and 3) (Zp.) are dignified and refined.

In Einar Melling and Catharinus Elling we have two highly attractive composers of the *Miniature*. Melling, overflowing with melody, writes in the refined Cosmopolitan style of Schütt. Of his interesting *Erotik* (Hals) and 6 *Lyrical Pieces*, *Op*. 3 (Zm.), the *Abendfriede* and *Vöglein* are very charming.

Elling writes in exceedingly dainty style. His *Mosaic* (No. 2, 7, 8 and 10) (Wa.) and *Op*. 50 (5 *Pieces*) (Hals) suggest a combination of the fairies of Mendelssohn and the sprites of Heller. They are Norwegian in style, melodious and original. The *Melodie* in *Op*. 50 is a gem.

Eyvind Alnaes seems to be one of the most promising of Scandinavian composers. His style is massive, as though founded on Schumann, but is fresh and healthy in tone as well as Romantic and melodious in style. The 4 *Pieces*, *Op*. 4, the original *Variations*, *Op*. 5 and 3 *Pieces*, *Op*. 9 (Wa.) are all effective and interesting, as well as showing Norse style, especially in the *Op*. 4.

The *Norwegian Suite*, *Op*. 22 (Aug.), *Op*. 30 and the Cosmopolitan *Op*. 32 and 37 (Hals) of Gaston Borch are tuneful but not individual in style.

The composer Halfdan Cleve writes somewhat after the manner of Sinding. His work is vigorous and full of technical interest.

We may also mention the meritorious Griegian *Legends* and

Nos. 1 and 3 of the *Traumbilder* of Inga Laerum (Wa.) ; the *Hallings* and *Slatt Dances* (Wa.) of Chr. Teilman, a tuneful and popular writer of *Norwegian Dances* ; also single Nationalistic Pieces by J. Haarklow and Sigurd Lie (Hals), the *Norwegian Suites* of Smith-Hald (Foetisch) and miscellaneous Pieces in Cosmopolitan style by Elise Wiel, Iver Holter, Peter Lindeman, Per Winge and Per Lasson.

The Pianoforte Music of Finland

Finland is the " land of the thousand lakes," the heath and the forest. As the most northerly country in Europe it is also inhabited by one of the most highly-educated of peoples. Its National epics, appearing first in written literature in the sixteenth century, and typified in the *Kalevala* and the *Kantele tar*, are sung to the Finnish lute. *Kantele*, with its limited

minor scale foundation, 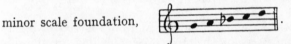 . That this

primitive scale has strangely influenced the National song is seen in the Sibelius Transcriptions of National Airs entitled *Finsk Volkvisen* (N.M.), five out of six being in that mode, one with the *minor* 7th, one with varying *major* and *minor* 7th, and one in the *major*. *Minum Kultani* runs thus:

The Collection of *Patriotic Songs* by F. Paccius (1809–91), the father of Finnish music and an opera composer, those of K. Collan and Kajanus, the Symphonist, though individual, lean somewhat to the Teutonic style, while the *Songs* of Sibelius (F. and W.), brilliantly transcribed by Melartin, Palmgren and Ekman, show him to be a follower of the characteristic National style, as appears also in the now popular orchestral *Finlandia* (B. & H.) built upon Finnish patriotic Themes.

The *Finnish Songs without Words* by Max Krook (J.A.) and Wilm's *Duet Paraphrase, Op.* 140 (Hs.), partly based on Finnish Folk-Song, may be referred to as well as the interesting and effective *Finnish Rhapsody* by Ilda Tilike (B. & H.) on 3 *Finnish Airs*.

The Finnish School, though still young, is specially indebted to the efforts of R. Faltin (b. 1855), Wegelius, Krolm and Genetz for their choral works, and to the symphonic and orchestral works of Melartin, Palmgren, Merikanto and Järnefelt.

Robt. Kajanus (b. 1856) initiated the National movement by his symphonic poem *Kullervo* (from the National epic *Kalevala*) and by an orchestral *Finnish Rhapsody* and *Summer Reminiscences* based on national Themes. The leading spirit in Finnish music, however, is Jan Sibelius (b. 1865), who studied under Wegelius and in Berlin and Vienna. Sibelius is a composer of real eminence who has brought out in his *Orchestral Legends* (*En-Saga, Finlandia* and *Elegie*), and especially in his *Songs*, the rugged earnestness of the Finnish nature, interpreted through the free characteristic rhythm, weird melodies and pungent harmonies which are associated with Finnish music. The Finn is said to be near akin to the Magyar. Be that as it may, the gloom of a land that knows no sunlight in December and January is seen in Sibelius' *Piano Pieces*, the *Barcarolle*, the *Romanze* (Bos.), the rich and sombre *Nocturnes*, the sad Schubertian *Andantino*, the *Idyll*, the arranged *Dance Intermezzo* and the popular *Valse Triste* (B. & H.). Also *Op.* 75, No. 5 (Wood edn.) and *Op.* 94, Nos. 4 and 5.

These are rendered interesting by their modern technique and by their unique, as it were, intensified *minor* element.

The *Sonata, Op.* 12 (B. & H.) contains very much of the elemental National vigour and gloom and is extremely interesting from this point of view, though lacking somewhat in cohesiveness.

The first movement opens in a Griegian manner, and a quaint, sad *Andante* and wild *Vivacissimo* complete the work.

The rich sombre passage here given is from the *Barcarola,*
Op. 38, No. 10 (B. & H.).

If the gloom of Finland is seen in the Piano works of Sibelius,
we have the sunlight in the more important works of E. Melartin,
who, in his very fine *Legends, Op.* 6 and 12, and the *Lyric Pieces,*

Op. 18 (B. & H.) combines National characteristics with a gift for melody and a richly harmonized style showing the influence of Liszt and Wagner. The *Legends* are somewhat after the style of Liszt's *Rhapsodies* and are very effective. The *Lyric Pieces* comprise a *Lied* in Folk-Song style—*On the Mountain, On the Shore, Twilight* and *Summer Evening* (Finnish Folk-Song) —all thoroughly interesting.

In conclusion, an attractive *Duet Prelude* by Järnefelt, *Valse Lente* by Merikanto, *Finnish Dance* by Palmgren, and his *Op.* 35 (Wood edn.) deserve mention.

CHAPTER XIV

THE recent renaissance of British Musical Art carries one's thoughts back to the time when this country was ahead of most others in its cultivation of music. From the earliest times Folk-Song and the Dance have flourished among the people of this country, the former occasionally influenced, as elsewhere, by ecclesiastical plainsong. In the seventh century a knowledge of the Harp and Part-singing was general, while English composers for the virginal and viols were supreme in the reign of Queen Elizabeth.

When Handel arrived in this country in 1710, he found a unique School of Church Music and Madrigals and the masterly compositions of Purcell, who had died fifteen years previously and had in his time been far ahead of his foreign contemporaries Carissimi, Schütz, Lully and others. The outlook for English music at that time had reached a climax, and great pride was taken in our National School of Composition. Unfortunately the arrival of Handel and the Italian Opera put an end to the prospects of our art until the recent re-awakening. Going back, however, to the mainspring of all National Art—the Folk-Song and Dance—abundant material exists for the foundation of a National School.

The gay humour of the Saxon and the dreamy and passionate moods of the Celt have found expression in stirring rhythms and, above all, in an overflowing fount of melody. As M. Paul Millien has said, " Melody found a shelter from scientific complications in England. English composers preserved their sensitiveness to the simple beauty of melody."

The rollicking old English Sea Songs, the old English Hornpipe and Morris Dance, the vigorous and fresh Lowland Scotch Folk-Song, the quaint and melancholy Gaelic airs of the north and west of Scotland, the buoyant harp-accompanied melodies of Wales, and, lastly, the cloying sweetness of Erin's airs, all form a rich heritage for him who can avoid the Germanisms of Mendelssohn and Brahms and the Slavisms of Dvořák and Tschaïkowsky, and combine with sound workmanship and modern harmony the many varied melodic and rhythmic characteristics of the music of his own country.

In treating of Modern British Pianoforte Music we shall classify its composers according to the qualities manifested, and deal first with the older School of writers showing strong Lyrical powers with, in some cases, the National tendency to the Idyllic.

The two *Sonatas* of Sir C. Hubert H. Parry (b. 1848, d. 1918) (No. 1, Ash; No. 2, Aug.), both early works, are essentially Lyrical in style, and modelled on Heller and Schumann (*see* Part III, Chapter XXI, on Modern Sonatas). No. 1 is the more attractive. The freedom of style of the *Sonatas* is less apparent in the vocally massive *Sonnets* and *Songs without Words* (also an early work) and the orchestrally-minded, ingenious and continuous 19 *Variations in quasi-Fantasia Form* (Ash) (Part III, Chapter XXIV); but the *Suite in F* (Nov.) and the masculine *Duo in E minor for Two Pianos* (B. H.) are written in masterly style and the latter shows strongly the influence of Bach, the *Finale* being a kind of *Toccata* in *Fugato* style. Mention should also be made of the *Concerto in F♯*.

Sir Charles Villiers Stanford (b. 1852) has, like Sir H. Parry, written comparatively little for the Piano. A resourceful and interesting *Toccata in C* (Cpl.) is an early work. His masculine style appears in the masterly *Variations for Orchestra and Piano* on the old English Theme, *Down Among the Dead Men,* in which the interest is well sustained, increasing especially in the Schumannesque 11*th Variation* and *Canonic* 12*th*, which leads to a brilliant *Finale* in the *major* mode. This work has been arranged for two Pianos by the composer. In the *Three Dante Rhapsodies, Op.* 92 (Houghton) we have remarkable nobility of style and a clear portrayal of the spirit animating the genius of Dante according to the chosen quotations, No. 1, *Francesca;* No. 2, *Beatrice;* No. 3, *Capaneo.*

> " Nessun maggior dolore
> Che ricordarsi del tempo felice
> Nella miseria."*

* " That a sorrow's crown of sorrow is remembering happier things."— *Tennyson,* " Locksley Hall."

The technique is Lisztian in style and effective. The work, as a whole, is individual and English in style. Born in Dublin, Sir Charles Villiers Stanford has also done much for Irish music by his arrangement of Irish melodies. Ireland was always a musical nation, though little has been recorded as regards Irish composers for the Pianoforte in the past. In 1768 were published *Six Sonatas* by a Mr. Bird of Dublin ; a *Concerto* by Harden Smith was published by S. Lee in Dublin in August, 1770 ; *Piano Pieces* by Barthelemon appeared in Dublin in 1771–72 and *Two Lessons* by Wm. Heron in 1772.*

In Arthur O'Leary (b. 1834, d. 1919), who was educated at the Royal Academy of Music and at Leipzig (and was a pupil of Mendelssohn) we have a gifted fellow-countryman of Field and Osborne, who wrote a charming *Barcarolle* (Bos.), *Valse Heureuse* (Aug.), characteristic *Wayside Sketch*, No. 3, and a *Berceuse* (Nov.) showing refined melody and modern style.

Algernon Ashton (born 1859 at Durham) was educated at Leipzig and was also a pupil of Raff. Ashton is a disciple of the Schumann-Brahms School. His tendency to nobility of style is unfortunately discounted by perpetual turgid writing, and his melody and harmony also lack distinction. The most acceptable of his works are the *Albumblätter* (Cz.), portions of the *Gedankenspiele* (K.), the *Fandango* (Aug.), the effective *English, Scotch* and *Irish Dances* for Duet, the fanciful *Berceuse* and the neatly-written *Perpetuum Mobile*.

The somewhat Mendelssohnian *Sonata, Op.* 45 (Aug.) of John Francis Barnett (b. 1837) is interesting and fresh, while his *Tarantelle* (Aug.), *St. Agnes' Eve*, Chopinesque *Valse Brillante* and *Valse Caprice* (B. & H.), as well as the pleasing *Intermezzo* and *Gavotte*, are modern in harmony, melodious and effective.

Francis E. Bache (1833–58), whose early death was a loss to English music, reminds one, in his youthful *élan* and spirit of Mayer and Wollenhaupt, as, for instance, in his brilliant and gay *Souvenir d'Italie*, No. 1 (Aug.), *L'Irrésistible* (Aug.) and the *Polonaise, Op.* 49 (Ash) ; while a fresh, healthy, Lyrical style pervades the attractive *La Penserosa* and *L'Allegro*, the 2 *Romances*, the *Barcarolle* (Aug.) and the 4 *Mazurkas*. These are all good instructive Pieces. Bache was taught by Sterndale

* I am indebted for these details to Dr. Grattan Flood, the leading authority on Irish Music.

Bennett and at Leipzig. He wrote also some pretty *Character-
istic Pieces* and a *Concerto*, etc. His younger brother, Walter
Bache, devoted his life to the propaganda of Liszt's music in
England.

Walter C. Macfarren (1826–1905) in his *Rondeau à la Berceuse*,
Album Leaf and *Rondino Grazioso* shows a graceful English
Lyric style, though lacking in distinctive harmonic effects. His
3rd *Tarantella* and 3rd and 4th *Polonaises* are among the best
examples of his useful teaching Pieces. The 12 *Studies* also are
well written and melodious.

Ignace Gibson (b. in London, 1826) has written pleasant Pieces
for teaching purposes, as in his *Meditations, Carmencita* (Ash)
and *Podolia* (Leonard).

Michael Watson (Jules Favre) excels in the attractive Old
English characteristic Dances—the *Morris Dance, Hornpipe,
Branle*, etc.

Henry Parker (b. 1845) is also known for *Sarabande* and
Pavan (Cramer) in the older style.

The Lyric and Idyllic style has been continued by the
following (mostly) younger composers :—

Josef Holbrooke (b. 1878), one of the most promising of
British composers, in his 4 *Pieces* (Hammond), *Air de Ballet*
(Vincent) and *Esquisses* (Leonard), possesses all the charm and
finish of the French School without being Gallic in conception.
His harmonies are original and modern.

S. B. Mills (b. at Cirencester, 1838) was a pupil of Sterndale
Bennett and at Leipzig, and settled in New York in 1859.
He died in 1898 at Wiesbaden. Mills was a brilliant pianist
and wrote some very attractive works, for example, his *Barcarolle
Op*. 12 (J.S.), 1st *Tarantella* and *Caprice, Op*. 24 (Pd.), which are
melodious, well written and effective.

Percy Sherwood (b. 1866, educated and resident in Dresden)
has written charming poetical *Miniatures, Op*. 9 (Kistner) and
a well-written *Capriccio* in the Idyllic style.

Charles Vincent in his modern *Valse Poétique* and *Allegro
Vivace*, Walford Davies, in his unpretentious but effective
3 *Pieces* (Or.), and H. W. Nicholls (born in Birmingham and
settled in America) in the emotional and curiously rhapsodical
Op. 22 (Rab.) and *Op*. 21 (B. & B.) also deserve mention.

Walter Fitton, in his attractive *Pastoral Romance* and *Meditation*, combines fresh melody with modern harmonies. Albert

Ketelbey's and Denis Dupré's very tuneful and graceful teaching Pieces also deserve mention.

We now come to those whose style is peculiarly English in tone.

Herbert F. Sharpe (b. 1861 and educated at the National Training School), in his *English Pastorals*, comprising *My Country, Pastoral, Country Revels, Elegy, Courtly Dance* and *Morris Dance* (Woolhouse) gives us the atmosphere of the typically English merry *Jig*, the *Maypole*, the *Morris Dance* and the salt-sea wave. He combines delicacy and skill with National characteristics. His 5 *Characteristic Pieces* for Duet (Woolhouse) are well written.

Arthur Somervell, in the charming *Spring Fancies* (St. Lucas), the 6 *Dances* for Duet (Leonard), the melodious *Romance of the Ball* and the *Pan Pipes*, No. 3, gives us overflowing melody and idyllic tone in the Pastoral Pieces and quaint gambolling in the Dances.

Ed. German (Jones) (b. 1862 of Welsh descent) has not written much Piano music. His beautiful *Abendlied* (S.L.), *Graceful Dance* (Ash) and four-hand *Caprice* (Suite) are specially melodious.

The well-known Sir Frederic H. Cowen (b. 1852), in his few Piano works, the *Months* (Nov.) and the *Concertstück* for Piano and Orchestra, *Romance* and *Scherzo*, shows individual Lyric style.

Another class of the younger generation has caught something of modern Romance and manifestsit in addition to natural Lyricism. The late lamented Wm. Y. Hurlstone (1876-1906), who died full of promise, is at present known by his charming *Miniatures, Op.* 8 (J.W.) in which he shows originality of idiom and piquant harmonic effects. Hurlstone was trained at the Royal College of Music, and had written a *Concerto, Capriccio* (performed from MS. in 1902) and other works.

John B. McEwen is known for his important, well-developed and attractive *Sonata in E minor* evincing a command of modern technique ; while the intellectual and modern *Concerto* of Donald Tovey has been successfully performed in public. In the 9 *Preludes* of Paul Corder (Avison) we have dramatic Sketches in modern style tending towards the ultra-modern phase of Impressionism. In No. 5 he shows striking *harmonic* effects.

Benjamin Dale has written a remarkable *Sonata in D minor*

Avison), full of passion and modern feeling and Lisztian technique combined with a tendency to over-elaboration.

Norman O'Neill, in his *Op.* 4, *Four Pieces* (Forsyth) and an original *Gavotte* (Scht.) shows a fund of quaint melody combined with modern style (*see* Irish Composers).

George H. Clutsam (born in Australia) in his *Études Pittoresques* (En.) excels in the dreamy Romantic style; while Louis Rée, a pupil of Leschetitzky, who lives in Vienna, displays strength, melody and originality in his *Op.* 7 (5 Pieces).

In the Pianoforte works of W. Wolstenholme, the blind organist, we find a beautiful and original *Liebeslied*, a Gallic *Spanish Serenade* and a sentimental though refined *Melody in F* and *Romanza* (Lengnick). He has also made essays in the Antique style.

A number of commendable individual works may be mentioned:—the *Caprice Valse* (En.) in French style, of Herbert Bunning; the *Petites Danseuses* (Un.) of Herbert Botting; the dignified and modern *Album Leaf* (Ash) by Ch. Dunkley; a *Nocturne* by Cliffe Forrester (Wl.); a *Romance* (Aug.) by E. Duncan; Noontide Reveries (Un.) by H. Blair; a *Serenade* by Hopekirk (Patterson); a *Barcarolle* (S.L.) by Mary Carmichael; a Romantic *Sonata* and tuneful *Valse Arabesque* (Aug.) by Horace Barton (born in Port Elizabeth, Cape Colony); *Four Sketches* by Ethel Barns (Cramer); a modern and impressive *Prelude* (Hammond) and various instructive Pieces by Albert Ketelbey; and an attractive *Suite* for Duet by S. P. Waddington. The melodious and well-written *Barcarolle* and *Jagdlied* (B. & H.) by J. A. Jeffrey; the cultured *Pensées Lyriques* (Laudy) of R. K. Armitage; the *Cabalette* (Scht.) by Percy Godfrey; the effective *Variations on a Swedish Air* by Theodore Holland (educated Royal Academy of Music., resident in Berlin); the *Humoresque* by Martin Shaw; and the *Impressions* (Cary) by H. Jervis Read are also worthy of notice.

There are graceful pieces in Sydney Rosenbloom's *Sketch Book* (Bos.), and he has composed a well-written *Barcarolle* (Avison), *Serenade* (Cary) and *Op.* 6 (1 and 3) (Aug.), which are interesting both in melody and harmony. A. H. Brewer's 3 *Pieces* (Aug.) are tuneful and the *Old English Dances* by Edward L. Bainton are very attractive.

Perhaps the best-known of British composers in the Romantic style is " Anton Strelezki," the *nom de plume* of Mr. Burnand, a

cousin of Sir Francis Burnand, who was born in 1859 at Croydon
and trained at Leipzig.

Mr. Burnand also has written much in the educational Salon
style under the *nom de plume* of " Stephan Essipoff."   His most
familiar works in this country are those in the style of *Serenades*,
full of *con amore* melody with wide-sweeping *arpeggio* accompaniments and resounding low bass foundation, as, for example,
in his delicately finished *Spanish Serenade* (J.W.).   Mr. Burnand
has, however, cultivated other styles most successfully and with
Lisztian technique in the brilliant and effective *Op.* 120 (No. 2)
(P. & M.), *Op.* 91*, *Op.* 89 (Nos. 3, 7*, 8*, 5 and 1), (R.F.) in
the Chopinesque *Nocturnes*, *Op.* 104 (R.F.) and *Op.* 120 (No. 1*)
(P. & M.), and in the *Valses Mignonnes*, Nos. 2 and 3 (R.F.)
written in the piquant French style.   (Those marked * deserve
special attention.)

Also in the expressive and lyrical *Op.* 89 (No. 2) (R.F.),
Landschaft and *Valse Poétique* (F.S.), *Songs without Words*
(U. Ed.) and *Eight Pieces* (Nov.) ; while local colouring is seen
in the *Mazurka*, *Op.* 89 (R.F.), the *Ungarisch* (J.W.) and the
Duet *Danses Espagnoles* (Aug.).

At the head of those who have written in the characteristic
style stands Graham P. Moore, whom younger composers, however, are now running close.   Moore was born in Australia
(1859), studied in Berlin, and was later Professor at the Royal
College of Music.   His earlier works belong to the Mendelssohn-
Heller School.   Of the collective volume of his works (B. & H.)
the *Valse Capricieuse*, *Pleading* and *Valse Poétique* are interesting, and two numbers of the *Chromatische Étuden* are useful.

The 1st Book of his *Op.* 12, *The Village Wedding*, is a happy
example of his power of characterization, and the *Weihnachts-
gabe*, *Op.* 39 (Christmas Gifts) are also delightful Pieces in the
same style.   The *Op.* 35, nine Clavier Pieces in Study form,
the *Rhapsodie Polonaise*, *Op.* 41, the *Tarantelle*, *Op.* 22 and
Album Miniature (all B. & H.) are excellent virtuoso pieces,
fresh and interesting, effective and grateful to play.

One interesting section of the Characteristic is shown by
Oliver King in his imitation of the styles of Grieg, Henselt,
Heller and Liszt in his 3rd Book of *Miniatures*, the first being
the most successful ; while Percy C. Buck evinces sterling merit
in his attractive Schumannesque Album *Seven Days of the
Week* (Metzler).   Two well-written sketches, *The Old Castle* and

The Wishing Well by Katharine E. Eggar show considerable descriptive power. The piquant and individual *Minuet* and *Humoreske* by Martin Shaw (Lengnick) may also be mentioned.

H. Farjeon, in his *Night Music, Pictures from Greece, Tone Pictures*, Part IV and *Swan Song* (Aug.) shows the gift of dainty melody and characterization. He has written a Brahmsian *Sonata, Op.* 43 (Ash) and has breathed the spirit of the Dance into the *Miniature Sonata*. The characteristic element is also strongly in evidence in his interesting *Concerto* and in the *Four Winds* for orchestra and piano (Aug.). Ernest Austin (b. 1874) excels in the poetical *Miniature*, as in his interesting and refined 37 *Short Pieces for a Musical Calendar* (M.S.), and in a five-sectioned *Musical Poem, Op.* 28 (M.S.). Lindsay Kearne, a composer of Chamber music, in his 7 *Short Pieces, Sylvan Song* and *B minor Nocturne* (M.S.) shows refined melody and powers of expression. Joseph Hathaway and Alfred H. Barley are also cultivating this style.

" Florian Pascal " (*nom de plume*) has also successfully culti-vated local tone colour in his four *Spanish Rhapsodies* and 5 *Sketches* in the Irish style (J.W.). Geehl's *Suite Espagnole* and F. A. Armstrong's *Autumn Leaves* (Nov.) may also be mentioned.

Frederick Nicholls, in his pretty *April Melody* (B.F.W.), *Fairy Gold*, No. 3 and *Op.* 40, No. 1, shows talent. Frank William Baines' *Four Sketches* (3 and 4) (Banks) deserve attention. Alec Rowley builds on a good foundation in his *Georgian Suite* with their gratefully British and old-world flavour. In his *North Sea Fantasies* a breath from the rolling sea is inhaled, and he is equally at home in the glamour of the fairy world, as shown in *From the Fairy Hills* (Rogers). Roger Quilter in his *Three Pieces, Op.* 16, shows originality combined with a reflective spirit.

Reginald Steggall, in his 5 *Pieces* (*Op.* 18) and *Prelude* and *Valse* (S. & B.) presents a virile and modern—though some-what chromatic—style. Eric Fogg's *Album* (Bos.) of broad, simple, pretty *Sketches* may be commended; while attractive and well-written work will be found in Mr. Joseph Speaight's *Three Pieces* (S. & B.) and *Tone Pictures* (Rogers). Charming examples of the cult of the light heart are present in Thomas J. Hewitt's *Ballet Suite Columbine, Four Trifles*, and *In Downland* (K. & P.).

In W. J. Fenney's *Early Spring* we have a charming Sketch—but withal an overcrowded canvas; and Gustave Lind has attained popularity in his poetic *Sketch Albums*, such as the *Silent Mere*.

We now come to the British Impressionist School, which, like that of the French, is beginning to be of some importance.

Tobias Matthay, in his *Monothemes* (Patterson) was one of the first to appear in this style. His *Lyrics* (Patterson), *Moods of a Moment* (Ascherberg) and *Preludes* (Weekes) are all examples of that elusive charm which arises rather from a succession of beautiful suggestive harmonies than from any defined melody or development of form—a style which does not always make itself clear on a first hearing. His more transparent *Love Phases* (J.W.) and *Elves* (Weekes) are charming examples of their style. Matthay's *A minor Concert Piece* for orchestra and piano has been performed at the Bournemouth Symphony Concerts.

In Cyril Scott (b. 1889, in Liverpool) we have one of the leaders of this School. In *Dagobah* (Forsyth) we are initiated into Egyptian mysteries and the *Andante Pastorale* is an example in this style of the thickening of what would otherwise be simple passing notes by the addition of chords, thus giving rise to a corruscating succession of subordinate secondary harmonies weaving their way betwixt those of the thereby obscured principal Theme.

Similar qualities are also found in the interesting *Solitude* and *Vespérale* (Forsyth).

Perhaps the most lucid are the *English Waltz*—an early work—and the *Passacaglia* from the *Pastoral Suite*.

The later *Ballade, Rondeau de Concert* and *Sonata* (*Op.* 66) are good examples of the absolute incoherence which results from putting tonal atmosphere first and last with practically every chord in a different key, every discord unresolved and rhythm almost non-existent. Should not our Impressionists rather look to Debussy as a model?

Felix Swinstead reveals strength of purpose and the influence of Wagner in his *Prelude in D* (Avison), while the 6 *Preludes* (M.S.) and *Valse Caprice* (M.S.), show delicacy of style and new harmonic effects.

Balfour Gardiner makes striking use of successions of massed discords in his original *De Profundis*, in a really humorous

Andante molto espress. Dagobah, Cyril Scott, Op. 3.

Humoreske, an impassioned Sketch entitled *Mère* and the attractive *Two Simple Pieces*.

Percy Pitt's (b. 1870, in London, trained in Leipzig and Munich) Impressionist *métier* is revealed in the sombre colouring of his *Autumn Harmonies* (Nov.) especially in No. 3, *Crépuscule*, and also, though less decidedly, in an effective *Scherzo* (Aug.).

His refined and modern *Scène de Ballet*, *Op.* 4, *Lointain Passé* and *Scherzo Valse* display piquant harmonies and his *Op.* 11, 8 and 37 (Aug.) also deserve attention.

York Bowen (b. in London, 1884, trained at the Royal Academy of Music), shows a Lisztian virtuoso element combined with masterly modulatory effects in his *Miniature Suite* (Avison). His *Concerto* (M.S.) has been well received in public.

Frank Bridge, in his Minuet Idyll, *Dew Fairy* (Aug.), *Three Sketches* and *Four Characteristic Pieces* (Rogers), shows a bold, facile pen in the scintillating, kaleidoscopic harmonic effects. They have the merits and deficiencies of their class. His pretty *Miniature Pastoral*, No. 3, a simple Sketch, shows he is not lost to form and sense.

William Baines, in his *Seven Preludes* and *Paradise Gardens*, with their mystical half-lights, reminds one of Debussy. In Leo Livens' *Moorland Suite* (Rogers) there are some pretty bell effects in *Heather Bells*, produced by consecutive fourths, fifths and octaves. Gerard Williams, in his descriptive *Three Preludes* (Rogers) shows commendable sequence of thought, and secondary harmonies are not the only feature. In John Heath's *Six Inventions* (Rogers), which are pictures of various moods, we find daring experiments in harmonic colouring; while in John Ireland's *Preludes* (Rogers), *Island Spell* and *Chelsea Reach* (Aug.) the moods are forcibly expressed, almost every melodic note being driven home by a compelling dissonance. In this he resembles Cyril Scott—" strong meat " in both—but perhaps Ireland is the more coherent. In Arnold Bax's *Mountain Mood* (Chester) the usual chain of subsidiary harmonies gives place to subsidiary (and alien) melodic or contrapuntal accompaniments. He is best known by *In a Vodka Shop* (Aug.).

Eugene Goosens' *Nature Poems* (Chester) glow with gorgeous colouring.

In summing up this highly meritorious British Impressionist School it is, perhaps, ungrateful to observe that colours in an

Impressionist should not clash continually, and that there should not be a total absence of outline. These are faults in most Impressionists. We are confronted with gorgeous studies in the art of colour obtained by (1) chromatic harmony ; (2) an undercurrent of alien harmonies or alien melodies. Composers are apt to forget that melody is the unit and harmony but the accessory. No doubt it is an age of colour and in our own country the movement will have a good influence, since the weak point in British composition down to the time of Sterndale Bennett and Sullivan has been its backwardness in use of modern harmonies. Equally patent is it that the undercurrent was prompted by Wagner's wonderful polyphonic weft. But it is well to remember Wagner's own dictum : " Whenever a composer attempts to be a painter in music, he will succeed in producing neither good music nor a good picture."

British composers of Salon music are dealt with in the Chapter on " Salon Music."

The leading exponent of Scottish music is Sir Alex. Mackenzie (b. in Edinburgh, 1847), who, while excelling as a dramatic writer for the orchestra, has written some charming Pianoforte music.

His *Scottish Rhapsodies* and *Scenes in the Scottish Highlands* are fired by enthusiasm for the stirring rhythm and beautiful melodies characteristic of Scottish music. The very attractive little piece *On the Heather* is an example.

The *Scottish Concerto* (Kistner) is a very interesting work from a National as well as from an artistic point of view. It is cast in a Romantic mould and the Scottish atmosphere is maintained by the use of fragments of Scottish melodies skilfully developed.

The Theme *Green grow the Rashes* is used in both first and last movements, together with other Themes, as quoted on p. 346.

Hamish McCunn has a beautiful pathetic Pastoral *By the Burnside* and a piquant *Harvest Dance* in his own Arrangement of his *Highland Memories* (Aug.).

A. E. Moffat (b. in Edinburgh, 1866), the vocal composer, has also written several Pianoforte works.

Most interesting publications are the *Piano Lyrics* and *Sea Pieces from the Hebrides* (Boosey), also the *Scots Folk-Tune Suite*, arranged by Marjory K. Fraser after the style of the Old English and Continental Suites and consisting of (1) *Slow Strathspey;* (2) *Old Dance Song;* (3) *Celtic Coasting Song;*

(4) *A Lowland Lilt*, in which the Themes are appropriately set out.   No. 3, for example, is after the manner of Grieg.

1st Movement.   Scottish Concerto, Sir A. Mackenzie.

Tobias Matthay also, in his Concert Arrangement of *Scottish Dances and Melodies* uses the virtuoso method of Liszt as displayed in the latter's *Hungarian Rhapsodies*.

Another attractive and artistic method is shown in the interesting *Scottish Songs without Words* (Patterson) by Eugene Woycke (4 Books), in which a freely elaborated accompaniment is used. Examples of artistic Fantasias on Scottish airs are to be found in *In the Highlands* by D. R. Munro (Cary) and in the six *Schottische Weisen* by Gustave Lange (Challier).

The resources of the strikingly simple and pathetic airs of Wales, beyond the usual Potpourris and the Transcriptions of Brinley Richards (1817–85) ; trained at the Royal Academy of Music, in particular, do not seem to have been made much use of. Ed. German (Jones) has recently written a *Welsh Rhapsody* for Orchestra, but beyond this, Welsh composers at present seem to be absorbed in Vocal Music.

The characteristic and cloying pathos of Irish Folk-Song has been little exploited beyond the usual Potpourris and flimsy Fantasies—one exception being the *Souvenir d'Irlande*, a quasi-Concerto by Moscheles. Stanford has made some artistic Arrangements of Irish Airs and Norman O'Neill, in his very attractively written *Variations* and *Fugue for Two Pianos* (Scht.), has used as the foundation a beautiful Irish Theme. Signor Esposito (resident in Dublin) has also written artistic Transcriptions (Piggot, Dublin) and Carl G. Hardebeck (Belfast) has composed effective *Rhapsodies* on Irish Airs.

The names of the principal Irish composers of Piano music are Field, Osborne, Vincent Wallace (*see* " Salon Music "), O'Leary, Stanford, Augusta Holmes (born in Paris) and O'Neill.

[For the most recent compositions of the Modern British School *see* ADDENDUM, pp. 405 *seq.*]

CHAPTER XV

WHAT impresses one particularly in reviewing the mass of Modern American Pianoforte Music is its melodiousness and general attractiveness.

We note in it the absence of the ruggedness of the Norwegian and the Finn, the pessimism of the modern Italian and modern German, the triviality of the French style, and in its stead we note the presence of simple, unaffected melody—a characteristic also of the British School to which it is allied. American compositions also incline to the *effective* rather than to the *reflective* side of one's sympathies ; and consideration of this appeal to the effective moves one to ask whether the New World will lead the way in that aspect of the evolution of the fittest— the appeal to effectiveness ?

The influence of Nationality on Musical Art in America seems to be in a comparatively early stage of development, as compared with the state of affairs in Great Britain and Ireland, where we have an Anglo-Celtic basis leavened for a thousand years by Dane and Norman. America's Pilgrim Father basis has apparently not yet assimilated the other various nationalities who are settling in that vast country. So far, indeed, American-born composers of any repute seem to be of British origin. As regards sources of inspiration, there is always the vigorous, healthy British Folk-Song and Dance to fall back upon, especially since British composers themselves have largely neglected the birthright which lies at their own door. At least one may hope that American composers of the future will avoid the " isms " of the European States, and manifest and preserve their individual and National feeling as far as may be.

Ed. MacDowell (b. 1861 ; d. 1908), is not only a distinguished and original composer in Sonata form, but one thoroughly endowed with the spirit of the Romantic, especially in his interpretations of Nature. He is up to the present the most prominent composer that America has produced.

His *Waldstille* (Stillness of the Woods) in his *Wald Idylle* (K.)

348

strikes the keynote of his *Nature Studies*, and the Nature atmosphere appears to us at once in the *Driadentanz* of the same Collection, in the *Hexentanz*, *Op.* 17 (Bos.), and in the *American Wood Sketches*, *Op.* 51 (Elkin, A.P.S.). In purely poetical Sketches, too, as in the *Op.* 51, *To a Water Lily*, the *Serenade* (Siegel), the Impressionist *Sketches*, *Op.* 32 (*Four Little Poems*) (A.P.S.) and his *Sea Pieces* (especially " 1620," *i.e.*, *The Mayflower's Journey*) he is highly attractive.

The genius of MacDowell is meditative and, though his modern and striking *Sonatas*, showing the influence of Schumann and Brahms, especially the *Tragic* and *Keltic*, are very fine, he is at his best in smaller works and most inspired in the moods of Nature. The influence of the modern German School has been such as to incline him towards *Impressionism*, and his power is *harmonic* rather than *melodic* : *see* his *New England Idylls* and *Forgotten Fairy Tales* (Elkin), indicating a composer of the Characteristic worthy to rank with Schumann and Heller.

MacDowell has also written two sonorous and brilliant *Concertos* and two *Suites*. Altogether some sixty-four Pianoforte works of his have been published. For a detailed description of these the reader is referred to Gilman's *Edw. MacDowell*.

The composer is of British descent, his grandfather having been born at Belfast of Scoto-Irish parents. MacDowell himself was born in New York in 1861. In 1876, at the age of fifteen, he went to study in Paris, and for some twelve or thirteen years he studied and taught in Germany, not settling again in America until 1889. Through his death not only America but the whole musical world became the poorer.

Ernest Hutcheson represents in an able manner the Classical spirit in American Pianoforte Music. His *Andante Tranquillo*, *Capriccio* and *Sarabande* of the *Op.* 10 (Schirmer) are noble, refined and dignified in tone, besides being melodious and attractive generally.

Arthur Whiting, who was born at Cambridge, Mass., in 1861, and educated in the United States and at Munich, lives now in New York. His remarkably virile *Modern Suite* (S.R.M.) shows the influence of Schumann and Liszt.

The pretty and effective *La Fileuse* and the interesting *Bagatelle* and *Scherzino*, *Valse Brillante* and *Op.* 14, No. 3, are like the rest of his works, masculine and original.

J. K. Paine (b. 1839), together with G. W. Chadwick and

Arthur Foote, also represent the Conservative aspect of American music, though they have not contributed much of importance for the Pianoforte.

Paine has written a Book of *Characteristic Pieces* and also *Three Pieces, Op.* 41 ; Chadwick (b. 1854), some Miscellaneous *Pieces, Op. 7, Caprices* and *Waltzes ;* and Foote (b. 1853), 2 *Suites, Bagatelles,* 5 *Poems* and Miscellaneous Pieces. Paine and Chadwick both studied in Germany.

Horatio Parker (b. 1863) has contributed some characteristic *Pieces* and *Sketches,* while Ed. S. Kelley (b. 1857) has written some popular *Pieces* in individual style.

Of composers in the modern Romantic style, apart from McDowell, we place first William Mason (b. 1829), who, after studying in Germany, made a name as a virtuoso and settled in New York in 1855. His compositions entitle him to more than local or American fame. His *Rêverie Poétique* (Srm.) and 1st *Ballade* (J.S.) in the Romantic style ; the *Toccata* and *Dance Caprice* (E.S.), of technical interest, and showing the influence of Liszt, which appears in all his works ; and finally, the *Capriccio* (Srm.), *Minuet* and *Scherzo* in the Classic-Romantic style, all appeal to the hearer as refined, well-written, melodious and effective compositions.

Homer N. Bartlett (b. 1845) writes in refined style and with Lisztian technique. His *Le Matin Nocturne, Op.* 210, *Mazurka de Concert* (Dt.) and Étude *La Grace* (Pa.) are Romantic in feeling and charmingly written. His harmonic treatment is specially noteworthy.

Porter Steele is a skilful " characteristic " writer. His attractive *September Morn, Barcarolle* and *Petite Sérénade* (Srm.) have vigour, melody and elegance.

Howard Brockway's Schumannesque *Op.* 8 (6 *Pieces*) (Sl.) are very interesting, and the influence of his model is apparent in the attractive *Op.* 21, Nos. 1 and 3, the *March, Op.* 25, the *Slow Waltz, Op.* 25 (Srm.) and the delightful Suite of small Pieces, *Op.* 26 (Srm.). Brockway was born in Brooklyn in 1870 and educated in the States and in Berlin.

H. H. Huss, who was born at Newark, N.J., and educated in the States and at Munich, is a refined writer with a passion for ethereal and *una corda* effects, as, for instance, in *The Night,* the *Nocturne, Op.* 20, and the *Minuet, Op.* 18 (Srm.).

Wm. H. Sherwood, who was born in Lyons, N.Y., in 1854,

and educated in the States and in Europe, shows in his *Piano-forte Pieces* a richly ornamented style, as, for example, in his *Autumn* (Dt.).

Ethelbert Nevin (b. at Edgeworth, Penn., 1862, and educated in the States and in Europe) is the well-known composer of the Romantic and charmingly modulated *Narcissus*. Possessing a fund of grateful melody, *recherché* harmony and transparent style, his charming Pieces, *Shepherds All* and *Lullaby* from the *Pastoral Scenes, Op.* 16 (St.), the *Suite Maggio in Toscano* (Barchetto-Notturno), the *Il Rosignuolo* and *Barcarolle* of the *Op.* 13, together with the *Narcissus* and *Barghetta* from the *Water Scenes* are highly attractive in the best sense.

Wilson G. Smith (b. in Ohio State, 1855) is the composer of some pleasantly written Pieces, *Op.* 88 (Srm.), the *Romance* and *Valse, Op.* 9 and an *Arabesque* (Dt.).

J. H. Rogers displays a genius for the " Characteristic " and a bold melodic style in his attractive *Op.* 53 (1 and 2) and *Air de Ballet* (Dt.), and also in the *Toccatina* (Pd.).

R. H. Woodman's melodious and poetical *Brook and Spring Song* (Dt.) and John Orth's pleasant melodious *Romanza* and *Brookside* (Dt.) should be mentioned.

Charles Denée (born in Oswego, 1863) has written *Suites, Characteristic Pieces* and smaller Pieces.

Mrs. H. H. A. Beach's (b. 1867), *Sketches* and *Children's Carnival;* Hy. Hadley's elegant *Tone-Pictures* (Dt.) ; E. R. Kroeger's 3rd *Sonnet* (F.S.) ; Arthur Bird's *Valse Noble* (Jn.) ; Gr. Schaefer's *Gondoliere* (C.F.S.) ; D. G. Mason's *Elegy* (Metzler) ; E. Schelling's *Variations* (Srm.) ; N. J. Hyatt's *A Frolic* (Dt.) and *Serenade;* and the well-written *Pieces* of Marie von Hammer (Dt.) deserve notice.

American Pianoforte composers seem to have the faculty of writing attractive educational Pieces, and in this connection we may mark those by J. F. Gilder, (*Tarantelle* and *Carnival Dance*) (Dt.), the energetic Pieces of B. C. Henry (Dt.), the refined *Op.* 41 (No. 4) and *Op.* 42 (No. 1) of A. G. Salmon (b. 1868), the *Op.* 10 of Rudolph Ganz (A.P.S.), L. E. Orth's Pieces (Dt.), and those of Frank Lynes (b. 1858), Stephen Emery, G. W. Marston, A. D. Turner and Templeton Strong.

The Spanish American element in Pianoforte music is repre-sented by Ernest Redon and Louis Moreau Gottschalk, both born in New Orleans, the former in 1835, the latter in 1829.

In the interesting *Chants Créoles, Op.* 35, by Redon, and Nos. 1
and 3 of the *Chants d'Amitié* we have the languorous element of
the South set forth with charm and refinement, as well as in
the attractive *Deux Préludes* and *Reflets d'Orient* (Cs.).

Redon afterwards retired and settled in Bordeaux.   Gottschalk studied in Paris with Hallé and toured as a virtuoso.
His works, which are of a refined Salon type, lean to the sentimental side and require a sympathetic touch.   His *Last Hope,
La Jeunesse*, etc. (Dt.) are well known.

Other Spanish-American composers are Ernest Guiraud, also
born at New Orleans (1837) and died in Paris (1892), who wrote
some effective Pieces ; R. Espadero (b. 1835 at Havana in Cuba),
a composer of brilliant Pieces ; and A. Rogues, author of a
Capricho Español (A. Becker, Santiago, Chili).   C. Heuser
(*Konzertwalzer*), E. Pons (*Spirito Aereo*, Kirsinger, Santiago),
and D. Sequeira (a piquant *Atlantida*, A.P.S.) may also be
mentioned.

In the following Section we deal with the work of the English
negro-composer, Coleridge Taylor, whose excellent choral work
Hiawatha is well known.   In Grant Schaefer's *Tales of the Red
Man* (A.P.S.) we have charming Sketches utilizing quaint
melodies of the Red Indian.

It may seem a far cry to the Far East from the New World,
but the subject justifies the mention here of W. Niemann's
Orchid Garden, Op. 76 (Simrock)—ten interesting Impressions
of the Far East, giving the appropriate atmosphere of India,
Java, China, etc.

THE NEGROID ELEMENT

With the growth of the National element in music we must, at
no distant date, look for a greatly enlarged sphere of activity.

In S. Coleridge Taylor (b. 1875, d. 1912) we have the herald
of an art movement, the limits of which it is difficult
to foresee.

The father of Coleridge Taylor was a full negro.   He was a
native of Sierra Leone and was educated as a doctor in London.
He married an Englishwoman, and their son was born in London
in 1875 and trained at the Royal College of Music.   His 24
Transcriptions of Negro Melodies (Rogers) and (Dt.), taken from
the South-East, South and West Africa, from the West Indies

and from the Plantations of America, are extremely interesting. Coleridge Taylor's purpose is best explained in his own words : "What Brahms has done for the Hungarian Folk-Music, Dvořák for the Bohemian and Grieg for the Norwegian, I have tried to do for these Negro melodies." The plan adopted here has been almost without exception that of the *Tema con Variazioni*. The Transcriptions are cleverly set forth and have just enough ornamental work to entrance without overwhelming the simplicity and beauty of the original Themes.

Coleridge Taylor, in his Introduction, makes the interesting statement that : "The native music of India, China, Japan, and, in fact of all non-European countries, is to our more cultivated ears most unsatisfactory in its monotony and shapelessness. The music of Africa is a great and noteworthy exception. Primitive as it is, it nevertheless has all the elements of European Folk-Song." This fact the writer can bear out as the result of a stay in South Africa.

The virility and freshness of the Themes and the masterly treatment by Coleridge Taylor make them well worthy of study.

Coleridge Taylor has also a gift for the Characteristic, as, for example, in the *Oriental Valses* (Fs.), the 4 *Characteristic Valses* (Nov.), etc.

CHAPTER XVI

A GROUP OF STUDY WRITERS—CLASSICAL SCHOOL

" The three great inseparable requisites of the art of playing the piano-forte are: correct fingering, good style, and graceful execution."—Em. Bach.

THE reader of the Chapter on the " Educational Aspect " will realize that, prior to the nineteenth century, the study of the pianoforte was not systematized in any particular way, apart from the omniscient and very-much generalized " methods " then in vogue.

Isolated efforts, it is true, had been made. Couperin, in his *L'Art de Toucher*, provides progressive Exercises, Preludes and movements from his own works for purposes of study, and these were improved upon in the *Méthode* of Rameau. J. S. Bach also wrote *Progressive Preludes*, *Minuets* and *Allemandes* for his sons' use. The *Lessons* of D. Scarlatti (originally *Esercizi*) seem to have an educational purpose—though, perhaps, an ill-defined one. Coming to the beginning of the nineteenth century, the *Caprices* of Müller, though more or less in *Sonata* form, are in the style of *Études* and refer principally to the crossing of hands in the style of Scarlatti.

It was also about this time, 1804, that the much superior first *Studies* of Cramer appeared.

John Baptist Cramer came to England as an infant in arms in 1772. At the age of twelve he was taught by Clementi, who also resided in London, and with whom he shortly took part at a Concert, in a *Duetto for Two Pianofortes*, duly announced as played by " Master Cramer and M. Clementi."

Young Cramer, then nineteen, also appeared in 1791 with Master Hummel, then aged twelve, in another Concert at which Haydn was present.

Cramer's world-famed *Studies* appeared in 1804. It is curious to note that Clementi's *Gradus*, which is altogether in an earlier style of technique—the polyphonic—did not appear till fifteen

354

years later. It is also quite natural that Beethoven, whose technical style had been developed from Clementi's *Sonatas*, should declare that the *Studies* of Cramer, which were further advanced in style, " were the chief basis of all genuine playing." Beethoven was so far interested in Cramer's *Studies* that he annotated a Selection from them—now reproduced as the *Beethoven-Cramer Studies* (Aug.) and edited by the late Mr. J. S. Shedlock. Cramer later became a Professor at the Royal Academy of Music. As a performer, Cramer had a perfect *legato* and singing velvety touch, and he was the means of introducing Mozart's *Concertos* to English audiences. Dying at the age of eighty-seven, he was a connecting link between the pre-Beethoven era and that of the Rhapsodian Liszt.

The *Gradus ad Parnassum* of Clementi appeared in 1817. Before this, however, his Sonatas had set the pattern for the pianoforte *technique* of his time. Clementi's own execution was described by a contemporary as " marvellous in its correctness and regularity—the hand keeping motionless ; the fingers alone, supple, active, independent, of incomparable equality, drew from the clavier harmonious sonority and exquisite charm." As has been mentioned, Clementi's *Gradus* represents the older *polyphonic style* of execution, and some of the numbers of this and the whole of his *Preludes and Exercises* are still valuable for that style, and especially for (1) independence of the fingers, (2) florid fugal works ; (3) double-third passages. Cramer's *Studies*, though more advanced, are founded on Clementi and are useful for *cantabile* and *broken-chord* work. For the continuation of the Clementi-Cramer style we must look to another of Clementi's pupils, Ludwig Berger, whom he took with him to St. Petersburg in 1804, and who subsequently became the teacher of Mendelssohn, Taubert and Henselt.

Berger's *Op*. 12 and 22 have the Clementi solidity and make progress in extensions, repeated notes and shakes. Berger ultimately settled in Berlin. Daniel Steibelt, composer of trashy *Battle Pieces* and fashionable Classical Pieces, who settled in St. Petersburg in 1810, in the time of Field's sojourn there, wrote some excellent *Studies* (*Op*. 78) of the Clementi type.

Kalkbrenner was trained at the Conservatoire in Paris, where he was later (as also in London), in great demand as a fashionable teacher. The 12 *Studies* belonging to his *Method*, in which he newly advocates octaves to be played from the wrist, are in the

Clementi-Cramer style. They teach nothing new, however, except Solos for the left hand, which Kalkbrenner was the first to exploit. Hummel (d. 1837) also wrote *Studies*, a few of which, in florid style, survive. The *Studies* of Aloys Schmitt, upon which Mendelssohn was brought up, are modern and tuneful and partly in Cramer's style. They are useful for broken-chord work and simpler passages in double-thirds. The best Selection is that of Germer (Bos.). Schmitt was established mostly at Frankfort, where he taught Hiller.

The Romantic Chopin speaks of his " excellent Studies," but mentions that he composes " eighty-years-old music."

Bertini's *Studies*, *Op*. 29 and 32, which were written as preparatory to those of Cramer, are notable as being probably the first Studies in phrasing, *staccato*, expression, etc. Some of these, as well as the *Op*. 100 for small hands (probably his first *Elementary Studies*) are still useful. *See* Buonamici, *Selection* (Lit.).

Bertini was born in London (1798) but ultimately settled in Paris, where he was trained. The style of Bertini was continued in the works of Lemoine (d. 1854), Duvernoy (d. 1880), Burgmüller (d. 1874), Concone (d. 1861), Heller (d. 1888), Ravina (d. 1818) and Lack, all of whom taught in Paris. Those of Lemoine, Duvernoy and Bürgmüller are mostly elementary in grade and very useful for their purpose. The Studies in style of Burgmüller and of Concone, the Italian composer of vocal *Solfeggios*, are piquant but not so expressive as those of Heller, [*see Germer Selection* (Bos.)], who still stands *facile princeps* in this branch. (*See* Part III, Chapter X.) The " artistic " *Studies* of Ravina and Lack are also admirable in their way.

The general and " characteristic " *Studies* of Löschorn, the *Études Poésies* of Haberbier, who lived mostly in St. Petersburg, the *Bravura Studies* of the Bohemian Seeling, the excellent *Studies* of Schytte the Dane (residing in Vienna) and of Gurlitt, who settled in Copenhagen, have done much to carry on this branch of the art.

The Classic style of Schmitt reappears at its climax in the *Op*. 70 of Moscheles which, with its added polish and style, is on the whole the most prominent work of that kind since Cramer. As, however, nearly every Study illustrates a different branch of technique, concentration is not possible, and some additional work is needed. Moscheles' *Op*. 95 may be added to the list of

Characteristic Studies, though they have not the spontaneity of the earlier *Op. 70.*

Moscheles was at one time greatly esteemed as a virtuoso. Born in Prague in 1791, he settled in London in 1826, where he was much in request. After twenty years' residence in this country, Moscheles, at Mendelssohn's request, joined the staff of the Leipzig Conservatoire. Though a prolific composer, he will be mainly known to posterity by his *Concertos* and his *Studies.*

The *Studies* of Kessler are in Clementi's stiff, unwieldy style, but useful numbers for the cultivation of endurance can be found in the Selection compiled from *Op.* 20 and 100 by Germer (Schles.). Kessler was born in Augsburg (Bavaria) and resided mostly in Poland and Vienna. His energetic style is continued in Hiller's *Studies*—a few of which serve the same purpose.

Louis Köhler (1820–66) has been called the " heir of Czerny." His style, however, follows the unbending style of Clementi, and, as a consequence, his elementary works are rather ungrateful. He wrote in all branches of technique and always to the point, and some of his advanced *Studies* are valuable—especially *Op.* 270 (Senff) and his *Repetition* and *Virtuosity Studies.* Köhler settled and taught in Königsberg. He was known as a clever writer on educational matters. In similar style the modern works of C. H. Döring, of Dresden (b. 1834), Albert Biehl (b. 1833) and Bernard Wolff are valuable.

Carl Czerny (1791–1857), the Czech pedagogue, pupil of Beethoven, and tutor of Liszt, Döhler and Thalberg, who devoted practically the whole of his life to teaching in Vienna, was the composer of some 800 books of *Studies.* He may be esteemed the real founder of modern technique. The result of his work, as seen in Liszt, together with the individual technique of Chopin, represent all that is best in this framework of the art.

Czerny wisely made the mental aspect of his Studies of the slightest, so that all attention could be concentrated on the technical figures on which they are built. His style is lighter, more natural and spontaneous than that of Clementi—partly as the result of the lighter action of the Viennese piano.

Czerny's works, unlike those of his predecessors, cover every branch of technique and all styles, and many of them are indispensable to the modern student. His *School of the Legato and Staccato, School of the Left Hand, The Virtuoso School* and the *Art of Execution, Op.* 740, deserve special attention. Czerny was also an industrious composer of Symphonies, Concertos and numerous other works which, however, have not survived. Chopin speaks of him thus : " He was, as he always is (and to everybody) very pliable, and asked, ' Hast fleissig studiert ? ' (Have you studied diligently ?). He has again arranged an Overture for 8 pianos and 16 performers, and seems to be very happy over it."

Charles Mayer (1799–1862) was only eight years younger than Czerny. He was taught by Field in St. Petersburg, where he resided for some twenty-six years. Mayer grasped something of the poetical and lyrical style of his master as opposed to the contrapuntal *métier* of Clementi—Field's own tutor. This accounts for the fact that Mayer's graceful and interesting *Studies of Velocity* (Germer, Lit.) and *Op.* 305, 119 and other works (Germer, Lit.) stand in the same relation to Czerny as Moscheles does to Clementi, but Mayer's work is much more comprehensive and systematic. It also explains why his works form a direct link with those of Chopin and Henselt.

Mayer spent the last twelve years of his life in Dresden, where he died in 1862.

As regards style, the light and brilliant Czerny was soon improved upon in the *Studies* of Chopin (b. 1810) and the Viennese School—Thalberg (b. 1812), Henselt (b. 1814), Döhler b. 1814) and Liszt (b. 1811).

The technique of the piano matured wonderfully quickly. While Czerny and Mayer were at work, Chopin had already, in 1827, written the first Book of his famous *Études, Op.* 10. It is difficult, indeed, to realize that this was only ten years after the appearance of Clementi's *Gradus.* England at that time seemed to be the home of the older technicians, Clementi, Cramer, Kalkbrenner and Moscheles, while the newer and more perfect style was matured in Paris. Chopin and Liszt not only summed up in themselves a new and matured technique, but in addition they showed the perfect union of the poetic and artistic element.

The *Studies* of Chopin show the best aspect of his work—a feeling of glowing Romanticism, whether in the stormy *C minor,* composed after the fall of Warsaw, or the beautiful lyrical *E major (Op.* 10, No. 3), which Liszt declared he would have given four years of his life to have written, or the $A\flat$ (*Op.* 25, No. 1), which Schumann likened to a vision, or the glittering Study on the black keys. They appeal equally to the people and the musician as unique inspirations of their kind.

The *Studies* of Liszt, represented by the clever *Paganini Caprices*, the *Transcendantes*, and the *Concert Studies* are not so deeply poetical as those of Chopin, but they carry the bravura element to its greatest height, combined with powerful descriptive faculty as shown, for instance, in the forcible *Mazeppa* and *Wild Hunt* Studies or in the ethereal *Twilight Harmonies*.

Liszt's more advanced style was partly the result of, and dates from, the almost supernatural performances of Paganini on the violin in 1830. These inspired alike the *Paganini Caprices* of Liszt, of Schumann (1833-5 ; poetical style) and of Brahms— the latter being purely technical. Whether in those of Liszt, in the well-known *Campanella*, built on the *Bell Rondo* of Paganini, or in the *Venetian Carnival* (last number), which, as Schumann says, should glide past the hearer " like the scenes of a Marionette show," they reach almost a climax as regards difficulty.

Ed. Dannreuther, in his excellent edition of Liszt's *Études* (Aug.), says that " no pianist can afford to ignore Liszt's *Études ;* and, though the appeal more often than not is " to the hearer's nerves," " the methods employed . . . are so very clever and altogether *hors ligne* that a musician's intelligence, too, may be delighted and stimulated."

In technique, at least, Liszt's contemporaries and rivals, Thalberg and Döhler, were left far behind. The former, in his melodious (but not poetical) *Op.* 26, lays himself out to produce more variety of technique than in his smooth-fingered compositions, and some numbers are still useful (*see* Part III, Chapter XIV), as are also some of those by Döhler dealing with scales and trills in his Nocturne-like style. Technically speaking, the *Studies* of Henselt stand between those of Chopin and Liszt ; like those, they are also poetical in style. In some respects, as in the use of extensions, Henselt goes beyond Chopin. In style he approaches Chopin in his *Si Oiseau j'étais*, and resembles Liszt in his powerful *Thanksgiving after a Storm* (Part III, Chapter XIV).

The light-fingered technique of Czerny, combined with modern style and expression, has been academically continued by many composers. Among these, the works of Berens, Battmann and Löschorn stand out prominently. Löschorn (1819–1903) was a pupil of Berger and resident in Berlin. His excellent *Studies* comprise all styles and are melodious and elegant as well as practical. Berens (1825–80), a Norwegian, lived mostly in Stockholm, and is the author of a meritorious *Velocity School* and *Studies for Left Hand*.

J. L. Battmann (1818–86), one of the French pedagogues, was an Alsatian, who resided in Belfort and wrote excellent *Studies* (Leduc) in the above-mentioned style.

Space will not allow more than a mention of the leading Pedagogues and Apostles of Technique : the virtuoso Tausig (d. 1871), Beringer, who settled in London in 1871, and Germer (b. 1837), who is resident in Dresden.

The *Variations* and the *Paganini Études* of Brahms may be considered, like those of Chopin, as constituting an exposition of his own peculiar technique.

What impresses one in the consideration of various books of *Études* is that probably not one in itself serves the general needs of the pupil. The too universal 101 *Exercises* of Czerny, now it is to be hoped extinct (as a whole), are a specimen of the *dilettante* presentation in miniature of many different branches of technique, none of which is more than touched upon. It has remained for Editors recently to gather the best of each kind from various sources and to put them into progressive order in different Collections, according to the capacities of various pupils. In this way great educational help has been rendered by Franklin Taylor, Germer, Thümer and Reinecke ; and, in a lesser way, by Bülow, Buonamici, Pauer and others in the excellent Collections connected with their names.

CLASSICAL SCHOOL.

Couperin, *L'Art de Toucher* (1717).
J. S. Bach (d. 1759), *Inventions*, etc.
D. Scarlatti (d. 1760), *Lessons*.
A. E. Müller (1767–1817), *Caprices*, *Method* (1804).
Cramer, *Studies* (1804–10).
Clementi, *Gradus* (1817).
Berger (1777–1822), *Op.* 12 and 22.
Steibelt (1765–1823), *Fifty Studies*.
Hummel (1778–1837),*Method*(1828).

Kalkbrenner (1788–1849), *Method*, based on Müller.
Aloys Schmitt (1788–1866), *Op.* 16, etc.
Köhler (1820–86), *Studies.*
Moscheles (1794–1870), *Op.* 70 (before 1830), *Op.* 95.
Kessler (1800–72), *Op.* 20 and 51.
F. Hiller (1811–85), *Twenty-four Studies* (1831).
Döring (b. 1834), Biehl and B.Wolff.

MODERN SCHOOL.

Czerny (1791–1857), *Op.* 740, etc.
Mayer (1799–1862), *Studies.*
Thalberg (1812–71), *Op.* 26.
Döhler (1814–55), *Op.* 30 and 42.
Henselt, *Op.* 2 and 5 (before 1814).
Chopin, *Op.* 10 (1827), *Op.* 25 (1836).
Liszt, *Paganini Caprices* (1831–5),
 Études Transcendantes (1835–9),
 Études de Concert (1849).
Löschorn (1819–1903).
Berens (1825–80).
Battmann (1818–86).

Characteristic Studies.
Bertini (1798–1876).
Burgmüller (1806–74).
Concone (1810–61).
Heller (1815–88).
Ravina (b. 1818).
Haberbier (1813–69).
Seeling (1828–62).
Gurlitt (b. 1820).
Schytte (b. 1850).
Franklin Taylor.

CHAPTER XVII

THE EDUCATIONAL ASPECT

Methods and Technique

" Consider technical exercises as the daily physical exercise which is necessary to keep you in health."—*Schumann.*

GREAT composers and artists have, more or less, in the past been disinclined to present the fruits of their experience in methodical form, both as regards the purely introductory stage of pianoforte playing and the necessary systematic arrangement of the technical material used. It is, therefore, to the patient teacher that we must mostly look for results in this direction.

An Italian work by Doni (b. 1593) is about the first *Method* of importance on record, the next being Couperin's practical *L'Art de Toucher*, 1717, and Rameau's more advanced *Méthode*, 1724. Em. Bach's *The True Art of Playing the Clavier* (1753) was praised by Haydn and Clementi and is still highly esteemed for its historical value and " as representing the high-water mark of the clavier before the advent of the pianoforte " (Dannreuther).

The work is divided into two parts. The first contains sections on (1) Fingering ; (2) Embellishments ; and (3) Rendering ; the second Part treats of (1) The Art of Accompaniment ; (2) Free Improvisation ; and (3) Harmony. The most important of these is the section on Embellishments and the graces prevalent in older music ; and though Em. Bach's interpretations of the signs in his father's works may be misleading, this Section as a whole is, according to Dannreuther (*Ornamentation*), of considerable value. (Students should see Schwenker's *Beitrag zur Ornamentik*, Univ. Ed.)

Marpurg's *Method* appeared in 1765 and that by Türk, embodying the results of both the preceding, was published in 1789. The latter is noteworthy as marking the transition period in technique between clavichord and pianoforte. It treats especially of Fingering, for which ten rules are given [*see* Kullak's *Æsthetics of Pianoforte Playing* (Schirmer)] and it also gives some hints which are still worthy of notice, one of which is that "keeping time is more important than the development of velocity." Other Chapters—notably those on "Performance and Rendering"—are useful, including one point, much overlooked in this breathless age, *viz.*, the necessity of pauses similar to those employed in rhetorical declamation. Türk points out also the interpretation of National style ; the French—a light style ; Italian—medium ; and German— "heaviest of all."

The *Méthode* by Adam (*c.* 1802) refers to the "hammer clavier" or pianoforte, the others apparently being more concerned with its predecessors. Adam is particularly interested in *touch ;* he recommends that the aim of the pupil should be "to imitate as far as possible the singing tone, developed by great masters on all instruments, and the manifold inflections of the voice which are so tender and affecting." He recommends also, with regard to style, that "each composer must be interpreted according to his character, the one with deep feeling and forceful rendition, the other in a gay, romantic, often fantastic spirit."

The *Clavierschule* of Cramer was for a long time popular for its treatment of the elementary part of the subject, but is now, along with the *Methods* of Hummel (1828), Kalkbrenner and Czerny, entirely out of date.

Hummel introduced for the first time a large number of *Exercises*, and technique is, with him, more systematically developed ; but in one point—the treatment of the pedals—he is rather behind the times, remarking, as he does, that "Mozart and Clementi did not need this help to win fame as the most expressive players of their period."

Kalkbrenner, on the other hand, complains, on a Concert tour, that most of the German instruments have no pedals at all. Kalkbrenner, in his *Method*, adds the study of the wrist to technique, and has some trenchant remarks on expression, rhythm and touch, as, for instance, that "all notes foreign to the keys or notes with accidentals, tied or syncopated notes must be more marked," that "repeated notes must be shaded in tone," that "the manner of striking the key must exhibit innumerable variations," that "one must now caress the keys, now pounce upon it, as the lion hurls himself upon his prey."

Czerny's *Method* (*Op.* 500) is the more complete and scientific, and it forms the practical foundation of all modern technique. Among general rules, he mentions that " the most convenient fingering is the best," and he gives also special attention to the fingering of the chromatic scale.

This voluminous work, now (from its size) out of date, treats at great length of Beethoven's style of rendering, of Fugue-playing (giving eleven rules), of the virtuosi, besides Chapters on " Transposing," " Playing from Score," " Preludizing," " Improvising," etc. Other *Methods*, by Moscheles, Fétis, Lebert and Stark (1858) have appeared, but those have been mostly occupied in the grouping of Studies to a certain end.

The well-known *Technical Studies* of Plaidy (1852) formed the first practical and comprehensive work brought within reasonable limits. Other aspects have been dealt with by A. Kullak (1855) in the *Art of Touch*, by L. Köhler's *Mechanical Training as the Foundation of Technique* (1857), by Marx, incidentally, in a treatise on the treatment of the music of Bach and Beethoven, and by Thalberg's *Art of Singing on the Pianoforte*, where he recommends that " For simple, tender and graceful melodies one should knead the keys, so to speak, pressing and working them as with a boneless hand and fingers of velvet." Also, in Wieck's *Method* (Simrock), which takes the *Cantabile* tone as a basis, and in Riemann's comparative *Theoretical and Practical Pianoforte School*, which is intended as a general guide.

Tausig's *Studies* were the next important factor in educational technique ; not that, in themselves, they provide systematically arranged study, but because this has been provided by others on the principle acted upon by Tausig, *viz.*, the use of similar fingering in similarly constructed phrases. This principle, which involves the free use of the thumb and little fingers on the black keys, was advocated by Liszt, Bülow, Klindworth, Scholtz and Riemann, and was further carried out in the work on *Technique* by Germer (1877) and the later work of Beringer. As the latter remarks, " Chopin's advent knocked the first nail into the coffin of the Clementi and Cramer system of fingering. It has now become entirely inadequate and obsolete for the rendering of the works of modern composers for the pianoforte."

A valuable guide to Germer's *Technics* (Hug, Bos. ; in the four-course Edition) is his *How One Ought to Study Piano*

Technique (1902) (Hug, Bos.). The theoretical basis can be studied also in Germer's *Tone Production in Pianoforte Playing* (1896), which treats of the various kinds of touch and of style and gives practical examples of the same for study. Germer's *Ornamentation* attached to his *Technics* is reliable and concise.

That the artistic rendering is also receiving attention is evident from the valuable works recently published on the subject, especially in England and America. Franklin Taylor, whose little book on *Pianoforte Playing* (Macmillan) has been translated into German, has also written a treatise on *Technique and Expression* (Nov.) in which he also treats lucidly of Fingering, Rhythm, Phrasing, Ornaments and Methods of Study.

Gordon Saunders' valuable *Art of Phrasing* (Hammond) expatiates also on Phrasing, Fingering and Embellishments, giving some 350 examples. Matthay's *Principles of Teaching Interpretation* (Bos.) is the leading book on the subject. Adolph Carpé similarly treats of *Grouping, Articulating and Phrasing in Musical Interpretation* (Bos.) and of *The Pianist's Art* (B.F.W.), the latter work dealing with *Pianoforte Literature.* Tuft's *Technique and Notation* (Summy), containing hints on Technique and Phrasing, and Amina Goodwin's *Hints on Technique and Touch* (Aug.) are useful. Much can be learnt as to musical interpretation from Lussy's *Musical Expression,* 1873 (Nov.), while Adolph Kullak's *Æsthetics of Pianoforte Playing* (Schirmer) is valuable for its general historical and critical view of the whole subject.

Riemann touches on the old and new systems of Fingering and Phrasing in his *Catechism of Pianoforte Playing,* 1880–90 (Hesse, Aug.). Useful hints may be also gathered from Ehrlich's (Editor of *Tausig*) *How to Practise* (Schirmer), Hortense Parents' *L'Étude du Piano,* 1871 (Hachette), Klauwell's *Musical Execution* (Schirmer), and (especially on the Trill) from F. Kullak's *Beethoven's Piano Playing* (Schirmer).

The two most useful modern practical works dealing with elementary technique and touch are Graham Moore's *First Principle of Technique* (Bos.) and Johnstone's *How to Strike the Keys of the Pianoforte* (Hammond). Mason's *Touch and Technique,* Part I (Presser) is similar but more advanced. It had already been pointed out by Brendel that Hummel's tone was not full owing to his finally bringing the finger-nail over the keys, and that Field pressed with perpendicular fingers to the bottom of the key. Early masters had always adhered steadily to a certain position of the hand. Modern technique, however, demands more freedom in style.

The touch which suits one instrument does not always suit another. Similarly, the touch may vary with the technical requirements and particular style of the composition, just as it is recognized that the most convenient fingering is the best. Something of this freedom of action is discerned in the *Leschetitzky Method*, Prentner (Curwen)—a work somewhat opposed to the recent *First Principles of Pianoforte Playing* by Tobias Matthay (Longmans), which, with his *Act of Touch* and the illustrative *Muscular Relaxation Studies* (Bos.) deserve serious study.

Of late years the tendency has been to cultivate the muscles employed in playing, apart from the keyboard, as in the use of the Virgil clavier, the *Techniquer*, the *Hand Gymnastics* of Prentice (Nov.), the " McDonald Smith " system, and the *Rhythmical Exercises* of Parsons (Schirmer). Elementary training is now proceeding on better lines than before. The inculcation of ear-training, perception of rhythm, sight-reading, etc., are dealt with, for instance, in Mrs. Curwen's *Method*, and theoretically discussed in C. B. Cady's *Music Education*, 2 vols. (Summy) ; while the Psychological side is treated in Mrs. Curwen's able *Psychology* and in Dr. Warriner's *Art of Teaching* (Hammond). This leads us to the various modern practical educational works, and since no mere enumeration is of value in itself, their *relative* position and value will be disposed in order, as follows :—

Technical Course.

The best modern foundation for fairly advanced pupils is that of Germer or Beringer (Bos., 1915 Ed.), built upon the *Tausig* principles. Philipps' Edition of Cesi (Ricordi) is also useful. A good shorter course is Philipp's *École du Mécanisme* (Janin) (octaves and chords very good). Franz Kullak's *Die Höhere Klaviertechnik* (Leuckart) is useful for fingering of 3rds, 6ths and octaves. Rosenthal and Schytte's *School of Higher Pianoforte Playing* (Fürstner) is representative and modern (thumbwork good) but not well classified. The *Tausig Vorstufe* (Tausig Preparation) (St. Ed.), though crowded, is valuable (scale passages good, but more double-third work required). Manhire's double-thirds (Larway) and the Germer system of double-third scales are to be recommended. Langley's *Student's Chart* (Aug.) is useful as a concise survey of the whole field of technique.

For the use of younger or less apt pupils (1) Moore's *First Principles of Technique* (Bos.) ; (2) Süss' *Academic Studies*, Part I (very clear) (Lit.) ; or (3) Hartung, *Op.* 34 (Kaun) are valuable ; (4) the modern *Mayer-Mahr Technik* (Sim.), excellently designed work, co-ordinating both Technical material and Studies from the elementary to the difficult stage. Good comprehensive works, but not reaching the higher stages, are the (1) *Eccarius-Sieber System* (Lit.) (very good) ; (2) Süss, *Academic Studies*, II and III (Lit.) ; or (3) Breslaur, *Technische Grundlage* (B. & H.) (well graduated scale work).

Preparatory foundation work is available in (1) Schmitt, *Preparatory Exercises* (Hammond) ; (2) Rie, *Five-Finger Exercises* (very good) (Leduc) ; or (3) Kullak, *Technical Studies* (Schirmer) ; which can be extended by (1) Bellairs' *Elements of Technique* (Enoch) (very good) ; or (2) Cyril Scott's *Modern Finger Exercises* (Elkin) ; or (3) Schultze, *Technical Studies* (Lit.).

With the scales as a basis, Hougounene's *Mécanisme* (Hachette) or Solway's *Exercices Journaliers* (Katto), in conjunction with Bellairs' *Short Scale Studies* (Enoch) are recommendable.

Other useful foundation systems with wider scope are the excellent Hanon *Pianist Virtuoso* (Junne) (in sequential form) ; Krause, *Op.* 38, 1 and 2, or Pischner *Studies*, Rehberg Edition (Eul.) (mostly with fixed notes).

For fairly advanced pupils not working on any particular system there are Henselt's *Exercices Préparatoires* (Schles.), which are very good, or the *Suite* (sequel) to the same, which are not so good. Also there is Philipp's *Une Heure d'Exercice* (Costallat).

The following graded works are best used for *keeping up* practice upon a regular course : (1) Gurlitt, *Op.* 78 (Cranz) ; (2) Czerny, *Forty Daily Studies* (Schles.). To extend the course, Czerny's *Virtuoso School* (Lit.) or Joseffy's *School* (Schirmer) are best.

The best work for the *left hand* is that by Pauer in four Parts (Aug.). For the *weak fingers* and thumb there is a good work by J. O'Neill (Nov.), Schroeder (Cranz, 57 and 58) or Falkenberg, *Six Études* (Leduc). For *independence of finger* we have the work by Phillips (Schirmer) and Philipp's admirable *Exercices Préparatoires*, 2 vols. (Hain), Marchisi's *Seventy-Four Exercises* (Capra), Krug (Nov.) and Döring, *Op.* 69 (Eul.) ; while Vaillant's *Exercices Progressifs* (Ricordi) and Fowles' *Studies in Part Playing* (Aug.) are excellent.

For polyphonic work the best introduction is to be found in the *Collections* of Bellairs (Ash) or Leede (Bos.), or, for more advanced students, in the *Bach-Vorschule* (Lit.).

Graduated *wrist-work* is available in Williams' *Wrist and Forearm Studies* (Schirmer), Krug's *Wrist Studies* (for weaker pupils) (Nov.) or Bellairs (Ash) ; and more advanced wrist-work in Taylor's *Chord Studies* (Nov.) and Pauer's *Gradus* (Aug.).

For the important branch of octave playing there is Germer's excellent *School* (three Parts) followed by Part III of Kullak (Schles.) or the more modern Philipp *School* (Part III) (Schirmer). The *Schools* of Löschorn (Peters) and Gurlitt (Cranz) require preparatory work. Excellent extended octave Studies are found in *Collections* of Taylor (Nov.), and in Pauer's *Gradus* (advanced) (Aug.), or in B. Wolf, *Op.* 100 (Lit.) and Coenen (Nov.)

A course of double notes can be best prepared for in Gurlitt's *School of Thirds* (Cranz) and continued in Taylor's *Studies* (Nov.) and Philipp's 10 *Studies in Double Notes* (Leduc) ; preparatory 3rds and 6ths in Krause, *Op.* 57, II (Cranz), or 6ths alone in Gurlitt's *Op.* 100, II (Cranz). The best sequel to these is Philipp's *Double Notes* (Schirmer).

The more fully developed Study forms a link between the plain technical material and the *Piece*. The perfect Study should make little mental demand on the student. Excellent and unsurpassed general courses are to be found in the *Collections* of Taylor (Divisional) (Nov.) and Thümer (mixed) (Aug.). Of strictly preparatory Studies the best are Holmes and Karn I (Ash) and Gurlitt, *Op.* 187 (J.W.). In the next grade Rowley's 12 *Little Fantasy Studies* (Rogers), Taylor's *Progressive Books* Nos. 1 and 5 (or *Selected*, Bk. I), Holmes and Karn II (Ash), Leduc, 25 *Studies* and Sartorio Bk. I (Ash) (*cantabile* style) are very good.

The easy *velocity* Studies, Gurlitt, *Op.* 141 (Aug.) and Biehl, *Op.* 170 (R.F.) come first. Good and really elementary Studies in *style* are not easy to find. Concone's *Op.* 24, Matthew's graded Course II (Presser) and Rowley's *2nd Year Fantasy Studies* (Rogers), the latter also as an introduction to polyphonic work, are perhaps the best. Following the easy Velocity Studies, Thümer's Bk. II, Lemoine, *Op.* 37 (Lit.), Löschorn *Selected Studies*, II (Presser) or Germer's *Selection from Schmitt* (Bos.) are recommendable.

In the next grade, Taylor's *Progressive Studies*, Nos. 3 (Scale) and 14 (Arpeggio) are excellent. Instead of the *Arpeggio Studies* the easier Germer, Schmitt, or Ebor *Bk.* III can be used. The best *mixed Studies* here are Thümer, *Bks.* III and IV ; for *velocity*, Le Couppey, *Op.* 20 (Ed. Wood); for *polyphonic work*, J. Vogel, 6 *Studies*, *Op.* 15 (Foetisch), and for *expression*, Ebor IV and Heller, 30 *Select Studies* (Presser).

Foundation work, continued as before, but amplified by Taylor, No. 6 or 7, broken chords, wrist-work and easy double notes. The best *mixed Studies* are Taylor's *Selected*, *Set* I, No. 4, Karn V and VI, or Vogt, 24 *Studies* (Schles.). For *velocity* there is Biehl, *Op.* 179, I (R.F.) or Berens, *Newest School* (Aug.) ; while for *expression*, Heller or Burgmüller, *Op.* 109 (Aug.) are best.

In the next grade, Taylor's *Velocity VI*, *Arpeggio III*, *Double notes* and *wrist-work*, or the pleasant Phillip's *Études Classiques* (Leduc) are useful for a foundation ; while of *mixed Studies* Thümer, XA and XB, *Ebor Series*, V and VI, Karn VII, or the Bülow-Cramer (Univ. Ed.) (broken chords and double notes) are the best. For *style* Heller's *Studies*, MacDowell's 12 *Studies*, *Op.* 39 (Elkin), Lack's *Études Artistiques* (Lemoine) or Haberbier (Lit.) are available.

For the difficult grade we recommend a continuation of the above or Pauer's *Gradus* (scales and *arpeggios*) (Aug.) amplified special courses in polyphonic, wrist, and double notes. The *Mixed Studies* of Thümer, XI to XIV, or Reinecke, *Schule der Technik* (B. & H.) are very good, or selections can be made from Tausig's *Clementi* (Univ. Ed.), Mayer's modern *Op.* 168 (Pauer Ed., Leuckart) or Czerny's *Op.* 740 (R.F.). Moscheles, *Op.* 70 (Aug.) is useful for *style*. The best introduction to the more difficult Chopin works is through Philipp's *Études Techniques* (Ricordi, 2 vols.) mostly on the black keys, the Germer Selection of Mayer (Lit.) or the Heller-Chopin *Studies* (Ash).

Suitable preparatory material for the Concert Room is to be found in Augener's *Études de Concert* and in works by Geo.

Schumann (Hop.) and Seeling (Aug.), in Philipp's *Caprice,
Op.* 14 (Ham.) and Georges Beach, 4 *Études* (Foetisch).   The
highest grade includes specialization in wrist and polyphonic
work with Selections from the Studies of Chopin, Thalberg,
Op. 20 (Ash), Henselt, *Op.* 2 (Aug.) and Liszt's *Concert Studies*
(Aug.).   The separate Studies in *Petit Gradus* and the *Nouveau
Gradus* of I. Philipp (Leduc) are very useful.   Philipp's *Études
de Perfectionnement* (Leduc),   Joseffy, *Selected Studies* (Schirmer)
and Thümer, Bks. XV and XVI also are useful.

Somewhat allied to the *Study* in style or expression is the
modern *Prelude*, which is mostly designed on a technical figure
and indued with artistic feeling.   It is distinguished by vague,
unfettered form, considerable poetical feeling and charm.

The Russian School excels in the *Prelude* and Scriabin and
Wihtol stand out pre-eminently in this delightful class of
composition, with their interesting rhythmical peculiarities
and Chopinesque technique (*see* Part IV, Chapter VI).   The
Preludes of Liadow, Glazounow, Stcherbachew, Antipow,
Blumenfeld and Schütt are likewise interesting.   (*See* Part IV,
Chapter VI.)

Of the attractive *Concert Études* which are suitable for the
Concert Room Liszt's and Liapounow's *Transcendant Études;*
and the *Concert Études* of *Aus der Höhe* (Schirmer), Stradal (J.S.)
and E. Kullak (Schles.) may be mentioned, in addition to the
standard *Poetical Studies* of Chopin.   We have not space to
mention more than leading works dealing with special branches
of technique, but these are : Scale Work, Kullak, *Hints* (Aug.) ;
Arpeggios, etc., Taylor, and Pauer's *Gradus;*   Extensions and
Skips, by Philipp (Leduc), Pauer's *Gradus* and Taylor;
Repetition, Pauer's *Gradus* and Taylor ; the Shake, Philipp's
La Trille (Leduc) ; Alternation of Hands, Schytte, *Op.* 75,
Bk. 4 (Hansen).

The right use of the pedals is important.   Whiting's *Pedal
Studies* (Schirmer), coupled with the *Guide to Pianoforte Pedals*
(Examples from Rubinstein's Programmes) (Bos.) are sufficient.
The works on Phrasing by Saunders (Hammond), Taylor (Nov.)
and Carpé (Bos.) are very useful ; while practical phrasing studies
(a neglected branch) can be found in Matthew's *Studies in
Phrasing*, 2 vols. (Presser), in Czerny's *Legato and Staccato* (Lit.),
in Germer's *Selection from Heller* (Bos.) and Presser's *Selection
from Concone* (Presser).

For Rhythm, Germer's *Rhythmical Problems* (Bos.) and Reinhold's *Op.* 57 (Dob.) are the best. In the insufficiently cultivated branch of Sight-Reading, works by Geehl (Ash), *Scale Melodies* (Hammond), Charles de Beriot's advanced *Lecture de Piano* (Leduc), Somervell's *Sight Reading*, 6 vols. (Swan) and Harrison's *Sight Reading Tests* (Weekes) are all useful.

The reviving art of Improvisation can be studied in Czerny's *L'Art d'Improviser* (Leduc) with his *L'Art de Préluder* and Sawyer's *Improvisation*.

The very practical and interesting method of studying classified extracts from the works of the masters is adopted in Bülow's *Applied Piano Technic* (Bos.), in Philipp's more complete *Études Classiques*, 3 Parts (Leduc), in the admirable but advanced *Exercices Journaliers*, edited by I. Philipp and in his preparatory *Exercices Pratiques* (Dur.), in Buonamici's *Passages from Beethoven* (Venturini), in Langley's *Selections* from Wollenhaupt (Aug.), in Heller's *Chopin Studies* (Ash) and in Henselt's difficult *Meister Studien* (Challier).

We now leave the technical side and proceed to general instructive works.

Many methods exist, but it is still difficult to select really good works interesting to the average pupil.

Pt. I and II of the *ABCDarian* (Aug.)—the most elementary introduction—*Piano Methods* by Beringer (Duet System) (Bos.), Mrs. Curwen (very exhaustive) and *The Art of Pianoforte Playing* by Jackson and Ed. Duncan (Dent & Sons) may be specially mentioned. Good Collections of elementary material are to be found in Alec Rowley's *First Year at the Piano* (Swan), Tapper's *Graded Course* (Ditson), Spurling's *Miniatures* (Aug.), *Pieces* by Bath (Curwen and Nov.) and G. Newton's *Woodland Dances*, Classical work in the *Classisches Jugend-Album* (André), Germer's *Sonatina Playing* (Bos.) and Philipp's *Petite Bibliothèque Classique* (Ja.). and Recreative work in Carl Hein's *Blumenlese* (Harris) and in Gurlitt, *Op.* 120 (Lit.). Selections from Schumann's *Kinder-Album* and Schytte's *Op.* 94, 96 and 97 (Hansen) also are most valuable. Recommendable instructive Collections in the 2nd Grade are Tapper's *Courses* II and III (Ditson), the Recreative *Zuschneid*, *Op.* 42 (Siegel) and Espen, *Freudvoll and Leidvoll* (Portius). In the 3rd Grade there are the *Sonatina Album* (Lit.), Germer's *Teaching Material*, II and III (Bos.), *Sonatinas* by Von Wilm, *Op.* 20 (Univ. Ed.) and by

Beringer (St. Lucas), Poetical and Recreative work by Heller, *Op.* 138 (Ash), Behr, *Op.* 310 (Lit.) and Henrique's *Bilderbuch*, II (Rahter). For lists of separate instructive Pieces, graded in order of difficulty, one must refer to Webbe's *Primer* (Forsyth) or to the Ruthardt (Bos.) and *Eschmann Guides* (Foetisch).

We might mention finally representative *Duet Collections* in graded order.   In the Elementary Grade, *ABCDarian*, I and II (Aug.)—*Claviermaterialien*, I, Hartung (Kaun), Gurlitt, *Op.* 81 (Donajowski), E. Low, *Duet School*, I (Lit.), and, further advanced, Gurlitt's *Grateful Tasks* (Aug.).   Second Grade, Low, Part II (Lit.) and Diabelli, *Sonatinas*, I, etc. (Lit.).   For Recreation, 10 *Easy Duets*, Moffatt (B. & F.) and Hein's *Travel Pictures* (Harris). Third Grade, Hartung, *Clavier Material*, IV and V (Kaun).   Poetical, Low, *Op.* 150 (Lit.) and Gurlitt, *Op.* 202 (Lit.).   After these may follow Selections from Beethoven *Duets* (Lit.), Schubert *Rondos*, etc. (Lit.), Weber, *Duet Compositions* and Schumann, *Oriental Pictures* (Lit.).

The American *School of Four-Hand Playing* (Presser) and Tapper's *Graded Four-Hand Course* (Ditson) are also generally useful.

CODA

We now come to the conclusion of our work, and by way of Coda would ask ourselves in what direction Pianoforte Music is tending, and what is its future.   Unmistakably the tendency at present is the development of National modes of thought and the substitution of new features, both melodic, harmonic and rhythmic, for the now well-worn and until recently universal models.

Peering more closely into the future, we see that the most likely factors are the influence of (1) the orchestra ; (2) the opera, and (3) a new keyboard.

The organ and vocal styles have had their day in Pianoforte music ; the orchestra is now to the fore.   From an " effective " point of view the orchestra's influence is certainly nugatory. Beethoven blended the Thematic and Orchestral styles in his Sonatas with passable pianistic results, while Liszt, through his widened technique (in his own words) contrived that " a man's ten fingers are enough to render the harmonies which are brought out by the combined efforts of hundreds of musicians."

Mere fulness or power does not, however, add materially to the resources of the composer, and Pianoforte works written in the language of the orchestra are usually ineffective.

The Opera, again, with its ever-changing dramatic situations and its kaleidoscope of the emotions, does not favour the reasoned detail of Thematic treatment, but it would seem to have an important influence on the evolution of new and more intense harmonic combinations. From this and from the compositions of the Impressionist School there is no doubt that we may see in the future the evolution of new and entrancing harmonization in combination with the new melodic and rhythmic characteristics of the various National Schools.

The next step in the future may be a revived interest in Thematic work, stimulated, perhaps, by the appearance of a future Beethoven who will write Pianistic works endowed with the new and charming features just mentioned.

The new Janko and Emmanuel Moor keyboard, with added mechanical devices, such as prevailed in the harpsichords, *viz.*, octave stops, additional row of keys and pedal keys, may also add to our technical resources, and to variety of tone and effect and fulness or power.

The artistic conscience, however, desires, above all, *not quantity but quality*—and we, for our part, while welcoming the facilitation of difficult works, would be inclined to favour the composer of the future who does not attempt to rival the organ or the orchestra, but is able to sketch with the pen of a Chopin or Heller a simple but charming Prelude ; or, on the other hand, can make us realize that music is the " archetype of all the arts," the " perfect identification of form and matter " (Pater) as applied in all artistic sincerity to the most universal form of Art—Pianoforte Music.

APPENDIX.

Modern methods for young children have been enriched by S. M. Livsey's *Children's Musical Moments* (Wood ed.), in which all melodies have nursery rhymes added, and by Alec Rowley's *Child Heart, Duet Albums* (Ash) founded on nursery folk-songs.

Dr. Bellairs' admirable *Primer* (Enoch) is also based on the Duet principle. Felix Swinstead's *First Lessons* (A.F. Co.) begins on the Great Staff principle.

Good elementary Pieces, endued with good melody and avoiding cacophony, have appeared by M. E. Marshall, T. F. Dunhill, Julius Harrison, and Markham Lee (all Curwen). Good material will be found in similar Pieces by Cyril Jenkins, and Carl Hemann (Cary), Harold Craxton (A.F. Co.), Dr. Cuthbert Harris, Gladys Cumberland (Warren and Phillips), the *Four Album Leaves* by Felix Swinstead, E. L. Bainton's *By Wave and Shore* (A.F. Co.), and in Dr. Bellairs' *Progressive Pianist* (Enoch). This is a sphere in which Alec Rowley stands to the front. Further works by him should be mentioned in the *Seven Little Pieces, Mosaics* and *Fragments* (Ash) ; also in his very imaginative *Goblin Suite*, poetic *Shepherd's Calendar*, the invigorating *English Dance Suite* and *Punchinello Suite*, the melodious and refined *Six Impromptus* and the *Rivulet* (all Ash). Further select material should also be named in the fresh and melodious *Five Sketches* by Reg. H. Hunt (St. & B.), R. Richard's *Souvenirs* (Wood edn.), Dr. Darke's *Miniatures* (St. & B.), *Playtime Pleasures* by Alg. Ashton (Ricordi), and an attractive *Our Holidays Suite* (Lg.) by Cecil Hazlehurst.

To selected elementary studies should be added the excellent series by Cuthbert Harris (W. & P.), the *Poetical Studies* by Alec Rowley (Ash), and for the classic style Alg. Ashton's *Eight Studies* (Aug.).

Coming to special Studies, there are, as an addition to Julia O'Neill's invaluable *Weaker Finger Studies*, her *Picturesque Technique* (S. & B.), and its sequence, *Melodious Technique* (Nov.). For the Left Hand, Moskowski's work (Enoch) and Litta Lyn's *Night Song* (Wood's edn.) provide useful material. For Alternate Hands there is the attractive *Op.* 2, 3 and 5 by Caroline Crawford (Wood's edn.). Regarding Double-Note Scales, Manhire's Chart (Larway) should be supplemented by Moskowski's *School* (Enoch), while to *Concert Studies* a useful example by Leonard Peck (Banks) and a virtuoso *Toccata* by Tobias Matthay (A.F. Co.) can be added.

In Matthay and Swinstead's *First Music-Making*, elementary technique is taught on Mr. Matthay's system.

Noteworthy Pieces : M. E. Marshall, *Three Sketches* ; Reg. King, *Second Arabesque* ; G. Devers, *Canzonetta* ; and the Scandinavian Pieces by Olaf Petersen (all Jos. Williams).

APPENDIX

SELECT BIBLIOGRAPHY

I. LITERATURE CLASSIFIED.

II. MODERN EDITIONS.

III. JOURNALS FOR PIANISTS.

IV. PUBLISHERS OF PIANO MUSIC.

PART I

LITERATURE.

Histories of Pianoforte Music.

1842-45.—Whistling, *Handbuch der Musical. Literatur* (Hoffmeister).

1863-87.—Weitzmann, *Geschichte des Klavierspiels und der Klavier-litteratur.* Lessmann Ed. 1887 (Breitkopf & Härtel).

1884.—Prosniz, *Handbuch der Clavier Literatur,* 1450-1830. 2 vols. (Doblinger, Vienna).

1895.—Pauer, *Dictionary of Pianists* (Novello).

1897.—Dr. Baker's Translation of Weitzmann (Schirmer, New York).

1898.—Max Seiffert's revised and enlarged (3rd) edn. of Weitzmann, vol. I : to 1750 (Breitkopf & Härtel).

1899.—Oscar Bie, *History of the Pianoforte and Pianoforte Players.* Translated and revised from the German, by E. E. Rellett and E. W. Naylor (Dent).

1901.—Villani, *L'Arte del Clavicembalo* (Fratella-Bodia, Turin).

1904.—J. C. Fillmore, *Pianoforte Music* (Presser, Philadelphia). Ridley Prentice's edn. of above (no date ; Reeves).

1910.—H. E. Krehbiel, *The Pianoforte and its Music* (Scribner, New York ; Murray, London).

CLASSIFIED GUIDES—EDUCATIONAL.

1888.—Eschmann-Dumur, *Guide* (Foetisch).

1900.—Webbe, *Pianist's Primer and Guide* (Forsyth)—valuable encyclopædic work.

1900.—Parent, *Répertoire Encyclopédique*—16th Century to Schumann—with Biographies. (Hachette).

1905.—Ruthardt (Hug-Bos) Enlargement of Eschmann. Best general Guide ; but deficient in British, American and Modern National School of Composers.

1905.—Georgi, *Pianist's Guide* (lithographed) (Pabst—Breitkopf & Härtel).

Marmontel, *Vade Mecum* (Paris).

Löschorn, *Führer.* (Guide)—concise (Breitkopf & Härtel).

1894 and 1905.—Köhler, *Führer* (Breitkopf & Härtel).

Wysman, *Vade Mecum* (Stumpf & Koning).

1886, in German.—Reinecke, *What shall we play ?* (Presser).

General Pianoforte Study.

Fr. Taylor, *Technique and Expression* (Novello). (Technique, Fingering, Rhythm, Phrasing, Expression, and Ornaments).
Parent, *How to Study the Piano* (Presser).
Pauer, *The Art of Pianoforte Playing.* 1877 (Novello).
Fisher, *The Pianist's Mentor* (Curwen).
Vincent, *The First Year's Study* (Vincent).
Friskin, *The Principles of Pianoforte Practice* (Gray).
J. F. Cooke, *Great Pianists on Piano Playing.* 1913–17 (Presser).

General Technique.

Ad Kullak, *Æsthetics of Piano Playing.* 1861 (Schirmer). (I : Historical ; II : Technique ; III : Rendering). Additions by Bischoff, 1876 and 1889.
Fr. Taylor, *Primer of Pianoforte Playing* (Longman). Also in German.
Davenport and Baker, *Guide to Pianoforte Students* (Longman).
Amina Goodwin, *Technique and Touch* (Augener).
S. Vantyn, *Modern Pianoforte Technique* (Kegan Paul).
Langley, *Students' Chart of Technique* (Augener).

Systems of Technique.

Germer, *How Ought One to Study Technique* (Bos). Guide to author's *Technics.*
Ehrlich, *How to Practise* (Tausig system) (Schirmer).
Prentner, *The Leschetitzky Method* (Curwen ; Presser).
Melasfield, *The Hand of the Pianist* (Leschetitzky Method).
Ehrenfechter, *Technical Study* (Deppe System) (Reeves).
——, *Delivery in Pianoforte Playing* (Reeves).
Amy Fay, *Musical Study in Germany* (Deppe System) (Macmillan).
Bettina Walker, *My Musical Experiences.* 1890 (Bentley).
Mason, *Touch and Technique.* 4 Vols. (Presser ; Curwen).
Tuft, *Technique and Notation* (Summy).

Physical Training.

R. Prentice, *Hand Gymnastics* (Novello).
Stoewe, *Die Klavier Technik.* 1886 (Berlin).

On Touch and Fingering.

O. Klauwell, *Der Fingersatz des Klavierspiels.* 1885.
A. Richter, *Das Klavierspiel* (Breitkopf & Härtel).
Riemann, *Catechism of Pianoforte Playing* (Augener).
M. Faell, *Der Anschlag* (Breitkopf & Härtel).
Germer, *Tone Production* (Bos).
T. Matthay, *First Principles of Pianoforte Playing* (Longman).
——, *Muscular Relaxation Studies* (Bos).
J. A. Johnstone, *How to Strike the Keys* (Hammond).
——, *Touch, Phrasing and Interpretation* (Reeves).
Wm. Townsend, *Balance of Arm in Pianoforte Technique* (Bos.).

Interpretation, Phrasing and Expression.

Lussy, *Musical Expression* (Novello). Foundation work.
O. Klauwell, *On Musical Execution* (Schirmer).
Riemann, *Catechism of Pianoforte Playing* (Augener).

Wieck, *Clavier und Gesang*. Translated by Krüger, of Aberdeen.
Carpé, *Grouping, Articulating and Phrasing* (Bos.).
——, *The Pianist's Art* (B. F. Wood).
Christian, *Principles of Expression* (Presser).
J. A. Johnstone, *Phrasing in Pianoforte Playing* (Ashdown).
G. Saunders, *Art of Phrasing* (Hammond). Very good.
J. B. McEwen, *The Principles of Phrasing and Articulation* (Augener).
Mathews, *Studies in Phrasing*. 3 Vols.; practical (Presser).
T. Matthay, *Interpretation* (Jos. Williams).
J. A. Johnstone, *The Art of Expression* (Weekes).

WORKS FOR TEACHERS.

Mrs. J. S. Curwen, *Psychology Applied to Music Teaching* (Curwen).
Dr. Warriner, *Art of Teaching* (Psychological) (Hammond).
Wm. Wallace, *The Threshold of Music* (Macmillan). The development of the musical sense.
——, *The Music Faculty; its Origins and Processes* (Macmillan).
Cady, *Music and Education*, 2 vols. (In general) (Summy).
Lavignac, *Musical Education* (4th American Ed.) (Putnam).
Marmontel, *Conseils d'un Professeur*. Paris.
Em. Bach, *Die Wahre Art das Clavier zu spielen*. 1753 and 1761; new Ed. by Niemann (Breitkopf & Härtel). Nine Chapters are given in Dannreuther's *Ornamentation*, Pt. II (Novello).
Plaidy, *The Piano Teacher* (Reeves).
Le Couppey, *Piano Teaching* (Reeves).
Riemann, *Theortisch-Praktische Klavier-Schule*, 2 vols. (Rahter).
Eccarius Sieber, *Handbuch der Klavier-Unterrichtslehre* (Viewey).
Eschmann, 100 *Aphorismen*. New Ed. (Raable and Plothew).
Mrs. Curwen, *The Teacher's Guide to Mrs. Curwen's Method* (Curwen).
Presser, *Suggestions in Modern Methods* (Gratis) (Presser).
Mathews, *Teacher's Manual of Mason's Technics* (Chicago).
J. A. Johnstone, *The Art of Teaching Pianoforte Playing* (Reeves).
Chas. W. Pearce, *The Art of the Pianoforte Teacher* (Rogers).
H. Antcliffe, *The Successful Music Teacher* (Augener).
Woodhouse, *Pianoforte Pedagogy of to-day* (Kegan Paul).
Horrocks, *Pianoforte Teacher*.
Ernest Fowles, *Harmony in Pianoforte Study*, 2 vols. (Curwen).

WORKS ON FORM.

Pauer, *Musical Forms* (Novello).
Jadassohn, *Musical Forms* (Breitkopf & Härtel).
Prout, *Form and Applied Forms* (Augener).
Anger, *Form in Music* (Rogers).
Peterson, *Handbook of Musical Form* (Augener).
Cornell, *Musical Form* (Schirmer).
Stewart Macpherson, *Form in Music* (Jos. Williams).
Mathews, *Primer of Musical Forms* (Schmidt, Boston).
Goetschius, *Lessons in Musical Form* (Ditson).
Henderson, *How Music Developed* (Murray).
M. H. Glynn, *Analysis of the Evolution of Musical Form* (Longman).
Prescott, *About Music and What it is Made of* (Methuen).
Mathews, *How to Understand Music*, 2 vols. (Form and Biography) (Presser).

HISTORY OF MUSICAL FORMS.

The Sonata.

Shedlock, *The Pianoforte Sonata* (Methuen).
Hadow, *Sonata Form* (Novello).
O. Klauwell, *Geschichte der Sonata.*
Bagge, *Die Geschichte der Entwickelung der Sonata* (Breitkopf & Härtel).
Grove's Dictionary. Article on " Sonata."

The Concerto.

Daffner, *Die Entwickelung des Klavier-Konzerts bis Mozart* (Breitkopf & Härtel).
Shedlock, *Mozart's Pianoforte Concertos* (Musical Record, Nov. and Dec., 1906).

FORM ANALYSIS.

Stewart Macpherson, *Studies in Phrasing and Form* (Jos. Williams).
Bertenshaw, *Rhythm, Analysis and Musical Form* (Longman).
Bannister, *Musical Analysis* (Bell).
Goodrich, *Musical Analysis*, 2 vols. 1889 (Schirmer).
Statham, *Form and Design in Music* (Reeves).
Fisher, *Pianist's Mentor* (Form ; Analysis, etc.).
A. E. Hull, *Questions on Musical Form* (Augener).

APPLIED ANALYSIS.

R. Prentice, *The Musician*, 6 grades (Curwen).
Perry, *Descriptive Analyses*, 2 vols. (Presser).
Holmes & Karn, *Analyses*, 4 pieces (Weekes).

ANALYSED EDITIONS OF MUSIC.

Dr. G. Saunders, Annotated Editions of the Classics (Hammond).
Dr. E. Turpin, Student's Edition of the Classics (Weekes).
Bülow Edition of Beethoven's Sonatas, Op. 53—in Cotta Edition.
Editions of Bach's 48 Preludes and Fugues by Lott (Ashdown) ; Reinecke, (Breitkopf & Härtel); Stade's Open Score Edition (Steingräber) ; Vincent's Open Score Edition (Vincent) ; Saunders' Edition (different-sized notes) (Hammond) ; Boekelman's Edition (coloured entries of subject, etc.).

DESCRIPTIVE ANALYSIS OF THE CLASSICS.

Analysis of Mozart's Sonatas, by Janet Salisbury.
Analysis (Form, etc.) of Bach's 48 Preludes and Fugues, by Iliffe (Novello) ; Riemann, 2 vols. (Augener) ; Van Bruyck (Breitkopf & Härtel) and Sampson (Digest of—in 3 sections) (Vincent).
Analysis of Beethoven's Sonatas, by Elterlein (Reeves) ; Nagel (1903), in German (Langens). Harding—Detailed Formal Analysis (Novello).
How to Study the Pianoforte Works of Beethoven, by Herbert Westerby (Reeves).
Descriptions. See Reinecke's *Letters to a Lady* (Augener), and Lenz's *The Three Styles.*

Descriptions and Critiques.

Herbert Westerby, *Piano Works of the Great Composers* : *Bach and Handel to Beethoven*, 1 vol. ; also 7 Parts (Reeves).

Marx, *Beethoven's Piano Works* (trans.—Summy, Chicago).

F. Kullak, *Beethoven's Pianoforte Playing* (Concertos, etc.) (Schirmer).

Lorenz, *Mozart als Klavier Componist* (Leuckart).

Reinecke, *Zur Wiederbelebung der Mozartschen Clavier-Konzerte.*

Schumann, *Music and Musicians*, 2 vols. (Reeves).

Vogel, *Schumann's Klavier Ton Poesie* (Hesse).

Jansen, *Die Davidsbündler* (Breitkopf & Härtel).

Kleczynski, *Greater Works of Chopin* (Reeves).

——, *How to Play Chopin* (Reeves).

Jonson, *Handbook to Works of Chopin* (Heinemann).

Naylor, *An Elizabethan Virginal Book* (Breitkopf & Härtel).

Pauer, *Three Historical Performances* (Recital Notes) (Augener).

Henderson, *Preludes and Studies.* 1891 (Evolution of Piano Music, etc.) (Longman).

J. A. Johnstone, *Modern Tendencies in Musical Art* (Schumann, Chopin, etc.).

Bülow, *Studien* (Notes on various works) (Luckhardt).

Niecks, *Programme Music* (Novello).

Jeffrey Pulver, *The Ancient Dance Forms* (Musical Association Lectures, 1914).

Ornamentation.

Harding, *Musical Ornaments* (Weekes).

Fowles, *Studies in Musical Graces* (Vincent).

Germer, *Ornamentation* (now added to his *Technics*) (Bos.).

Dannreuther, *Ornamentation*, 2 vols. (Novello).

Schwenker, *Ein Beitrag zur Ornamentik* (in Em. Bach's works), Universal Edition.

Dolmetsch, *The Interpretation of the Music of the 17th and 18th Centuries* (Novello).

Ehrlich, *Ornamentation in Bach's Works* (St. Ed.).

——, *Ornamentation in Beethoven's Works* (St. Ed.).

Sight Reading and Memorizing.

Dr White, *Reading at Sight* (Curwen).

Mott Harrison, *Sight Reading Tests* (Weekes).

Somervell, *Sight Reading*, 6 vols. (Swan).

Scale Melodies, 4 Parts (Hammond).

C. de Beriot, *Lecture du Piano* (Leduc).

Parent, *Lecture Musicale* (Hamelle).

Shinn, *Musical Memory* (Vincent).

Tapper, *Sight Reading and Memory Lessons* (Schmitt, Boston).

Fisher, *Pianist's Mentor* (Memorizing, etc.) (Curwen).

Accompaniments.

Newton, *Song Accompaniments* (Gould).

Glen, *How to Accompany* (Cocks).

A. H. Lindo, *The Art of Accompanying* (Rogers).

Evans, *The Art of Accompanying at the Piano* (Reeves).

Reinecke, *Aphorisms on Song Accompaniments* (Gebr. Reinecke).

MUSICAL APPRECIATION.

Scholes, *The Listener's Guide* (Oxford Univ. Press).
Kobbé, *How to Appreciate Music* (Sisley).
Antcliffe, *How to Enjoy Music* (Kegan Paul).
St. Macpherson, *Music and its Appreciation* (Jos. Williams).
Dickinson, *The Art of Listening to Good Music* (Reeves).
Henderson, *What is Good Music ?* (Murray).

THE PEDALS.

Rubinstein, *Piano Pedal Studies* (Bos.).
Schmitt, *The Pedals of the Pianoforte* : trans. (Presser).
J. A. Johnstone, *How to Use the Pedal* (Ashdown).
A. H. Lindo, *The Art of Pedalling.* 1923 (Kegan Paul).

ORCHESTRAL SCORE READING.

Riemann, *Playing from Score* (Augener).

RHYTHM.

Germer, *Rhythmical Problems* (Practical) (Bos.).
M. H. Glyn, *The Rhythmic Conception of Music* (Longman).

EXTEMPORIZATION.

Sawyer, *Extemporization* (Novello).
Czerny, *L'Art d'Improviser* (Leduc).
——, *L'Art de Préluder* (Leduc).

HISTORY OF THE PIANOFORTE.

Hipkins, *The Pianoforte* (Novello).
Weitzmann, *History of Pianoforte Playing, etc.* (Schirmer).
Paul, *Geschichte des Klaviers* (Payne).
Oscar Bie, *History of the Pianoforte* : trans. (Dent).
Southgate, *English Music* (Evolution of Piano, etc.) (Scott).
Ruthardt, *Das Klavier* (Origin ; Style ; Technique) (Hug).
Marmontel, *Histoire du Piano* (Influence on Composers) (Paris).

GENERAL MUSICAL HISTORY.

Concise Histories : by Davey, 1s. (Curwen) ; Hunt, 3s. 6d. (Bell) ; and
    Riemann (Augener).
Parry, *Summary of Musical History* (Novello).
Colles, *The Growth of Music,* 2 Parts (Clarendon Press).
Dickinson, *Study of the History of Music* (Scribner ; Reeves).
J. E. Matthew, *Handbook of Musical History* (For Authorities) (Grevel).
Oxford History of Music, Vol. III : The 17th Century ; Vol. IV : Bach
    and Handel ; V : Viennese School ; VI : Romantic Period (Clarendon
    Press).
Stanford and Forsyth, *History of Music* (Macmillan).

MUSICAL CRITIQUE.

Streatfeild, *Modern Music and Music* (Palestrina to R. Strauss) (Methuen).
Hadow, *Studies in Modern Music*, 2 vols. 1893 (Schumann to Brahms) (Seeley).
Huneker, *Mezzotints.* 1900 (Chopin, Brahms, Liszt studies, etc.)(Scribner; Reeves).
Mason, *Beethoven and his Forerunners* (Macmillan).
——, *The Romantic Composers* (Schubert to Liszt) (Macmillan).
——, *From Grieg to Brahms* (Includes also Dvorák, Saint-Saëns and Franck) (Outlook Co.).
Gilman, *Phases of Modern Music* (McDowell; Grieg, etc.) (Harper).
Filson Young, *Mastersingers.* 1901 (Hallé; Saint-Saëns; etc.) (Reeves).
Rubenstein, *Music and its Masters* (Augener).
Elson, *Modern Composers of Europe* (Page, Boston).
Niemann, *Musik and Musiker des 19ten Jahrhunderts* (Senff).
Riemann, *Geschichte der Musik seit Beethoven* (1800–1900) (Spemann).

GREAT PIANISTS.

Lahee, *Great Pianists* (Putnam). (Very good).
J. F. Cooke, *Great Pianists on Piano Playing* (1913–17) (Presser). (Very good).
Ehrlich, *Celebrated Pianists* (Presser).
Lenz, *Great Piano Virtuosos* (Liszt; Henselt; etc.) (Schirmer).
Marmontel, *Les Pianistes Célèbres* (Heugel).

MUSICAL BIOGRAPHIES.

BACH. By Parry. 1909 (Novello). By Spitta, 3 vols. 1884–5 (Novello).
BEETHOVEN. By D'Indy (Boston Music Co.). By Romain Rolland. 1917 (Kegan Paul).
BENNETT (Sterndale). By J. R. S. Bennett. 1907 (Camb. Univ. Press). By O'Leary. 1881 (Mus. Assoc. Lecture).
BRAHMS. By Colles (Lane). By Deiters. 1888 (Unwin). By Fuller Maitland. 1911 (Methuen). By Florence May, 2 vols, 1905 (Arnold).
CHOPIN. By Huneker. (1900) 1903 (New York). By Niecks, 2 vols. 1888 (Novello).
DEBUSSY. By Cortot (*The Pianoforte Music of Debussy*) (Chester). By Le Cas (Breitkopf & Härtel). By Liebich. 1908 (Lane).
DVORÁK. By Markham Lee (Lane).
FRANCK (César). By Derepas (Breitkopf & Härtel). By D'Indy (Lane).
GRIEG. By Finch. 1906 (Lane).
HALLÉ. Autobiography (Macmillan).
HANDEL. By Streatfeild (Methuen). By Rolland (Kegan Paul).
HAYDN. By Hadow (*A Croatian Composer*) (Seeley).
HELLER. By Barbadette (Ashdown).
HOLBROOKE. By Lowe. 1920 (Kegan Paul).
HULLAH. By Leschetitzky (Lane).
LISZT. By Calvocoressi (Paris). By Hervey (Lane). By Huneker (Chapman & Hall). By Ramann, 2 vols. 1882 (Reeves). By Wohl. 1887 (Ward & Downey).
MACDOWELL. By Gilman. 1905 (Lane). By Porte. 1922 (Kegan Paul).
MOSCHELES. By his Wife, 2 vols. 1873 (Hurst & Blackett).
MOZART. By Jahn, 3 vols. 1883 (Novello). By Wilder (Reeves).

MUSORGSKY. By Calvocoressi. 1919 (Kegan Paul).
RUBINSTEIN. By M'Arthur. 1890 (Reeves).
SAINT SAËNS. By Neitzell (*Die Harmonie*). By Watson Lyle, 1923 (Kegan Paul).
SCHUBERT. By Hellborn, 2 vols. 1869 (Longman), Article "Schubert" in Grove's *Dictionary*.
SCHUMANN. By May (Arnold). By Reissmann. 1886 (Bell).
SCOTT (Cyril). By Hull. 1918 (Kegan Paul).
SCRIABIN. By Hull (1916) 1920 (Kegan Paul).
TCHAÏKOWSKI. By Newmarch (Grant Richards).
WEBER. Article "Weber" in Grove's *Dictionary*.
See Appendix to Webbe's *Pianist's Primer and Guide* (Forsyth) for "Books for Musicians;" also Articles in Grove's *Dictionary*, 5 vols. (1879–88) 1904–10 (Macmillan) and the :—

> New Library of Music Series (Methuen).
> Master Musician Series (Dent).
> Living Masters of Music Series (Lane).
> Music of the Masters Series (Lane).
> Library of Music and Musicians Series (Kegan Paul).
> The Musician's Book Series (Kegan Paul).
> Miniature Series of Musicians Series (Bell).
> Great Musicians Series (Sampson Low).
> Les Maîtres de Musique Series (Paris).
> Musical Booklets Series (Weekes).

WORKS OF REFERENCE.

Baker, *Biographical Dictionary* (Schirmer).
Grove, *Dictionary of Music*, 5 vols. 1909 (Macmillan).
Riemann, *Dictionary of Music* (Shedlock ; Augener).
——, *Dictionary of Russian Composers* (Longman).
Schytte, *Nordisk Musik Lexicon*. 1888 (Scandinavian Composers) (Copenhagen).
Fetis, *Biographie*. 1863 ; Supplement 1878 (Paris).

THE NATIONAL ASPECT.

Engel, *The Literature of National Music*. 1879 (Novello).
Niemann, *Musik und Musiker des 19ten Jahrhunderts* (Senff).
Crowest, *British Music*. 1896.
Davey, *History of English Music* : new Ed. 1922 (Curwen).
Maitland, *English Music of the 19th Century*. 1894.
Scholes, *Introduction to British Music* (Palmer & Hayward).
Browne and Stratton, *British Musical Biography* (Vincent).
Grove, *Dictionary* : Articles on "Scottish and Irish Music."

America.

Elson, *History of American Music*. 1904 (Macmillan).
Mathews, *A Hundred Years' Music in America*.
Ritter, *Music in America*. 1883 (Reeves).

Germany.

Maitland, *Masters of German Music*. 1884.
Soubies, *La Musique Allemande* (Paris).

France.

Hervey, *Masters of French Music* (Osgood, Boston).
Jean Aubry, *French Music of To-day* (Kegan Paul).
Hargrave, *The Earlier French Musicians* (Kegan Paul).
Expert, *Maîtres Musiciens de la Renaissance* (Paris).
Servière, *La Musique Française* (Franck ; Saint-Saëns, etc.) (Harvard Fils).

Russia.

Nathan, *Introduction to Russian Music* (Palmer & Hayward).
——, *Contemporary Russian Composers* (Palmer & Hayward).
A Pougin, *Short History of Russian Music* (Chatto & Windus).
Cui, *La Musique en Russe.* 1880 (Paris).
Articles on Russian Composers in Russian Edition of Riemann's Dictionary (Jurgenson).

Finland.

Flodin, *Musik in Finnland.* 1900 (Söderstrom, Helsingfors).
Newmarch, *Jan Sibelius* (B. & H.).

Scandinavia.

Niemann, *Die Musik Scandinaviens.* 1906 (B. & H.).
Og-W. Behrend, *Panum Hortense,* 2 vols. 1905 (Norway ; Sweden ; Denmark).
Soubies, *L'Art Scandinave,* 3 vols. 1874 (Paris).
Schytte, *Nordisk Musik Lexicon.* 1888 (Copenhagen).

Bohemia.

Hostinsky, *Musik in Bohemia* (Urbanek, Prague).
Soubies, *Histoire: Bohème* (Paris).
Mackenzie, *R.A. Lectures* (Internationale Musikgesellschafts Magazine).

Hungary.

Kaldy, *History of Hungarian Music* (Reeves).
Soubies, *Histoire: Hongrie* (Paris).
Liszt, *Die Zigeuner und ihre Musik in Ungarn.*
Ilona de Gyory, *Hungarian Music* Musical Assoc. Lecture. 1902.

Netherlands.

Soubies, *Histoire: Belgique,* 2 vols. ; *Hollande* (Paris).
Cobbett, *Music and Musicians of Walloon Provinces* (Musical Assoc. Lec. 1901).
Courier Musical, Paris, Feb.,1904. *L'Ecole Flamande.*
Van der Straeten, *Musique des Pays Bas avant le XIX. Siècle* (1867-85).

Switzerland.

Becker, *La Musique en Suisse.* 1874.

Italy.

Villani, *L'Arte del Clavicembalo.* 1901 (Fratelle-Bodia, Turin).
Torchi, *L'Arte Musicale in Italia,* 5 vols. (Bodia).

Spain.

C. van Vechten, *The Music of Spain* (Kegan Paul).
Cart, *Spanish Music* (Musical Assoc. Lect., 1906).
Soubies, *L'Histoire de la Musique en Espagne,* 3 vols. (Paris).
——, *L'Histoire de la Musique en Portugal* (Paris).
Pedrell, *Dictionary of Spanish and Portuguese Musicians.*

Reference.

See Articles on Music of various nationalities in the American magazines,
Étude and *Musician,* and in the German *Die Musik.* *See also* the
Universal Handbook of Musical Literature (annual) (Augener), and the
Monatsbericht (Hofmeister) which contains monthly announcements
of new music.

MODERN EDITIONS.

"Look upon the alteration or omission of anything or the
introduction of modern ornaments in the works of good composers as a
contemptible impertinence."—R. Schumann.

The modern Edition of Standard Pianoforte works may be said to
date from the publication of the Cotta Edition. No doubt this Edition
was a great advance in the way of giving educational help, on what had
gone before. Since that time, however, quite a generation of well-equipped
Editors has come to the front, and much progress has been made. We
may put down the following as being essential to good modern editions of
any work :—

1. Good paper and bold, clear print.
2. Correct phrasing.
3. Modern Fingering.
4. Suitable Pedal signs.
5. Rational Expression Marks—where not provided by the Composer.
6. Intelligible Analysis in Analytical Editions.

Of many well-known Editions several offend against one or other of
these requirements. Several of our British Editions take front rank, and
of the foreign Editions probably the Germer Editions are the best.
Riemann's Editions are too subtle and overcrowded. Buonamici is prodigal
of Pedal Indications, while, going further back, Henselt (Edition of Weber)
and Tausig, on paper, like Liszt, in actual practice, took many liberties
with what they attacked. Perhaps, the addition of rational phrase marks
is the most important point. Germer, O'Leary, Agnes Zimmermann and
Conrad Kuhner, among others, have earned distinction in this way. It is
greatly to be desired in the interests of clear phrasing that mere legato
playing should no longer be indicated by the slur ⌒. As regards the
Pedal, perhaps, the best sign is ⌐, one which is fast growing in favour.

———

PART II
Chief Collective Editions of the Classics.

N.B.—Other Collective Editions are mentioned in the various chapters.

Chopin : Valses (contains posthumous numbers) (Jos. Williams).
Couperin : Brahms and Chrysander, 4 vols. (Augener).
  Les Maîtres de Clavecin, 13 pieces (Lit.).
  Old French Composers (Augener).
Rameau : Les Maîtres de Clavecin, 12 pieces (Lit.).
  Old French Composers (Augener).
  Concertos (Steingräber Ed.).
Scarlatti : Compositions (70), Ed. by Barth, 4 vols. (Univ. Ed.).
  Sonatas (60) (B. & H.).
  8 Suites, 24 pieces (Ed. by Longman) (Rather).
  New Collection (Ed. by Pedrell) (Barcelona).
  12 Sonatas (Hug.).
Old Italian Composers. Ed. by Pauer, 117 pp. (Augener).
Old German Composers. Ed. by Pauer, 114 pp. (Augener).
Early English Composers. Byrd ; Bull ; Gibbons. Separate vols. (Augener).
Later English Composers. Blow ; Purcell ; Arne. Separate vols. (Augener).
Early English. Fitzwilliam Virginal Collection (B. & H.).
—— ——. Rimbault's Reprint of Parthenia (1611 A.D.). Byrd ; Bull ; Gibbons (Reeves).
Later English. Henry Purcell, Suites, 4 vols. (Ed. by Squire) (Chester).
General Early Classics . Les Maîtres de Clavecin, Vol. I . German Master (Lit.) ; Vol. II . English, Italian, French (Lit).
Alte Klavier Musik (B. & H. ; Simrock).
Golden Treasury, 2 vols. (Schirmer).
From the 18th Century's, 2 vols. (Ed. by McDowell) (Elkin).
Le Petit Claveciniste (Ed. by Philipps) (Ja).
Froberger, Adler Collection (B. & H.). Nieman Selection (Senff).
Em. Bach :—Compositions (14 Sonatas, and Rondos) Ed. by Schenker.
  Baumgart Edn., 6 Books (Leuckart). Concertos (Steingräber Edn.).
W. F. Bach : Polonaises and Fugues (Peters). 4 Fantasias (Kistner).
  Concertos (Steingräber Edn.).
Handel :—5 vols. (Univ. Edn.), 3 vols. (Peters), 3 vols. (B. & H.), 1 vol. (Lit.). Compositions (Kistner) ; Suites Ed. by Reinecke (Schweers and Haake) ; Easy Pieces, Ed. by Bülow (Augener).
Seb. Bach :—Bachgesellschaft Edn., 5 vols. (B. & H.). Bischoff Edn., 7 vols. (Steingräber) ; also Editions in Peters, Litolff, B. & H. and Augener Collections.
Bach's 48 Preludes and Fugues. Germer Edn. (Lit.). Busoni Edn. (Schirmer). Saunders Edn. (Hammond). Lott. Edn. (Ash) ; also Novello Edn.
Haydn.—Sonatas. Riemann Edn. (Augener) ; also Lit., Peters (Augener) ; B. & H. Edn.
Mozart :—Gesammtausgabe (B. & H.), vols. 16, 19–22 ; also Peters, Lit., Cotta., Steing., and Simrock Edns. The Concertos (Peters and B. & H.) ; also 5 for 2 Pianos (St. Ed.), 3 (Peters). The Sonatas (Augener, Bos.) ; Novello Edns.
Beethoven :—Gesammtausgabe (B. & H.), vols. 9, 15–18 ; also Peters Edn. and Lit. Variations, 2 vols (Univ. Edn.). Sonatas. Germer Edn. (Lit.) ; D'Albert Edn. (Forberg) ; Cotta Edn. ; also Novello, Augener and Gebr. Reinecke Edns.

Beethoven and Mozart:—Sonatas: analytical edn., ed. Macpherson (J. Williams).
Clementi :—Aug.; Univ. Edn.; Lit. (B. & H.); Holle Edns.
Hummel :—Lit., B. & H., Peters; Concertos, St. Ed., Univ. Ed.
Weber :—Peters, Augener, Wouters Edn. (Katto). Concertos. Lit. and St. Edn.
Schubert :—Gesammtausgabe (B. & H.). Sonatas, Augener and Univ. Edns. Works vol 1802 (Peters). Duets Lit. Edn. Impromptus (Lengnick).
Mendelssohn:—Complete (Nov.) (unfingered); Gesammtausgabe (B. & H.). Concertos. St. Edn. *Lieder ohne Worte* Klindworth Ed. (Novello and Augener). B. F. Wood Edn. with Titles.
Schumann :—Gesammtausgabe (B. & H.) Lit., Novello and Augener Edns. Neitzels Edn. (Rühle).
Chopin :—Univ. Edn. (Peters), Augener and B. & H. Edns.
Field :—Nocturnes and Concertos (J. Schubert Edn.).
Bennet :—Augener, and Ashdown.
Brahms :—Simrock Edn.
Dvoràk :—Simrock Edn.
Reger :—Univ. Edn.; Lauterbach and Kuhn.
Thematic Catalogues in B. & H. Edn. of Em. Bach, Beethoven, Chopin, Liszt, Mendelssohn and Mozart.
Phrased edition of Bach in Wood's and Berner's edns.; and of Gade in the new Litolff edn.

PART III.

CHIEF MUSICAL JOURNALS FOR PIANISTS.

Great Britain :—*Musical Record* ; *Times* ; *Opinion* ; *News* ; *Standard* ; *Music Teacher*.
America :—*Music* ; *Etude* ; *The Musician*.
Germany :—*Der Klavier Lehrer*; *Die Musik* ; *Allgemeine Musik Zeitung* ; *Neue Musik Zeitung* ; *Signale* ; *Musikalisches Wochenblatt* ; *Neue Zeitschrift für Musik*.
Austria :—*Neue Musik Presse* (Vienna) ; *Musiker Zeitung* (Vienna).
Bohemia :—*Dalibor* (Prague).
Switzerland : *La Musique en Suisse* ; *Schweizerische Musik Zeitung*.
Netherlands :—*Le Guide Musical* (Brussels) ; *Caecilia* (The Hague) ; *De Muziekbode* ; *Tydschrift der Vereenigung* ; *Weekblad fur Muziek*.
France :—*Le Ménestrel* ; *Le Monde Musical* ; *Revue Musicale*.
Italy :—*Il Pianoforte* ; *Rivista Musicale Italiana* ; *La Nuova Musica* ; *La Cronaca Musicale* (Pesaro) ; *Musica e Musicisti*.
Russia :—*Am Klavier* (Riga) ; *Russkaij Musij kaalja Gazeta*.
Sweden :—*Svensk Musiktidnung*.
Finland :—*Finsk Musikrevy*.
Spain :—*Revista Musicale Catalana* (Barcelona).
Bavaria :—*Kunstwart* (Munich).
Hungary :—*Zenevilag* (Budapest).
Poland :—*Musikal Novitäten* (Warsaw).
Roumania :—*Romania Musicale*.

Particulars of the above can be found in Hesse's *Musik Kalender* (Leipzig).

PART IV.

Publishers of Pianoforte Music.

Great Britain.

	ABBREV.
London—Anglo-French Co., 95 Wimpole Street, W.1.	A.F.
Ascherberg, 16 Mortimer Street.	Ac.
Ashdown, 19 Hanover Square.	A.
Augener, Great Marlborough Street.	Aug.
Bayley & Ferguson, 2 Great Marlborough Street.	By.
Boosey, 295 Regent Street.	B.
Bosworth, 8 Heddon Street, W.	Bos.
Cary, 13 Mortimer Street.	Cr.
Chappell, 50 New Bond Street.	Cp.
Chester, 11 Great Marlborough Street.	Ch.
J. Church, 105 Great Russell Street, W.1.	J.C.
Cramer, 139 New Bond Street.	Cm.
Curwen, 24 Berners Street.	Cw.
Duff, Stewart & Co., 51 High St., Bloomsbury, W.C.2.	Df.
Elkin, 8 Beak Street, W.	Ek.
Enoch, 14 Great Marlborough Street.	En.
Forsyth, 34 Berners Street, W.1.	Fs.
Gould, 24 Poland Street.	G.
Hammond, 6 Kingly Str., W.	Hm.
F. Harris, 40 Berners Street.	Hr.
Laudy, 8 Newman Street.	Ld.
Lengnick, 14 Berners Street.	Lg.
Leonard, 47 Poland Street, W.1.	Ln.
Metzler, 142 Charing Cross Road, W.C.2.	M.
Murdoch, 23 Princes Street, W.1.	Mur.
Novello, 160 Wardour Street, W.	Nov.
Orpheus Co., Moorgate Street Arcade.	Os.
Reeves (Literature), 83 Charing Cross Road.	R.
Ricordi, 283 Regent Street.	Rc.
Schott, 48 Great Marlborough Street.	Sht.
Stainer & Bell, 58 Berners Street.	S.B.
Swan, 288 Regent Street.	Sw.
Warren & Phillips, 24 East Castle Street, W.1.	W. & P.
Weekes, 14 Hanover Street.	W.
Wickins, New Bond Street.	Wk.
B. Williams, 26 Goodge Street, W.	B.W.
J. Williams, 32 Great Portland Street.	J.W.
Winthrop Rogers, 18, Berners Street.	W.R.
B. F. Wood, 84 Newman Street, W.1.	Wd.
York—Banks, Stonegate.	Bn.
Edinburgh—Patterson, George Street.	Ps.
Dublin—Pohlman, 40 Dawson Street.	Ph.

Germany.*

Berlin—Bote & Bock, Leipziger Strasse, 37.	B. & B.
Challier, Beuth Strasse, 10.	Ch.
Fürstner, Kronen Strasse, 16.	Fr.
Ries & Erler, Kurfürstendamm, 32.	R. & E.
Schlesinger, Franz Strasse, 23.	Schles.
Simon, Markgrafen Strasse, 101.	Sm.
Simrock, Friedrich Strasse, 171.	Sr.

* Most foreign music can be imported through Novello, or Augener, London.

ABBREV.

Leipzig—Belaieff, Rabenstein Platz, 3.   Bl.
    Bertram.   Bm.
    Bosworth, König Strasse, 266.   Bos.
    Breitkopf & Härtel, Nürnberger Strasse, 38.   B. & H.
    Brockhaus, Quer Strasse, 76.   Bk.
    Dieckmann.   Dk.
    Eulenberg, König Strasse, 8.   Eu.
    O. Forberg, Stephan Strasse, 10.   O.F.
    R. Forberg, Thal Strasse, 19.   R.F.
    M. Hesse, Eilenburger Strasse, 4.   M.H.
    Hofmeister, Quer Strasse, 13.   Hf.
    Hug, König Strasse, 20.   Hg.
    Junne, Thal Strasse, 21.   J.
    Jurgensson, Thal Strasse, 19.   Jr.
    Kahnt, Nürnberger Strasse, 27.   K.
    Kistner, Rabenstein Platz, 3.   Ks.
    Klemm, Neumarkt, 28.   Kl.
    Lauterbach & Kuhn, Ross Strasse, 18.   L. & K.
    Leuckart, Dresdener Strasse, 11.   L.
    Pabst, Neumarkt, 26.   Pb.
    Peters, Thal Strasse, 10.   P.
    Portius, Quer Strasse, 8.   Pr.
    Rahter, Rabenstein Platz, 3.   R.
    Geb. Reinecke, Felix Strasse, 4.   G.R.
    Rieter Biedeman, Gerichtsweg, 3.   Rb.
    A. P. Schmidt, Gerichtsweg.   A.P.S.
    Fr. Schubert, junr., Markgrafen Strasse, 8.   F.S.
    J. Schubert, Dörrien Strasse, 1.   J.S.
    Bartholf Senff, Ross Strasse, 22.   B.S.
    Siegel, Dörrien Strasse, 12.   Sg.
    Steingräber, Seeburger Strasse, 100.   St.
    Zimmermann, Quer Strasse, 26.   Z.
Braunschweig—Litolff. London Agent, 57, High St., W.2.   Lit.
Bremen—Fischer, Katharinen Strasse, 30.   F.
    Praeger & Meier.   P. & M.
    Schweers & Haake.   S. & H.
Breslau—Hainauer.   Hn.
Dresden—Brauer, N. Haupt Strasse, 2.   A.B.
    L. Hoffarth.   L.H.
Hameln—Oppenheimer.   O.
Magdeburg—Heinrichshofen.   Hs.
Mainz—Schott.   St.
Offenbach-am-Main—J. Andre, Don Strasse, 21.   J.A.
Regensburg—M. Cohen.   M.C.
Strassburg—Süd-Deutscher Musik Verlag.   SD.
Stuttgart—Cotta Edn., Cotta Strasse, 13.   Ct.

AMERICA.

New York—Schirmer, 3, E. 43rd Street.   Srm.
    Pond & Co., 148, 5th Avenue Street.   Pd.
    Schubert & Co., 23 Union Square, West.   E.S.
    H. W. Gray, 2 W. 45th Street.   Gray
Chicago—C. F. Summy, 220 Wabash Street.   C.F.S.
    J. Church, 200 Wabash Avenue.   J.C.

	ABBREV.
Cincinnati—G. B. Jennings.	Jn.
Milwaukee—Rohlfing.	Rh.
Philadelphia—Presser, 1712 Chestnut Street.	Ps.
Hatch, Locust Street.	Hh.

CANADA.

Toronto—Anglo-Canadian Co., 88½ Yonge Street.	An. C.

AUSTRIA.

Wien (Vienna)—L. Doblinger.	Db.
Weinberger, I. Maximilian Strasse, 11.	Wn.
Universal Ed., I. Maximilian Strasse, 11.	U. Ed.
Eberle (late Spina), Augustiner Strasse, 1.	Er.
Gutman, Hofoper, 1.	Gt.
Robitschek, Bräuner Strasse, 1.	Rc.
Innsbruck—Grosz, Landhaus Strasse.	Gr.

BOHEMIA.

Prague—Urbanek, Ferdinand Av., 14.	Ur.

HUNGARY.

Buda Pest—Rozsavolgyi, Christopher Platz.	Rz.
Bard & Bruder, Kossuth Lajos Strasse.	Brd.
Harmonia, Waitznerg, 20.	Ha.

SWITZERLAND.

Zürich—Hug & Co.	Hg.
Neuchâtel—Sandoz Jobin.	S.J.
Lausanne—Foetisch Frères.	F.F.

FRANCE.

Paris—Sulzbach (late Benoit), 13 Faubourg St. Martin.	Sb.
L. Gregh, 78 Rue d'Anjou (London Agent : Ricordi).	L.G.
Lemoine, 17 Rue Pigalli.	Lm.
Grus, 116 Bd. Hausmann.	Gs.
Gallet, 6 Rue Vivienne.	Gl.
Hamelle, 22 Bd. Malesherbes.	Hl.
Bellon Ponscarme (late Baudoux), 37 Bd. Hausmann.	B.P.
Durand, 4 Place de la Madeleine.	Dr.
Societé Nouvelle (late Dupont) 24 Rue des Capucins.	S.N.
Costallat (late Richault), 15 Chaussée D'Antin.	Cs.
Noel, 22 Passages des Panoramas.	Nl.
Leduc, 3 Rue de Grammont.	Lc.
Librairie Hachette, 79 Bd. de St. Germain.	L.H.
Heugél (Au Mènestrel), 2 bis Rue Vivienne.	Hn.
Joubert, 25 Rue d'Hauteville.	Jb.
Fromart, 40 Rue d'Anjou.	Fm.
Choudens, 30 Bd. des Capucins.	Chd.
Lyons—Janin Frères.	Ja.
Clot Fils.	Ct.

HOLLAND.

Amsterdam—Nieuwe Muziekhandel, Leidsche Straat, 24.	Mz.
De Algemeene Muziekhandel, Spin, 2.	A.M.
G. Alsbach & Co., Musiekhandelaren en Uitgevers.	As.
Seyffardt, Damrak.	Sy.

ABBREV.

Rotterdam—W. C. de Lange, Schiedsingel, 16.   Lng.
    W. D. Lichtenauer, L. Blaak, 44.   Lht.
The Hague—G. H. van Eck, Vlamingstraat.   V.E.
Utrecht—G. A. H. Wagenar, Ondkerkhof.   Wa.
    H. Rahr.   Ra.
    Rennes, Maria Plaats.   Re.
Middleburg—Noske.   Ns.

RUSSIA.

Petrograd—Belaieff (also Leipzig).   Bl.
    Bessel, Nevsky, 54.   Bes.
Moscow—Jurgenson, Neglumy, 14.   Jr.
    Idzikowsky.   Iz.
Riga—Neldner.   N.

POLAND.

Warsaw—Gebethner & Wolff.   G. & W.

DENMARK.

Copenhagen—Nordisk Forlags.   N.F.
    Hansen.   Hs.

NORWAY.

Christiania—Brödrene Hals, Storthingsgade, 24.   Hals.
    Haakon Zapfe, Carl Johannis Gade, 23.   Zp.
    Warmuth, Muzikhandel.   Wa.

SWEDEN.

Stockholm—A. Lundguist, Malmtorgsgaten, 8.   A.L.
    Elkam & Schildknecht.   E. & S.

FINLAND.

Helsingfors—Nya Musikhandel Forlag.   N.M.

SPAIN.

Barcelona—Vidal Llimona de Boceta.   Vl.
    Sindicato " Dotésio," 1 y 3 Puerta del Angel.   S.D.
San Sebastian—Casa Erveti, 28 San Martin.   C.E.

PORTUGAL.

Lisbon—Neuparth & Carneiro, 97 Rua Nova do Almado.   Na.

ITALY.

MILAN—Ricordi (*see* London).
    Carisch & Janichen.   C. & J,
    Al Pigna, Viale Manza, Sesto St. Giovanni.   Pg.
Florence—Bratti, Via de Martelli, 7.   Bra.
Turin—Marcello Capra.   M.C.
Rome—Venturini.   Vn.

BELGIUM.

Brussels—Ges. Oertel, Rue de la Régence, 17.   G.O.
    Katto, Rue de l'Ecuyer, 46.   Ko.
    Aynssa, Rue Neuve, 92.   Ay.
    Schott & Co.   Sht.
    Cranz & Co.   Cz.
Liège—Muraille, Rue de l'Université, 45.   Mu.
Ghent (Gand)—Beyer, Digne de Brabant, 14.   By.

INDEX OF COMPOSERS

SUBJECT INDEX

A

" Act of Touch," T. Matthay's, 366
Agrément, 22
Alberti Bass, 29
Allemande, 9
Allmaine, 13
Alman, 9
American Pianoforte Music, 348
" Art of Teaching," Dr. Warriner's,
  366
Austrian Composers, 270
Ayre, 13

B

Ballade, Grieg's, 210, 325
Ballades, Brahms', 145, 148
——, Chopin's, 235
Ballet Music, Chaminade's, 274
" Bible " Sonatas, 41
Bohemian Pianoforte Music, 247
Bourrée, 14
Branle, 9
Bravura Element, 101
—— School, 152

C

Canzoni, 12, 24
Capriccios, Mendelssohn's, 110, 217
" Carnival," Schumann's, 117
Chaconne, 14
Characteristic Music, 120, 122, 132
—— Pieces, Bennett's, 123, 139
—— ——, Gade's, 303
—— ——, Hägg's, A., 312
—— ——, Hiller's, 123, 132
—— ——, Schumann's, 116, 122
—— ——, Tchaïkowsky's, 265
—— ——, Winding's, 303
Chichona, 13
Classical School, Decay of, 94

Classicists, Modern, 167
Clavecin Music, French, 17
Clavicembalo, 5
Clavichord, 5
Componimienti, 41
Composers, Later English, 33
Concerto, The, 187 ff.
Concertos, Bach's, 188
——, ——, Em., 188
——, Beethoven's, 190
——, S. Bennett's, 193
——, Brahms', 149, 196
——, Great, 48
——, Grieg's, 194, 324
——, Henselt's, 195
——, Liszt's, 163
——, Mackenzie's, 197, 345
——, Mendelssohn's, 109, 193
——, Moscheles', 193
——, Mozart's, 189
——, Rameau's, 19
——, Rimsky-Korsakoff's, 255
——, Rubinstein's, 196
——, Saint-Saëns', 196
——, Schumann's, 194 ff.
——, Stenhammar's, 319
——, The Study of, 200
Contrapuntal Element, Modern, 172
Coranto, 9, 13
Courante, 9
Cuckoo Capriccio, 27
——, Toccata, 27
Czechs, Music of the, 248

D

Dance Forms, Modern, 211
Danish Pianoforte Music, 300
Danse-basse, 9
Duet Collections, 372
Duets, 201
——, Instructive, 204
——, Schubert's, 202
——, Schumann's, 202
Duet Sonatas, 201
—— Suites, 203
Dumka Dance Form, 248

401

ADDENDUM TO CHAPTER XIV

Those seeking inspiration in Scottish music will delight in Granville Bantock's *Three Scottish Scenes* (Swan), as built on Scottish melodies ; and in Henry Geehl's " 1745," five episodes No. 1, *The Gathering of the Clans* ; etc. (Swan). Music of the best British type we find in Balfour Gardiner's *Sailor's Piece*, and in Nos. 2 and 4 of *Shenadoah* (Forsyth) with their invigorating melody and modern harmonies, in which also Roger Quilter runs him close in his *Country Pieces* (Rogers). The same bracing atmosphere is found in York Bowen's tuneful *Three English Dances* (Swan) ; Alec Rowley's *Elizabethan Portraits* (Swan) in diatonic mode ; and in W. F. Arnold's *Call of the Sea* (Swan).

Of notable contributions to the school of the *characteristic* we must mention Alec Rowley's very attractive *Three Lyrics* and *The Sea* (Ash), and his *Festival of Pan* (Swan) ; also one by Percy Godfrey, who, in his *Oberon's Court* (Swan), writes good modern " fairy music." York Bowen, in the piquant Nos. 4 and 6 of his *Hans Andersen's Fairy Tales* (Swan) and invigorating *At the Play House* (Ascherberg) and *Three Serious Dances*, also shows mastery of the characteristic. Coleridge Taylor's individual style is seen in his popular *Three Fours Suite* (Aug.), his *Intermezzo*, and *Three Dream Dances* (Asch).

With Cecil Hazlehurst's very captivating *Scherzo* (Elkin), his *Petite Suite, Impromptu, Valse Caprice* and *Fughetta*, are associated attractive melody, rhythm, and harmonic effects, while a modern and elusive charm also characterizes James Lyon's *Water Mirror Suite* (Rogers). Sir Edward Elgar appears in lighter vein in his *Rosemary*, and in the *Starlight Express Suite* (Elkin) ; his masterly individuality is also seen in *Carissima*.

Other able composers in the characteristic style are Percival

Driver, in his effective *Four Sketches*, and Paul Corder, who has written a fine *Heroic Elegy*, and *Nine Preludes ;* there is also a very good modern *Interlude* by Felix Swinstead (A.F. Co.). Similar effective compositions are the delicately wrought *Three Preludes* and *Vignettes* by John McEwen, and the highly refined and poetical Miniatures of Tobias Matthay in his typical *Album Leaf*, *Op.* 2, and *Sketch Books*, *Op.* 24 and 26 (A.F. Co.).   Of Leo Livens' virtuoso bizarre compositions his *Sing a Song of Sixpence* and *Sunset* are effective.

These also are commendable : Herbert Howell's *Street Dancer* (Snapshots) (Swan) ; Percy Fletcher's *Idyllesques* (Swan)—in modern mood.   Fredk. C. Nicholls' *Autumn Song* (Stainer and Bell), Welton Hickins' *Suite Mignonne* (A.F. Co.), and Alg. Ashton's *Two Characteristic Pieces* (Aug.), written in classical style.

The British Impressionist School has grown in power, and in Cyril Scott's *Handelian Rhapsody* (Elkin) we have bold outlines enriched by modern secondary harmonies.   Of his *Three Vistas,* "*A Lonely Dell*" aptly describes itself, while in his attractive *Lotus Land* (Elkin) dank, sweet vapours hang low.   In John Ireland's *Merry Andrew* (Asch.) appears a masterly sketch. Harry Farjeon has depicted real Eastern atmosphere effects in his *Moorish Idylls* (A), as has also Arnold Bax in *The Slave Girl* (A.F. Co.).   The *Worcestershire Suite* of Julius Harrison (Enoch) effectively portrays a mystical atmosphere, and Chris. M. Edmunds in *Pan's Garden* proves a capable disciple of Debussy. John R. Heath also proves to be deeply immersed in his Debussean harmonic rhapsody, *A Rune* (Enoch), while H. V. Jervis Read shows that it is possible to combine melody with the new harmonic effects in his *Little Preludes* (Elkin).   J. Gerrard Williams, in *The Isle* from *Three Miniatures* (Curwen), also creates a good effect.

To turn to the more serious aspect—York Bowen's *Short Sonata* (Swan) presents a corruscating succession of secondary harmonies of great interest, but one feels the atmosphere to be unfavourable to the development necessary to a work of this kind.   One can, however, commend his *Mood Phases* and a brilliant *Lisztian Polonaise in F♯* (A.F. Co.).   By way of contrast, Landon Ronald's *Three Compositions* (Swan) interest in another way, as putting ideas first.   Ideas, too, masterly and noble, characterize the *Preludes* by Sir Ch. V. Stanford (Swan).

In the 48 numbers (in 7 Books) are to be found material for interesting Suites, Studies, etc.

Josef Holbrooke's dramatic style is best seen in No. 4 *L'Orgie. Fantaisie Bacchanale* from his Suite, *Op.* 18 (Cary). His genius is essentially orchestral, and can be clearly seen in his Piano Transcriptions of his Variations on *The Girl I Left Behind Me* and the *Pierrot Ballet Suite* (Nov.). He has also transcribed his Preludes to *Bronwen, Dylan, The Raven* and *Pontorewyn*.

To the *Variations* mentioned in Chapter XXIV one should add the ably written and very effective ones written *On an Original Theme* by R. Walker Robson (Nov.).

Printed in Great Britain by MACKAYS LTD., Chatham.